The Ruling Passion

British Colonial Allegory
and the Paradox
of Homosexual Desire

Christopher Lane

Duke University Press

Durham and London, 1995

© 1995 Duke University Press
All rights reserved
Printed in the United States of America on acid-free paper ∞
Designed by Silvia Steiner
Typeset in Times by Tseng Information Systems, Inc.
Library of Congress Cataloging-in-Publication Data appear
on the last printed page of this book.

Advertisement for Pears' Soap, *McClure's Magazine*
13 (Oct. 1899).

Oh, East is East, and West is West, and never the twain shall meet,
Till Earth and Sky stand presently at God's great Judgment Seat.
But there is neither East nor West, Border, nor Breed, nor Birth,
When two strong men stand face to face, tho' they come from the ends
of the earth!
— Rudyard Kipling, "The Ballad of East and West"

The contact with pure unmitigated savagery, with primitive nature
and primitive man, brings sudden and profound trouble into the heart.
To the sentiment of being alone of one's kind, to the clear perception of
the loneliness of one's thoughts, of one's sensations — to the negation
of the habitual, which is safe, there is added the affirmation of the unusual, which is dangerous; a suggestion of things vague, uncontrollable,
and repulsive, whose discomposing intrusion excites the imagination
and tries the civilized nerves of the foolish and wise alike.
— Joseph Conrad, *Tales of Unrest*

What a paradox was to me in the sphere of thought, perversity became
to me in the sphere of passion.
— Oscar Wilde, *De Profundis*

If it was love that was to bring him back he must be an exile for ever.
— Saki, *The Unbearable Bassington*

Someday we must write the history of our own obscurity — manifest
the density of our narcissism, tally down through the centuries the
several appeals to difference we may have occasionally heard.
— Roland Barthes, *Empire of Signs*

Contents

Preface

> Those who read these lines will hardly doubt what passion it is that I
> am hinting at. *Quod semper ubique et ab omnibus* — surely it deserves a
> name. Yet I can hardly find a name which will not soil this paper.
> —John Addington Symonds[1]

The challenge facing any book that takes British colonialism and male homosexuality as its subject is one of restricting their textual and cultural frame.
The decisions that shaped this book were often arbitrary, and the exclusions
perhaps glaring, but the final choice of period, geography, culture, and gender
seemed to me most emblematic of tensions and anxieties circulating within
Britain's empire at the turn of the last century.

At its inception, I wanted this book to include texts about lesbianism,
greater emphasis on Victorian literature, and more varied accounts of southern Africa; this at least was my stubborn ideal. I would attribute some of the
problems I experienced including this material to the diffuse and voracious
expansion of British colonialism. The impact of this diffusion and voracity on
an unsuspecting reader can usefully defeat assumptions that British colonialism was historically and internally coherent; this is only one of many lessons
I have learned in the course of writing this book. Indeed, the book could not
properly begin until I had relinquished the fantasy of uncovering or recovering a single and self-evident "colonial homosexuality" in British literature. In
this respect, the extent to which lesbianism is generally tangential to this account should be considered not as indifference or uninterest but as avoidance
of too hasty an inclusion, which would have created more epistemological
damage than it could have countered. I hope these readings support the aim
of an established field of colonial inquiry and a growing body of literary and
historical work on same-sex representation.

In the spirit of its subject, this book was conceptualized in Zimbabwe, researched and written in Britain, and revised and published in the United States; it has become a testament to my geographical displacements and a record of the many intellectual and personal debts I have incurred along the way. Jacqueline Rose supervised the project as a doctoral dissertation, many drafts ago, providing insight, encouragement, and much needed caution with warmth, subtlety, and brilliance; my intellectual and personal debt to her is inestimable. In their diverse ways, Geoffrey Bennington, Homi Bhabha, Rachel Bowlby, and Jonathan Dollimore at the University of Sussex also shaped my thoughts by providing a constant resource of interpretation and valuable contention. Morag Shiach, at Queen Mary and Westfield College, University of London, was an excellent reader of earlier drafts of the Forster and Firbank chapters. My colleagues at the University of Wisconsin-Milwaukee shared ideas and friendship in equal measure, and I warmly thank Herbert Blau, Jane Gallop, Bernard Gendron, Lawrence Hoey, Gregory Jay, Lynne Joyrich, Andrew Martin, Jeffrey Merrick, Panivong Norindr, Marina Pérez de Mendiola, Patrice Petro, and Kathleen Woodward. Tim Dean was a friend and resource throughout, and Jason Friedman untangled many of the manuscript's conceptual and syntactical knots; I cheerfully absolve him of any that remain.

Other bodies and individuals provided generous financial and practical support: I am grateful to Carol Tennessen and the staff and research assistants at the Center for Twentieth Century Studies, UWM, for their assistance during my fellowship in 1993–94, and to the graduate school at UWM for grants over the summer of 1993 that enabled me to complete research in London and Austin, Texas. I thank also Paul Julian Smith at Cambridge University and Steven Connor at Birkbeck College, University of London; my graduate students at UWM; former colleagues and students at Roehampton Institute, London; the British Academy; staff and former students at Marondera High School, Mashonaland, Zimbabwe; the Ministry of Education in Harare; and the documents and interlibrary loans staff at the Universities of Sussex and Wisconsin-Milwaukee for enduring an endless stream of requests. I am also grateful to Leo Bersani, George Chauncey, Laura Chrisman, Richard Dellamora, Diana Fuss, David Halperin, Michael Moon, Bart Moore-Gilbert, Vincent Samar, and Brian Street for advice on the project, and to Ken Wissoker at Duke University Press for much encouragement about its completion. Family and friends in London, Edinburgh, Brighton, and Milwaukee sustained me throughout with generous affection; I thank especially my brother, Rob Lane, in London for unyielding support, and Zackie Achmat in Johannesburg for endorsing my suspicions and waiting patiently for some explanations to emerge.

I acknowledge the trustees of the Joseph Conrad Estate in London and the Harry Ransom Research Center at the University of Texas at Austin for permission to cite previously unpublished passages from *Victory*. Earlier versions of chapters 3, 6, 7, and 8 appeared in *ELH, Discourse, Literature Interpretation Theory,* and *Raritan* respectively; a shorter version of chapter 6 also appeared in *Writing India, 1757–1990*. I thank Anita Roy at Manchester University Press and the editors of these journals for permission to reprint.

Milwaukee, Wisconsin

Introduction:

Theorizing "The Empire of the Selfsame"[1]

Passion: suffering of pain (earliest, of the sufferings of Jesus Christ); being acted upon; powerful affection of the mind; outburst of anger; amorous feeling; sexual impulse; strong predilection. — (O)F. — ChrL. *passiō,* pp. stem of *patī,* suffer.[2]

To the clear-sighted, failure was the only goal. We must believe, through and through, that there was no victory, except to go down into death fighting and crying for failure itself, calling in excess of despair to Omnipotence to strike harder, that by His very striking He might temper our tortured selves into the weapon of His own ruin.
— T. E. Lawrence[3]

This passage from *Seven Pillars of Wisdom: A Triumph* (1926) argues, quite unusually, for an approach to colonialism based on political failure, betrayal, and treachery. Lawrence's strategy is pertinent to this book in his attempt to read two largely incompatible trajectories: the allegorical dimension of British imperial thought and the persistent force of homosexual desire that often underwrote this thought, or compelled it into a hostile and antagonistic silence.

In light of Lawrence's claim for a politics of colonial failure, it is necessary to ask whether British colonialism promoted a successful sexual project, or whether central components of sexuality emerged from that proj-

1

ect's deficiency. If we conceive of sexuality in a functional relation to colonialism, we might answer the first question in the affirmative, convinced that the repression of unconscious elements of the empire upheld its political function. For instance, Ronald Hyam has argued that "the driving force behind empire building was . . . the export of surplus emotional or sexual energy," not the export of surplus capital.[4] However, if we uncouple sexuality from hydraulic definitions of desire, in which sexual repression appears amenable to political service, Britain's empire would lie in the midst of a complicated and indeterminate field of "unamenable" desires. No longer the object of critiques about successful sublimations and productive dissociations, the empire would yield an opaque and varied picture of colonial rule shrouded by doubt, ambivalence, and antagonism. This second version of colonial sexuality is the subject of this book, which focuses on the failure of self-mastery, the insufficiency and overabundance of drives to colonial sublimation, the relation between imperialism and the death drive, the service that colonialism performed in the realm of sexual fantasy, and the influence that all of these factors brought to bear on the symbolization of masculinity and homosexuality during Britain's volatile years of world power. For clarification of this argument, consider the following passage from Conrad's *Nostromo* (1904): "The confused and intimate impressions of universal dissolution which beset a subjective nature at any strong check to its ruling passion had a bitterness approaching that of death itself." [5]

Since I follow Conrad's conviction that sexual desire is often unproductive in an economic and political sense, but of immense value in conceptual and interpretive terms, I will use the term "allegory" to refer to a rhetorical structure that substitutes partial and fragmentary emblems for subjective entities, thus organizing otherwise disparate groups and individuals into effective political units.[6] Concurrently, and in direct opposition to this structure, I am interested in a counterforce that shatters national allegory by introducing unassimilable elements of homosexual desire. This counterforce resembles Lawrence's bid for failure in his assertions about colonial fantasy and national treachery; *The Ruling Passion* elaborates a similar argument that the radical inutility of desire frequently conflicted with Britain's colonial allegories. Consequently, this book is a study in sexual ambivalence, political contention, self-antagonism, and national and racial dispute; it shifts the focus of colonial and gay studies beyond the obvious proposition that homosexuals were an important component of the British Empire, and that the empire provided opportunities for sexual expression that were denied at home.[7]

Although this argument is important to consider, it interprets the empire at the level of the ego—that is, in terms of conscious and apparently coherent meaning—without addressing the unconscious antagonism that often erupts between national and sexual identification. As Jacques Lacan once argued, "Sexuality is established in the field of the subject by a way that is that of lack." [8] *The Ruling Passion* begins from this premise by engaging the diverse subjective and symbolic meanings of masculine identity and desire that surfaced at the turn of the last century. In this book, interpretation of different texts moves from conventional attention to the signified (the object of narrative representing what a text logically and conceptually "means") to that of the signifier (the element producing meaning, which is available for interpretation on several different levels). Lacan clarified this distinction's psychic consequences in his account of Freud's essay on "Repression" (1915) when he argued, "what is repressed is not the represented of desire, the signification, but *the representative,*" which is to say, the signifier (217). The difficulty of turning this distinction into a critical procedure emerges from the fact that the first (conscious) register tries to displace and supersede the second, while the second (unconscious) register is readable only at the level of effect and influence, not empirical cause. Following the difficulty of all interpretation, this book therefore engages what Lacan once called the treachery of a certain *"hermeneutic demand"* (7).

If we uphold this precarious but vital gap between external effect and psychic cause, how can we gauge the influence of ambivalence and self-antagonism on British colonial literature? What specifically do these factors contribute to our understanding of national identification, racial desire, and colonial fantasy? How, moreover, do crude, often nebulous political symbols mobilize people into groups? By engaging these questions, I want to challenge a form of historical and literary criticism that interprets the British Empire as a set of coherent policies and events whose social and political meanings are apparently self-evident; I argue that we miss a crucial element of colonial history when we ignore or dismiss the influence of unconscious identification, fantasy, and conflict on these political events.

The Ruling Passion tackles the assumption that undisputed ties of affiliation and mandates of power organize national groups and armies; this book argues instead that a nation's organization derives from its use of allegory, and that citizens understand themselves as part of a wider set of political initiatives only when this structure identifies them rhetorically. Since this inclusion hinges on citizens' willingness and ability to identify with national allegory, I argue that colonial theorists have not paid sufficient attention to group and racial identification. In alignment with the radical changes that are now reshaping the "affective ties" of groups and nations across the world, we must surely consider how unconscious identifications disturb national allegory to clarify contrary and antagonistic histories of imperial policy and national unity; this may be the best way of grasping the radical, internal turbulence of Britain's—and other European countries'—colonial past.

In the readings that follow, I interpret the influence of resistant and generally unassimilable homosexual drives, proposing that sexual desire between men frequently ruptured Britain's imperial allegory by shattering national unity and impeding the entire defeat of subject groups. In this respect, I refer less to a model of "integrated" homosexuality (the integration was generally a fantasy), in which proponents of the empire such as Rhodes and Kitchener bolstered the most egregious imperialist strategies by rejecting or sublimating their physical desire for other men. The "paradox" of my title refers more to the representational and political mobility of homosexual drives, insofar as these drives resisted the allegedly unifying principles of colonialism by invoking suspicion, antagonism, and betrayal. Although this strategy has some resemblance to recent concerns about the implied treachery of lesbians and gay men in the U.S. military and British intelligence services, I place more emphasis on the symbolic roles and fears that British culture attributed to homosexuality—specifically, homosexuality's ability to demonstrate what is precarious and *lacking* in heterosexual meaning and national formations.[9] In this book, I suggest that homosexuality was and still is *symbolically* disposed to this purpose, though it represented only one of several sexual and identificatory dilemmas for the British Empire. Thus, while I focus on "conservative" and "radical" lineages of homosexual desire, the second interests me primarily because its tension with "the Empire of the Selfsame" helped to unmake some of Britain's imperialist policies by fostering a contrary interest, or counterallegiance, with the colonized. We have only to recall Melville's horror at this possibility in "Benito Cereno" (1855) to consider its far-reaching consequence: "Who [had] ever heard of a white so far a renegade as to apostatize from his very species almost, by leaguing in against it with negroes?"[10] For Melville, the question was officially so preposterous that it supplied an immediate, negative answer.

To clarify this argument about counterallegiance, which renders "radical" homosexuality one of many interrogative positions, *The Ruling Passion* interprets several representational lineages of homosexuality between 1888 and 1942. At the risk of simplification and of giving these positions false coherence, I would argue that some of these lineages emerged at the frontiers of imperial defense, supporting national loyalty by apparently sublimating same-gender desire into proficient military relations; others were intermediary, falling between the nation and the colony, with often considerable ambivalence toward each; numerous others surfaced disruptively and defiantly within the nation by confronting charges of criminal obscenity when publicly accused, and legal injunctions when detailed explicitly in literary text.

Although every lineage produced a corresponding sexual practice, I argue that we must also distinguish them in literary and perceptual terms to avoid three critical assumptions. The first conflates these diverse forms of homosexuality into a single phenomenon, in which colonial and national representations of same-gender desire seem distinguishable only by the extent of their "dishonesty." [11] The second concerns the symbolization of this desire in literature, presuming that this dishonesty enters the text by veiled allusion or deliberate obscurity.[12] The third extends this principle by attempting to explain retroactively all forms of textual obscurity by the general inadmissibility of its author's desires.[13] This last example is of greatest relevance to my argument since many critics transform their discovery of homosexuality—whether disguised, dishonest, or latent—into a key to all biographical enigma and an elemental truth that pervades literary representation.

Although the question of homosexuality's "unspeakability" is central to this book, I suggest that these explanations fail to address the symbolic variability of same-gender relations during this period; that we cannot easily describe the significance of its sexuality by contemporary terms or assumptions of a hidden gay identity; and that the pursuit of homosexual truth places an impossible demand on this period's diffuse constituents and diverse representation of same-gender desire. In my attempt to avoid the pitfalls of these approaches, I foreground the period's multiple elaboration of homosexual desire by retaining a necessary undecidability about this elaboration's meaning. I also emphasize the importance of reading moments in which the text becomes elliptical about desire, without trying to give that desire an absolute position, especially not one that would endorse the most intractable proscriptions of the time. By interpreting how homosexuality acquired a distinct—and often unreliable—legibility in British literature, I ask what that desire came to signify in colonial mythology, and what meanings and fantasies it brought to the fore. Thus I begin from a premise similar to T. S. Eliot's account of opacity in "The Hollow Men" (1925): "Between the idea/ And the reality/ Between the motion/ And the Act/ Falls the Shadow." [14] This is not a "shadow" that we can flesh out with form or meaning by rendering it simply as a latent and coherent homosexual icon. Following Lacan, I approach the question posed by this "shadow" by the way it determines "impediment, failure, split" in the colonial subject (25).

Although the following proposition may appear self-evident to many, it seems important to reiterate that—like all forms of sexuality—we cannot readily assume, uncover, or retrieve homosexuality's diverse meanings; successive cultures have formulated and reframed the complex significance of this desire under different historical circumstances with radically different aims. This statement does not deny, for instance, that British law and society have credited homosexuality with an overdetermined meaning for about the past one hundred years as part of an endeavor to unify its description—as contrary, wayward, and unnatural. Instead, we must emphasize the turbulent incongruencies *between* homosexual desires and masculine identities precisely because no single signifier is adequate to their representation. Thus, I hope to arrest the mythology that homosexuality carried one perverse and deviant meaning during this period by disputing the notion that its "corollary"—heterosexuality—sustained greater coherence as "nature's" expression of sexual desire.

Unlike many constructivist accounts of homosexual desire, this book does not offer an account of the explicit or empirical meanings of "colonial homosexuality"—a point that would lend it a Foucauldian emphasis on structure, surveillance, and the "incitement to discourse";[15] it concerns a more difficult passage between internal and external fields of meaning by engaging a conflict between social and subjective perceptions of desire. Although these representations often work in conjunction with specific historical events and political initiatives of the time—for instance, the Crewe Circular of 1909, which I interpret in chapter 6—I do not offer a history of homosexuality in the colonies by assuming that these meanings are simply available for the record, or that history is a succession of events whose order and meaning is stable and conscious; I draw instead on the attention and significance that psychoanalysis has attributed to its subjects' drives, aims, and objects for an account of the precise variability and volatility of colonial fantasy and identification.[16]

Psychoanalysis is clearly implicated in historical change, but it is neither the sole cause nor the most exemplary symptom of transitions in the "deployment" of a sexual regime, or *"dispositif de sexualité."* [17] As Jacques-Alain Miller argued recently, "The notion that sexuality is historical is by no means shocking to a psychoanalyst." [18] Although materialist and psychic fields of inquiry influence one another, the subject's internal apprehension of desire often varies with public testimony and cultural symbolization; it may also testify to acute levels of ambivalence, hostility, even disgust. Critical accounts of this period that stress only discursive and political patterns tend to overlook these elements or assume that cultural intolerance and opprobrium adequately explain their wayward patterns. I contend that this interprets only one side of the proverbial story: since my interest lies in the difference between what is said or announced in these texts, and what is *heard,* I am concerned less with materiality than with a register Lacan once described as "the empire of the dream" (68).[19] I would claim that this study's focus on the unreliable and asymmetrical relation between the signifier and signified is appropriate and necessary because literature's inscription of desire was such a contested and difficult phenomenon at the turn of the last century.[20]

Given the historical and conceptual problems surrounding this project, how can readers interested in this period approach its literature's complex encoding of desire? Certainly, the idea of gaining direct access to a period, or recovering a history untarnished by loss, seems doubtful if we consider, contra Jeffrey Meyers, that desire was not successfully "liberated" by the civil rights movements at the end of the 1960s,[21] and that the signifier for every manifestation of desire in general is never adequate to the drive it represents. Many accounts of homosexuality in modern writing ignore this difficulty by representing homosexuality unproblematically as a transhistorical phenomenon; when discussing some of the texts and writers that I interpret here, they focus on either homosexuality or colonialism. While the latter has received much sophisticated and rigorous attention, a reading across and between both subjects has been less common, as if analysis of one required the other's occlusion.[22]

The texts I have chosen to interpret bear an interesting relation to an already established canon of modernist writing. Though critics have perceived such figures as Conrad and Forster as central proponents of British modernism, their analyses of homosexuality have returned to a select number of these writers' texts, thus repeating without question the assumed criteria by which the canon became known as such. Ironically, what this procedure omits is the very question modernism posed to received notions of the literary, the aesthetic, and their canonization—an interruption that emphasized the precise contingency and asymmetry of these phenomena. Since critics have often ignored this interruption when discussing homosexuality in these writers, the relation between homosexuality, colonialism, and modern writing remains an active question throughout this book, both for the critical reception of "modernist" homosexualities and for the figurative and allegorical work that homosexuality performed in turn-of-the-century writing. Following my interest in the shattering potential of homosexual desire, I contend that homosexuality often brought into relief a significance that British culture attached to sexuality and subjectivity, and that it dramatically transformed the encoding of each. Thus the texts I interpret push the representation of these phenomena toward crisis, establishing a need for homosexuality to fall out of representation so that other meanings can prevail.

We might read this representational crisis historically and fantasmatically as a paradox, in which the vast body of writing that sexologists, criminologists, and medical practitioners produced about homosexuality at the turn of the century was numerically disproportionate to this period's fictional accounts of homosexuality. As a result, the discursive influence of theoretical inquiry consigned many literary accounts to anonymity, censorship, and silence. Jeffrey Weeks has estimated, for instance, that over one thousand books were written about (predominantly male) homosexuality between 1898 and 1908.[23] If theory frequently displaced the literary forms of a "love that *dare not* speak its name," an array of "experts" nonetheless addressed this love, and spoke on its behalf, with relentless passion and seemingly unarguable authority.

Thus far, I have stressed that the problem of theorizing homosexual *desire* is central to my reference and critical procedure. I suggest that readers of British colonial fiction have uncritically repeated assumptions about this desire's singularity and coherence that intrude as blind spots within their analyses. Recent work in Lesbian and Gay Studies provides important exceptions to this problem; it has also enlivened interest in turn-of-the-century literature. However, this work has not always alleviated the question of sexual formulation and interpretation; if anything, the sheer quantity of analyses now engaging this literary period has intensified the urgency with which we must examine its historical, conceptual, and interpretive underpinnings.

One example of criticism that has influenced this book is Eve Kosofsky Sedgwick's work on sexual and gender paradigms. Sedgwick's use of the term "homosocial" has advanced our ability to interpret alleged heterosexual rivalries; the term has also pushed discussion beyond impoverished notions of latency, dishonesty, or inference. In an article published several years ago, Sedgwick provided the following definition of "homosocial" exchange: "The male homosocial structure [is that] whereby men's 'heterosexual desire' for women serves a more or less perfunctory detour on the way to a closer, but homophobically proscribed, bonding with another man."[24] In light of this definition, the concept of homosocial exchange inevitably has difficulty reading situations in which women — or indeed men — are absent.

Recent use of the term has intensified this difficulty by reintroducing Lesbian and Gay Studies to an element it has immense difficulty theorizing: conjecture; the term "homosocial" now refers largely to men *potentially* identifiable as homosexual and less commonly to a precarious *structure* that regulates same-gender relations by ensuring the relative stability of heterosexual exchange.[25] This raises a problem about bonding between men (and between women) that falls short of sexual significance, but which also resists conforming to a "more or less perfunctory detour" of desire for a woman (or man). This problem prevails when same-gender institutions—such as the military, the missionary school, the church, and government bureaucracies and administrations—define the "detour" these men and women adopt. Many historical accounts attest that during Britain's imperial sovereignty, men and women expressed fanatical support for these institutions.[26]

The difficulty of using the term "homosocial" to denote a situation in which no exchange of gender occurs makes the word slightly anachronistic for the process I interpret. That the "social" is never simply "homo" because alterity constitutes it; that the term obtains from an etymological confusion; and that I consider the social not only as exterior and empirically verifiable, but also as violently interior, renders inapplicable—because of its imprecision—some of the critical nomenclature of Lesbian and Gay Studies. Part of the first chapter outlines new ways of conceptualizing this relation in colonial armies and bureaucracies; the significance of the institution also returns in discussion of the Crewe Circular in chapter 6 and in a reading of Sassoon's and Saki's relations to the British army in the penultimate and final chapters.

Since my interest lies predominantly in the violent effect of sexual desire on ontology, and the way that psychoanalysis emerged in the service of a commensurate inquiry, I explore this dimension through psychoanalytic accounts of projection, displacement, fantasy, sublimation, resistance, and identification. I should stress that my argument is not reducible to one methodology or psychoanalytic term—it often demonstrates that literature and psychoanalysis fail in their respective accounts of social and sexual meaning. However, psychoanalysis is invaluable to this study *because* it foregrounds this failure as a generic difficulty about representing desire; psychoanalysis also explores the ambivalence a desired object can precipitate for a subject, the complex disjuncture that emerges between external mandates and internal fantasy, and the traumatic gap that prevails between a subject and its drives. Adam Phillips put this well when he argued recently, "It is impossible to imagine desire without obstacles." [27] Taking issue with commonsense assumptions about pleasure and satisfaction, Phillips argued: "The desire does not reveal the obstacle; the obstacle reveals the desire [because] the object of unconscious desire can be represented only by the obstacles to the conscious object of desire." [28] Phillips suggests that we need to place more emphasis on unexamined resistance and unconscious patterns of desire because "to think of resistance as the construction of an obstacle might lead us to redescribe resistances as peculiarly inventive artifacts." [29]

Freud's paper on "Instincts and Their Vicissitudes" (1915) is central to my use of this argument—and a structuring possibility for this book—because it clarifies the diffuse constituents of subjectivity, in which the drive is not reducible to an impulse, nor the object of desire necessarily commensurate with its subject's aim.[30] As Lacan notes of Freud's title (*Trieb und Triebschicksale*), "*Schicksal* is adventure, vicissitude" (162); in the colonial scene, effectively, we are already involved with the "adventure" of the drive. Lacan elaborated: "When you entrust someone with a mission, the *aim* is not what he brings back, but the itinerary he must take" (179). This study puts Lacan's point to work in a number of literary texts. Freud also clarified the effect of this argument about psychic turbulence on sexual orientation in his presentation of the case history of the "Rat Man" (1909), when he made the following, astonishing claim: "In no case is it permissible to classify someone as homosexual or heterosexual according to his object." [31] As Lacan recently corroborated, with an argument that has profoundly antiheterosexist and anti-imperialist implications for Lesbian and Gay Studies, the question is not so much *what* is one's desire as *where* it can be found (253–55):

> This is what Freud tell us. Let us look at what he says—*As far as the object in the drive is concerned, let it be clear that it is, strictly speaking, of no importance. It is a matter of total indifference.* One must never read Freud without one's ears cocked. When one reads such things, one really ought to prick up one's ears.
>
> How should one conceive of the object of the drive, so that one can say that, in the drive, whatever it may be, it is indifferent? (168; original emphasis)

The question is certainly worth considering. Lacan responded provocatively to Freud's challenge by considering the "*objet a* [as] *cause* of desire"; that is, not as an object to which the subject can freely and voluntarily attach (168).[32] In this respect, Freud and Lacan refute biological *and* culturalist definitions of desire as volition, decision, or conscious performance; they reframe desire as irrevocably tied to alienation: "*manque-à-être,* a 'want-to-be' " (29). Given this emphasis, we might infer that criticism that evacuates the unconscious from literature and history as the principal site of sexual fantasy necessarily produces an imperialist politics of the ego. Hence, for instance, Freud's insistent critique of "His Majesty the Ego." [33]

The Ruling Passion interprets these conceptual and procedural difficulties with cause and demand in colonial literature by emphasizing the subject's conflicted relation to its drives. My purpose in using Freud and Lacan is to clarify the forms of ontological meaning, violence, and crisis that colonialism often precipitated in relation to its subjects' demand. The questions that I address (in part, modifying Lacan's apparent rejection of the object's specificity) concern not only what homosexuality signifies in political terms and how it manifests conceptually as an object relation, but also how this desire registers as the effect of specific identifications and orientations. Following my reading of Lacan here, the point perhaps is less How can one write history or engage politics after his claim? than How could one entertain these cultural and political arguments without engaging the treacherous and often impalpable fields of demand, alienation, and symbolization that give them meaning?

This question of the object's bearing on the subject is one of emphasis; clearly, the object as cause is profoundly important insofar as it engages the logic of the drives. I contend that Lacan is not dismissing the object's importance out of hand in the passage above, and thus the relevance of the subject's rapport with ostensibly "same" and "different" genders—psychoanalysis in general cannot fail to discuss objects; [34] he is taking issue with conventional, philosophical assumptions about intersubjectivity and subject-object reciprocity, with which he entirely disagreed: "I have long stressed the specious character of this supposed altruism, which is pleased to preserve whose well being?—of him who, precisely, is necessary to us [i.e., the subject, 'ourselves']" (191–92). Consistent with my emphasis here on the difficulty of broaching historical and cultural continuity in terms of sexual identification, Lacan usefully challenges the fantasy that homosexuality overrides problematic breaks between different historical epochs and, let me emphasize this, *between different subjects.* As he once implied, in a statement that punctures much romantic mythology, "the number two delights at being odd" (194). In relation to the other, he critiqued the common refrain: "*What value has my love for you?* the eternal question that is posed in the dialogue of lovers. . . . It belongs to a dialogue that may be defined, in many respects, as a masculine phantasy" (192; original emphasis). Finally, in relation to transference and denial, he claimed: "In persuading the other that he has that which may complement us, we assure ourselves of being able to continue to misunderstand precisely what we lack" (133). Thus, Lacan would surely engage the question of homosexuality not as a realtight identification that bonds lesbians and gay men with automatic ease, but as a question of psychic drives that culminate in different, unreliable, and sometimes even untenable "orientations."

With all of these issues in mind, the first chapter, on Kipling, is the book's most sustained discussion of the fantasies underlying "conservative" or "integrationist" models of colonial desire: it interprets the anxiety surrounding Kipling's elaboration of sexual desire, and the way he used legal categories as a point of appeal against its vicissitudes and unruly influence. The second chapter examines the sexual and psychic dimension of the adventure tale in several lesser-known texts by Haggard and A. E. W. Mason, which place masculine affiliation in relation to the "colonial frame of homophilia." Chapter 3 emphasizes homosexual anxiety in the context of late-nineteenth-century Britain, arguing that James, Wilde, and Beerbohm found various tropes of masculine desire and seduction appropriate to the productive and interpretive labor of painting. My fourth chapter examines the influence of memory and repetition in Conrad's *Victory,* unraveling this novel's extraordinarily dense inflections by focusing on its preoccupation with drives, sexual difference, and racial equivalence. I argue that Conrad's emphasis on the psychic field denatures some of the biological privilege of Western heterosexuality, allowing the narrative to explore violent and challenging components of sexuality. Chapter 5 follows in the wake of this reading by interpreting the meaning that Maugham's novel *Of Human Bondage* attached to several triangular relationships, and the difference psychoanalysis brings to existing models of homosocial criticism. This chapter argues that the text's impossible relation to homosexuality exceeds conventional accounts of jealousy with one's rival by attributing a physical symptom to its protagonist, thus relieving him and the narrative of responsibility for his desire. Chapters 6 through 9 concern a more identifiable presence of homosexuality in writing by Forster, Firbank, Sassoon, and Saki: the first two chapters in this group interpret the influence of fantasy, displacement, and exile in Forster's short stories and Firbank's novellas; the latter two examine the theme of binding and diffusing homosexual desire in Sassoon's diaries and memoirs and in Saki's short stories.

Due to my emphasis on Sassoon's and Saki's ambivalent relation to the First World War, chapters 8 and 9 shift this book's focus onto the precarious relation between British nationalism, masculine identification, and homosexual desire. For this reason, and with the exception of my reading of

Saki's *The Unbearable Bassington* (1911–12), these chapters' engagement with British colonialism is largely secondary to *intra*national and domestic concerns. My reason for downplaying their emphasis on empire is both historically and conceptually important: not only did Britain's imperial dominance wane quite dramatically after the First World War, but questions of imperial rule are also inseparable from a country's internal conditions. Chapters 8 and 9 reengage conceptual issues that emerge in my opening chapters on masculine identification and national and psychic betrayal. The book closes by questioning the legacy of this identification in contemporary Britain and the persistence of a national transference that Britain has not adequately relinquished or mourned.

The central proposition of this book is that a rhetoric emerged at the turn of the last century that struggled to contain the diverse phenomena of masculine identification, colonial practice, and same-sex desire within a comprehensive set of terms and a coherent logic. Britain has used this rhetoric for many decades to determine national policy, behavioral mandates, and culturally proscribed fantasies, though I would argue that it is now time to decode these condensed meanings and to unravel their drives if we intend to shatter Britain's colonial legacy, once and for all.

1

The Incursions of Purity:

Kipling's Legislators

and the Anxiety

of Psychic Demand

Impurity and Expropriation: The Colonial Impulse to Power

Now, this is the road that the White Men tread
When they go to clean a land . . .
Oh, well for the world when the White Men tread
Their highway side by side!
—Rudyard Kipling[1]

A stone's throw out on either hand
From that well-ordered road we tread
And all the world is wild and strange.
—Kipling[2]

It's curious the fascination that white men feel drilling queer
material into shape.
—Kipling[3]

In their speeches and writings, many British Victorian colonials raise concerns about the successful implementation of law and authority. Their anxiety resonates beyond imperial governments and legislative structures; it also questions the internal coherence of colonial rule.[4] In interpreting this anxiety,

I suggest that a conflict between desire and mastery prevailed on what I shall term Britain's "colonial impulse to power."

This oscillation between desire and mastery clarifies an uncertainty that surfaced in many colonial texts about how to inhabit and symbolize colonialism's political and psychic registers; it also foregrounds the drives and fantasies that propelled Britain's ongoing bid for global sovereignty. Kipling often referred to the "breaking strain" that stymied his protagonists, for instance, when their national loyalty created intolerable fatigue and confusion over the precise meaning of the labor.[5] Although this "breaking strain" implies that acts of personal sacrifice glorified Britain's empire, many historians tell us that Britain's drive to secure political and economic sovereignty also intensified and sexualized relations between men, projecting antagonism and hostility onto those outside its franchise.[6] Since Britain's colonial mastery generated profound ambivalence toward its subjects, British women may have represented supports and vanishing mediators whose partial absence allowed forms of colonial mastery to prevail.

This account, however, is only one side of an uncertain and contested story. If Britain's colonial power was as absolute and secure as its politicians maintained, how should we explain so many colonials' suspicions that Britain's power not only was vulnerable but also, on another level, already lost? This anxiety between colonizer and colonized, and between men and women, at the turn of the last century differed greatly from the full weight of Britain's administrative power. It produced a paradox over the way that prominent colonials understood political instability at the level of ontological, group, and national fantasy, and the reason Britain's authority turned on a nebulous and quite precarious hinge between external security and internal control.

Before we consider Kipling's engagement with these psychic and rhetorical dilemmas, let us first turn to several prominent exemplars of colonial doubt: in his military speeches, for instance, Lord Horatio Kitchener—friend to Kipling, administrator in South Africa, political rival to the viceroy of India, and discreet homosexual—considered this psychic rigidity a precondition for military success: "No soldier who is unable to exercise due restraint in these matters can expect to be entrusted with command over his comrades. . . . Every man can, by self-control, restrain the indulgence of these imprudent and reckless impulses that so often lead men astray."[7] Kitchener urged the soldier to examine and manage his "reckless impulses" to prevent him from being "led astray." When this policy failed, as it often did, Kitchener proposed genocide and brutal subjugation as a corrective for a paucity of domestic and internal control. Calls for askesis and sexual chastity influenced not only this ferocious and unappeasable command, but also the premise that the native would not submit to outside rule without evidence of the colonial's self-restraint.[8] Adopting this paradox of controlled violence, Kitchener considered the vigilant internal discipline of passions as a valuable quality for export.

Recent critics have documented the colonial perception of indigenous peoples as lawless, seditious, and sexually promiscuous; this work provides an impetus for my study. However, critics have paid less attention to the dynamic that was integral to Britain's "Empire of the Selfsame," and have often framed this dynamic by appealing to historical events. Contrary to this single emphasis on historical materialism, I suggest that an unremitting dread of external defiance *and* internal unmaking propelled Britain's drive for global mastery; that the unappeasable quality of this drive created a fervent ambition that many colonialists tried to temper and vindicate by ethical appeals. Let us consider more examples: Robert Needham Cust, a civilian who served in the Punjab in the 1850s and 1860s, acknowledged that "the first sweet taste of unbounded power for good over others, the joy of working out one's own design, the contagious pleasure of influencing hundreds, the new dignity of independence, the novelty of Rule and swift obedience, this and the worship of nature in the solemnity of its grandeur and the simplicity of its children, were the fascinations which had enchanted me."[9] Henry Lawrence, who directed many of Britain's contemporaneous policies in the Punjab, elaborated on this point without appearing to jeopardize his command's authority: "It is all nonsense, sticking to rules and formalities, and reporting on foolscap paper, when you ought to be on the heels of a body of marauders, far within their own fastness, or riding into the villages and glens consoling, coaxing, or bullying as it may be, the wild inhabitants."[10] Finally, let us cite James Fitzjames Stephen, an influential imperialist of the time, because his sentiment influenced Kipling's later demands for colonial appropriation: "The sum and substance of what we have to teach them [amount to] the gospel of the English. . . . It is a compulsory gospel which admits of no dissent and no disobedience. . . . If it should lose its essential unity of purpose, and fall into hands either weak or unfaithful, chaos would come again like a flood."[11] Despite the confidence of these statements, each appears haunted by anxiety that a counterforce can unmake and usurp their authority from within. We could describe this force as colonial *jouissance* since it underpins each declaration and dissipates labor and power.[12] In considering the full influence of this counterforce, we also might argue that it obliged the colonial to compete with a corresponding impulse to self-dispossession whenever he bid for a country's possession. Thus the anxiety fueling the colonial's ambition to possess a country may have precipitated a significant number of internal crises for the colonial and his administration.

Since masculine rigor seemed amenable to channeling discipline into an incitement to power, many colonialists deemed it a suitable force to check these destructive impulses. For instance, Fitzjames Stephen gendered force as the expression of resolute masculinity: "Strength in all its forms is life and manhood. To be less strong is to be less of a man, whatever else you may be."[13] However, Stephen never clarified the referents to this "whatever else"; they conflict with central axioms of colonial masculinity.

These examples demonstrate that by the time Kipling came to theorize imperialism, inexorable laws of progress, hierarchy, and evolution appeared to determine the foundational logic of Britain's empire, presenting "mankind" as the governor of Nature's ordinance: "Nothing is gained by coddling weak and primitive men. The law of survival applies to races as well as to the species of animals. It is pure sentimental bosh to say that Africa belongs to a lot of naked blacks. It belongs to the race that can make the best use of it. I am for the white man and the English race."[14] This appeal to natural law generated a frame of categories and roles able to proscribe acceptable behavior by condemning their infraction. The law seemingly resolved the problem of antagonistic and self-destructive drives by fostering an ideal by which to measure the subject's deficient relation to each political mandate. Kipling's imperial law established a "transcendental signifier" against which to defend the empire from the manifest dissent and chaos of its unruly impulses.[15]

Kipling often connected this anxiety with the process of writing and the general production and dissemination of colonial meaning; his fiction relies on an analogous injunction to expel all of its detrimental elements. Kipling termed this radical excision "Higher Editing"; he sought to leave only a text's essential elements: "A tale from which pieces have been raked out is like a fire that has been poked."[16] However, his attempt to reduce the proliferation of meaning in his narratives inadvertently produced an elliptical and "modernist" style that stressed allusion, inference, and interpretation as a means to withstand "the pressure of the absent."[17] Additionally, the excised is never absent in Kipling's writing; the pressure of a "burden incommunicable" amplifies the precise limits of his narrative control.[18] In the opening sentence of a description of his "Working-Tools," for instance, Kipling argues that "Every man must be his own law in his own work."[19] The narrator of "False Dawn" later demonstrates the practical impossibility of this ideal: "No man will ever know the exact truth of this story . . . so the tale must be told from the outside—in the dark—all wrong" (67).

With its appeal to law over desire's vicissitudes, Kipling's writing mirrors a defensive structure that tries to expel sexual intimacy and miscegenation from the text; this attempt repeatedly surfaces and fails in the readings that follow. Benita Parry foregrounds Kipling's reliance on *parataxis*, for instance, arguing that the trope "organizes incommensurable discourses in ways that obscure and conceal the antagonism of their ideas." [20] The brevity of Kipling's fictional endings indicates the urgency with which he tried to disband the shattering chaos of desire; this brevity also foregrounds anxious moments of colonial authority by displaying his tenuous control over the text's periphery. Kipling's "nostalgia for a center" [21] often manifests as an extensive fraternal diaspora, for instance, that relieves the uncertainty of "race" by promising a reprieve from horrific formlessness: solidarity among white men provides at least imaginary defense against "impure" elements of racial difference and sexual desire. Yet Kipling's fiction is never stable in this regard because the displacement of "impurities" compels them to haunt their original structure. Let us therefore examine this difficulty of desire, and its uncertain resolution, in one of Kipling's most interesting narrative failures.

The Aim of Desire and the Passion That Fails

> He must be a man of decent height,
>   He must be a man of weight,
> He must come home on a Saturday night
>   In a thoroughly sober state;
> He must know how to love me,
>   And he must know how to kiss;
> And if he's enough to keep us both
>   I can't refuse him bliss
> —Rudyard Kipling [22]

> He was beginning to learn, not for the first time in his experience, that kissing is a cumulative poison. The more you get of it, the more you want.
> —Kipling (182)

There are many lies in the world, and not a few liars, but there are no liars like our bodies, except it be the sensations of our bodies.
　—Kipling [23]

Critics generally condemn Kipling's first novel, *The Light That Failed* (1891), as a lamentable failure. While enigma and thematic irresolution riddle the work, the narrative splits between two remarkable and dissimilar endings. In the first, the protagonist Dick Heldar dies in the arms of his closest male friend, Torpenhow; in the second, amended version, Heldar forms a precipitous marriage to Maisie, a woman who has from the novel's outset expressed almost unmitigated hostility toward him. The narrator must emphasize her uninterest in Heldar because their artistic rivalry disrupts the romantic attachment, creating an agony of unrequited love. Although neither version is successful in realist terms, Kipling preferred the first but proffered the second as a hasty revision to renew the interest of his disaffected readers.

This revision is incongruous because Maisie's abrupt change of heart and spontaneous repentance contradicts the narrator's emphasis on her and Heldar's incommensurate demands. On the one hand, the narrator censures Maisie's preoccupation with painting as a selfish disregard for her "suitor's" plight. On the other, her resistance is central to the narrative because it upholds the novel's basic concerns: the relentless unpleasure of Heldar's creativity, the extent to which he succeeds in convincing himself (if not the reader) of his passion for an "unworthy" woman, and the self-destructive impulses that represent all heterosexual interest in the novel.[24] Maisie illustrates all of these themes because the novel projects her as the reprehensible cause of Heldar's misery.

In this respect, the novel's split between two endings is not an exception to, but rather an emblem of, a wider narrative difficulty; the split documents the novel's resistance to sexual desire. *The Light That Failed* represents a crisis of object choice for which the classic scenario of the unavailable woman—and her conventional indictment—seems inadequate to explain its failure.[25] Maisie and other women in the text are recipients of an embittered misogyny, but the antagonism of desire that beleaguers Heldar not only precedes his involvement with Maisie, but also transforms her lack of interest into a conflict to which she has no obvious connection.

Thus, the text follows a split in Heldar between his desire's aim and the object that receives it—the object which he considers its *cause*—

although his desire's character falls elsewhere, within the purview of masculine relations, and particularly the arms of one man whose attraction prevails throughout. We can attribute many critics' complaints about this text's flaccidity to a conflict between aim, desire, and object because the text exists irrespective of Kipling's metaphysical explanation for Heldar's despondency and the author's misogynist rejection of women as the principal cause of Heldar's misery. The phrase "spoilt my aim" recurs in this text (10, 11–12, 14, 206), for instance, an example and symptom of Heldar's psychic impotence and as a precursor to his eventual blindness—an illness that stages his need for Torpenhow's specular assistance, allowing him to focus on what otherwise he cannot see about his desire.

We can further illustrate Heldar's dilemma by the significance he attaches to kissing.[26] His obsession for Maisie begins—like Philip Carey's similarly hopeless "demand" for Mildred in W. Somerset Maugham's *Of Human Bondage* (1915)—from an apparent lack of intimacy (see chapter 5 for discussion of Maugham). Their first kiss occurs after his gun has misfired, its aim spoilt: "Considered as a kiss, that was a failure, but . . . it was the first" (13). By granting Heldar only one kiss, Maisie makes each request exorbitant, leaving Heldar furious and later incapacitated by its "cumulative poison" (182); the demand always exceeds her response—and, one might suggest, his need. While Maisie constrains oral gratification in *The Light That Failed,* several bizarre and equivalent incidents represent this pleasure between men and between women. For instance, Heldar and Torpenhow hear the refrain from the musical—cited as an epigraph to this section—during their reuniting walk. Although the narrative curiously disembodies this stanza, it is not, as Kipling claims, a "music-hall refrain" (141), but rather an example of his own verse whose inclusion gives this scene particular significance: it encourages Heldar to sign up for military service, though the narrator never explains why a regiment of men would sing their desire for a man who "must know how to love me, / And he must know how to kiss; / And if he's enough to keep us both / I can't refuse him bliss" (141). Later, Heldar receives an unsolicited kiss from a female acquaintance and comments, as if to reiterate this refrain: " 'The amount of kissing lately has been simply scandalous. I shall expect Torp to kiss me next' " (196). In fact, this homosexual possibility recurs throughout Kipling's work as the most feasible limit—or point ad absurdum—to same-gender contact. To put this issue another way, we could say that it recurs as the jocular expression of a wish that expands one man's affectionate interest for another, from the specific concerns of object choice to the generic field of homophilia. Thus Mulvaney, in "With the Main Guard," reports a soldier's comment to his officer as follows: "The Staff Orf'cer wint blue, an' Toomey makes him pink by changing to the voice ov a minowderin' woman an' sayin': 'Come an' kiss me, Major dear, for me husband's at the wars an' I'm all alone at the Depot.' "[27] Similar and unaccountable homoerotic rejoinders punctuate Kipling's short story "Love-o'-Women": "He might as well have said that he was dancing naked," comments Mulvaney to Ortheris incongruously to explain his sergeant's behavior[28]; Mackenzie later declares of another soldier: "I knew there was no callin' a man to account for his tempers. He might as well ha' kissed me" (184).

Heldar's remarks about the scandal of kissing therefore are not exceptional to Kipling's economy of masculine desire; they are arguably that desire's most logical epiphany. Heterosexual desire characteristically disrupts the intimacy that men foster for each other, compelling same-sex friendship (or homophilia) bitterly to engage with the "disloyalty" that cross-gender interest precipitates.[29] When Heldar's obsession for Maisie seems most chaotic and self-destructive, for instance, his relationships with men begin to fracture; in turn, they insist that he remain faithful to their group—masculine loyalty ensures his salvation. Fraternal bonding thus is a redemptive camaraderie against the debilitating influence of women: " 'But a woman can be—' began Dick unguardedly. 'A piece of one's life,' continued Torpenhow. 'No, she can't' " (103).

The idea that intimacy with women can destroy Heldar's creative talent is consistent with this paradigm; such intimacy creates an instability that threatens all of his male friendships. Heldar's relationship with Torpenhow is contrary to this impulse, however, because it fosters creative talent and psychic stability, generating a productive cohesion between sublimation, group loyalty, and self-discipline. As the narrator remarks of this split between male and female objects: "Torpenhow came into the studio at dusk, and looked at Dick with eyes full of the austere love that springs up between men who have tugged at the same oar together and are yoked by custom and use and the intimacies of toil. This is a good love and, since it allows, and even encourages strife, recrimination, and the most brutal sincerity, does not die, but increases, and is proof against any absence and evil conduct" (58). If love between men is "good" when it is "austere," shaped by "the intimacies of toil," and able to ward off women's "evil conduct," heterosexual love tortures Heldar because it frustrates his pursuit of "higher" goals. Homophilia thus is regenerate, pure, and sublime, while heterosexuality is degenerate, impure, and abject. The narrator corrects any assumption that women's "evil conduct" is merely an external threat; woman's repression also prevents fraternal bonding from corrupting *philia* into *eros*. As an appropriate analogy here, Freud argued that the "Primal Horde" of brothers had to maintain a similarly vigilant "esprit de corps" against the legacy of their presocial and homosexual barbarism.[30]

Heldar's defense cannot properly excise evil conduct and comply with the colonial demand for askesis, however; neither painting nor the regiment can draw off the remainder to this novel's desire. Instead, the desire tips first toward a "bad" love for Maisie and then, with less compulsion and self-destruction, toward a "love" —that is, approval, respect, and loyalty— for Torpenhow. Even this figure of salvation cannot foreclose a demand for physical contact; he represents this demand with additional intensity:

> "Steady, Dickie, steady!" said the deep voice in his ear, and the grip tightened. "Bite on the bullet, old man, and don't let them think you're afraid." The grip could draw no closer. Both men were breathing heavily. Dick threw his head from side to side and groaned.
> "Let me go," he panted. "You're cracking my ribs. We—we mustn't let them think we're afraid, must we—all the powers of darkness and that lot?"
> "Lie down. It's all over now."
> "Yes," said Dick obediently. "But would you mind letting me hold your hand? I feel as if I wanted something to hold on to. One drops through the dark so." Torpenhow thrust out a large and hairy paw from the long chair. Dick clutched it tightly, and in half an hour had fallen asleep. Torpenhow withdrew his hand, and, stooping over Dick, kissed him lightly on the forehead, as men do sometimes kiss a wounded comrade in the hour of death, to ease his departure. (137–38)[31]

The first version of the novel seems to be this passage's logical epiphany because the aim of Heldar's desire finally reaches its object—another man—when Heldar collapses and dies in Torpenhow's arms. In this ending's revised version, however, Kipling recasts intimacy between the two men as a passionate friendship, while an alternative path—love between women—replaces this unwritable fantasy. The substitution of lesbianism for male homosexuality was a frequent trope of the art deco movement two decades later; as I argue in chapter 7, Ronald Firbank adopted this trope throughout his fiction for similar reasons.[32] In *The Light That Failed,* "the love which dare not speak its name" [33] also emerges from another sexual scene as desire for Maisie from the unnamed "red-haired girl." It appears that the second ending was the narrative solution to what Heldar and Maisie heterosexually resist, and what Heldar and Torpenhow find homosexually impossible: "The red-haired girl drew her [Maisie] into the studio for a moment and kissed her hurriedly. Maisie's eyebrows climbed to the top of her forehead; she was altogether unused to these demonstrations. 'Mind my hat,' she said, hurrying away, and ran down the steps to Dick waiting by the hansom" (68).

As with the earlier question about the music sung by the passing regiment, the narrator does not comment on this incident, though it fulfills an important function in this novel. The narrator does not name or develop the "red-haired girl" as a character, though she models for Maisie's painting, so her presence encourages a mild form of sexual rivalry between Heldar and Maisie for the same woman. The "red-haired girl" also voices an agony of homosexual longing, as if representing the displaced expression of an impossible love between Heldar and Torpenhow. Having kissed Maisie, for instance, she erupts at her cleaner with unaccountable rage: "The woman fled, and the red-haired girl looked at her own reflection in the glass for an instant and covered her face with her hands. It was as though she had shouted some shameless secret aloud" (72). Although we last hear the "red-haired girl" urging, "Maisie, come to bed" (150) — Maisie's inability to sleep results from her insoluble relation to Heldar — the persistent cultural disavowal of women's sexual desire in late-Victorian friendships suggests that this incident does not intentionally signify lesbianism.[34] However, it does indicate a link between an impulse and the desired object at the close of *The Light That Failed* that is equivalent to the two men's final embrace and consistent with homophilia's exchange for marriage's conventional resolution in its revised ending.

This secondary "lesbian" relationship displaces erotic interest between Heldar and Torpenhow by representing their intimacy as a defense against women's "cumulative poison" (182).[35] For instance, Heldar's life improves when he relinquishes his obsession for Maisie, and it coheres entirely when he returns to the brotherly fold. Having pursued Torpenhow to the Sudan for military service, Heldar also finds the inspiration to paint scenes of war, while the company of men re-solders his life's disparate aims, leaving him "wild with delight at the sounds and the smells [of war]" (201). The narrative implies that his regiment is reparative in psychic terms because it gives him purpose instead of abjection and reassurance after hopeless instability: "The clank of bayonets being unfixed made Dick's nostrils quiver. . . . 'Oh, my men! — my beautiful men!' " (141). Since this reintegration takes place abroad, in military conflict and by the death of "Fuzzies" (Sudanese soldiers), it also indicates what is at stake in each narrative and psychic pattern of expurgation: war allows Heldar to feel "master of himself" (196) and "good to be alive again!" (192). Since one of this text's most distressing and inexplicable scenes is the recollection of an incident in which Heldar and Torpenhow happily ridicule the death of a Sudanese soldier, Heldar's epiphany and ritualized purification are also the grotesque effect of colonial subjection and racial slaughter: "Then came to his mind the memory of a quaint scene in the Sudan. A soldier had been nearly hacked in two by a broad-bladed Arab spear. For one instant the man felt no pain. Looking down, he saw that his life-blood was going from him. The stupid bewilderment on his face was so intensely comic that both Dick and Torpenhow, still panting and unstrung from a fight for life, had roared with laughter, in which the man seemed as if he would join, but, as his lips parted in a sheepish grin, the agony of death came upon him, and he pitched grunting at their feet. Dick laughed again, remembering the horror. It seemed so exactly like his own case" (126–27). With the exception of Kipling's most recent biographer, Martin Seymour-Smith, who claims that this scene "has power as a true metaphor of how Kipling felt," [36] critics have thoroughly condemned this passage. Notwithstanding the problem of "true metaphor," it is imperative to ask why Kipling's metaphor took this form in establishing an analogy between his depression and his fantasies of racial violence. For other critics, Heldar's memory indicts British barbarity by enlisting the death of a Sudanese man as a source of pleasure and contemptuous laughter for white men. The idea that "stupid bewilderment" could be "intensely comic," that being "hacked in two" would produce a "sheepish grin," and that "the agony of death" could bolster the memory of a "quaint scene" is itself so obscene that it has impeded further inquiry. However, the argument that this scene illustrates only Kipling's callous indifference seems inadequate in this context; the link between humiliation and mirth—and that the respondents are virilized and sexualized by their laughter—demonstrates the *jouissance* maintaining their intimacy as it fuels their fascistic bid for power.[37]

A less extreme, if no less racist, example of projection arises before Heldar returns to the army, when he considers the inspiration for one of his paintings—the portrait of a woman he began during a sea voyage from Lima to Auckland; her image configures every conceivable fantasy and prejudice: "She was a sort of Negroid-Jewess-Cuban; with morals to match . . . who served as the model for the devils and the angels both—sea-devils and sea-angels, and the soul drowned between them" (98).

Following the topography of E. M. Forster's short story "The Other Boat" (1915–16), which I interpret at length in chapter 6, Heldar produces the painting "on the lower deck" (98) to signify difficult and inaccessible fantasies, and to allow the woman to figure desires that seem unwritable elsewhere. Since femininity and race condense a threat that Heldar flees, I suggest that this "Negroid-Jewess-Cuban" also embodies *The Light That Failed*'s narrative logic by compelling Heldar's return to the army and Torpenhow. The spectacle of the grotesquely mutilated Sudanese soldier indicates the violence that is necessary to represent—and then annihilate—each "opposition," whether it amplifies concerns about gender, race, or both. By adopting a principle of permanent antagonism, the "Empire of the Selfsame" uses defensive structures to purify its center and unify its diffuse impulses. As *The Light That Failed* illustrates, however, this antagonism returns desire to itself, keeping it within the apparent safety of an enclosure that admits no alterity. Less by intent than by default, this enclosure also creates a reactive homoeroticism: the empire manifests an *erotics* of the "same" rather than sexual desire for one man whom other men perceive differently. In this way, the novel promotes the idea that masculine imperialism glorifies phallic power and authority without resonating entirely of homosexuality. The novel eroticizes Torpenhow, for instance, because he represents an ideal whose physical realization never occurs. The narrative impedes the expression of Heldar's palpable desire for him, using the principle of de-eroticized friendship to withstand the pressure of this "burden incommunicable." [38] As the publication history of this novel testifies, however, the text could not sustain this ideal; it tried instead to resolve this idea by writing first the suicide of its protagonist, then Maisie's marital conversion in a way that disbands Kipling's primary support for homophilia. Kipling's decision to leave *The Light That Failed* heterosexually "secure" is thus contrary to the fundamental erotic path of this novel. Generally, though, he privileged the austere "rigor" of colonial masculinity over the debilitating effects of marriage and the effeminacy he perceived the Victorian dandy as embodying. As he declared in the poem "In Partibus," in a passage that attests to the impetus of his other writing:

> It's Oh to meet an Army man,
> Set up, and trimmed and taut,
> Who does not spout hashed libraries
> Or think the next man's thought
> And walks as though he owned himself,
> And hogs his bristles short.[39]

Carving Up, Cutting Up: Frontiers and Disfiguration

I won't make a nation . . . I'll make an empire! These men aren't
niggers; they're English! Look at their eyes—look at their mouths.
Look at the way they stand up. They sit on chairs in their own houses.
They're the Lost Tribes, or something like it, and they've grown to be
English. . . . We shall be Emperors—Emperors of the Earth! . . . I'll
treat with the Viceroy on equal terms . . . and we'd be an empire.
—Rudyard Kipling [40]

I am a barbarian. I believe with Ruskin that all healthy men love to
fight, and all women love to hear of such fighting . . . I love the big and
simple. . . . Expansion is everything. . . . These stars . . . these vast
worlds which we can never reach. I would annex the planets if I could.
—Cecil Rhodes [41]

As earlier sections of this chapter demonstrate, Kipling often staged
a conflict between colonial law and sexual desire, representing the first as a
point of appeal against the vagaries and vicissitudes of the second. The resulting tension clarifies a limit to the British colonial project by demonstrating
that colonial and psychic mastery fundamentally are untenable.

Kipling's short story "The Man Who Would Be King" (1890) elucidates this limit by tracking an imperial mission by two white men—Dravot
and Carnehan—that the author both validates and disparages: while the story
endorses their commendable ambition, this drive is also so excessive that it
tips into the very barbarism both men set out to master. Dravot and Carnehan's ambition ultimately corrupts their colony because they fail to exercise
restraint; instead, they unleash an authoritarian *jouissance* that ruins all principles of government. By carefully tracing the points where their empire
stymies, Kipling distinguishes "proper" legislation from crude opportunism,
vindicating the former over the latter's vulgarity. However, this distinction
between proper and illicit authority is unpersuasive; the logic of synecdoche
indicates that Britain endorsed similarly crude impulses to power by establishing white supremacy in the "legal" colony of India. Indeed, "The Man
Who Would Be King" maintains this similarity by linking the two buccaneers—by a shared bond of brotherhood—with the journalist who assists and
then reports them: all three are Masons. This bond connects each character

to his version of colonial history; it also defeats Kipling's aims of separating barbaric impulse from political righteousness.

The journalist first meets Carnehan on a train, and with a Masonic pledge reluctantly offers to help him defeat Kafiristan.[42] Carnehan and Dravot annex this kingdom, but after a short period of absolute sovereignty in which they pretend to be gods, the buccaneers inadvertently disclose their humanity when Dravot bleeds: a rebellion ensues during which Dravot dies. Carnehan returns to the journalist to dictate his version of their calamitous rise and fall.

If initially in this text the Masonic bond fosters a link between official practice and unofficial desire, it later represents a binding pact between Dravot and Carnehan that they write on "a greasy half-sheet of notepaper" as their social contract:

> "*This Contract between me and you persuing witnesseth in the name of God—Amen and so forth.*
>
> *(One)   That me and you will settle this matter together; i.e., to be Kings of Kafiristan.*
>
> *(Two)   That you and me will not, while this matter is being settled, look at any Liquor, nor any Woman black, white, or brown, so as to get mixed up with one or the other harmful.*
>
> *(Three) That we conduct ourselves with Dignity and Discretion, and if one of us gets into trouble the other will stay by him.*
>
> *Signed. . . . Both Gentlemen at large.*" (65–66)

This contract signifies a formal declaration of intent for Dravot and Carnehan, which ratifies their will to power. Loyalty to each other is this contract's primary condition; it prevents "Liquor nor any Woman" from corrupting their ambition. The journalist copies the contract (correcting Dravot and Carnehan's misspelling of the term "Contrack"), which Kipling encloses in turn by his own narrative, as if to foreclose the possibility that it might seep into the larger colonial text and soil its integrity. For instance, the journalist appeals to Kipling's administrative law at the beginning and end of Carnehan's narrative, as if to stabilize his colonial infraction and legislate the correct boundaries of political conduct: the sentence "The Law, as quoted, lays down a fair conduct of life, and one not easy to follow" (57) introduces the journalist's account of meeting Carnehan, while "And there the matter rests" (86) represents his hasty bid to conclude it. Despite this precaution, Dravot's death creates such symbolic and thematic unrest in this text that Kipling clarifies how barbarism is central to every colonial project—whatever "Dignity and Discretion" it claims for itself—by demonstrating that colonialism cannot sustain distinctions between the buccaneer and the authentic "Gentlemen at large."

Once they have successfully usurped power from the Kafiristanis and set up their own administration, for instance, Dravot and Carnehan's empire struggles to repress its founding violence by establishing a beneficent government. Carnehan smoothes out their unruly beginnings while the journalist, in turn, corrects their spelling and copies and authorizes their "greasy half-sheet of notepaper." This sequence recurs throughout the tale as different registers of writing and speech map out corresponding grammatologies of power. Since the narrative takes the form of a palimpsest, it allows each register to recede in a series of concentric circles that begin with the colonial writer and the transcribing journalist. The narrative then moves into the interior and inferior spaces of the text, with the "contract" and its writers, Dravot and Carnehan, who are only part literate; it finally withdraws into the innermost fold of the illiterate natives onto whom Dravot and Carnehan impose each successive piece of legislation. Kipling also forces a correspondence between himself and the journalist because a description of the latter's procedure signifies an authorized version that the reader could otherwise dispute: "the last type was set . . . and the machines spun their fly-wheels two or three times to see that all was in order before I said the word that would set them off" (62).

Kipling provides the reader little opportunity to contest the master narrative in this tale because he displaces its authority onto subsidiary terms: by the time the "Contrack" (64, 66) [sic] has reached the indigenous people, its jurisdiction has fractured into discrete phonetic units:

> "The letter?—Oh!—The letter! Keep looking at me between the eyes, please. It was a string-talk letter, that we'd learned the way of it from a blind beggar in the Punjab."
>
> I remember that there had once come to the office a blind man with a knotted twig and a piece of string which he wound round the twig according to some cipher of his own. He could, after the lapse of days or hours, repeat the sentence which he had reeled up. He had reduced the alphabet to eleven primitive sounds, and tried to teach me his method, but I could not understand. (74)

Dravot and Carnehan make a concerted effort to learn the language of Kafiristan and give directives "in their lingo" (74)—a policy that European administrators modified by compelling the colonized either to adopt their own language (as did the French, Spanish, and Portuguese), or to use a two-tier language system on the understanding that the European's tongue would be the colony's official discourse (e.g., the Flemish and Germans), or, more curiously but wholly in line with their policy of segregation and racial purity, to superimpose the official language *and* actively resist the colonized's efforts to communicate in the master tongue for fear that the colonized would corrupt it (e.g., the British).[43]

Since much of "The Man Who Would Be King" elaborates concentric spheres of influence and their accompanying nomenclature of power, it sets up a distinction between the colonial's "correct" practice and the charlatan's corrosive ambition. Contrary to their initial similarity with the journalist, for instance, the buccaneers appear fraudulent when they overstep the proper bounds of legislation. Dravot and Carnehan's appropriation of Kafiristan exceeds Kipling's conceptual limits because they inaugurate a shift from benign paternalism (government on behalf of the incapable and unruly) to despotic intervention (dictatorship by a selfish and primitive subjugation).

This split between the journalist and the buccaneers is a critical hinge on which the outcome of this story turns. Kipling pits one system of government against another to distinguish the characteristics seemingly "appropriate" to each race. The story emphasizes that the illicit quality of Dravot and Carnehan's colony is an effect of their degenerate aims because their behavior rescinds their contract. Both men also corrupt British dignity by mocking the totemic system of Kafiristan and by assuming an omnipotence that challenges the word of God, the "Primal Father": "Dravot says— 'Go and dig the land, and be fruitful and multiply,' which they did, though they didn't understand" (72). Finally, the narrative reveals their exorbitant desire for power as not only fascistic—which might seem, in Kipling's terms, almost tolerable—but heterosexual—which in this context is not: Dravot's desire for a woman introduces the "trouble" that the second clause of their contract anticipates; it also ruins the brotherhood that its third clause ratifies. When Dravot orders one of the chiefs to find him an eligible wife, for instance, she rejects his advances by biting him, thus causing him to bleed. This discloses both men as mortal; the Kafiristanis expel them in psychic and symbolic terms from their kingdom.

I interpret Dravot and Carnehan's usurpation of Kafiristan as colonial *jouissance* because their reign over Kafiristan illustrates a central psychoanalytic principle of mastery and transference: both men accede to power and occupy the place of the Father by representing themselves as phallic authority. They achieve public adoration so easily because the Kafiristanis perceive them to *embody* the law: "We thought you were men till you showed the sign of the Master" (80). However, this fantasy of omnipotence precipitates their political and psychic castration after engendering an almost psychotic delirium. Dravot's demand for a woman ruins their charade by returning *jouissance* to the place it was formerly denied.[44] Consistent with the "cumulative poison" of kissing in Kipling's later novel *The Light That Failed,* the kiss Dravot receives from his wife also repeats Kipling's association between castration and a generic, female menace:

> "She'll do," said Dan, looking her over. "What's to be afraid of, lass? Come and kiss me." He puts his arm round her. She shuts her eyes, gives a bit of a squeak, and down goes her face in the side of Dan's flaming red beard.
> "The slut's bitten me!" says he, clapping his hand to his neck, and, sure enough, his hand was red with blood. Billy Fish and two of his matchlock-men catches hold of Dan by the shoulders and drags him into the Sashkai lot, while the priests howls [sic] in their lingo—"Neither God nor Devil but a man!" (82)

By repeating this point in *The Light That Failed,* Kipling argues that heterosexuality—and specifically women—are responsible for unmanning men because both compel them to betray homophilia. In *The Light That Failed,* this betrayal surfaces throughout the text; in "The Man Who Would Be King," the narrative writes this betrayal formally into Dravot and Carnehan's contract. In both narratives, however, heterosexual desire usurps the authority of each man's ego by instigating a furious return of *jouissance.*

With its impulse to master new and sublime heights (Kafiristan is a mountainous kingdom in an "out-of-the-way corner of the Empire into which [the journalist] had not penetrated" [57]), "The Man Who *Would Be* King" also reads as a struggle to master subsidiary and psychic drives. Dravot and Carnehan's journey may signify the ascent into an equivalent psychic topography, for instance, because the narrator describes it as one of "the dark places of the earth, full of unimaginable cruelty" (59–60). Like Conrad's *Heart of Darkness* (1902), in which external colonization is part congruent with internal crisis, Kipling's story corresponds to Freud's description of the aim of psychoanalysis four decades later. In "The Dissection of the Psychical Personality" (1933), Freud argued that psychoanalysis tries to empower the ego with sovereignty over previously unconscious drives: "Where id was, there ego shall come to be";[45] a task he considered as "not unlike the draining of the marsh lands of the Zuider Zee" in the Netherlands because it replaces swampland with firm and fertile ground. The analogy is not gratuitous here; Freud also likened the personality to geography in the same lecture, and argued earlier in *Inhibitions, Symptoms and Anxiety* (1926) that ego-organization resembles a "frontier-station with a mixed garrison," since it regulates the transposition of impulses between unconscious and preconscious systems.[46] By maintaining secure defenses against the "foreign" and "alien" (Freud's metaphor for the symptom),[47] the ego guarantees the abreaction of drives whose beneficence it recognizes; it also forbids entry to those whose aim and intensity appear suspicious and hostile.

Earlier in *Inhibitions, Symptoms and Anxiety,* Freud explained the vertiginous warfare prevailing between the ego and the id by representing consciousness as a volatile colony: "Let us imagine a country in which a certain small faction objects to a proposed measure the passage of which would have the support of the masses. This minority obtains command of the press and by its help manipulates the supreme arbiter, 'public opinion,' and so succeeds in preventing the measure from being passed." [48] In chapters 2 and 6, I elaborate on this metaphoric link between the unconscious and presumptions of indigenous "savagery." Here, we should note that, unlike Kipling, Freud's metaphor aligns the indigenous or colonized with revolutionary defiance and insurrection; the ego's law in this instance represents potential tyranny since it exploits the manifest docility of "public opinion."

Psychoanalysis has often described the psychic register by metaphors common to colonial administration and writing. Freud used the theme of buried treasure in H. Rider Haggard's *King Solomon's Mines* (1885) to signify preoedipal pleasure;[49] as I recount in chapter 2, he also recommended Haggard's *She* (1886) to a patient for its symbolization of "the eternal feminine, the immortality of our emotions. . . ." [50] This analogy between the psychic and political-historical project renders each register blurred and indistinct—particularly in Kipling's writing. For instance, when Dravot speaks of his and Carnehan's desire to construct an empire as "Kings in our own right" (64), both men must clearly secure equivalent dominion over an internal landscape whose collapse they interpret as the cause of their political failure.

That Kafiristan is a colonial outpost lying "beyond the border" of existing sovereignty (68) appears to strengthen its need for internal control; the passage beyond the known leads the "frontier–station with a mixed garrison" into ungovernable and intolerable terrain. The dilemma recurs in Kipling's poem "Arithmetic on the Frontier," when he describes "A scrimmage in a Border station— / A canter down some dark defile. . . ."[51] "The Man Who Would Be King" insists, however, that its protagonists must never reach this beyond; in this instance it is responsible for unleashing a ferocious violence that culminates in tyranny and massacre. Nevertheless, Kipling's vision of bogus colonialism and violent misrule cannot *stay* "beyond the border"; comparable tendencies lie within the realm of even the most correct administration that irrupt as dramatic, internal insurrections.

The problem of colonial influence that "The Man Who Would Be King" raises is considerable but not exhaustive; it recurs in many Kipling stories as compulsive activity and a frantic reconsolidation of power. "At the Pit's Mouth" (1899) certifies the punishment of a "Man's Wife and a Tertium Quid" (or extra third) for enjoying an affair. The tension is so unbearable for the Tertium Quid that he decides to spur his horse over the edge of a precipice to fall into the oblivion beneath. Although inscrutable and ludicrous, this ending represents a tension in Kipling's fiction that surfaces whenever his characters' impulses disempower them and geographical impasses represent their crises. While ravines, pits, and wells haunt his landscapes, sudden turns of circumstance (*peripeteia*) brutalize and destroy his characters.

We can develop this analogy in Kipling between physical and psychic topographies because the first often substitutes for the second, as if the colonial drive leads its subject inexorably toward ruin and death. When Freud likened the ego's regulation of the unconscious to "a man on horse-back, who has to hold in check the superior strength of the horse," [52] he unwittingly endorsed the most common allegorical structure of Kipling's fiction. The rider in "At the Pit's Mouth" suffers from an equivalent drive to relinquish control, for instance, as if his ego realized the futility of its struggle and submitted instead to the convulsive bliss of self-sabotage—a *jouissance* ride into the hole of oblivion and the brink of the real. [53]

In "The Strange Ride of Morrowbie Jukes" (1895), this release of tension allows *jouissance* to perform a similar function, though Jukes's flight is not upward toward the colonial sublime, as in "The Man Who Would Be King," but downward toward the abject elements that fashion what is culturally and subjectively within. [54] Jukes falls into a pit on the outskirts of a desert workcamp and finds that the sand walls, swamp, and quicksand prevent him from escaping. More to the point, the pit is inhabited by the living dead—those "who did not die, but may not live"—because they are social and religious outcasts. [55]

This tale recounts a colonizer's nightmare of being led to a place in which his law, race, and caste contain no meaning. Jukes eventually realizes that the pit levels men and women to a common denominator, that their fight for survival prevails over all established "Rules" of culture. Perversely, the text seems intent on confronting the forces lying just beyond or outside

British legislation; it recounts the "sensation of nameless terror [that Morrowbie] had in vain attempted to strive against," which eventually "overmaster[s him]" (178). Thus the imposition of colonial laws on a country is virtually inseparable from accompanying fantasies of its violation and dissolution. Morrowbie struggles to avoid "imaginary traps" (169), but his task proves impossible because the text itself falls into one.

"The Strange Ride of Morrowbie Jukes" is a peculiar and interesting tale because it represents the horror of being ensnared and annihilated by colonialism's underside—the realm of dirt, corporeal excrescence, sexual license, and political chaos that British imperialism set out to expurgate and master.[56] As I demonstrate in chapter 4, Axel Heyst—Conrad's protagonist in *Victory* (1915)—complains similarly of "disgust at my own person, as if I had tumbled into some filth hole";[57] in Kipling's tale, though, a loyal Indian servant eventually "hauls [Jukes] out" from the "Village of the Dead" (199) and—so the inference must follow—returns him to the realm of law, discipline, and hierarchy. The drama of Jukes's "strange *ride*" is rather less obvious, however, because the narrative struggles to rationalize his decision to climb onto his horse to chase—and then kill—the wild dog howling outside his tent: Jukes has a slight fever, the moon is full, he is slightly delirious. According to the narrative, his "strange ride" is the culmination of illness and a generic Indian malaise that takes him to the very brink of insanity. Jukes's delirious ride also connects illness to specific and imaginary topographies: the colonial outpost and the abject pit beyond it. The impulse that precedes this "ride" therefore is mysterious because it is never as rational as the narrator implies. The pit seems less the entrapment of an unfortunate adventurer than the logical fulfillment of Jukes's self-destructive fantasy.

By framing the tale in this way, I intend to bracket immediate focus on India and Jukes's apparently symptomatic delirium to assess the status of the "beast" he chases, the reason its cry enrages, and the significance of slipping into a hole from which escape is virtually impossible. My interest lies in the repeated imposition and convulsive unmaking of legislation that barely succeeds in keeping colonial discipline and its subjects in check—the same phenomenon that led Heldar to destitution over a woman he could not love (*The Light That Failed*), Dravot and Carnehan to renege on their contract ("The Man Who Would Be King"), and the Tertium Quid to leap into a ravine to avoid the shame of adultery ("At the Pit's Mouth").

Once Jukes decides to "slaughter one huge black and white beast" (170), he prepares his horse to "mount and dash out as soon as the dog should again lift up his voice" (170). As in Freud's analogy of the horse rider to the ego, Jukes appears to give chase as soon as an unruly impulse enters his consciousness; the beast, however, is able to elude him:

> The brute bolted as straight as a die, the tent was left far behind, and we were racing over the smooth sandy soil at racing speed. In another we had passed the wretched dog, and I had almost forgotten why it was that I had taken horse and hog-spear.
>
> The delirium of fever and the excitement of rapid motion through the air must have taken away the remnant of my senses. (170)

While Jukes ruminates on the baleful consequence of his "mad gallop" (171), his ride also "o'erleaps" its object because the chase presents its own demented rationale. As "the wretched beast went forward like a thing possessed, over what seemed to be a limitless expanse of moonlit sand" (171), it leads him to a sharp incline of sand and invites him to fall into the crater beneath.

In line with my reading of "The Man Who Would Be King" and "At the Pit's Mouth," I suggest that this ride connects deliberately and paradoxically with the crater and its accompanying meanings of psychic immolation and racial entrapment. After the Indian servant rescues Jukes, Kipling extols the virtues of control and legislation by first elaborating and then allegedly resolving the "nameless terror" of incarceration. However, this terror is so extensive in this tale that Kipling cannot control it; the hole has a tendency to evacuate the ego by destroying its control of the environment. By allegorizing colonial and psychic impulses, Kipling exacerbates, rather than relieves, the anxiety at the center of his texts. Since quicksand sections off the crater, it compels Jukes to traverse the crater to escape. Here, he falls prey to "an indescribable drawing, sucking motion of the sand below. Another moment and my leg was swallowed up nearly to the knee. In the moonlight the whole surface of the sand seemed to be shaken with devilish delight at my disappointment. I struggled clear, sweating with terror and exertion . . ." (188). In a moment of sheer panic and profound paranoia, Jukes personifies the environment as hostile, intent on inflicting an indescribable injury on him.

The extent of this crisis indicates that "The Strange Ride of Morrowbie Jukes" announces the aim of the colonial drive, not the object that leans upon it.[58] The precarious compound of colonial aim, drive, and object splits to expose the raw constituents of what would otherwise bind and assemble them. In Kipling's more conventional tales, the object leads the subject to this peril, as if desire can shatter a protagonist's tenuous control of its environment and interiority. Thus, "Beyond the Pale" (1888) represents a Portuguese man's desire for a black woman as the cause of his downfall; Kipling warns him in these notorious opening lines: "A man should, whatever happens, keep to his own caste, race, and breed. Let the white go to the white and the black to the black. Then, whatever trouble falls is in the ordinary course of things—neither sudden, alien, nor unexpected." [59]

Taking no heed of this warning, Trajego's desire for Bisera leads him so far beyond accepted limits that the narrator's opprobrium promptly upbraids him: "This is the story of a man who willfully stepped beyond the limits of decent everyday society, and paid for it heavily" (43). Beyond the infamous prejudice, what is notable in this tale is Kipling's concern to protect "decent" elements of society from the "willful" impulses that spoil its "civilized" rules. Given the fate of Morrowbie Jukes, Dick Heldar, and Dravot and Carnehan, the consequence of this desire seems startlingly familiar. As Trajego reaches out to embrace "the black dark Bisera," he discovers the punishment her family has already inflicted on her: "both hands had been cut off at the wrists, and the stumps were nearly healed" (47). This racial castration cuts both ways, however, serving as a double prohibition; as Bisera bows and cries, for instance, "someone in the room grunted like a wild beast, and something sharp—knife, sword, or spear—thrust at Trajego in his *boorka* [gown]. The stroke missed his body, but cut into one of the muscles of the groin, and he limped slightly from the wound for the rest of his days" (47). An almost identical outcome prevails in the short story "Dray Wara Yow Dee" (1890), in which the protagonist swears an eternal and homoerotic "lust of vengeance" against his rival: "I will follow him as a lover follows the footsteps of his mistress, and coming upon him I will take him tenderly—Aho! so tenderly!—in my arms. . . . What love so deep as hate? . . . There is no madness in my flesh, but only the vehemence of the desire that has eaten me up. . . . Surely my vengeance is safe! . . . for I would fain kill him quick and whole with the life sticking firm in his body.[60]

The violent consequence of ungovernable desire compels Kipling to insist that the colonial fold must repudiate first miscegenation, then all sexual desire per se. Apparently, it is not enough to avoid contact with the colonized; one must abstain from all sexual relations to stay faithful to one's racial fraternity. Paradoxically, though, Kipling's rejection of the sexual is itself highly sexual; the way his protagonists suffer from this rejection encourages desire to return from without with increasingly manic and violent consequence. Sexual contact also haunts and exhausts them because they exert formidable energy in repressing each catastrophic propensity to lose control. In similar ways, the narrative concludes its often wild oscillations of fantasy by shunting unmanageable heroes into ravines and craters.

These scenes of abstention and violence in "Beyond the Pale" and "Dray Wara Yow Dee" partly explain why Kipling invests the other with a formidable power to unmake and destroy colonial authority. His dread often a specific fear of unmanning: Bisera's uncle leaps out of the darkness in "Beyond the Pale" with a vengeance that injures and emasculates Trajego. In a related story, "The Mark of the Beast" (1891), an Indian leper performs a similar retribution against Fleete, an English colonel, when Fleete desacralizes a Hindu temple by stubbing out his cigar on "the red stone image of Hanuman." [61] The narrator uses the leper to invoke "some of the more unnecessary horrors of life in India" (195). Indifferent to life and self-injury, the leper apparently embodies India's infection and decomposition as the empire's burden or White Man's symptom. His eerie disfiguration also relieves him of fixed identity by allowing him to support whatever fantasy the British project onto him. In other words, the leper—whom the narrator describes as "the Silver Man"—bears whatever mark of "beast[liness]" most resembles Fleete's racial anxiety:

> When we confronted him with the beast the scene was beyond description. The beast doubled backwards into a bow as though he had been poisoned with strychnine, and moaned in the most pitiable fashion. Several other things happened also, but they cannot be put down here. . . . I understand then how men and women and little children can endure to see a witch burnt alive; for the beast was moaning on the floor, and *though the Silver Man had no face, you could see horrible feelings passing through the slab that took its place,* exactly as waves of heat play across red-hot iron—gun-barrels for instance.
>
> Strickland shaded his eyes with his hands for a moment and we got to work. This part is not to be printed. (205; my emphasis)

At the tale's end, Fleete assumes the same properties as the leper and "snarl[s] like a wolf" at his former friends (202). "The Mark of the Beast" is an extraordinary account of colonial metalepsis (metonymic substitution) that betrays the social and psychic proximity between the colonizer and the colonized: after Strickland and the narrator maim and kill the leper, Fleete's "soul" returns to him; he becomes "civilized" again. However, the narrator completely ignores the murder's brutality and the colonel's frenzied delirium.

With its stress on purity and colonial askesis, "The Mark of the Beast" demonstrates that Kipling often represented his dread of contagion in racial terms. In "His Chance in Life" (1890),[62] a confluence of infection and racial inmixing generates an obsession with boundaries and defenses that recalls the narrative caution of "The Man Who Would Be King" by mapping the question of racial influence in crass geopolitical and psychic-corporeal metaphors: "If you go straight away from Levées and Government House Lists, past Trades' Balls—far beyond everything and everybody you ever knew in your respectable life—you cross, in time, the Borderline where the last drop of White blood ends and the full tide of Black sets in. . . . The Black and the White mix very quaintly in their ways. Sometimes the White shows in spurts of fierce, childish pride—which is Pride of Race run crooked—and sometimes the Black in still fiercer abasement and humility, half-heathenish customs and strange, unaccountable impulses to crime" (91). In this passage, the narrator perceives race not only as an *interior* coloration but also as a specific influence on psychic drives, as if the black surpassed qualities that are "proper" to the white by tinting the colonizer with an otherwise foreign instability. While this tale describes the psychic as a racial characteristic, "The Mark of the Beast" explains that this fantasy is also quite untenable.

Although ostensibly the story of an Indian man who gains the approval of a "Native Police Inspector," "His Chance in Life" never loses its obsession with measuring colonial talent by "racial" blood; the narrator attributes Michele's promotion entirely to this factor: "Michele was a poor, sickly weed and very black; but he had his pride . . . he looked down on natives as only a man with seven-eighths native blood in his veins can" (92). Michele's "chance" hinges on his precarious one-eighth of nonindigenous blood because this apparently visible distinction sustains his civic responsibility: "[T]he Police Inspector [was] afraid, but obey[ed] the old race-instinct which *recognizes* a drop of white blood as far as it can be diluted . . ." (94; my emphasis). The remaining seven-eighths of Michele's blood appear to gain the upper hand, however; "Responsibility and Success" so overwhelm him that by the time he meets a proper "Sahib" (white man), he collapses in hysterical tears—the childishness that apparently befits his prevailing nature: "Michele felt himself slipping back more and more into the native. . . . It was the White drop in Michele's veins dying out, though he did not know it. But the Englishman understood . . ." (95).

Kipling obviously was comfortable with the idea that races possess discernible characteristics and qualities, and seldom tired of repeating it to those willing to listen. From the despotic interventions I cited earlier in this chapter to the apparently benign paternalism that shrouds "His Chance in Life," Kipling upheld Britain's right to political sovereignty by arguing that it promoted cultural and religious salvation. In this way, he managed to off-set the barbaric violence of colonialism by its capacity (if not rapacity) to redeem each cultural vacuum.

By infantilizing the colonized, Kipling found another way to vali-date Britain's intervention: "Never forget that unless the outward and visible signs of Our Authority are always before a native he is as incapable as a child of understanding what authority means, or where is the danger of disobeying it" (93). Under the influence of such an administration, the colonized clearly had little opportunity to forget this imposing authority. The remark, however, is notable because the omnipotence of "Our Authority" recalls the ambition of "The Man Who Would Be King," which gives the white man a messianic right to interfere. Considering Kipling's ambivalence toward paternal authori-ties, and his strong identification with children and adolescents in *Mowgli, The Jungle Book, The Just-So Stories, Stalky & Co.,* and even *Kim,* this citation illustrates a form of imperialist advocacy that Kipling subtly undermined by the nostalgia and sentiment he devoted to his children's fiction.[63] The severity of the former position may even have served as the precondition for this sen-timent to emerge: Kipling encouraged protagonists like Stalky and Kim to transgress the limits of authority before they finally bow to national loyalty. While Kipling supported extreme policies for the empire without regard to their often brutal consequence,[64] he was cheerfully idealizing the canny de-fiance of youth as it gleefully wreaked havoc on "Our Authority." Clearly Kipling permitted this violence only because the protagonists in question were white, but this permission nevertheless raises important questions about Kipling's legislation of empire and the meaning of his fictional accounts of race for children. In the following section, I interpret the consequence of this sanctioned rebellion and its effect on Kipling's brief period of colonial and paternal ambivalence.

Re/Signing to Law: Affiliation "In the Interests of the Brethren"

Now this is the Law of the Jungle—as old and as true as the sky; And the Wolf that shall keep it may prosper, but the Wolf that shall break it must die.
—Rudyard Kipling[65]

'E was all that I 'ad in the way of a friend,
An' I've 'ad to find one new; . . .

Oh, passin' the love o' women,
Follow me—follow me 'ome!
—Kipling[66]

It is not only that . . . Mr Kipling . . . celebrate[s] male virtues,
enforce[s] male values and describe[s] a world of men; it is that the
emotion with which these books are permeated is to a woman
incomprehensible. . . . So with Mr Kipling's officers who turn their
backs; and his Sowers who sow the Seed; and his Men who are alone
with their Work; and the Flag—one blushes at all these capital letters
as if one had been caught evesdropping at some purely masculine orgy.
—Virginia Woolf[67]

By the time Kipling wrote *Kim,* in 1901, the severity of his distinction between support for the empire and idealization of rebellious youth
had softened, and the frame of racial opposites—hitherto a structuring principle to his work—notably was less pronounced. The poems "Recessional"
and "The Islanders" illustrate this shift in tone and nomenclature by their
respective accounts of imperialism. Although "Recessional" vindicates Dar-
win's principle of racial evolution by representing the empire as God's command over "lesser breeds without the Law," [68] "The Islanders" acknowledges
the "Strife" of colonial administration as a troubling addition to the "White
Man's burden." [69]

Considering this second position, *Kim* may be further evidence of
Kipling's brief reprieve from an otherwise remorseless authoritarianism; it
clarifies points of tension and anxiety that have dogged his intransigence all
along. Kim's confusion about his racial status arguably derives from the fact
that a proleptic uncertainty surrounds this novel's racial significance: *Kim*
represents a transition between the unequivocal logic of "Recessionals' " perspective on imperialism and the more fluid scene of racial identification that
surfaces in "The Islanders." As the Irish Kim declares: "I am *not* a Sahib. I
am thy *chela* [disciple], and my head is heavy on my shoulders" (319; original emphasis).

By repeatedly challenging the demand of his elders that he affiliate
to British power, Kim measures the price of this shift from imperial identity
to political identification. Though he is poor, Irish, and white, Kim identifies
as the *chela* to a Tibetan lama, and defies the pressure to follow the "appropriate" path of his race by offsetting the benefit of nomadic freedom against

the visible constraints of British education. The meaning of race is therefore functional and surfaces in this text because the narrative cannot conceive its properties as discrete and innate. Since Kim is a hybrid of conventional racial markers, the text dismantles the antinomies that define colonial subjectivity, generating a diffuse set of codes that formally resist coherence. If *Kim* represents an intermediary place in Kipling's oeuvre, its eponymous hero inhabits a liminal space between spurious racial polarities by insisting on their intermediary and diverse points of identification.

It is possible to see this text as attempting to deconstruct the simple logic of Occidental and Oriental difference; the narrator complicates Kim's racial properties in the second paragraph of the text: "*Though* he was burned black as any native; *though* he spoke the vernacular by preference, and his mother-tongue in a clipped uncertain sing-song; though he consorted on terms of perfect equality with the small boys of the bazar; Kim was white—a poor white of the very poorest" (49; my emphasis). Each qualifier represents a tension between the role he now occupies and the place from which others represent his identity by illustrating the power and fantasy that are necessary to keep them apart. The declaration "Kim was white" invokes, but cannot guarantee, the colonial authority that this position traditionally represents. Nonetheless, *Kim* also resists formal deconstruction by impeding the critique it engenders; the text encounters a limit point that compels it to reassemble the identificatory gap between the individual and its national structure by restoring the meaning of racial difference. While Kim's loyalties may therefore be in doubt, Kipling's finally are not. This suggests that Kim's hybridity performs a co-optive masquerade by trying to incorporate and assimilate both the other's difference and colonialism's unconscious fantasies. (We might clarify the terms of this co-option by the fact that as readers we cannot reverse them, enabling the lama to usurp the Sahib's symbols—a notion to which Kipling would likely have responded with horror.)

Recent critics tend to disagree on the meaning and effect of this strategy of racial masquerade: Benita Parry argues that it is thoroughly co-optive while Edward Said upholds a generous reading in which the text cautiously unbinds the racial dichotomy that Orientalism maintains.[70] Reading this text in either way can blind us to the importance of its internal work, however, as the text's central crisis devolves on Kim's identity. To Kipling— at least at this moment (1901)—the questions that beset Kim (Who and what am I?) may elaborate and flounder on the outer limits of possible identification. For instance, Kim's identity is enigmatic whenever colonialism reaches a conceptual or epistemological impasse. When the narrator of an earlier tale, "The Conversion of Aurelian McGoggin" (1890), considers this problem of national identity, the very logic of the empire turns awry: "If the Empress be not responsible to her Maker—if there is no Maker for her to be responsible to—the entire system of Our administration must be wrong. Which is manifestly impossible." [71] Kim's decision to spy for the British by disguising himself as an Indian is consistent with this text's problematic of national identity and racial loyalty, however; spying temporarily submerges his Western identity as he examines, from the place of the other, the point where this "Selfsame" principle of identity is least credible and secure.[72]

Doubt jeopardizes the radical and reactionary implications of this text as an intractable narrative obstacle. This obstacle surfaces for Kim whenever he lets his mind "go free upon speculation as to what is called personal identity" (233) by generating profound isolation and uncertainty: "I am Kim—Kim—Kim—alone—one person—in the middle of it all" (273). This statement persists as the syntactical echo "Who is Kim—Kim—Kim?" (233) before it produces only a partial understanding of self-definition: "I am Kim. I am Kim. And what is Kim?" (331). The final question represents the crisis of each previous speculation because *what* Kim is in racial terms is grounds for determining *who* he is in social terms. Each query is also syntactically unusual for Kipling; the em dashes fracturing Kim's declarative statement impede Kipling's "realist" style. Kim's *cogito* stalls between a desire to fix his identity by reducing it to the limit of his name and an impossible struggle to represent "alone—one person—in the middle of it all" without including the wider frame of racial symbols in his purview. Thus, the question "What *is* Kim?" follows the tautology "I am Kim" precisely because the narrative cannot consider his isolated ontology without an accompanying crisis of colonial epistemology. Despite its radical difference from other texts by Kipling, *Kim* illustrates a now familiar split between legislated terms and fantasized acts. Though the narrative returns Kim to the fold of law, Kipling seems to obscure Kim's self-examination by shielding him from the question not only of who he is but also, more urgently and radically, of what it is that he wants.

This problem of demand is worth considering because critics often represent *Kim* as a text without desire insofar as women traditionally represent objects of desire, and Kim more or less consistently rejects women.[73] This rejection largely repeats the dogmatic misogyny of most of Kipling's texts, whose protagonists avoid women to protect their integrity and withstand unmanning. For instance, "I have seen something of this world . . . and there are but two sorts of women in it—those who take the strength of a man and those who put it back" (325); "Thus do foolish women drag us from the Way!" (274); "it is by means of women that all plans come to ruin . . ." (225), et cetera. Since there are no white women in *Kim,* the novel's problem of temptation may conflate an already volatile threat of racial usurpation with a palpable sexual antagonism—any forays into intimacy are strictly with Indian women. While the narrative outlines a naive and idealistic fantasy of social and racial harmony, the binding askesis of masculine friendship strongly resists sexual intimacy. As in "The Man Who Would Be King," the basic social contract of *Kim* comprises loyalty to homophilia, mentorship, and the authority of the brother. Once the narrative has secured this contract, investigation can proceed into racial difference by rescuing the white man's ontological status with a pact of masculine friendship: " 'I have known many men in my so long life, and disciples not a few. But to none among men, if so be thou art woman-born, has my heart gone out as it has to thee—thoughtful, wise, and courteous; but something of a small imp' " (118).

Homophilia's fundamental irrevocability in *Kim* enables Kipling to take his protagonist far into uncharted racial terrain to test the meaning of his cultural identity. Seen in this light, *Kim* may indicate Kipling's still unresolved tension toward the empire—not the idea of it, which fundamentally was never in question,[74] but rather Kipling's personal experience of the empire, and the immense task that often beleaguered and overwhelmed his solitary administrators. Their fatigue prevails throughout Kipling's colonial tales, as harassed subalterns suffer from estrangement and despondency, and are frequently either compulsive about their labor or suicidal about its impossible completion.

Considering this reading, *Kim* loses much of its radicalism, offering only a brief excursus into the meaning of race for the British Empire before concluding with an endorsement of imperialist allegiance. This may partly confirm Parry's concern about co-option, though it is significant that *Kim* achieves its imperial orthodoxy by detailing the precise limits of identity, and by demonstrating that its protagonists cannot presuppose affiliation with their race. Thus, we can see the vicissitudes of Kipling's novel as resulting from a conscious and deliberate strategy; we cannot explain the frequent and more challenging slips of identity so easily, and the redolent unconscious emphases of Kipling's writing. If the meaning of race is disputable in *Kim,* the text also designates a split between racial identity and political identification that leads it into potential crisis even as it insists that each is finally commensurate.

Once Kipling had written *Debits and Credits* (1918)—a collection whose title alone seems to calculate the price of this allegiance—he had, at least consciously, sealed the gap between race and imperialist politics; his maxim had all but become "The Fatherhood of God, an' the Brotherhood of Man; an' what more in Hell *do* you want?" [75] If we consider Britain's tenuous post–World War I hold over the empire alongside the crisis that female suffrage engendered for men like Kipling, we might characterize this flight to conservatism as an anxious retreat into a highly contested order. This may explain the vehemence of Kipling's question, though I have stressed that this resistance also resonates in many other examples of his work. We might characterize Kipling's final turn by the title of his story about Masonic bonding, "In the Interests of the Brethren." The tale recalls the contract of brotherhood in "The Man Who Would Be King"; it also anticipates the antidemocratic and profoundly homoerotic logic of "As Easy as A.B.C." (1912), in which a band of men joins a vigilante group to halt the decline of conservative values and the pernicious growth of antipatriotic feeling. [76]

The complexity and ambivalence of Kipling's many positions indicate a difficulty in assessing or discarding him on any one of these pronouncements; [77] it seems more useful to interpret the actual and/or imaginary objects to which they stubbornly adhere. Therefore, I have emphasized the various oscillations of national allegiance in his fiction because the titles of *Limits and Renewals* (1932) and *Traffics and Discoveries* (1904) alone demonstrate the diversity and flexibility of his symbolic frame. Kipling criticism has not addressed the reason for this oscillation—or adequately interpreted the drives that inform it—whose racial tension, sexual anxiety, and colonial doubt Kipling tellingly enumerates. If this doubt is largely responsible for his narratives' strange resolutions, as I have claimed, it is perhaps no surprise that Kipling came full circle in his career by producing texts that prioritize the voice of law over the vicissitudes of desire. Thus he wrote a mandate in 1893 to create a rule that would structure—and, paradoxically, undermine— the logic of almost all of his later work:

> Hold ye the Faith—the Faith our Fathers sealèd us;
> Whoring not with visions—overwise and overstale.
> > Except ye pay the Lord
> > Single heart and single sword,
> Of your children in their bondage He shall ask them treble-tale!
>
> Keep ye the Law—be swift in all obedience—
> Clear the land of evil, drive the road and bridge the ford.

Make ye sure to each his own
That he reap where he hath sown;
By the peace among Our peoples let men know we serve
the Lord! [78]

2

The Fate

of the Pioneer:

Mason, Haggard,

and the Colonial Frame

of Homophilia

Introducing the Pariah

And alien tears shall fill for him
Pity's long-broken urn
For his mourners will be outcast men,
And outcasts always mourn.
— Sir Jacob Epstein [1]

There still remained the question, what was Harry
Feversham, disgraced and ruined, now to do? How was he to
recreate his life? How was the secret of his disgrace to be most
easily concealed?
   "You cannot stay in London, hiding by day, slinking
about by night," he said with a shiver. "That's too like ——"
and he checked himself.
— A. E. W. Mason [2]

Since it was written in 1924 about a drama set in 1822, this epigraph from
A. E. W. Mason's *The Four Feathers* could easily convey the unhappy conse-

quence of a homosexual scandal; similar words resonate in Wilde's *De Pro-fundis* (1905) and anticipate the agony of several scenes in Forster's *Maurice* (1913–14). Yet Mason's novel does not include a scandal about homosexuality; it represents the public scrutiny and private shame of a man disgraced by military cowardice. Still, the links between military cowardice and homosexual scandal are important to consider because *The Four Feathers* compares pacifism with socially unacceptable desires. The recent furor over the visibility of lesbians and gay men in the U.S. military confirms that it is still possible to be praised for killing another man in wartime and reviled for going to bed with one.[3] Accordingly, this chapter argues that homosexuality and military shame are related, even intimate, concerns.

The opening scene of *The Four Feathers* explores this intimacy by capturing the thoughts of a peripheral character, Lieutenant Sutch. A gathering of British ex-officers and soldiers invites Sutch to join it in reminiscing about military victories in South Africa. Emphasizing their characters' unusual aspects, the scene recalls Henry James's short story "The Liar" (1888), which I interpret in the following chapter. As General Feversham recounts his military exploits, his speech captivates Harry, his son: "[Harry] sat quiet under the compulsion of a spell" (14). While the officers indulge their colonial nostalgia, the boy finds the tale distressingly vivid: "Harry Feversham sat listening as though the incidents thus carelessly narrated were happening actually at that moment and within the walls of that room. . . . Even his face grew pinched as though the iron frost of that winter was actually eating into his bones" (11–12, 13). To the narrator, this overidentification implies a worrying degree of sensitivity and an effeminate "gift of imagination" (19); Sutch also anticipates the boy's troubled relation to "virility" when he realizes that Feversham takes after his mother. The consequence of this maternal influence and the agony it induces in Feversham are the principal subject of *The Four Feathers,* which highlights a traumatic gap between the general's military ideal for his son and the obstacles that prevent the boy from realizing it. With various intentions, the novel represents this default within masculine and colonial relations.

General Feversham first manifests this default in an after-dinner anecdote: a man conscripted for military service in North Africa accepts his undertaking with pleasure, though he later refuses to fight and hides in Britain until his unit has boarded its ship. As the general amplifies, the ignominy of this decision surpasses inconvenience for the army and loss of status for the soldier: it reduces the man to a pariah. The general explains: "He was broken, of course, and slunk back to London. Every house was closed to him, he dropped out of his circle like a lead bullet you let slip out of your hand into the sea. The very women in Piccadilly spat if he spoke to them; and he blew his brains out in a back bedroom off the Haymarket. Curious that, eh?" (15). Although disturbing to the other officers, this anecdote demonstrates that cowardice defines the standards of military prowess. Specifically, the anecdote introduces an element of fear and disgust into *The Four Feathers* that surfaces whenever Feversham's doubt troubles the meaning of heroic acts and colonial virtue. As the narrator observes, in a tone of melodrama quite risible to modern readers: "Even upon these men, case-hardened to horrors, the incident related in its bald simplicity wrought its effect. From some there broke a half-uttered exclamation of disbelief; others moved restlessly in their chairs with a sort of physical discomfort, because a man had sunk so far below humanity. Here an officer gulped his wine, there a second shook his shoulders as though to shake the knowledge off as a dog shakes water" (16).

This anecdote affects Feversham so profoundly, it reduces him to a "savagery of despair. . . . [H]is cheeks white as paper, his eyes burning and burning with ferocity. He had the look of a dangerous animal in the trap" (16). Following a toast in which the general hails his son as his military successor, Feversham is sent to bed, though he pauses in the portrait-lined hallway to anticipate his forebear's derision. With astute sensitivity, Sutch follows him out of the room, finding him paralyzed beneath portraits "as though in that dark void peril awaited him. And peril did—the peril of his thoughts" (17). The narrator explains: "There was not one man's portrait upon the walls which did not glisten with the colours of a uniform, and there were the portraits of many men. . . . They were men of one stamp; no distinction of uniform could obscure their relationship—lean-faced men, hard as iron, rugged in feature, thin-lipped, with firm chins and straight level mouths, narrow foreheads, and the steel-blue inexpressive eyes; men of courage and resolution, no doubt, but without subtleties, or nerves, or that burdensome gift of imagination; sturdy men, a little wanting in delicacy, hardly conspicuous for intellect; to put it frankly, men rather stupid . . ." (18–19). This reflection on stupidity enlists Sutch's sympathy for Feversham by disparaging the military ideal his father compels Feversham to adopt. As the text develops, however, the narrator's antipathy for combat and colonial "stupid[ity]" becomes increasingly difficult to hear. Caught between the ignominy of public shame and the relative "stupid[ity]" of fighting, the narrator urges Feversham to renounce sensitivity and cowardice for military valor. At this point in his youth, however, the text partially indicts his father for the "iron discipline under which the boy lived" (14) and the coercive "voice [that] bid him play the man, if only in remembrance of his fathers" (14).

Similar to a poignant scene in Conrad's *Victory* in which Axel Heyst cowers beneath a portrait of his father to postpone his subjection, Feversham projects onto his family's portraits a demand that he repeat their military careers. Like Heyst's, his resistance manifests as a desire to reject combat and rescind even limited identification with his forebears. However, General Feversham's anecdote of the soldier's abjection haunts this novel as an allegory of masculine ridicule; the anecdote anticipates Feversham's anxiety and misery when he fails to become an officer.

Since military combat overlays a prior and unresolved problem about filial obligation and deference, I return to this scene and its ramifications later in this chapter. Here we should note that colonial loyalty compels the soldier or pioneer to repeat a filial conflict. In Mason's novel and related fiction, the soldier's and pioneer's conflicts reproduce a haunting, often insoluble, crisis of domestic and familial meaning; the drives and fantasies they try to assuage seem to influence, if not determine, their field of adventure and conquest by repeating remnants of an earlier anxiety.[4] This chapter's task is to interpret the relation between these primary and secondary dramas.

General Feversham's anecdote about cowardice and stigma resonates with contemporaneous accounts of homosexual scandal that Mason is likely to have read. Historically close to the trials of Oscar Wilde in 1895 and the publication of *The Picture of Dorian Gray* four years earlier, in 1891, Mason's account of his "coward" being shunned, spat at, and pushed toward suicide generates an intriguing subtext in *The Four Feathers*. Wilde's punishment is worth considering as an influence on the shudders and revulsion that Feversham elicits from his father and acquaintance; as Wilde remarks of Dorian Gray, "His extraordinary absences became notorious, and, when he used to reappear again in society, men would whisper to each other in corners, or pass him with a sneer, or look at him with cold searching eyes, as though they were determined to discover his secret."[5] The eponymous hero of *Teleny; or, The Reverse of the Medal* (1893), a novel many critics attribute to Wilde and his friends, suffers a more extreme fate. Teleny remarks: "Like Cain, it seemed as if I carried my crime written upon my brow. I saw a sneer upon the face of every man that looked at me. A finger was for ever pointing at me; a voice, loud enough for all to hear, was whispering, 'The Sodomite!' "[6]

When Feversham decides to marry Ethne Dermod, declining to fight in the Sudan, he receives three white feathers that symbolize cowardice, effeminacy, and social exclusion. To this Ethne adds a fourth that not only cancels their likelihood of marriage but also jeopardizes his sexual identity: since in this novel heterosexuality relies on active military service, Feversham's inability to marry generates a level of confusion about his sexuality that other characters signify by a shudder of disgust.

I suggest that Feversham and Dorian Gray share analogous positions as reviled, but functionally necessary, components of colonial and masculine identity. Although the relation between Feversham and Mason may be more tenuous and conjectural than that between Wilde and Dorian Gray, *The Four Feathers* represents a script that Mason seemed concerned to remember, if only to recall his propensity to enact a similar drama. Mason acknowledged, for instance, that much of his early fiction was autobiographical; he also conveyed in his writing an element of wish fulfillment for objects and activities that were otherwise unattainable.[7] More compelling is the absence of personal detail in Roger Lancelyn Green's 1952 biography of Mason, which unfolds in the tradition of literary anecdote, narrative summary, and personal reminiscence with only a fleeting discussion of Mason's private life. Although Green does not comment on his subject's confirmed bachelorhood, his remarks about Mason's idealized rapport with women are difficult to square with Green's insistence that they constitute passionate affairs. Mason did not marry, nor did he have any notable or durable relationships with women; he devoted his attention almost exclusively to men, whether in travel abroad or in London's gentlemen's clubs. Mason sustained two important and passionate relationships with men—one was Hugh Warrender, his companion for nearly thirty years on almost all his foreign visits, to Morocco, India, Egypt, and South America.[8] Green declines to comment on this relationship and spectacularly ignores the effect on Mason of Warrender's death, which appeared to cause him much grief and to exacerbate his fervent need to travel.

Halfway through this biography, however, Green notes that "Mason's love affairs seem to have been a standing joke among his friends at the time—they are said to have been many and varied."[9] Though it is unclear whether the "joke" refers to their number or instability, J. M. Barrie, one of Mason's long-standing friends, wrote to Mason's devoted Oxford mentor, Sir Arthur Quiller-Couch, explaining that "his heroines . . . are always drawn from the lady he is then in love with, and by the time I see the proofs it is always off but he keeps her in, and roars his great laugh when attention is drawn to the circumstances."[10]

Clearly, we cannot deduce from this material Mason's sexual preference. Were such an "answer" even available, it could not guarantee either the meaning or enigma of his writing. However, these remarks about Mason by his bachelor friends raise important questions about the status of women and courtship in his fiction, confirming the suspicion of readers like Barrie that they performed a disingenuous role in his literature and life. When Green writes, for instance, that "in the period of the Great War, Mason was in and out of love with gay abandon, enshrining the lady of the moment in whatever he chanced to be writing," [11] he makes an important point about *The Four Feathers*'s Ethne Dermod, the woman for whom Feversham determines to redeem his honor. Green elaborates: "Of his heroine, Ethne, it is harder to speak. She is better studied than many of his female characters, who are so apt to sacrifice individuality to charm, but she leads the story into its only blemish: the excessive sentimentality of her second farewell to Harry." [12] Considering this remark, Ethne appears so studied an object for Feversham's ardor, she does not engender an appropriate passion for Feversham's task.[13] Green's comments have particular bearing on Mason's characterization of Durrance, Feversham's "rival" for Ethne's affection: according to Green, Mason modeled Durrance on his companion, Hugh Warrender, "[a] born soldier, born wanderer, with all the preciseness and method with which Durrance is credited." [14]

The proximity between Feversham's and Dorian Gray's abjection clarifies the influence of Wilde's trials on Mason's intimate literary group of friends. Although I examine Max Beerbohm's relation to these trials in the next chapter, Mason was involved tangentially with the *Yellow Book,* Oxford's decadent journal, and dined periodically with Wilde at the Café Royal before Wilde was imprisoned in 1895. Though the precise effect of Wilde's trials and imprisonment on Mason is impossible to determine, I suggest that the ensuing controversy amplified sexual anxiety and social derision for Mason and contemporaneous writers, and that Mason explored the implications of this crisis in *The Four Feathers.* As my reading of this novel suggests, Mason sought to resolve a comparable crisis of homosexuality and cowardice, which for him became almost synonymous terms.

The shame and contempt that beleaguer Dorian Gray and Feversham demonstrate profound concern over national health and loyalty because the dual "sins" of desire and cowardice eat into Britain's symbolic fabric. When Dorian Gray contacts Alan Campbell to assist him in destroying Basil Hallward's body, for instance, his friend comments: "I don't care what shame comes to you. You deserve it all. I should not be sorry to see you disgraced, publicly disgraced. How dare you ask me, of all men in the world, to mix myself up in this horror?" [15]

How does this analogy between homosexuality and public disgrace influence *The Four Feathers*? I suggest that it elaborates an insidious mechanism of gender control by conflating Feversham's default on masculine identification with a powerful stigma and taboo. The fates of Dorian Gray and Wilde seem to function for Mason's narrator as primitive and punitive horrors compelling Feversham to form a successful alliance between colonialism and masculinity. Nevertheless, the text closely monitors Feversham's desperate, even frenzied, attempt to regain Ethne's affection; his drive to retain honor and sexual respectability exceeds the knowledge or even interest of the woman for whom he carries out these tasks. Green touches on this point when he remarks: "The first idea of it was nearly as old as Harry Feversham: but this time it was love and the mistaken choice in the moment of temptation which was to lead the hero down the path of shame. And behind this idea was another which, almost from the first, was part of it: the hero must have an hereditary example for his choice of dishonour, and an example, too, of how that dishonour could be wiped out." [16] Although the narrative pursues a frantic course to redeem Feversham's dishonor, it is not clear what this second, honorable example amounts to. Since a form of handicap troubles every man in the novel, *The Four Feathers* has no obvious representative of colonial virtue: the narrator initially mocks Feversham's family for its crass and "stupid" obedience to orders, and criticizes the general for his rigidity and callous rejection of his son. The reader may infer that dishonor is "wiped out" only by the text's concern to structure the protagonist around a taut and unyielding standard of masculine virtue. Green's description of Feversham's impulse toward "cowardice" as a "moment of temptation" indicates the counterpressure needed to return him to the "right path." When Feversham decides to follow his battalion to the Sudan, for instance, he creates a series of solitary tasks that "aton[e] for this one act of cowardice" (233); in his father's words, "he committed the sin, and he must pay" (269). Feversham hopes to impress the three friends who gave him feathers and to influence Ethne into taking back the fourth so that they can marry. The price of this "aton[ement]" (233) is a furious internal pressure that condemns him more thoroughly than his peers' spoken or symbolic rejection; this pressure also registers as the cost of straying from "normalcy" and the energy he expends in attempting to regain it: "Despair kept him company at times, and fear always. But from the sharp pangs of these emotions a sort of madness was begotten in him, a frenzy of obstinacy, a belief fanatical as the dark religion of those amongst whom he moved, that he could not now fail and the world go on . . ." (104). Although Feversham achieves his aim and Ethne rediscovers her love for him, a "perpetual menacing companion" (65) haunts him. This voice taunts him with reminders of prior lapses of cowardice that resemble Lacan's formulation of the hectoring superego—the "noxious neighbor."[17] Feversham's ambition is a bitter imperative and a furious vindication of his cowardice; he cannot forget the imminence of his social and sexual unmaking: "It was proof that in this story there was to be no failure" (154).

Despite its often crass interpretation of human emotions, *The Four Feathers* is valuable in documenting internal tyranny. The need to express this tension and the commensurate social demand to repress it torment every point of the novel's triangle—that is, the lover, beloved, and rival: while "Durrance . . . schooled himself not to wince" (33), "Harry . . . schooled [him]self into contentment" (95) and "[Ethne] schooled herself to omit Harry Feversham from her thoughts, and to obliterate him from her affections, [although] the cry showed to her how incompletely she had succeeded" (148). This final remark indicates how self-deception not only obstructs every subject's relation to desire by introducing an unwelcome element of "failure" (154), but also crucially enables them to function: the narrator deems Feversham's mission to reclaim his honor "the mere vainglory of a man who continually deceived himself" (105) since it can restore but never conceal his social and sexual humiliation. This dynamic recurs throughout my reading of Maugham's novel *Of Human Bondage* (1915) in chapter 5; in Mason's novel, however, it foregrounds a problem about the position and object Feversham strives to recover. As he admits to Ethne with uncharacteristic honesty, "always you exceed my thoughts of you" (39). If he means that her strength and beauty continually surprise him, this statement actually reveals a gap between his expectation and realization of passion for her. By analogy, the narrative's comment on "how incompletely she had succeeded" is an adroit remark on Feversham's failed "recovery" to heterosexuality, as if his entire mission is a protracted and risible masquerade.[18]

The Four Feathers demonstrates how few of its characters live "authentic" roles; it also shows how tension emerges from the impossible repression of its characters' emotions: the narrator acknowledges a multitude of "sacrifices which must not be mentioned, and which no sign must betray" (26).[19] Though the protagonists rarely express this agony, they often find other ways to convey it: Ethne plays a haunting line of melody on her violin to represent "unformulated longings [that lie] beyond the reach of words" (31–32). Later, during a period of acute despair, the narrator remarks that "the violin seemed to squeal with pain" (185). By charting these limits and eruptions, the narrator expresses a tension between every intention and action, or—to elaborate on Freud's theory of psychic drives—between the "pressure" of a need and the crisis accompanying its subject's spoken demand.[20]

To implicate Freud's argument with colonial masculinity, let us return to the tension surrounding General Feversham's toast to his son's military success, at the beginning of the novel, and the boy's anticipation of his wrath in becoming a lamentable failure. The general's expectation sets up a pressure that his son will be "true" to his lineage, will inherit and repay his father's "debt" (by his reputation), and finally will exceed his military legacy. While Feversham's ensuing torment derives from this pressure, his father's decision to disown and disinherit him rings a strangely contemporary note. My earlier analogy between Feversham and Dorian Gray, and between Mason and Wilde, renders this opening scene—with its explicit hope that Feversham will become a fine soldier—similar to many parents' unquestioned expectation that their son or daughter will marry and give them grandchildren. The first half of *The Four Feathers* resembles 1950s coming-out stories, with their belabored clues about the protagonist's difference, accounts of his or her tormented longing and furtive glances, and an epiphany that explains the sexual secret and its possible management.[21] According to their author's preference, the reader can celebrate or pity these protagonists, but the narratives generally settle the enigma and resolve the problem by explaining and/or banishing the "sexual deviant."

When Durrance ponders the meaning of Feversham's resignation, for instance, he observes a solitary man by the river who resembles his friend and rival. To Durrance, the man's face is "stamped with an extraordinary misery, the face of a man cast out from among his fellows" (37). Later, Lieutenant Sutch observes Feversham wandering aimlessly around London, and urges him to meet him the next day. Uncannily echoing the man his father first derided, Feversham responds: " 'Good God, not there!' . . . in a sharp low voice, and moved quickly into the roadway where no light fell directly on his face. . . . 'I do not go out in the daylight. . . .' He imagined contempt on every face which passed him in the street. . . . 'At night I prowl about the streets or lie in bed waiting for the Westminster clock to sound each new quarter of the hour' " (62–63). Like the misery of a man who is "cast out from among his fellows," Feversham's crisis mirrors Dorian Gray's rejection by men who "pass him with a sneer" and women who "grow pallid with shame or horror" when he enters a room.[22] In ways that also repeat Wilde's text, Feversham's mentor holds himself partly responsible for the misery of his creation: "If only I had spoken . . . I might have saved you many unnecessary years of torture. Good heavens! What a childhood you must have spent with that fear all alone with you" (65). The narrator later corroborates this fear by confirming retrospectively the secret misery of Harry Feversham's life: "The long years of childhood, and boyhood, and youth, lived apart . . . in the presence of the uncomprehending father and the relentless dead men on the walls had done the harm. There had been no one in whom the boy could confide. The fear of cowardice had sapped incessantly at his heart. He had walked about with it; he had taken it with him to his bed. It had haunted his dreams. It had been his perpetual menacing companion. It had kept him from intimacy with his friends lest an impulsive word should betray him" (65).

With its emphasis on the number of "impulsive word[s]" that later "betray him," *The Four Feathers* probes this secret by forcing it to be heard. When Feversham seems able to succeed in his mission, however, the text becomes a colonial thriller, losing most of its subtlety by endorsing Feversham's "heroic" project. The text lays aside the narrator's previous indictment of war and Feversham's railroaded masculinity: Sutch—always a yardstick for this text's dilemmas because he monitors their social and psychic effect— "nurse[s] with a most pleasurable anticipation a hope that, in the end, Harry would come back to all that he once had owned, like a rethroned king" (87).

When Feversham secures his right to marry and is gratefully "rethroned" to heterosexuality (paradoxically, as a queen?), the narrative does not disband his secret, but displaces it onto his rival's shoulders:[23] as Feversham luxuriates in the glory of his reputation, Durrance vows never to marry to preserve his imaginary bond with Ethne. Despite the narrator's care in documenting the price of this decision, the narrative insists that it can give the "throne" of heterosexuality to only one man; the rival correspondingly must become a pariah and receive his community's taunts and insults. Durrance later turns to Sutch for advice; he assumes that Sutch's handicap (an injured foot) can diminish his own—blindness: "The same sort of lonely life lay stretched out before Durrance, and he was anxious to learn what alleviations could be practised, what small interests could be discovered, how best it could be got through" (257).

Considering this homology between bachelor and outcast, life without marriage—and the respectability and status it confers—is something that Mason's protagonists must learn to "g[e]t through." Though this "affliction" curses several men in the novel, apparently it must afflict at least one: it seems impossible for both Durrance and Feversham to marry. Lieutenant Sutch is also more than a mentor; he guides each man through the hardships of confirmed bachelorhood, or, as John le Carré put it more recently in *Tinker,*

Tailor, Soldier, Spy, at a similar point of marital agony for George Smiley, a failed British spy, the lonely life of "a solitary queer." [24]

Although *The Four Feathers* corrects its protagonist's unbalanced gender makeup (too much of his mother's sensitivity, too little of his father's courage), it seems unable to repair this problem without noting both the protagonist's accompanying distress and the "surplus" of gendered doubt and anxiety that diminishes when another man assumes it. Although this burden falls on the character who most resembles Mason's devoted companion, Hugh Warrender, the narrative loses interest in Feversham the moment he completes his task; Durrance takes up the challenge of a narrative enigma and an unrealizable sexual goal.

This complicated dynamic resonates in Mason's other fiction, particularly *The Philanderers* (1897) and *The Broken Road* (1902).[25] The latter novel recounts the fantasies and antagonisms that surface between two men (Linforth and Shere Ali) over a woman who intercedes (Violet Oliver). This novel also concerns colonial labor and interracial relations: Shere Ali is born in India into a wealthy caste and educated at Eton and Oxford for the purpose of returning to India to assist the British in subjecting his people. After Violet rejects his proposal of marriage as "impossible" (128) — it would violate "the natural law that white shall mate with white, and brown with brown" (129) — Ali returns to India to lead a campaign against the British. When the British defeat him, they recall his former rebuke with vehement political disappointment and punish him as a cross-cultural failure: " 'England overlaid the real man with a pretty varnish,' [Ralston] said. 'That's all it ever does. And the varnish peels off easily when the man comes back to the Indian sun. There's not one of these people from the hills but has in him the makings of a fanatic. It's a question of circumstances whether the fanaticism comes to the top or not. Given the circumstances, neither Eton, nor Oxford, nor all the schools and universities rolled into one would hinder the relapse' " (239). Despite its egregious stereotypes of cultural and racial difference, *The Broken Road* is an interesting account of cultural displacement: the illogic of Britain's empire troubles and disorients Ali because it trains him to be, but never properly includes him as, a member of its ruling elite. Predictably, British rulers and Indian natives alike undermine his authority; he falls between the binary distinguishing colonial master from colonial subject.

Shere Ali's confusion over this putative racial binary complicates Frantz Fanon's more recent account of collaboration: Ali does not mimic the implied treachery of a "black skin, white mask";[26] nor does he simply live with a "black skin" without troubling the cultural subordination it confers.

Ali ruins this associative link by introducing a dimension of cultural psychosis that places him outside symbolic relations. Drifting in a liminal space between colonizer and colonized, Ali suffers a trauma that Mason cannot represent and critics should not idealize; the failure of colonial meaning renders him a racial anachronism, embodying the troubled and isolated space of the sexual pariah in Mason's earlier novel, *The Four Feathers*.

Mason's colonial melodramas represent a double vision of travel and mastery, in which the expropriation of outside elements mirrors the repression of internal and "foreign" elements. This oscillation between "inside" and "outside" aspects of the colonial scene not only reminds us of the difficulties that beset Kipling's protagonists, detailed in the previous chapter, but also anticipates discussion of interracial fantasy, ambivalence, and internal war in later chapters on Forster, Firbank, and Saki. For now, we should consider this oscillation as colonial restoration and psychic reparation: Mason and H. Rider Haggard constantly represent and try to resolve disruptive and threatening forces, especially those affecting masculine identity and colonial homophilia. The following section on H. Rider Haggard's novel *Nada the Lily* (1892) interprets the pioneer's figurative and psychic meaning in the context of comparable familial and social turbulence about racial identification.

The Lay of the Land

The Frontier has been my wife, my children, my home, my one long and lasting passion.
— A. E. W. Mason, *The Broken Road* (31)

The pioneer in a new country doesn't bring testimonials with him invariably.
— Mason, *The Philanderers* [27]

The world is a thorny wilderness, my daughter, and its thorns are watered with a rain of blood, and we wander in our wretchedness like lost travellers in a mist; nor do I know why our feet are set upon this wandering.
— H. Rider Haggard, *Nada the Lily* [28]

Perhaps the most striking aspect of Haggard's fiction is his repeated claim that the pioneer inhabits a state of exile. By investigating this proposition, I do not wish to ignore that a pioneer often acts as an envoy for his or her domestic culture, or the disturbing esteem in which critics often held Haggard for endorsing Britain's colonial policies and fantasies. Since the pioneer and the fugitive stand at opposite ends of the political spectrum, we cannot ignore their difference: the first chooses the journey and departure; the second finds the journey enforced by compelling and life-threatening reasons. However, the political difference between the pioneer and the fugitive may not override their psychic similarity; both figures tend to perceive themselves as social outcasts. With due regard to this proposition's contentiousness, I will elaborate on the tension between these figures' symbolic and political differences by exploring their occasional fantasmatic similarities.

Critics of Haggard's fiction have often commented, without much difficulty, on his repeated use of a small number of tropes: the task of the journey, the inevitable conflict with an enemy, the reward of treasure and other significant discoveries, and the figurative meaning of women, especially the female body. *King Solomon's Mines* (1885) and *She* (1887) endorse this reading because they uncannily and obsessively repeat these tropes.[29] Allan Quartermain's account of his journey between Sheba's two breasts—Haggard's name for two mountains in southern Africa—and his pursuit of a hidden mine, in which lies a plethora of valuable jewels, makes this relation somewhat overdetermined.[30] Indeed, Quartermain's wish to encamp on "the nipple" of one of these "breasts" raises an important fantasmatic relation between the pioneer and the land, which amplifies Barbara Johnson's recent question, "Is male to female as land is to figure?" [31]

Haggard's fiction is clearly amenable to the suggestion that its feminine embodiment of Africa metaphorizes colonialism as a sexual project. By conjoining racial slavery with sexual mastery, Haggard proposes a horrific—but also, for him, historically convenient—analogy between women and Africans that justifies the subordination of each to European law. Not only are women domestic slaves in his fiction, but all non-Caucasian races are stereotypically feminized as weak, unruly, and in need of discipline.[32] Anne McClintock, David Bunn, and Brian Street have demonstrated that Haggard's position received the full support of biological and medical discourse in the 1870s and 1880s because Britain's conceptual hierarchy of race placed Caucasian men at its pinnacle and black women at its base.[33] This discourse calculated gradations among races and subcategories of gender to determine a mathematics of European sovereignty, in which God and Nature appeared to countenance exploitation. Once biology and medicine had assigned each race a specific character, stereotypes of civilizations and subcontinents could proliferate on the anecdotal basis of cranium size, musculature, and physiognomy.

Britain invested heavily in these stereotypes because its colonies formed a vital part of its national and imperial wealth; Britain also adapted these hierarchies to its own empire by defining its colonized's "character" and constituency. Although it is difficult to gauge these fantasies' effect on prominent authors of the time, Haggard reiterates many of the assumptions that eugenic, evolutionary, and sexological theorists like Carl Vogt and Max Nordau were then promulgating.[34]

Although the influence of medical and biological science on contemporaneous writers was considerable, we cannot simply formulate a rigid schema in which Haggard's fables reproduce, or appear as equivalent to, the scientific rhetoric informing them. Critics who read Haggard this way render him as a transparent proponent of his culture by assuming a functional relation between his literature and other discursive registers. This version of literature simplifies the dynamic and conflictual nature of all social formations by conflating the author with his or her symbolic structure. Other critics of Haggard follow the reverse principle of overemphasizing the gap between different discourses, which isolates his literature into a creative enclave, untarnished by scientific racism. Neither position is satisfactory: if Haggard endorsed and influenced many popular opinions about race and cultural stereotypes, he was also not merely an unqualified apologist for Britain's colonialist policies and its absolute supremacy over Africa. Haggard often punctured this assumption by invoking an unequivocal relativism among races, which appealed for authority to the tenets of another "scientific" discourse of the time: psychoanalysis. Haggard wrote, for instance, that "sexual passion is the most powerful lever with which to stir the mind of man, for it lies at the root of all things human." [35] His belief in the power and potential damage of "sexual passion" was so extensive that he saw it as compromising society's foundations. Consider Allan Quartermain's lament in this eponymous novel (1887):

> Ah! this civilisation, what does it all come to? . . . I say that as the savage is, so is the white man, only the latter is more inventive, and possesses the faculty of combination. . . . It is a depressing conclusion, but in all essentials the savage and the child of civilisation are identical. I dare say that the highly civilised lady reading this will smile at an old fool of a hunter's simplicity when she thinks of her black bead-bedecked sister. . . . And yet, my dear young lady, what are those pretty things round your own neck? . . . I might go on

for ever, but what is the good? Civilisation is only savagery silver-gilt. . . . [S]upposing for the sake of argument we divide ourselves into twenty parts, nineteen savage and one civilised, we must look to the nineteen savage portions of our nature, if we would really understand ourselves, and not to the twentieth, which, though so insignificant in reality, is spread all over the other nineteen, making them appear quite different from what they really are, as the blacking does a boot, or the veneer a table.[36]

If the savage and civilized human are for all purposes "identical," Haggard cannot sustain stable assumptions about racial or national difference. The "civilized" fraction of human identity is so diffuse and nebulous that the European woman cannot represent her nature "as quite different from what [it] really [is]"; Haggard suggests that people's underlying nature will prevail, regardless of race. As he once wrote of childhood, in *Nada the Lily,* "I sought one youth, and I have found many evil spirits" (123).

Haggard's views on human nature often challenged British orthodoxy by undermining the racial "logic" of its foreign policies. Haggard also challenged the assumption that by mastering their own savage propensities, the British could somehow teach others to do the same. If Britons were only one-twentieth "civilized," Haggard implied, how could one hide their military excesses, or excuse their evangelical desire to "bring light" to a "dark continent"?[37] Additionally, what violent affinity might emerge when Haggard illuminated the "dark continent" of his home soil, when he reintroduced his readers to desires they sought to project onto Africa?

All the evidence suggests that the influence of psychoanalysis on colonial literature cut both ways, and that Haggard brought his own paradoxical impact to psychoanalysis by clarifying how its theories of the unconscious consistently imbricated with colonial fantasies of "savagery." As I observed in the previous chapter, Haggard's *She* (1887) and *Heart of the World* (1895) fascinated Freud, for he lent the former to a patient to convey "the eternal feminine, the immortality of our emotions. . . ."[38] Haggard's novels so affected Freud's dreams that he once awoke in a "mental fright" after a night of late reading.[39] In his account of this dream, Freud describes seeing himself in a laboratory, dissecting his own pelvis and legs to rid himself of "thick flesh-coloured protuberances."[40] The scene changes to a perilous journey that takes Freud through a landscape peopled by savages ("Red Indians or gipsies").[41] At the journey's end, Freud is forced to cross a chasm on narrow planks, a task that precipitates immense anxiety in the dream. He interprets the dream as a resistance to self-analysis. Jung also drew on *She* to interpret the feminine archetype and undiscovered aspects of the self.[42]

By detailing my reservations about certain functionalist approaches to Haggard, I do not wish to rescue him from misinterpretation or recast him as a vociferous opponent of Britain's empire. As this section will demonstrate in its reading of *Nada the Lily,* Haggard gave colonial violence so much support there is no hope of his political redemption. Nevertheless, his arguments about the relative similarities among races shift the terms of colonial support from biology (an intractable element of human nature) to politics and economics (an unappeasable European greed), and this deserves attention. Ultimately, his stress on the universality of savagery tended to endorse imperialism on a global scale; what the European colonial renounced of civilization, he (rarely she) could regain by seizing wealth and disseminating power. In a selective reading of Freud—disturbing for its indifference to Freud's arguments about social ethics and the need selectively to renounce instinctual gratification—Haggard drew on psychoanalysis to vindicate the savagery of colonialism and Darwinian theories of evolution to transform colonialism into an axiom of nature. However, Haggard's support of British imperialism exhibits a number of prominent tensions that undermine his ability to adopt a single and unified approach to Britain's colonial practice.

Nada the Lily is similar to Haggard's preceding novel, *Eric Brighteyes* (1891), in the virtual uniformity of its racial composition: with the exception of one unnamed "White Man," *Nada* documents the fate of South African tribespeople while its corollary, *Eric Brighteyes,* represents almost exclusively Anglo-Saxon characters. As Norman Etherington remarks, however, "Except for the skin color, . . . the books are almost interchangeable."[43] Though *Nada* refers to the massacre the Zulus suffered under the Boers in Natal, the narrative describes Boers abstractly and only by the Zulu term, *Amaboona.* Thus, as the narrator admits, *Nada* consistently de-emphasizes the white man's status: "Some years since—it was during the winter before the Zulu War—a White Man was travelling through Natal. His name does not matter, for he plays no part in this story" (1).

It may seem odd that the narrator declares this on the first page of the novel, and that Etherington represents so crucial a difference as race by a qualifier so tenuous as "except"; race is surely the critical factor on which any colonial drama turns. However, Haggard's relativism may disturb colonialism's antinomic logic: despite his arguments for the survival of the fittest nation and the promise of a global free-for-all, the fantasy relation between Britons and Zulus in these texts is unusually close.[44] As the narrator of *Nada* explains: "It is obvious that such a task has presented difficulties, since he who undertakes it must for a time forget his civilization, and think with the mind, and speak with the voice of a Zulu of the old *régime*. All the horrors perpetrated by the Zulu tyrants cannot be published in this polite age of melanite and torpedoes; their details therefore have been suppressed" (x).

Certainly, we could read this passage as arguing that rapacity and aggression belong in principle to the Zulus, and that Haggard used this extreme to conceal some of British imperialism's egregious excesses. However, texts like *King Solomon's Mines* demonstrate that white men are quite capable of practicing and enjoying this violence; the farther they move from Britain, the less its culture impedes their aggression, and the easier it is for them to discard any semblance of "civilization." Ultimately, this point rebounds on Britain's prominent "tribalism." As Etherington notes: "First to go is the top five percent of official civilization. . . . Beneath the layer of official civilization brothers are always rivals, sisters are sworn enemies, sons are rejected by fathers whom they subsequently replace, homosexual love is as common and as passionate as the heterosexual variety. Still deeper, beneath the second layer of personality lurks a third, elemental and horrific, which is literally unconscious." [45] On several occasions in *King Solomon's Mines,* the surface layer of Britain's "civilization" (one-twentieth of human nature) is so slight that a psychotic lust to kill overwhelms the novel's white protagonists. The following passage is consistent with, not exceptional to, the remainder of the novel: "There he stood, the great Dane, for he was nothing else, his hands, his axe, and his armour all red with blood, and none could live before his stroke. Time after time I saw it sweeping down, as some great warrior ventured to give him battle, and as he struck he shouted 'O-hoy! O-hoy!' like his Bersekir forefathers, and the blow went crashing through shield and spear, through head dress, hair and skull." [46] Although we must not overlook how African "barbarism" measures the wayward violence of every Briton, the proximity between colonizer and colonized in *King Solomon's Mines, She,* and *Nada the Lily* suggests that Britain's cultural demand for violence offset these rapacious accounts of tribal violence as an imperial wish fulfillment. If Haggard's readers grew up to desire—but not always to practice—comparable behavior, British culture could be intolerant of this violence at home, and manifest it eagerly as a national concern for global power.[47]

To clarify this argument further, Ludwig Horace Holly, the protagonist of *She,* also represents a dramatic, physiological and apparently evolutionary distance from Leo Vincey, whom the novel's editor remarks is "without exception the handsomest young fellow I have ever seen. He was very tall, very broad, and had a look of power and a grace of bearing that seemed to him as native to him as it is to a wild stag." [48] Already conspicuous for his lack of family and "misanthropic and sullen" bachelorhood (8), Holly describes his own figure as "short, thick-set, and deep-chested almost to deformity, with long sinewy arms, heavy features, deep-set eyes, a low brow half overgrown with a mop of thick hair, like a deserted clearing on which the forest had once more begun to encroach. . . . Like Cain, I was branded—branded by Nature with the stamp of abnormal ugliness, as I was gifted by Nature with iron and abnormal strength and considerable intellectual powers. So ugly was I that the spruce young men of my College [at Cambridge University] . . . did not care to be seen walking with me. . . . I was set apart by Nature to live alone . . ." (8). The reference to Cain repeats a trope I interpreted earlier in writing by Mason and Wilde. Like Harry Feversham and Dorian Gray, Holly's intellect briefly mitigates the catastrophe of this mark, though his use of such words as "native," "deformity," and "abnormal" eventually places him in a similarly tenuous position. In *She,* Holly represents a precarious hinge between masculine "civility" and "savagery"; in Haggard's day these terms frequently conjoined to invoke both sexual and racial degeneration. Like the evolutionary and masculine hierarchy that Conrad invokes in *Victory* (1915) between Jones, Ricardo, and Pedro, which I discuss in chapter 4, Haggard often represents trios of British or European men at various stages of evolutionary "decline." In *She,* for instance, not only is Holly described as a "monster" who confirms for one female observer "the monkey theory" (8), but also with Leo Vincey (his ward) and Job (their effete and mannered servant), he represents an avuncular "beast" (8), whose Simian features allow him to discard all pretense at civilization, and so "descend" into the *jouissance* of manic violence. Unlike the above citation from *King Solomon's Mines,* however, the following passage from *She* is remarkable for juxtaposing Holly's frenzied self-defense with the projected judgment of his former British colleagues:

> . . . two others sprang upon me. . . . They were strong men, but I was mad with rage, and that awful lust for slaughter which will creep into the hearts of the most civilised of us when blows are flying, and life and death tremble on the turn. My arms were round the two swarthy demons, and I hugged them till I heard their ribs crack and crunch up beneath my gripe [*sic*]. . . . I slowly crushed the life out of them, and as I did so, strange as it may seem, I thought of what the amiable Head of my College at Cambridge (who is a member of the Peace

Society) and my brother Fellows would say if by clairvoyance they could see me, of all men, playing such a bloody game. (103)

This juxtaposition between southern Africa and Cambridge temporarily disbands all distinction between the traveler and the indigenous, or the colonizer and the colonized, by relativizing the hearts of men to a common aggressive denominator. Considering this imaginary proximity, it may be useful briefly to suspend discussion of Haggard's racism by foregrounding the effect of his accounts of Britain's tribalism. If the racial composition of *Nada the Lily* is almost irrelevant on one level, the intertribal conflicts it elaborates may—and perhaps should—be read as symbolic infractions against British society. If we interpret *Nada* this way, we must rescind the idea that race is an absolute and unifying category in Haggard's writing, and temporarily ignore the novel's South African location, to recognize analogous social and psychic conflicts prevailing in Britain. As the narrator of *Nada* explains: "The writer of this romance has been encouraged in his task by a purpose somewhat beyond that of the setting out of a wild tale of savage life" (ix). The precise *familiarity* of this scene poses a dilemma for the subject's fate, its ambivalence to parents, peers, and surrounding structures, and its future uncertainty—all of which recall, and then disband, a similar fantasmatic drama for the British reader. This identification by the reader requires an indifference to race because the reader cannot fix the tribespeople of *Nada* as basically white or thoroughly different. Identification with the Zulu may realize a drive to power and incorporation; it may also retrieve a pleasure of recollection that Haggard makes available to his reader by the romantic properties of this colonial saga.[49]

Dennis Porter has usefully clarified some of the psychic determinants of colonial melodrama by arguing for a careful reading of pleasure and repetition: "Psychoanalysis . . . helps us to understand the strength of the investments individuals make in this country or that through the theory of transference. Unconscious desire, as Lacan frequently reminded us, insists on reproducing itself in scenarios of our adult life that are retransfigurations of early fantasmatic scenarios. . . . Decisions concerning flight or exile from the 'homeland' along with the embracing or rejection of the countries through which one travels, often derive from identifications dependent less on objective factors than on the projection of early prototypes onto geographic space." [50] We could neatly summarize this perspective by the opening words of L. P. Hartley's *The Go-Between* (1953): "The past is a foreign country; they do things differently there." [51] However, Porter asks us to read the pioneer or émigré allegorically; that is, to interpret both figures as symbolic outcasts drifting between or across imaginary and symbolic registers. In this respect, we might consider these figures as not only suffering from social rejection but also repeating in this rejection their separation from the maternal body. Consider, for instance, Allan Quartermain's remark in *King Solomon's Mines:* "Yet man dies not whilst the world, at once his mother and his monument, remains." [52]

What impact has this reading on feminist critiques of Haggard's work? Without fundamentally disagreeing with Rebecca Stott's and Anne McClintock's readings of *King Solomon's Mines*—for whom colonial adventure signifies a penetration of Africa's passive and feminized "body"—it seems to me a mistake to claim that this body's "interior" is quite dissimilar from the colonizer's. To sustain this reading of gender and topography, it may not be enough to literalize colonization as a heterosexual act or to represent the landscape/object of this penetration as irremediably "other"; [53] the tension between Haggard's advocacy of colonialism and his support for psychoanalysis derives from an exploration of properties that are also internal and integral to the explorer. Although Haggard often attaches this ambivalence to fantasies of ferocious or acquiescent women, the control that his colonial quests desire and practice is usually less specific. In many of Haggard's texts, for instance, the colonizer identifies with the other's demonic qualities, though he uses this identification to quell the horror of a similar insurrection in himself. In this respect, it is impossible to ignore the ambivalence that circulates around male intimacy and penetration, or to dismiss the sense that inhabiting the other, in Haggard's texts, is also a means of dispelling anxieties about racial and sexual similarity. Finally, his narrative's national and ethnic turbulence may signal the limits of colonial epistemology by asserting a logic that often fails to comply with the dictates of colonial rule.

The type of erotic scene I am describing resembles Kaja Silverman's astute formulation of the "double mimesis," in which colonizers briefly disidentify with their national group by forming an attachment to the group their leaders intend them to punish. [54] Haggard's texts do not conform precisely to Silverman's analysis since skin color, not clothing, determines his frequent identification with Zulus and other South African tribes. Unlike T. E. Lawrence—Silverman's example—whose "reverse" identification established a semiotics of race through fetishized objects, Haggard produced an analogy between the colonizer and colonized by insisting that the latter's "character" mirrors that of the former. In this respect, Haggard's texts often displace race by other, comparable attributes like aggression and desire.

Etherington's contention that *Nada the Lily* is virtually indistinguishable from *Eric Brighteyes* is notable in this regard because similarities emerge between *Nada* and *The Four Feathers* concerning the meaning each attributes to exile and the perspective of the outcast. Drawing on Etherington's argument, I contend not that race is an empty category in *Nada* but rather that the novel adds a *familiar* emphasis to patterns of ambivalence about paternal authority and filial tyranny, membership in the tribe, and the difficulty of integrating a love object with responsibility to the community. This familiarity tends to collapse or postpone racial oppositions by accentuating the consistency of sexual difference: for instance, Ignosi leaves Quartermain, Good, and Sir Henry in *King Solomon's Mines* by stating, "Farewell, my brothers, brave white men," after Sir Henry has decapitated Ignosi's tyrannical brother, Twala, while Quartermain earlier declares in an odd moment of racial leveling: "Women are women, all the world over, whatever their colour." [55] By the end of the novel, however, when Good and Foulata appear quite inseparable, Quartermain volunteers that her death is politically fortuitous: "I am bound to say that, looking at the thing from the point of view of an oldish man of the world, I consider her removal was a fortunate occurrence, since, otherwise, complications would have been sure to ensue. . . . No amount of beauty or refinement could have made an entanglement between Good and herself a desirable occurrence; for, as she herself put it, 'Can the sun mate with the darkness, or the white with the black?' " [56] Although Good and Foulata's attachment is undesirable to Quartermain due to Britain's intolerance of miscegenation, their relationship demonstrates that racial dissimilarity is precisely "desirable" for the couple. Thus, consistent with this novel's premise of interracial brotherhood, there are moments in Africa when miscegenation is quite insignificant; the problem represents a difficulty only when Good and Sir Henry return to Britain.

By endorsing many of these familial assumptions, *Nada* elaborates an extraordinary number of tribal negotiations and resolutions, the majority of which carry parental meaning for its protagonists. The novel's primary concern hinges on the possibility of family against its values' prominent destruction. Opponents of family values in this novel foreground the family's ethical integrity against its *unheimlich* parody: the despot, Chaka, publicly executes his mother when she opposes his will—he refuses to produce an heir from the belief that it will in turn kill him. The hero, Umslopogaas, almost kills his surrogate father, Mopo, though he insists in repentance that he did not consciously intend his death. [57] More importantly, since it precipitates the "domestic" conflict that propels the narrative toward resolution, Mopo flees his home and tribe because his brothers are so envious of his intelligence, they "poison the mind of [his] father against [him]" (12). As Mopo explains, "I learned . . . that my father had ordered out all the men of the tribe to hunt for me on the morrow and to kill me wherever they found me" (18).

Following a predictable turn of events and a thoroughly overdetermined relation to the myth of Oedipus, Mopo becomes a fugitive from his father's wrath and endeavors to make peace with Chaka, though he discovers that his second father is more tyrannical than his first. Mopo also adopts Umslopogaas, Chaka's true heir, by vowing to protect him from his father's murderous aims. Finally, Mopo's daughter, Nada, is a woman whose beauty makes her vulnerable to tribal despots. Against this scene of rivalry and familial conflict, a constellation of "virtuous" characters emerges with respect for lineage and community and a desire to restore the "correct" balance of power. This second group includes Galazi since he avenges his father's death by murdering his killer. When Galazi and Umslopogaas befriend each other in exile, they form a virtuous partnership as "blood-brothers," swearing to honor rather than undermine their fathers' authority.

Given the form and violence of these domestic conflicts, the narrative resembles Freud's *Totem and Taboo* (1913) in its description of the Primal Horde's murder of their Father to end his homo/sexual jealousy; the Horde create a "brethren" from his legacy.[58] Like Freud's text, *Nada* constantly engages tensions among fathers, sons, and brothers; it also shares with *The Four Feathers* a concern for the "true" path of masculine identification by encouraging the "virtuous" son to distinguish authority from usurpation. *The Four Feathers* raises this concern by associating cowardice with sexual ambivalence; *Nada* advances a similar rhetoric of virility, which resonates beyond the gendered and sexual conflict of *The Four Feathers* because its account of masculinity is fundamentally at odds with heterosexuality. While *The Four Feathers* champions heterosexuality by disbanding a contrary "effeminacy," *Nada the Lily* portrays heterosexual desire in opposition to the basic tenets of homophilia—specifically, the "brotherhood" joining Umslopogaas to Galazi. In Haggard's text, erotic friendship outlasts and surpasses conventional romance between men and women: " 'Stay awhile, Umslopogaas,' cried Galazi; 'stay till we are men indeed. . . .' [T]hey made them blood-brethren, to be one till death, before all the company of ghost wolves, and the wolves howled when they smelt the blood of men" (118). As "Wolf-Brethren" (120), Umslopogaas and Galazi tame animals and defeat human enemies; their pact diminishes the threat of their surroundings. Conversely, heterosexuality renders a man and woman vulnerable to attack and oblivious to danger because they lose all sense of the enemy: "Umslopogaas was so lost in his love for the Lily that he forgot his wisdom, and thought no more of war or death or of the hate of Dingaan" (270).

If the central complaint of Mason's novel attaches to a man, the drama of Haggard's novel turns bitterly on the influence of women. Though they represent opposite ends of the homosocial spectrum, Mason's and Haggard's texts indicate an insecurity about masculine identity's *noninevitability* against the strictures that lay down its uniformity.[59] *Nada* also amplifies the threat that "bad" fathers and sexual women pose to masculine subjects; it clarifies that masculinity is socially and psychically possible only when it represses or displaces these threats. These conditions of possibility raise questions about the resistance to masculine identification in Mason's novel, and normativized versions of gender in Britain's colonial fiction at the end of the nineteenth century.

By emphasizing Mopo's and his sister Baleka's exile from their father, Galazi's from his brethren, and Umslopogaas's and his cousin Nada's from Chaka (his father), *Nada* recounts the symbolic trajectories of male and female characters alike by presenting every character as a traveler. The narrator attaches allegorical importance to the survival, conflict, and difficulty of his tribe by suggesting that Umslopogaas "would have reigned as a king, not wandered an outcast in strange lands I know not where" (238). When members of a Zulu tribe exclaim, "Ha! ha! . . . now your journey is done, little man" (99), they refer to the symbolic home from which he fled and the place to which he yearns to return. Finally, Baleka's statement about the danger awaiting Umslopogaas's tribe carries psychic importance by pronouncing the fate of every subject, irrespective of gender: "Death is behind us and before us — we are in the middle of death" (27).

Stymied by their violent origins, the protagonists of *Nada the Lily* face constant threats of danger. Their negotiation and resolution of this danger compose an axiom joining Haggard's and Mason's texts; every register of violence represents subjectivity's unremitting task and labor. In this respect, the relation between land and femininity that McClintock, Bunn, and Stott elaborate is not only a sexual appropriation of the colony by the white man, but also a relation between the subject and its origins, and between the subject and the territory defining its home and orientation. Regardless of their race and nationality, every character in *Nada* confronts this relation's shifting terms: when Galazi recounts his father's premonition that he will be "a wanderer for the few years of [his] life" (94), for instance, his nomadic longing represents exile, *oikos,* and origin: "Perhaps you know the place, my father. In it is a great and strange mountain. It is haunted also, and named the Ghost Mountain, and on the top of it is a grey peak rudely shaped like the head of an aged woman" (66). Since this description is central to the text's development, and thoroughly overdetermined by oedipal imagery, it is worth quoting at length:

> Then I rose and plunged into the forest. The trees are great that grow there, stranger, and their leaves are so thick that in certain places the light is as that of night when the moon is young. Still, I wended on, often losing my path. But from time to time between the tops of the trees I saw the figure of the grey stone woman who sits on the top of Ghost Mountain, and shaped my course towards her knees. . . . At times, also, I caught glimpses of some grey wolf as he slunk from tree to tree watching me, and always high above my head the wind sighed in the great boughs with the sound like the sighing of women. . . . So I climbed up the steep rock, where little bushes grow like hair on the arms of a man, till at last I came to the knees of the stone Witch, which are the space before the cave. I lifted my head over the brink of the rock and looked, and I tell you, Umslopogaas, my blood ran cold and my heart turned to water, for there, before the cave, rolled wolves, many and great. Some slept and growled in their sleep, some gnawed at the skulls of dead game, some sat up like dogs and their tongues hung from their grinning jaws. I looked, I saw, and beyond I discovered the mouth of the cave, where the bones of the boy should be. (100–2)

Galazi and Umslopogaas tame these wolves by attaching fur to their own backs; Galazi also carries a powerful sword he names "The Watcher" because it avenges the scene he witnessed in the cave. The allegorical conflict between territory and usurper that the old woman and pack of wolves describe is not exclusive to this passage; it persists throughout the text as a "melodrama of beset manhood." [60] When the narrative stages this conflict between competing parental imagoes, for instance, protagonists must defend themselves and the "womb" against the incursion of a foreign enemy.[61]

The tools of this defense are weapons symbolizing potency and phallic omnipotence; the pact between Galazi and Umslopogaas also represents an ideal tribal contract. Though swords enact this defense, the text reveals how identification with other men upholds the political and imaginary power of the phallus. Describing his vision of "The Watcher," for instance, Galazi admits that "a great desire came into my heart to possess it" (97); the power of Umslopogaas's own weapon so bewitches him that he names the sword "The Groan-Maker": "Umslopogaas . . . held up the great Groan-

Maker, the iron chieftainess, and examined its curved points of blue steel, the gouge that stands behind it, and the beauty of its haft, bound about with wire of brass, and ending in a knob like the knob of a stick, as a lover looks upon the beauty of his bride. Then before all men he kissed the broad blade and cried aloud" (134). When Umslopogaas appears to possess "The Groan-Maker," ten rivals challenge his authority. The sword and Galazi come to his defense, however, and his leadership over the community of wolves represents a sea change for the tyranny of his estranged father, Chaka.

This novel's predictable development and crass metaphors render its psychoanalytic reading almost unnecessary. What interests me is less the social competition between Galazi and Umslopogaas than their sexual conflict and jealousy. This conflict extends beyond the novel's obvious misogyny by contesting the traditionally stable relation between heterosexuality and the community:[62] Umslopogaas cannot easily choose between Nada and his male friends because the narrative sexualizes Galazi as a competing love object. Umslopogaas's choice between marriage and "brotherhood" stymies, for the erotics of male friendship deny exclusive object choice in *Nada*—its colonial romance expands to include both men and women, homophilia and heterosexuality. Even when "brotherhood" and male love are openly misogynist and women compete with men as sexual rivals, *Nada* is remarkably naive about the silence, reticence, and phobia that intensified as a crisis of masculine friendship only fifteen years after its publication, with the trials of Wilde.

Briefly to illustrate my point about *Nada*'s "nonexclusive" patterns of love, consider the tension that surfaces between Galazi and Umslopogaas when the latter marries Zinita and then falls in love with Nada. Although Umslopogaas's desire for each woman bitterly displaces Galazi, Zinita envies Galazi's affective power over Umslopogaas (194). When Umslopogaas tries to prioritize his relationship with Nada, however, he ignores matters of state, the community deteriorates, and the narrator promptly reverts to idealizing Galazi's solitary life in the woods (140). Since Galazi is indifferent to Nada's beauty (221, 275) and to women in general (139), her power over Umslopogaas becomes contentious because the narrator considers romance a consuming passion in which a woman is "foremost in [a man's] mind . . . [and] drives out all other desire—ay, my father, even that of good weapons" (126).

Increasingly troubled by Umslopogaas's neglect and inattention to his people's plight, Galazi laments: "Ah . . . changed is the Wolf King my brother, all changed because of a woman's kiss. Now he hunts no more, no more shall Groan-Maker be aloft; it is a woman's kiss he craves, not the touch of your rough tongue, it is woman's hand he holds, not the smooth haft of horn, he, who of all men, was the fiercest and the first; *for his last shame has overtaken him*" (267; my emphasis). Despite the unfortunate terms of this complaint, Galazi's indictment reverses the narrator's charge in *The Four Feathers,* in which loss of a woman defines masculine shame and marriage restores sexual ambivalence. Although both texts voice a taunt of effeminacy, *Nada* does so in respect of its protagonist's *heterosexuality.* The thirty-two years separating the publication of these books attests to a change in the insult, in which a gap between heterosexuality and masculinity in *Nada* is inseparable from a homphobic slur in *The Four Feathers.* Galazi's indictment in *Nada* indicates that in 1892, these phenomena were not identical, and that a structural tension in masculine friendship ensured that they temporarily remain apart. As the "Wolf Kingdom" further deteriorates, for instance, the narrator and Galazi lament the loss of this interstitial relation: "Galazi the Wolf . . . added this: that, like twin trees, they two blood-brethren had grown up side by side till their roots were matted together, and that, were one of them dug up and planted in Swazi soil, he feared lest both should wither, or, at the least, that he, Galazi, would wither, who loved but one man and certain wolves" (225). This image of "matted . . . roots" conveys a powerful suggestion of mutual masturbation. When Umslopogaas recovers his ability to fight and lead the "Wolf Kingdom," however, the narrator suggests that "his sense came back to him" (270), as if love for Nada makes him not only "insensible" but almost insane. Though Galazi and Umslopogaas fight together as "a glorious pair!" (279), their recovery comes too late and the enemy wounds both men. On the verge of death, Galazi declares his regret to Umslopogaas before he falls, in a swoon, on "a mat of men [he had prepared] to lie on" (281): "While it lasted our friendship has been good, and its ending shall be good. Moreover, it would have endured for many a year to come had you not sought . . . to complete our joy of fellowship and war with the love of women" (275). Umslopogaas's reply not only confirms this regret, but also thoroughly revises Haggard's definition of "colonial romance": "Perchance I did ill, Galazi, when first I hearkened to the words of Zinita and suffered women to come between us. May we one day find a land where there are no women, and war only, for in that land we shall grow great. But now, at the least, we make a good end to this fellowship" (276). For many colonists, the empire represented precisely "a land where there are no women" because marriage and conventional domesticity did not determine a pioneer's fate. Since Haggard often saw women as detractors from a masculine mission, the ensuing tension between heterosexuality and homophilia ensures that neither is possible in *Nada.* The desperate role this offers women in his fiction, as demanding objects and valuable depositories, urges his protagonists both to engage and withstand the danger of female intimacy. We can attribute part of this urgency to Haggard's interest in the unconscious; his protagonists' ambivalent violence and desire confirm "the nineteen savage portions of our nature . . . not . . . the twentieth." [63] The remainder may result from Haggard's unusual concern with barbaric qualities in all "civilized" cultures, which apparently permits the pioneer to range his desire across a limitless terrain.

Although my reading of Haggard and Mason has stressed the conceptual turbulence of masculine friendship, "brotherhood," and exploration, I have also emphasized some of their psychic determinants to demonstrate the repetitive function of these phenomena. In this sense, I would qualify the O.E.D.'s definition of the pioneer as "one who goes before to prepare or open up the way"; "one who begins . . . some enterprise"; and "an originator . . . [or] forerunner." [64] In my reading, the pioneer defines his or her function against a prior journey that fails to reach closure. As Pierre Macherey argued cogently, "To explore is to follow, that is to say, to cover once again, under new conditions, a road already actually travelled." [65] Though Macherey maintains that "The conquest is only possible because it has already been accomplished," [66] I would argue that a conquest of other cultures and peoples is possible only when its psychic equivalent has not been completed.

3

Framing Fears,

Reading Designs:

The Homosexual Art

of Painting in

James, Wilde, and Beerbohm

The Desire and Truth in Painting

Consciousness, indeed, is quite inadequate to explain the
contents of personality. It is Art, and Art only, that reveals us
to ourselves.
—Oscar Wilde[1]

The truth, then, is no longer itself in that which represents it
in painting, it is merely its double, however good a likeness it
is and precisely other by reason of the likeness.
—Jacques Derrida[2]

There is no truth that, in passing through consciousness,
does not lie. But one runs after it all the same.
—Jacques Lacan[3]

Given the previous chapters' investigation of colonial law and desire, what
meaning and authority can we attribute to narrative truth? How, for instance,
can literature represent a lie when its procedures involve duplicity? When

applied to the fiction of Henry James, these questions trouble the meaning and authenticity of his characters. A reader's struggle to distinguish between James's accounts of truth and deceit asks us to consider not only his understanding of character and knowledge, but also how turn-of-the-century literature represents personality, fantasy, and desire; this is the task of the present chapter.

I want to examine the problem of desire in James's fiction by arguing that desire forms an intermediary category between knowledge and personal truth. The meaning that circulates between and among his characters cannot answer or resolve their enigma, or render their truth stable and legible. Despite their promise of coherence, James's narrative conclusions raise as many questions about his characters' ontology as they successfully close down. Specifically, they represent an indeterminacy about objects of desire and their gender that takes the reader beyond his narratives' resolution.[4] What meaning can we therefore attribute to enigma and sexual dissimulation in James's fiction? Are James's tropes of artistry, masquerade, and interpersonal deceit able to suspend the significance his narratives attach to friendship, physical desire, and even same-gender intimacy? Finally, is there a relation between James's protagonists' fantasies, taboo elements of homosexuality, and restrictions on masculine roles in turn-of-the-century literature and society?

"The Liar" (1888), one of James's most intriguing and little-discussed short stories, may serve as an introduction to this discussion because it offers a dynamic of sexual deceit, enigma, and apparent resolution.[5] Sir David Ashmore, an aging gentleman, commissions the artist of this tale, Oliver Lyon, to paint him at his country house in Hertfordshire before he dies. Sir David's temporary absence at a dinner party in his house gives Lyon an opportunity to scrutinize the other guests to see whether they would make appropriate subjects for painting. Across the table, he observes a former lover and her husband, Colonel Capadose, and their subsequent introduction renews emotions that he must veil from the colonel and other guests. Under the gaze of the public eye, Lyon and Mrs. Capadose interpret the change that has taken place in their relationship and accept the impossibility of admitting their desire or resuming their intimacy.

This conflict generates interest for the reader and the guests of the party when Lyon realizes that Mrs. Capadose has married a man who is often incapable of telling the truth. Indeed, the colonel's tendency to distort and exaggerate events, both real and imaginary, indicates a self-deception that borders on pathology. Curious about the colonel, and desirous of his wife, the painter falls into a drama as he struggles to understand the colonel's mendacity and his wife's concealment of each preposterous untruth. By acknowledging the extent of her complicity, Lyon reaches an understanding of his own and is able to relinquish her as his memory's haunting object.

Before the painter sees Mrs. Capadose, for instance, Lyon considers his own status as an unaccompanied bachelor (a fact of considerable importance to the colonel) as well as each guest's potential to be painted. This moment of observation is significant because it hinges on the painter's interest in his portrait candidates, his ability to capture their external role, and the measure of artistry that a transposition from interest to figuration entails—that is, the shift that occurs when the painter poses an individual as a "subject," before transforming him or her into a figure on canvas. In each substitution, the painter focuses on what each subject exhibits of himself or herself and what he or she is able to hide. The public correspondingly measures the painter's skill by his ability to read each act of concealment and the fantasy that a subject maintains between his or her external appearance and idealized self-representation. By observing himself watching others, Lyon thus is able "to lose himself in his favourite diversion of watching face after face. This amusement gave him the greatest pleasure he knew, and he often thought it a mercy that the human mask did interest him and that it was not less vivid than it was (sometimes it ran its success in this line very close), since he was to make his living by reproducing it" (386).

James writes frequently from an observer's point of view—Rowland Mallet in *Roderick Hudson* (1875) and Lambert Strether in *The Ambassadors* (1903) are notable examples. His observers' interest is determined largely by their shift from detached outsider to embroiled mediator, a shift that accompanies their movement from mystification (enigma) to discovery (epiphany) when they finally pass judgment.[6] Art is especially useful to this process because it obstructs and foils James's characters' designs with an intermediary project (painting).

Rather than establishing the subject's truth, however, art appears to indicate the discrepancy between one truth and another, and the variance of meaning in different spheres of representation—from the literary to the figurative and fantasmatic. I want to emphasize this split between James's subject and its representation because the split does not always correspond to the project of James's tale or agree with his broader definition of fiction: it produces meanings that each narrative is unable to explain or contain since their field of meaning—particularly sexual meaning—is not subject to authorial or narrative control. "The Liar," for example, consistently undermines the mimetic strategy advanced in "The Art of Fiction" (1884), in which James describes painting as a faithful copy of life: "The only reason for the existence of a novel is that it does attempt to represent life. When it relinquishes this attempt, the same attempt that we see on the canvas of the painter, it will have arrived at a very strange pass." [7] This impasse often resonates in "The Liar" as an excess of meaning that develops from intrigue and speculation about different characters.[8] Painting veils *and* discloses the erotic intrigue of "The Liar" because the subject of painting defines its personality by deciding what qualities to adopt, exaggerate, and conceal.[9]

The colonel is significant in this regard, and troubling to his painter, because whenever he lies his public character and speech differ dramatically from his self-representation. Since Lyon is a reader of "the human mask" (386), he exposes the colonel as an anomaly because the colonel's persona points too obviously to dissimulation; it is not a laudable role through which he can artfully realize his character. The result is a visible duplicity that foregrounds the colonel's indifference to maintaining an important social distinction for his friends between a "player and the part he represent[s]." [10] For the purposes of my reading, this indifference accentuates the masculine subject and its social and sexual symbolization at the turn of the century by indicating a deceit of which the colonel is only the most visible symptom. Lyon's fascination often exceeds him because the dinner guests' tacit support for the colonel's mendacity throws their definition of truth awry. This further indicates the difficulty of reading someone else because the factors that confirm or discredit public identity—speech and facial expression—are notoriously opaque and inscrutable: "Arthur Ashmore [Sir David's son] would not be inspiring to paint . . . ; even if he had looked a little less like a page (fine as to print and margin) without punctuation, he would still be a refreshing, iridescent surface. But the gentleman four persons off [Colonel Capadose]—what was he? Would he be a subject, or was his face only the legible door-plate of his identity, burnished with punctual washing and shaving—the least thing that was decent that you would know him by?" (386). The surface of the face is comparable to a piece of writing because it is legible and "punctuat[ed]" by meaning, though Lyon is doubtful whenever he ruminates on what is beneath that surface—the illegible and unwritable text of personality. Although he understands that the face can elicit or inhibit desire, he fails to note that the subject's speech also can sustain deception when it artfully agrees with its persona's truth.

When Lyon renews interest in the colonel's wife, he exposes the colonel's duplicity because the art of seduction tests and draws on a similar manipulation of truth and appearance—displaying what one wishes known, for instance, and postponing what one would rather leave unsaid. In other words, seduction encourages a temporary suspension of character by performing an ideal that the lover invariably betrays. Lyon admits that an individual's projection of honesty—though difficult to maintain—creates more intrigue when it flirts with a certain economy of truth without falling into cultivated dishonesty: thus, when another guest at the dinner party asks Lyon, " 'Do you mean I like people in proportion as they deceive?,' he replies: 'I think we all do, so long as we don't find them out' " (391).

The colonel's most amusing problem is that he is spectacularly found out each time he describes his past and ruling passions. On the one hand, he is the least interesting character insofar as he is the most obvious liar; on the other, his manipulation of truth is so egregious that it veils the dissimulation of others with outrageous effect: the guests at the dinner party acquiesce in his lies to maintain their secret dramas. Lyon, for example, resumes a discreet intimacy with Mrs. Capadose under the pretext of painting the colonel. By representing the colonel's falsehoods on canvas, Lyon clarifies his reason for lying and simultaneously conceals his own desire to understand—and even seduce—the colonel's wife.

This gap between subjective and social truth makes the colonel's motives difficult to establish. As Sir David suggests, the colonel's compulsion is intermittent, so his stories cannot all be dismissed as outright lies. Instead, the infrequency of his lies requires considerable vigilance on his listener's part because the colonel is likely to evince credibility whenever he tells the truth. The compulsion is also not sufficiently sporadic for the listener to consider it, like a parapraxis, a passing conflict between the colonel's statement and intention; his lies are always framed by anecdotes that copy the figurative process of writing: "His allusions were very quietly and casually made; but they were all too dangerous experiments and close shaves" (392). This final problem returns us to other characters' strategic dishonesty, and James's literary dissimulations, because the lie occurs precisely inside, not outside, the structure of representation. This proximity between representation and deceit makes interpreting the lie all the more difficult because it subverts any certainty that the listener or reader can recover, beneath the various layers of falsehood, an untainted ontological truth; deception radically inheres in the everyday vicissitudes of speech and identity.

The colonel's lies so entirely revoke assumptions about conscious dishonesty that we can trace their meaning only by his use of anecdote. A critical reading of these lies must therefore begin at the point where the colonel's fantasies exceed his narratives' veracity; it is here that his wild and impossible bid for authenticity seems least credible. For James, as a writer of such ontologically and homoerotically indeterminate narratives as "The Beast in the Jungle" (1903) and "The Jolly Corner" (1908), the tale—not the teller—ultimately ratifies narrative truth. Perhaps for this reason, criticism of James that tries to confirm this indeterminacy as homosexual opacity stalls when it argues that sexual meaning inhabits the narrative subject more visibly than the narrative's frame of reference.[11]

Although the colonel seems impervious to his compulsion, and others are wary of bringing it to his attention, the symptom of his self-disclosure seems impossible properly to obscure. Indeed, the colonel joyously discloses this compulsion, as Freud wrote of the paranoiac's delirium, because "the patients . . . possess the peculiarity of betraying (in a distorted form, it is true) precisely those things which other neurotics keep hidden as a secret." [12] The colonel cannot "be compelled to overcome . . . internal resistances" because by laying bare the mechanism of resistance that would otherwise restrict his speech, he allows a prior impulse fleetingly to be heard.[13]

Freud identified this declaration as a form of psychosis because the subject's delirium seems to blind it to its expression's truth. Rather than formulating this—or any other—character prognosis, I am interested in desire's social and psychic difficulty in James's fiction, and the way the colonel makes this difficulty palpable by demonstrating that his statements fall short of full or unmediated explication. Indeed, the colonel is fascinating because his allusions depend on a metonymic substitution of one idea for another. These allusions are "all too dangerous" (392) because each substitution carries the trace of its preceding term, allowing meaning to condense around a single, readable obsession. While the other characters in "The Liar" largely ignore this condensation of his discourse, the colonel's danger lies in his willingness periodically to blurt out a link they are more adept at concealing. The homonymic link between Lyon and liar, for instance, makes this apparent; Lyon partly "lies" when he paints.

James's tale gives much prominence to the colonel's distorted subjects and the circumstances—including the person addressed—that precipitate his egregious manipulations of the past. The tale incorporates six of these anecdotes, each representing a topic designed to increase the colonel's acclaim from a public whose interest wanes in proportion to each desperate and hilarious falsehood.

The colonel's past refers to a period he spent in the colonies before his marriage to Mrs. Capadose: "He has been a great deal in India—isn't he rather celebrated?" (387). These details generate interest for the reader—who initially is as gullible as Lyon—because he or she cannot verify them, and because the period to which the colonel's anecdotes generally refer is one he seems unable to broach without distortion. As we shall see, even the narrator appears to lie when he claims: "though there was a great deal of swagger in his talk, it was, oddly enough, rarely swagger about his military exploits" (412). The colonel transforms his past by creating an event that substitutes for a truth he always withholds. This absent referent is as significant as the fantasy for which the colonel partially exchanges it: "He had a passion for the chase, he had followed it in far countries and some of his finest flowers were reminiscences of lonely danger and escape. The more solitary the scene the bigger of course the flower. A new acquaintance, with the Colonel, always received the tribute of a bouquet" (412). The new acquaintance—like the potential lover—is most willing to believe, and least able to contradict, each claim the colonel avows. The colonel therefore defines himself by a past he constantly remodifies. As a corollary, Lyon (as guest) is most exposed to, and (as painter) best able to interpret, the fantasies of a man who often is indifferent to his deceit's effect: "The Muse breathed upon him at her pleasure; she often left him alone. He would neglect the finest openings and then set sail in the teeth of the breeze. As a general thing he affirmed the false rather than denied the true; yet this proportion was sometimes strikingly reversed. Very often he joined in the laugh against himself—he admitted that he was trying it on and that a good many of his anecdotes had an experimental character. Still he never completely retracted nor retreated—he dived and came up in another place" (412-13).

Although the colonel's tales are replete with "inconsistencies and unexpected lapses—lapses into flat veracity" (412), a pattern seems to develop as much from what he cannot say and visibly distorts as from what he desires and struggles to become. For instance, the first untruth concerns an experience in Ireland: the colonel claims he was thrown from a horse so that he "turned a sheer somersault and landed on his head" (392-93). Several days later, a person finds him lying among some pigs and takes him to an inn, where he lies close to death "without a ray of recognition of any human thing . . . [or] a glimmer of consciousness of any blessed thing" for "three whole months" (393). The colonel blithely claims, unaware of his inadvertent pun on "lying," "there was really no limit to the time one might lie unconscious without being any the worse for it" (392).

Boasting the colonel's resilience and his survival of what seemed imminent death, the following anecdote is even more extraordinary in its elaboration of fantasy. According to the colonel, a friend from his past was diagnosed with "jungle fever," immediately "clapped . . . into a coffin," and literally buried alive:

> "He was left there till I came and hauled him out."
>
> "*You* came?"
>
> "I dreamed about him—it's the most extraordinary story: I heard him calling to me in the night. I took upon myself to dig him up."
> (393–94)

The colonel claims to have rescued his friend from "people in India—a kind of beastly race, the ghouls—who violate graves" (394). Upon hearing his call, he gallops to the grave in a frenzy to ward them off. The colonel is just in time, for the surface of his friend's grave has already been penetrated: "a couple of them had just broken ground!" (394). He manages to scare them off with a couple of shots, recover his friend, and nurse him back to health.

Although hilariously improbable, both stories are startling in describing a liminal movement between life and death and a condition of unconsciousness from which the colonel makes an urgent bid for rescue. In the second tale, the projection of an enemy makes this rescue more desperate because it ratifies an act of heroic courage and affection. While the friend is susceptible to "violat[ion]" by a group of spirits, for instance, the colonel repeats the same act moments later—at least in fantasy—with apparently different intent. These acts are quite indistinguishable from each other, however: the colonel's fight to defeat "the ghouls" makes him covet his friend's body in performing the same violation. The projection of desire both in source (the ghouls) and in aim (rescue, not violence) nonetheless elides all question of how the colonel could *know* of his friend's danger:

> "He called to you in the night?" said Lyon, much startled.
>
> "That's the interesting point. Now *what was it?* It wasn't his ghost, because he wasn't dead. It wasn't himself, because he couldn't. It was something or other! You see India's a strange country—there's an element of the mysterious: the air is full of things you can't explain." (394)

Lyon's question presses crucially the imaginary source of the friend's demand and its internal meaning for the colonel. However, the colonel's failure of memory and his fumble for a credible answer lead Lyon, and the reader, to suspect that the colonel has simply "dived and [come] up in another place"; that is, substituted one improbability (the "mysterious" culture of the Orient) for another (the plea for rescue). Psychic deceit and historical distortion therefore coalesce on a trope of colonial discovery: "[Sir David] spoke of his portrait as a plain map of the country, to be consulted by his children in a case of uncertainty. A proper map could be drawn up only when the country had been travelled" (406).

Unable to sustain the demands of this "proper map," the colonel's substitution only partially occludes Lyon's suspicion that the friend does not exist; although the fantasy is empirically spurious, it is not in any simple sense *untrue*. In other words, the colonel's insistence, despite Lyon's protest, implies that the story sustains a truth for him because it has already occurred as an imaginary scenario. I want to emphasize the gap in this example between the imaginary and represented event because it draws our attention to a fantasy the text cannot encode in any other way. By the end of the tale, the narrative has tied each anecdote to other expressions of fantasy to produce a condensed frame of meaning: from unconsciousness to reawakening, and from an object's rescue to its subsequent vanishing, each anecdote elucidates a fantasy of contact, intimacy, and allegiance with another man. More generally, the colonel's distortions seem to clarify an opaque and troubled relation between his fantasies and the growing legibility of homoerotic desire in turn-of-the-century literature.

The anecdote of the lost friend in India is interesting in these terms because it encodes a demand for contact that is inversely analogous to the physical violation from which the colonel must protect his friend. By projecting the ghouls as the single source of danger, the colonel uses physical urgency to discharge, and even validate, his impulses: "I came and hauled him out"; "d[u]g him up"; "[to] get at him first"; "I took him out myself"; "he would do anything for me" (394). Having avowed an element of distortion, the narrative begs the questions of why the colonel lies and why this obsessive theme of desirable and impossible contact with another man prevails in his speech.

The colonel later recounts his fantasy that a ghost haunts Sir David's manor, and that this ghost is responsible both for "a skeleton [that was] found years before" (401) and the startled behavior of young men who sleep in that manor before anxiously departing the next morning. Each young man bears "an ill-concealed agitation [and . . .] an awfully queer face" (402–3) after passing a restless night. The colonel notes of the room in which the men stayed, "Of course it's a bachelor's room, and my wife and I are at the other end of the house" (402). The inclusion here of such an apparently gratuitous comment carries significance—at least on an imaginary register—because it connects the earlier fantasy of the buried friend with Lyon's marital status.

The detail appears so irrelevant that doubt must surround the reason for its expression. Moments earlier, Lyon had explained that a corridor leads beyond his room "for half a mile"; a remark the colonel confirms by insisting that the haunted room lies at the end of this corridor—that is, at furthest distance from his own quarters. The length of corridor, the gender of the guests, and the marital status of Lyon seem to emphasize the distance that the colonel must maintain between an impulse (proximity to a male guest) and its fulfillment (rescue from violation); hence his insistence on the half-mile of corridor that prevents his desire from ever reaching its object.

Although Lyon's realization that the story is fabricated partially revokes this fantasy's meaning, the anecdote's redolence withstands the colonel's embarrassed attempt to override it. When Lyon questions Mr. Ashmore later on the same subject, for instance, Mr. Ashmore corrects him:

> "Three days ago? What gentleman?" [. . .]
> "The one who got urgent letters and fled by the 10.20. Did he stand more than one night?"
> "I don't know what you are talking about. There was no such gentleman—three days ago." (404–5)

"The Liar" foregrounds Lyon's (and the reader's) desire for knowledge by drawing repeated attention to both the unsaid and oversaid elements of the colonel's desire and the impossibility of its accurate representation. Lyon's attempt to clarify this enigma compels him to collate the fragments of an imaginary drama to interpret the character of "the most mystifying figure in the house" (405). He does this by painting him—that is, by exploiting another form of representation—because portraiture renders Lyon "something of a psychologist" (409). In this sense, the narrator couches interpretation as seduction: by offering to fix a representable trope of his personality, painting tempts the colonel to lie. As each anecdote attests, language, in its diffuseness, can witness but never secure the "hidden shame . . . of . . . a man whose word had no worth . . ." (410). However, painting can elicit and fix this meaning because it captures the "queer habit . . . [of] such a rare anomaly" by marking "what manner of man he was" (409–10). Sensing the imminence of her husband's exposure, Mrs. Capadose tries to disband the project before she is forced to explain why she conceals his "most contemptible, [and] least heroic, of vices" (411):

> ". . . he's such a rare model—such an interesting subject. He has such an expressive face. It will teach me no end of things."
> "Expressive of what?" said Mrs. Capadose.

"Why, of his nature."

"And do you want to paint his nature?"

"Of course I do. That's what a great portrait gives you . . ." (418–19)

Painting, like psychoanalysis, reveals the subject to itself by representing aspects of identity and the past that consciousness has repressed. Painting also represents a truth that the symptom's obfuscations inform and partially veil—in this case, the compulsion to lie. What is thus a means of drawing forth ("I shall bring it out!" [419]) is also dangerously close to a violation of defense because the drive cannot—or must not—be told to another. As Mrs. Capadose remarks: "Nothing would induce me to let you pry into *me* that way!" (419). Her fear is related to concealing the truth of a man whose word is no longer reliable; a concealment that forces her in turn to recognize what her idealizing love for the colonel has engendered. As Lyon tries to establish the extent of Mrs. Capadose's complicity, he realizes, by default, his capacity to misrecognize her.

Painting is able to bring this chain of substituted truths to a halt because painting offers a signifier by which to represent the colonel's necessary distortion. Lyon gives the portrait a title, *The Liar,* after both its subject and the narrative that frames it, though he never shows the painting because it exhibits more than its viewers should know. The painting's surplus meaning is perhaps synecdochic of this tale's (and its period's) wider opacity, for the reader cannot identify the source of the lie—is it Colonel Capadose, Lyon, or James? Since it remains undisclosed, the colonel's secret compels the reader to speculate on the impulse that shapes it, and to adopt Lyon's perspective to see in the colonel "the least thing that was decent that you would know him by" (386).

Each of the colonel's lies emphasizes the importance of this "least thing that was decent." The enigma of the colonel's history in India, the oblique references to his past and military rank, and the pervasive homoerotic allusions that circulate around his tales place considerable weight on his secret's stubborn—if unreliable—silence. Certainly the colonel's deceit is both structurally necessary and impossible fully to decipher. James cannot specify the nature of this deceit because a precise signifier would lead a narrative built on speculation toward bathetic collapse. As in other texts by James such as *The Turn of the Screw, The Sacred Fount,* and "The Jolly Corner," the reader's collusion is a prerequisite to textual interest, because each narrative revokes assumptions about conscious deceit, retaining only its diffusion's enigma. Although the narrative cannot represent the entire truth of subjective desire, painting "hears" and reproduces desire's enigma as an unwritable aspect of personality. By constructing and dismantling "an inscrutable mask" (411)—a description the narrator gives to Mrs. Capadose that applies equally to the colonel, his painter, and even his author—painting, speech, and writing embody mediums that constitute and distort, elicit and then frustrate, according to their users' designs. As Lyon muses to himself: "It is art for art. . . . He [the colonel] has an inner vision of what might have been, of what ought to be, and he helps on the good cause by the simple substitution of a *nuance*. He paints, as it were, and so do I!" (411–12).

This admission is written into "The Liar" (the painting and its narrative); it also resonates with similar accounts of painting that contemporaneous writers like Oscar Wilde and Max Beerbohm elaborated. *The Picture of Dorian Gray* (1891) and *The Happy Hypocrite* (1896) provide similar insights into men's relations and resemblances as well as comparable accounts of their figural seduction. By their use of specific metaphors, these texts clarify the suggestion that painting corresponds to an impossible homosexual desire; they establish a congruency by compressing these meanings until they finally break apart under the strain of homology. These texts appear to represent the eroticism of painting only by forcing this eroticism to remain allusion. To this extent, painting paradoxically supports and destroys the very meanings its activity engenders.[14]

It should not surprise us that the colonel tells his final lie when a woman mysteriously appears in the room as he is being painted. The colonel explains her presence by a bizarre and incredible fantasy: "She had hold of a friend of mine ten years ago—a stupid young gander who might have been left to be plucked but whom I was obliged to take an interest in for family reasons. It's a long story—I had really forgotten all about it. . . . I cut in and made him get rid of her—I sent her about her business . . ." (425). The woman allegedly haunts the colonel for denying her a man over whom she had a prior claim, but whom the colonel again felt obliged to rescue. As in earlier anecdotes, a third term (ghouls, ghost, or woman) quickly explains the colonel's deceit, as if intimacy with the man were impossible without this pretext. The woman's symptomatic presence does not resolve this deceit; it veils another palpable and unspoken enigma. However, we can read the "truth" that surfaces between the colonel's urgent speech and the pressure of his silence from his syntactical breaks, where the colonel's fantasy interrupts one narrative by preventing another's emergence.

Since the colonel lies while he is being painted, Lyon captures his deceit on canvas. True to his previous claim to Mrs. Capadose, Lyon returns to the colonel, albeit in an inverted form, the image of his enunciation.[15] The portrait serves as a partial repository for the colonel's final lie because it supports a meaning that is unbearable to its beholder. As Lyon watches the colonel furtively unveil his image and confront the "truth" of his discourse, the colonel utters "a passionate wail—a sort of smothered shriek" that curses Lyon and/or himself (430). Lyon and the reader cannot know the curse's object because its exposure would undermine the ending's ambiguity. Taking a knife to the canvas, the colonel tears it to shreds as if performing "a sort of figurative suicide" (431): "He plucked it out and dashed it again several times into the face of the likeness, exactly as if he were stabbing a human victim" (431). Still, the narrative refuses to impart the painting's secret: "The portrait had a dozen jagged wounds—the colonel literally had hacked it to death. Lyon left it where it was, never touched it, scarcely looked at it" (431).[16]

Despite the narrative's opening promise, the portrait cannot clear up the "questions which hummed in [Lyon's] brain" (426); the painting's defacement is so complete that it fosters an elaborate excuse. Denying all knowledge of the incident, the colonel later gives himself away by blaming his symptom: the woman who tried to avenge herself on him. However, the text never declares the real—or less obviously dishonest—reason for his violence; it substitutes this mystery for another version of truth. At the end of the tale, Lyon blames Mrs. Capadose for her hypocrisy because he considers that by veiling her husband's deceit, Mrs. Capadose is also living a lie.[17] The closing words of "The Liar," "he had trained her too well" (441), therefore silence more interesting and finally unanswered questions: What precipitates the colonel's lie, and what enunciation does the lie obstruct and make impossible? By its inadequate response to these questions, "The Liar" demonstrates that the need to be opaque lies in exact proportion to the pressure to express sexual desire. From this interesting relation between the subject's secret and the character that constantly announces it, we can begin to flesh out the enigma of James's tale by examining its repetition in contemporaneous writing. We can also contradict the narrator's assertion that "the male face [does not] lend itself to decorative repetition" (405–6).

Making and Unmaking the Face

It is the common belief that all subjects from inverted instinct carry
their lusts written on their faces; that they are . . . oblique in
expression.
— John Addington Symonds [18]

The great field for new discoveries . . . is always the Unclassified
Residuum.
— William James [19]

Wilde's 1891 novel *The Picture of Dorian Gray* famously elaborates
a promise to reveal the truth of painting. In ways that bear an extraordinary
likeness to James's short story, Wilde demonstrates that this truth often corresponds to men's uncertain relations. In *The Picture of Dorian Gray,* the narrative frames this uncertainty by drawing on associated meanings of fantasy,
pleasure, and obsession. This encourages masculine desire to surface at points
where the narrative strategy fails, particularly at the end of the text, where
the pressure of the unrepresentable acquires an urgent and violent resonance.

By repeating aspects of "The Liar," Wilde's painting also serves as
a partial repository for information that is inadmissible to its painter and impalpable to its subject. The painting's relation to each character, however,
is both obscure and excessive. Basil Hallward, Dorian's painter, claims to
have conveyed too obvious an interest in his subject — "I really can't exhibit
it. I have put too much of myself into it"; "I had told too much" [20] — while
Dorian considers the painting an ideal that substitutes for his perfect beauty a
counterpart with dangerously conspicuous desires. Finally, Lord Henry sees
in Dorian an aesthetic object that the painting mediates and only stubbornly
conveys. In each example, the painting represents Dorian's "mind in . . . its
secret places . . . the most magical of mirrors. As it had revealed to him his
own body, so it would reveal to him his own soul" (120).

Although each character perceives the painting's significance by its
ability to hide (Hallward), recapture (Dorian), or be admired (Henry), the
narrative's principal point of view, and the meanings that carefully evade de-
tection and exposure, belong to Dorian. The peripheral figures of Hallward
and Henry are important only insofar as they precipitate — and partially interpret — Dorian's transformed identity. Transfixed by his image, Dorian is able
to realize his ideal by renouncing age and desire. This renunciation engenders

such turmoil, however, that the narrative surpasses a relatively simple discussion of desire; it examines and only partially rejects the signifiers sin and guilt because the former "is a thing that writes itself across a man's face. It cannot be concealed" (166). When Dorian attempts to exchange his identity for his painting's truth, his desire is initially undetected because it inscribes a trace elsewhere—on a canvas of ulterior identity that he hides from sight, with such apparent distance from his consciousness that its repression appears successful. Dorian's incorporation of the image's facelessness is thus the condition of his identification; it allows him to pursue pleasures that are unrepresentable: he yields to each temptation, and moves flawlessly between London's West End theaters and East End opium dens.[21]

As in Freud's analogy between the unconscious and the "Mystic Writing-Pad" (1924), where impressions surface on a second, hidden sheet, Dorian's portrait unfailingly records the *vanishing* of his desire;[22] it represents what is unconscious to Dorian by disfiguring his supplemental identity. Since the portrait bears the scars of this hidden work, it memorializes the discarded by retaining what is unwritable to him and, as yet, unrepresentable by the text.[23] By drawing his and our attention to its inscription on another representational field, this scarring constantly reminds Dorian and the reader why the script disappears.

Since the portrait begins as a form of seduction, it retains part of the painter's interest by turning Dorian into an object that redefines and misrecognizes himself. As in James's story, painting precipitates a crisis over the meaning of desire by engendering an interpretive struggle over what it is that Dorian really wants. Lord Henry undertakes part of this struggle by encouraging Dorian to realize his desire: "The moment I met you I saw that you were quite unconscious of what you really are, of what you really might be. There was so much in you that charmed me that I felt I must tell you something about yourself" (30). This impalpable "something" moves unannounced from the narrative to its supplemental manuscript (the portrait), though the interstitial passage records it as an interest in masculine beauty and pleasure and a capacity to curtail the persistent announcement of desire.[24] The novel's attention to this proximity between pleasure, pathology, and degeneracy indicates the cruelty and social dread that result from controlling each impulse: "The worship of the senses has often, and with much justice, been decried, men feeling a natural instinct of terror about passions and sensations that seem stronger than themselves, and that they are conscious of sharing with the less highly organized forms of existence" (145). As Wilde demonstrates, the terror that men and women associate with pleasure cannot limit these "passions and sensations"; terror actually encourages their fervent and compulsive resistance: "There are moments, psychologists tell us, when the passion for sin, or for what the world calls sin, so dominates a nature, that every fibre of the body, as every cell of the brain, seems to be instinct with fearful impulses. Men and women at such moments lose the freedom of their will" (210).[25]

I want to use this suggestion of losing "freedom of the will" to argue that *The Picture of Dorian Gray* interprets how a particular form of masculine pleasure represented a cultural hinge between allure and danger at the turn of the last century. The novel embodies what this culture considers most civilized (when refined and restrained), and most reviled and potentially degenerate (when immoderate and excessive) in each individual and the groups to which he or she belongs. As Lord Henry later testifies, the pleasure principle in this text obeys no obvious—or at least nonpsychic—law because "Civilisation is not by any means an easy thing to attain to. There are only two ways by which man can reach it. One is by being cultured, the other by being corrupt" (232). Since corruption precedes and exceeds civilization's limits, it is integral and extraneous to cultural laws. However, as Wilde keenly observes in his essay "Pen, Pencil and Poison" (1891), the public's fantasy that it can expel corruption brings civilization and corruption paradoxically closer: "There is no essential incongruity between crime and culture. We cannot rewrite the whole of history for the purpose of gratifying our moral sense of what should be." [26]

The Picture of Dorian Gray's complexity lies both in its examination of this nebulous distinction between culture and anarchy and its critique of the troubled field of enjoyment; the novel's account of seduction and hedonism repeatedly questions the definitions and tolerable limits of pleasure and satisfaction (in this novel, these phenomena seem to be nonidentical). Dorian spends much time considering both how to yield to and to resist temptation without generating a craving, and how to recognize what is illicit in pleasure, and ontologically inducive to unpleasure, without being expelled from the social body.[27] Too little and too much of a good thing create passions that consume Wilde's protagonist because each induces a craving in the context of a structural privation. Though Dorian's passion exceeds the precarious control he can exercise over his drives, for instance, Britain's frequent conflation of pleasure and vice at the turn of the century compounds his problem.

In *The Picture of Dorian Gray,* this proximity between enjoyment and crime is psychically resonant and insistently political because many of this text's inferred pleasures hold the status of a crime. Section 11, "The Labouchère Amendment," of The Criminal Law Act (1885), for instance,

made *all* male homosexual acts, whether public or private, illegal and pun-
ishable for a term not exceeding two years, with or without hard labor (previously, British Parliament designated only sodomy as illegal).[28] As historians
and literary critics have well documented, the infamous libel case brought by
the Marquis of Queensbury against Wilde for "posing as a somdomite [*sic*]"
led to Wilde's public humiliation and imprisonment, the termination of his
flourishing career, and his premature death only four years after *The Picture
of Dorian Gray*'s publication.[29] The scandal of Wilde's trials was so extensive
that it transformed juridical and public consciousness of homosexuality, and
arguably was the most powerful reason for the collapse of Britain's decadent movement, with its emphasis on dandyism, aesthetics, and a burgeoning
homosexual movement and literature.[30]

We must therefore set in relief Wilde's repeated attention to the
unsaid of masculine pleasure against the political and cultural anxiety surrounding this category in the 1890s. If pleasure among men seemed to hover
between an aesthetic and a pathology in Britain at this time, it is in part because many of its constituents had recently been criminalized. Dorian Gray's
portrait cannot support these meanings because it bears the additional scar of
public opprobrium; the painting's secret also renders this split between the
subject and its self-representation an expedient element of survival. Dorian's
elaboration of different personalities takes us beyond the performance of a
disunited and multifaceted ego;[31] self-splitting serves the interest of a (sexual)
impulse against the force of its public repression. The division of his identity enables Dorian to hide from others—and from himself—the acts that fall
short of verbal and visual testimony, without his being able to rescind their
accompanying enigma. Recall the passage I cited earlier in my account of
Mason's *The Four Feathers:* "His extraordinary absences became notorious,
and when he used to reappear again in society, men would whisper to each
other in corners, or pass him with a sneer, or look at him with cold searching
eyes, as though they were determined to discover his secret" (157–58).[32]

This partial renunciation and inadequate dissimulation of pleasure
persists throughout the fiction I examine in this chapter, directing my interest
in tracking the path of this deceit—whether by these texts' recourse to guilt
and a fantasy of identification, or by their complex evasion of pleasure and
subsequent engagement with ulterior and apparently dissociated concerns.
My interest in Dorian's portrait specifically pertains to the novel's suggestion that it is less the simple repository of a secret than the condensation of
a preceding and unrepresentable drama. By withholding its truth, the painting makes public dissimulation possible and imperative because Dorian can

act only when speech and painting fail to capture his actions' consequences. If we further consider this fraught relation between subjectivity and masculine pleasure, the capacity to lie effectively becomes the condition of a successful personality; Dorian's deceit generates an ontological demand for *prosopopœia*—that is the production of another face. Derived from the Greek for "face making," this trope designates a rhetorical procedure informing personification in ways that can usefully interpret homosexual pleasure and symbolization in late Victorian Britain. For example, it fosters the representation of an apparently seamless identity amid a dearth of publicly acceptable roles. *Prosopopœia* suggests how subjects could use personæ to veil or echo the difficulty of sexual representation in fin de siècle British culture.[33]

Every individual must put on an act when he or she is assigned a social role. Dorian Gray's problem stems from the fact that masculine pleasure's political turbulence made even a temporary correspondence between (psychic) imago and (cultural) symbol impossible. Dorian's demand for pleasure takes him beyond the terms of an adequate signifier compelling him to perform the remainder on a field that is hidden from the social.

Good acting veils this inevitable tension within subjectivity by fostering an illusion of symbolic consistency—however precarious and temporary—between the subject and its social frame. Playing a part is acceptable to Wilde if the actor chooses, and the audience permits, the role. The bad actor makes this breach between identity's inside and outside explicit by demonstrating the artistry involved in making them cohere. Sibyl Vane destroys the seamless illusion of her personality, for instance, when she indicates her performance's truth beside herself. As Lord Henry explains, the truth of her personality lies neither in nor out of her performance; it emerges in the transition between her onstage and offstage performances. In effect, she destroys Dorian's transference and spoils the intrigue of seduction by returning the sexual drama to its source: "The staginess of her acting was unbearable, and grew worse as she went on. Her gestures became absurdly artificial. She overemphasized everything that she had to say. . . . It was simply bad art. She was a complete failure" (95–96).

In this passage, Wilde does not indict Sibyl for being superficial or inauthentic; he argues that a wooden and inexpressive performance spoils her artistry. The criticism is less an appeal to a unified and essential subjectivity than a plea to enhance the performative success of her identifications. Following Basil Hallward's naive remark that "Love is a more wonderful thing than Art," for instance, Lord Henry archly observes: "They are both simply forms of imitation" (96–97). He then elaborates on this proximity between art, romance, and transference: "When one is in love, one always begins by deceiving one's self, and one always ends by deceiving others. That is what the world calls a romance" (61).

Sibyl Vane's acting does not demonstrate the inauthentic status of character or the frequent exploitation of the social field as public theater. Wilde directs his contempt at the dearth of acceptable public roles and the way in which the subject's theatrical relation to the social compels it to compromise the integrity of its performance.[34] If Dorian creates a persona beside his existing personality, it is perhaps because he has only the bland and increasingly anodyne signifier "gentleman" with which to represent himself. His performance is successful insofar as the public never fully detects it, but his obligation to dissimulate transforms acting from "good art" into an intolerable ontological crisis. As I argued earlier in my account of Mason's *The Four Feathers,* society's insistence that Dorian limit his desire to a drama of self-secrecy is poignant and tragic, for it demonstrates—beyond the phenomenon of acting—the absence of an alternative symbol or social practice.[35]

Dorian's shift from a lived to an ideal (or painterly) identification is redolent of a wider transformation of group definition and cultural allegiance during this period. His shift foregrounds a crisis over the meaning of pleasure and desire that is general and specific: general, because the assumption that an identity can be adequate to its subject's drives is always a fantasy; specific, because the suppression of drives oriented to and among men is the effect of a political demand that these drives be abolished from public consciousness, or a claim that they can uphold only criminal and pathological definitions.

When Dorian stabs his painter, these general and specific meanings return to the text as components divorced from his identity, which he projects onto the painting. Perhaps the return is chaotic because it shatters the terms of his ideal, forcing him to recognize an impulse, or vice, whose excision from his subjectivity was necessary for it to function. As I suggested earlier, the reader can understand the meaning of this impulse only by the demand that compels it to vanish. Incorporation of this impulse proves impossible because the painting represents a vestige of opprobrium and violence that Dorian cannot symbolize or survive. If the painting first traces this hysterical conversion of desire into deceit, it may finally designate an unrepresentable part of his identity that his consciousness forecloses.

Having killed Hallward, Dorian endures a painting that remembers what he would rather forget—a "monstrous soul-life" whose "terror" and "melancholy" are a remorseless sign of "conscience" (247). The narrative never identifies the acts or pleasures to which his remorse corresponds, but the murder of Hallward brings their associated meaning into relief: Dorian must confess and "suffer public shame" as part of his "public atonement" (246). However, the repression of the portrait, much earlier in the text, suggests that his "crime" precedes this murder; indeed, the idea of exhibiting the portrait seems intolerable because of its surplus content. No integration or revelation is possible, then, because punishment rests on a culture's assumption that it can recognize and understand crime, that guilt corresponds to an imaginary redemption when no referent can designate either. Since Dorian cannot display the painting's conscience without representing this hidden significance, he stabs and destroys it before it is shown in public. Unlike Colonel Capadose, who performed the same desperate ritual, the painting's destruction brings not relief but a death that is neither written nor observed.

The painting's death returns us to the moment when Dorian's identification with the painting introduced a traumatic gap between his desire and its representation. This moment generates conjecture about his desire's meaning, though it also attests to an inadequate range of public symbols. Since Dorian's desire is clearly unwritable to the culture he inhabits, he has no alternative but to dissimulate it. The novel's violent ending draws attention to this scission because Dorian's death can only collide with a public and psychic demand that he destroy and disfigure this identification. In other words, Dorian's death cannot clarify who he really is because death marks the full meaning of his identification only by its disparity with what the narrative and public forced him to become. By retaining this secret to its end, the narrative represents the truth of Dorian Gray by default and misrecognition; this "truth" issues precisely from his struggle to excoriate the meaning of his desire.[36] In the space between the subject's secret and his death, however, an unnamable factor seems to preside, the consequence of which we can grasp by its final effect: "Lying on the floor was a dead man, in evening dress, with a knife in his heart. He was withered, wrinkled, and loathsome of visage. It was not till they had examined the rings that they recognized who it was" (248).

The Happiest Hypocrisy?

Mask after mask fell from the countenance
And form of all . . .
— Percy Bysshe Shelley [37]

A mask tells us more than a face. These disguises intensified his
personality.
—Oscar Wilde [38]

Persona means the actor's mask through which his dramatic tale is
sounded. Since man is the percipient who perceives what is, we can
think of him as the persona, the mask, of Being
—Martin Heidegger [39]

Max Beerbohm's 1896 novella *The Happy Hypocrite: A Fairy Tale
for Tired Men* advances these questions of *prosopopœia* by graphically demonstrating the possibilities and impossibilities of sexual desire and masculine
identification.[40] Since its romance is ostensibly heterosexual, a reading that
tries to interpret the text's strategy as pure deceit (as the displacement of an
underlying homosexual desire by a heterosexual imperative) would overlook
the novella's contrary insistence that its potential for homosexual desire remain unwritten. However, the palpable tension that arises from what this text
avows and shows—a tension the novella captures in its title—repeats the conflict in James's and Wilde's texts over what narratives can express and what,
of the sexual, is ultimately representable.

This tension may support two readings: either that the text, through
meanings it resists and turns away, demonstrates a denial of homosexuality, or
that it clarifies the semiotic possibility of homosexuality in its elliptical reference to signifiers that represent the failure and indeterminacy of other sexual
relations. It is important to distinguish between these readings: the first assumes that an inexpressible secret organizes the narrative's meaning, which
invites the critic to speak on the text's behalf by clarifying what it knows but
cannot say. The second seems more productive because it binds sexual indeterminacy to the narrative's precarious, and often unsuccessful, encounter
with heterosexuality. A reading that begins from the second premise allows
us to question how Beerbohm's novella achieves a limit to hypocrisy. That
is, we can ask where hypocrisy is *not* present, and who manages to avoid it,
without dwelling on more conventional questions about what hypocrisy resists, displaces, or conceals.

Beerbohm's suggestion that an exemplary hypocrisy devolves on
a sexual relation now may seem unsurprising after my reading of Kipling,
Mason, and Haggard; their narratives often represent the nomenclature of
romance by unequal demand, unexpressed need, and repeated untruth—re-

call also Lord Henry's suggestion of romance as inexorable deceit. However, since Beerbohm conjoined the terms "sexual" and "hypocritical" in 1896, the question of their relation may extend beyond general controversies of the sexual because *The Happy Hypocrite* satirizes these terms with particular reference to Wilde's downfall.

Certain historical and biographical details are relevant here: Beerbohm's friendship with Wilde began at Oxford and evolved from their joint interest in the *Yellow Book,* a journal devoted to aesthetics, pleasure, and decadence. Several critics stress that during this period Beerbohm only tolerated homosexuality, and that while his association with different aesthetic movements (decadence, Bloomsbury) brought him into close, and almost exclusive, contact with homosexual writers and artists, he was attracted solely to women.[41] Yet his lifelong passionate friendship with Reggie Turner and, more importantly, his comments about Wilde's trials, indicate his considerable ambivalence toward the subject of homosexuality.

While Turner and many other homosexual men left for Paris when the public controversy about Wilde began in 1895, Beerbohm formed a number of "unconvincing" and idealistic attachments to women that he conducted without ardor or commitment.[42] According to recent critics, Beerbohm's engagement to Grace Conover "dragged on for several years," during which time the couple spent many months apart; Conover was superseded by the actress Constance Collier and then by Florence Kahn, whom he married in 1910 when he was thirty-eight.[43] Shortly after her death, Beerbohm married Elisabeth Jungmann, his secretary, but they established the marriage (much like the former one) principally to nurse him; it lasted only one month, Beerbohm himself dying in 1956.[44]

Beerbohm's letters that have survived the spring of 1895 demonstrate greater concern for the scandal of homosexual disclosure than for the well-being of its subjects (Henry James's response was almost identical). Many years later, and from a position of relative safety, Beerbohm continued declining invitations to review Frank Harris's *Oscar Wilde, His Life and Confessions* (1916) because Wilde's reputation apparently was still so tarnished that any association with him would entail, in Beerbohm's eyes, a "raking-up of the old Sodomitic cesspool — the cesspool that was opened in 1895. . . ."[45]

Before the trial, Beerbohm's allusions to Wilde's homosexuality were notably less reticent and considerably more arch in innuendo. In the 1894 essay "A Peep into the Past," he writes of a "constant succession of page-boys" passing through the Wilde household that "startle the neighbourhood."[46] Beerbohm amusingly renames *The Portrait of Mr. W. H.* — Wilde's speculative work on Shakespeare's *Sonnets* — as *The Theory of Mr. W. S.,* and an invitation to join Wilde in his study leads Beerbohm to speculate on "the quickly receding *frou-frou* of tweed trousers." Beerbohm continues: "but my host I found reclining, hale and hearty, though a little dishevelled, upon the sofa. With one hand readjusting the nut-brown Georgian wig that he is accustomed to wear, he motioned me with a courteous gesture of the other to an arm-chair." [47] Each example suggests that Beerbohm's tolerance of homosexuality in others never displaced his fear of public speculation on his own preference, a fear that seems valid in 1895 but not in 1920. Indeed, it suggests that in his intimate friendship with other men, Beerbohm idealized platonic affection to displace the possibility of homosexual intimacy.[48]

The problem of biography notwithstanding, the title of Beerbohm's *The Happy Hypocrite* clearly tropes on Wilde's fairy story "The Happy Prince" (1888), while the date of Beerbohm's novella (written in 1896 but published the year after) suggests that we should read it in the wake of the crisis Wilde's discovery, trial, and imprisonment precipitated in 1895. Wilde's fairy story recounts the plight of a "human" monument that tries to redeem its life of pleasure by offering its jewels and gold to an impoverished bird. With amusing inversion, Beerbohm's mock hero, Lord George Hell, is anything but repentant for his life's excesses. The narrator candidly exposes Lord George's "vices" (7) — gluttony, luxury, and a hint of debauchery — but any desire to "atone" for his past (8) derives from his infatuation with a young actress, not from an ethical concern for moderation. (Beerbohm describes Lord George in Greek, using the word *sketleos,* meaning "merciless, headstrong, and wretched." [49])

Although *The Happy Hypocrite*'s irony and burlesque never passes judgment on these vices — suggesting that there is no limit to his or its hypocrisy — Lord George's desire for the young débutante, Jenny Mere, is clearly inseparable from his pursuit of love for its own sake (99). In other words, George's desire for the other always indicates his own hedonistic narcissism. This implies that his desire's aim is ultimately more important than his object's marital status or gender.[50]

The novella seems to endorse this reading, for its romantic parodies turn every statement of desire into a cliché. Catching sight of Jenny on stage, George is almost literally struck by an arrow, and his response is a gestural devotion to Jenny that is otherwise devoid of emotion. In ways that mimic *The Picture of Dorian Gray,* George's sins are inscribed on his face by "a tarnished mirror" that distorts the look of his beholder (24). Insofar as his vice is visible, Jenny's conditional return of desire insists that his persona change —

that he wear the face of a saint and reflect more successfully the projection of her romantic demand.

The humor and intelligence of this tale demonstrate repeatedly that desire is most narcissistic when the subject intends it to be oblatory; the object represents to the subject nothing more than an image of its demand. This point endorses Lacan's insistence that "there is no sexual relation" because desire is only the effect of an asymmetrical relation between subjects.[51] Following Wilde's contention that there is no single truth about consciousness, Beerbohm implies that sexual reciprocity merely upholds the subject's imaginary drama. Thus George is devoted less to Jenny's affection than to the pleasure of receiving it, for he buys a mask that will show the qualities she most wants to see—the face of a saintly lover who never fails to portray sincerity. The mask fits his own face so closely that "all traces of the 'join' [are] obliterated" (42). George convinces and seduces Jenny, and the couple falls in love and retires to an idyllic house in the country. Again, we should note the irony accompanying the adoption of this public role, given Beerbohm's emphasis on the transience and treachery of love.

The shame that George experiences when considering the disparity between his appearance to Jenny and his self-representation soon complicates the couple's romance. In addition, La Gambogi—a woman who previously desired George, but whose passion he did not return—sees him buying the mask, and decides to avenge herself on George by destroying his and Jenny's illusion of love. As George struggles to forget "the vague record of infamy [that] assailed him" (57) in his and Jenny's pastoral sanctuary, he marries under a false name and compounds an already acute crisis of self-definition: "What name should he assume? Under a mask he has wooed this girl, under an unreal name he must make her his bride. He loathed himself for a trickster. . . . And yet, surely, it was not just that he, whose soul was transfigured, should bear his old name. Surely George Hell was dead, and his name had died with him. So he dipped a pen in the ink and wrote 'George Heaven,' for want of a better name" (60). In ways that mirror and parody *The Picture of Dorian Gray,* Beerbohm's narrative demonstrates that George's past is psychically ineradicable; he cannot write or perform its influence away. The fear haunts him that La Gambogi will return; that she witnessed his transformation (as Basil Hallward did Dorian Gray's) renders her, like the old woman in "The Liar," a symptom of his past deceit. When La Gambogi does return, she and George fight as she attempts to pull off his mask: "Vainly did George try to free himself from his assailant, who writhed round and round him, clawing, clawing at what Jenny fancied to be his face" (77).

The mask finally gives, only to display a face that seems the same (78). George's mask does not mask anything more than his desire to desire, to change, and to be desired. George's appearance corresponds with the apparent success of his psychic transformation because there is apparently no limit to dissimulation or the ability to substitute one identity for another in *The Happy Hypocrite*. Since George simply gives face to his fantasies, the only resistance he encounters — and it is extensive — is a decision to remain the same, his unwillingness to imagine a different personality, and his defense against another form of love. Psychic resistance and negativity, we might argue, have been projected outward as the haunting legacy of La Gambogi.

Once the fight is over, George and Jenny resume their attachment (he is, after all, the same "saintly" man she "fell in love with"), and the mask with which he seduced her silently melts in the sun, without a trace of his imposture. The disappearance of La Gambogi implies that she, like Mrs. Capadose, was always the cause of her beloved's deceit; by renaming himself "Lord Heaven," George designates La Gambogi as a "serpent" (75) that intervenes in his and Jenny's prelapsarian paradise: "Crawl from our Eden, ere you poison with your venom its fairest denizen" (76). Having figured La Gambogi as a "writh[ing] assailant," the narrator likens her to Milton's figure of Sin, with all its connotations of femininity, duplicity, and sexual distortion.[52] The analogy implies that the havoc of shattering a secret lies less with the subject that performs it than with the agent who finally detects it. In ways that repeat James and Wilde, the narrative bathetically empties the "secret" of sexual meaning, casting it as an experiential question about the truth and consistency of identity.[53]

In this final retort to the narrative's sexual enigma, George merely veils the duplicity of every other character; his mask does not represent the truth of his personality because dissimulation represents the subject's identificatory mechanism. The mask shop in *The Happy Hypocrite* therefore offers different, if limited, costumes of personality promoting one course of action — invariably adultery (30) — under the pretext of another.

Once the narrative has removed the other woman, the love affair in *The Happy Hypocrite* successfully sustains the projection of romantic fidelity. La Gambogi predicts this outcome when she declares to George: "Your wife's mask . . . is even better than yours" (75). Deception, however, does not produce an obvious homology between shame and dissimulation or truth and consistency in this text, for George's mask apparently rescinds all links between personality and psychic depth. Identity manifests both performance and resistance, not a simple masquerade of the inauthentic; when surface qualities are the truth of one's ontology, the public can judge a personality only by its attraction and consistency. Friedrich Nietzsche captured the strength of this paradox in *Beyond Good and Evil* (1886): "Everything profound loves the mask; the profoundest things of all hate even image and parable. Should not nothing less than the *opposite* be the proper disguise under which the shame of a god goes abroad?" [54] If "everything profound loves the mask," all that is complex must lie on the surface. The subject has no interior with an authentic truth, according to Nietzsche, because the interior is already an image of depth, a fabricated kernel resting on other identifications. *The Happy Hypocrite* plays out this irony by dissolving all distinction between the lover's ardent integrity and the charlatan's skillful dissimulation.[55]

Similar to Wilde and, to a lesser extent, James, Beerbohm enumerates and questions many cultural assumptions about ontological consistency and the truth of sexual fantasy. The significance of "The Liar," *The Picture of Dorian Gray,* and *The Happy Hypocrite* lies also in their concern to represent the sexual relation as a prominent untruth and a failure of symbolic reference. This failure emerges whenever these texts draw attention to the crisis underlining homo/sexual demand and the resistance that prevents this crisis from being heard and publicly represented.

Since hypocrisy is fundamentally ungovernable in *The Happy Hypocrite,* there is little, short of deliberate intervention and psychic resistance, to prevent the text from elaborating same-sex relations. There is also much to suggest that this elaboration represents George's deceit and the surplus of his sexual interest. As Beerbohm once remarked in a comment that would corroborate Wilde: "Too long has the face been degraded from its rank as a thing of beauty to a mere vulgar index of character or emotion." [56] If beauty is distinct from character, as Beerbohm implies, beauty may have an independent relation to gender and, more radically, the interest each subject creates, transfers, and projects onto its objects.

In James's "The Liar," this problem of identity's meaning and authenticity persists as an ontological and narrative enigma that the tale cannot resolve: the narrative encounters a hiatus, finds it intractable, and renames it either a pathology or a problem of subjective consistency—it suggests that Colonel Capadose is consistently untruthful even when Lyon sees and hears revelations that question this assumption. Wilde, however, implies that the gap between a subject's desire and its representation confirms a symbolic and psychic limit to both. He defines the truth a mask conveys as part of the subject's demand—for an object, more fantasy, or a greater number of public roles. The fates of Dorian Gray and Lord George appear to hinge on the conflict between their demand for homo/sexual objects and this scarcity of public roles. Wilde's willingness to represent this demand suggests that he undertook a twofold critique of identity: he demonstrated that identity is a performance that the subject can alter and revise according to its will. Yet his paradigm is not idealist or voluntaristic: the mask represents a limit to identification that the subject assumes when no other role is acceptable and when character proves inadequate to resisting its expression.

4

Fostering Subjection:
Masculine Identification
and Homosexual Allegory
in Conrad's *Victory*

Scenes of Crisis and the Danger of Equivalence

When once the truth is grasped that one's own personality is
only a ridiculous and aimless masquerade of something
hopelessly unknown, the attainment of serenity is not very far
off. Then there remains nothing but the surrender to one's
impulses, the fidelity to passing emotions which is perhaps a
nearer approach to truth than any other philosophy of life.
And why not?
—Joseph Conrad [1]

The use of reason is to justify the obscure desires that move
our conduct, impulses, passion, prejudices and follies, and
also our fears.
—Conrad [2]

Conrad's *Victory: An Island Tale* (1915) begins with—and entertains throughout—a proposition of similarity. On its opening page, the narrator invokes a
likeness between coal and diamond to describe a disused mining company
belonging to the protagonist, Axel Heyst; more radically, the narrator draws
on this likeness in comparing related, "chemical" properties of human sub-

jectivity. Although the diamond represents an exclusive sign of wealth, due to its scarcity, the more abundant coal is a source of constant "fascination," though it offers "a deplorable lack of concentration" (57). The comparison of carbon allotropes with their human counterparts recurs several times in this novel, though the analogy actually begins in its opening sentence, when the narrator represents the logic of chemical properties as a truth so widely acknowledged it is a non sequitur, something "every schoolboy knows in this scientific age" (57).

By suggesting that there are allotropic qualities of identification and desire, *Victory* offers a startling account of human sexuality whose risk does not assure conceptual success: the constituents of human relations, like the stocks and resources of the disused coal mine, are prone to evaporate. *Victory* nonetheless reiterates two founding axioms: psychic instincts or drives determine human nature, and social correspondence derives from a precarious balance between instinctual gratification and cultural obligation. To enter the social order, Conrad's subjects sacrifice instinctual freedom; his novels measure this sacrifice as an irremediable loss of pleasure.[3]

Recent critics of *Victory* have interpreted this sacrifice in biological and evolutionary terms as the renunciation of instincts for more acceptable, sublimated desire.[4] According to this reading, the sacrifice binds humankind in group relations, and individuals suffer only when they refuse to comply with this demand or relinquish the social bond in pursuit of recidivist aims. Although this reading presents an interesting account of cultural alienation and "racial" isolation, in which the instinctual urge reduces the subject to its constitutive "savagery," these critics argue that Conrad tried either to dismantle the colonial project by claiming that its logic is as savage as the people it set out to master, or the reverse—that he chose to affirm the West's defense against an indigenous "savagery" that it must, at all costs, suppress.[5]

This antinomy misses the novel's most radical proposition. Contrary to the idea that *Victory* endorses a redemptive account of colonialism, I want to suggest like the previous chapter, that the narrative primarily concerns the precarious nature of Western socialization. *Victory* engages with colonialism's accompanying difficulties of national identification, cultural formation, and psychic management by investigating—and part unsettling—terms that Western empires enjoined to specific geographies. My reading throughout this chapter claims that cultures and races generate *fewer* differences than Conrad—and many of his critics—acknowledge. If we properly consider this argument, *Victory*'s crisis of differentiation emerges not only between acultural instinct and social demand, but also at society's kernel. Thus Davidson,

Victory's narrator, unwittingly observes: "It flashed through Schomberg's mind that these two [Jones and Ricardo] were indeed well matched in their enormous dissimilarity, *identical souls in different disguises*" (159; my emphasis). Most critics have ignored the radical implications of *Victory*'s claim for relative equivalence "beneath" social masquerade; my suggestion that the novel interrogates biological imperatives and evolutionary assumptions displaces inquiry into the points of cultural meaning that trouble the text, forcing the issue to resurface elsewhere, on altogether less safe terrain: the topos of Heyst's exile on the island of Samburan.

Following a central problematic in much colonial literature, *Victory*'s symbolization of instincts, drives, and civilization is frequently inadequate to the meanings it struggles to contain. I suggest that the novel's representation of sociality on a remote and allegorical terrain is part responsible for this problem of signification, because the distance between colony and nation renders the meaning of each untenable and susceptible to violence. *Victory* is a socio-symbolic allegory that inadvertently exposes the cultural and psychic constituents of colonial and homo/sexual identity; in this novel, subjective desire and identification repeatedly coalesce with their colonial frame.

This chapter interprets the function of this allegorical frame, the meanings it permits and displaces, and the anxieties it seeks to allay. I suggest that these phenomena recur throughout the text without finding an adequate answer: the narrative confronts and then stymies the radical possibilities of equivalence among members of the same gender, culture, and race. My inquiry engages with the tension and fatigue of a colonial structure that relies on, and struggles to maintain, difference. By emphasizing points in the text where the narrator establishes and then revokes metaphors of racial and sexual similarity, I examine how the text asserts and disbands relations between its central protagonists. As the character Wang reflects: "All that he really knew was his own mind. He had made it up to withdraw himself and the Alfuro woman [his wife] from *the uncertainties of the relations* which were going to establish themselves between those white men" (304; emphasis mine).

By focusing on *Victory*'s marginal figures, I want to displace a procedure governing the text—and a criticism that endorses it—that represents conflict as either an internal division within the protagonist (Axel Heyst) or a soured romance between Heyst and his "partner," Lena.[6] By reading each peripheral figure's function, I suggest that this novel's work is more complex and opaque than criticism has allowed, and that the retention of this opacity permits the text's more obvious meanings to prevail.

The oldest voice in the world is just the one that never ceases to speak.
—Joseph Conrad (193)

But all the time he thought . . . , he was conscious of his father
following his thought, surveying it, making it shiver and falter. At last
he ceased to think.
—Virginia Woolf[7]

Most critics of *Victory* overlook the figure of Morrison or represent his relationship with Heyst as a rehearsal for a later, replete engagement between Heyst and Lena: Douglas Park describes Morrison as "a distant anecdotal figure," [8] while Ted Boyle argues that he "functions solely as a symbol of those impulses which Heyst's intellect will not recognize." [9] Even critics noting the remarkable parallels, in gesture and speech, between the two relationships downplay the first as the origin of a narrative pattern.[10] However, this pattern's repetition throughout *Victory* lends an importance to Morrison that, perhaps for equally significant reasons, critics have failed to interpret. The text goes to such lengths to permit this correspondence between Heyst's relationship with Morrison that it is difficult to ignore its influence on subsequent moments of intimacy.

This pattern does not begin with Morrison or conclude with Heyst's death; though the text begins with an account of Morrison's death, the origin of their intimacy recedes into Heyst's past, surfacing only later, when Heyst attempts to explain to Lena his fascination for Morrison. The attempt fails, raising questions that the text and Heyst obstruct and remain reluctant to broach thereafter. Since Heyst's displacement of each love object forms a narrative trace and a repeated resistance to expression, however, the two relationships' mutual resemblance becomes apparent at the precise moment of their substitution.

Before the narrator recounts the events that culminate in Morrison's illness, he describes Heyst's grief over Morrison's death. This "return" to clarify a prior enigma characterizes the narrative's procedure: an event's effect tends to anticipate its cause. This narrative, like many of Conrad's texts, often defers exposition of these events and, finally, in Morrison's case, disbands the project as impossible to tell. Although death and loss interrupt this cycle of projection and retroactive explanation by precipitating a demand for Morrison's significance to Heyst, the narrative broaches these issues only after Morrison has died, as if it can process the problem he represents only when he has disappeared.

This problem of significance surfaces when Morrison joins the expatriate community of Sourabaya. The narrator explains that "Heyst became associated with Morrison on terms about which people were in doubt" (62).[11] The expatriate community struggles for words adequate to these "terms," alternating between "partner" and "a sort of paying guest" (62), before the narrator cuts short their "prying eyes" (193) and inquiry in a manner designed to provoke more: "the real truth of the matter was more complex" (62). While the narrative promises to explain this complexity, "the real truth" is inaccessible in this text because it gestures beyond nomenclature to an interstitial region between friend and lover.[12]

Both men experience a similar difficulty when they attempt to name, with any precision, the terms of their affection. The friendship begins with a shared financial concern—a "(highly creditable) tangle of strong feelings" (71): Heyst rescues Morrison from bankruptcy with a loan when Portuguese authorities impound his ship, and Morrison returns the favor by proposing a commercial partnership whose terms the men never declare. Each of these moments—and the impulses that inspire them—are susceptible to figurative reading: when Heyst first sees Morrison on the island of Timor, he "accost[s]" him on a whim because Morrison seems to be "a man in trouble, expressively harassed, dejected, lonely" (114).

Since this imbrication of remote geography and mental dejection are tropes familiar to Heyst's past and future, the impulse to "accost" Morrison is less spontaneous than it first appears. Another figure influences this desire to connect—his father—whose death makes Heyst's intimacy with Morrison possible, though scarcely permissible. If Morrison's distress leads to Heyst's relief and gratitude, Heyst's offer of help bewilders him: "[It was] one of those things that don't happen. . . . He had no idea what it meant" (66). The narrator couches the men's "transaction" in secrecy, describing Heyst as "even more anxious to bind himself to silence" (69). Several paragraphs later, the deal resurfaces as a "conspiracy" that Heyst withholds under such psychic duress that a malicious rumor soon "leaks" their secret to a fascinated community: "Heyst, having obtained some mysterious hold on Morrison, had fastened himself on him, and was sucking him dry" (69). We can attribute the mystery of this "fastening" to a shift in nomenclature from "transaction" to "conspiracy": the first term denotes a mutually beneficial exchange, while the second illustrates an imperative to silence that the text is unable to sustain because it begs the question, Against what—or whom—do they conspire?

The source of this rumor, and the persistent questioner of their relationship, is a hotelier named Schomberg: "a big, manly, bearded creature of the Teutonic persuasion, with an ungovernable tongue which surely must have worked on a pivot" (69). In an obvious pun, Schomberg's tongue also "works on" an axle—or Axel, Heyst's proper name, though the names by which others later know him also is instructive: "the Utopist," "the pursuer of Chimœras," "the Spider," "the Enemy" (61). Heyst is also the pivot around whom narrative events circulate, a narrative hinge that structures its irregular vertices, and a prop on whom others append meaning, fantasy, and retribution. In particular, he bears the opprobrium of Morrison's death, and a residual—if irrational—guilt about being disloyal toward his father, whose moral precepts he feels he has betrayed.

"The tangle of strong feelings . . . for the service rendered . . . between man and man" (71) ratifies a contractual bind between Heyst and Morrison that persists in a web of unresolved and unnamable emotions. The narrator claims this "tangle" is "highly creditable," suggesting both virtue in Heyst's decision to rescue Morrison and the deal's emotional and financial costs: for Morrison, a burden of gratitude; for Heyst, an "interest" produced by the community's prurient curiosity, as well as the interest on the loan— or, one might argue, the surplus of desire accruing between his financial gift to Morrison as an unconscious demand (or heist), and its haunting return as a residual, and still unsatisfied, expectation for something more.

In these terms of interest and repayment, Heyst's and Morrison's affective currency consists of "assets" that "evaporate" before "liquidation," as the novel's opening page reminds. When Morrison returns to England after falling ill, he dies "with extraordinary *precipitation*" (72; my emphasis), though the remainder of desire between Heyst and him persists in a purer form after Morrison's death by condensing, and then effacing, his unnamable significance for Heyst.

Heyst's remorse over Morrison's death has puzzled many critics. F. R. Leavis considers it inexplicable because the circumstances of his death were beyond Heyst's control, "the merest matter of ill-chance";[13] Jocelyn Baines has described the guilt as "gratuitous" because Heyst's behavior is "blameless" and beyond reproach.[14] These responses fail to address the tangible guilt about Morrison's death that in the text precedes the relationship, which raises accusations of murder that trouble Heyst.[15] Although Schomberg touches on Morrison's disappearance with assiduous doubt, Heyst's "calumny" publicly represents an internal accusation that he has already made. As Janet Butler Haugaard usefully observes, "Heyst anticipates reproaches before they have even begun." [16]

The intimacy and indeterminacy of Heyst's and Morrison's relationship captivate Schomberg, whose prurient interest enables him to alight on something closer to a "truth": "there never were two such loving friends to look at as you two; then, when you got all you wanted out of him and got thoroughly tired of him, you kicked him out to go home and die" (226). In the following section, I want to return to Schomberg's interest. Here, we can note simply that his charge against Heyst holds in some measure, and that the narrative neither disputes nor elaborates on its accuracy. Schomberg's claim represents the community's silent consensus, though it shocks Heyst much later when Lena tells him what the public think: "So that's how the business looked from the outside" (221)—a statement suggesting that "Heyst had, at one point, accepted it as truth, and later denied it." [17] His immediate response is to consider it fiction: "And, moreover, nobody had ever believed that tale" (222). Whether we believe him is immaterial, though, because the disjuncture that his surprise signifies between the public perception of Morrison's death and his own is more instructive. It asks us to consider what his perception of Morrison's death was all along, and to question the factors influencing Heyst's relationships in its wake. Since they are central to understanding this novel's persistent trace of desire, these questions form the remainder of this chapter.

The first question is easier to identify in the text: the narrator observes Heyst's "immense . . . shock" (72) at the news of Morrison's death, and a subsequent period of erratic behavior. Neither response signifies mourning, for the subject arguably must remember and symbolize the loved object's importance before grief can pass.[18] For Heyst to acknowledge Morrison's importance, he must first recognize the figure who replaced him (Lena) as well as the fantasy that precipitated his initial "impulse" to rescue Morrison. Heyst refuses both admissions; he re-covers and deflects his loss by alternating periods of depression and maniacal activity; neither alleviates their cause. With a "sort of guarded attitude," he "disappear[s] . . . for a time" (72), staying with a doctor before "drifting amongst the islands, enigmatical . . . like an insignificant ghost" (73). Lassitude and withdrawal give way to a "sudden display of purposeful energy" (74), during which he "materialise[s] in this alarming way" (74) to establish the mining company that soon falls into insolvency. The text opens with this dereliction as if it corresponds to his psychic condition; the mine's insolvency also reminds us of the inscrutable and haunting terms of interest, repayment, and debt that carry over from previous moments of intimacy.

The proximity between this mine's beginning and end suggests that Heyst's experience with Morrison is so unbearable that he can realize the relationship's significance only by his traumatic resubmission to it.[19] After this second "liquidation," the narrator observes that Heyst "faded completely away. He had become invisible, as in those early days when he used to make a bolt clear out of sight . . ." (74).[20] Davidson later visits him on the island of Samburan, where he lives amid its desolate "ruins," profuse jungle, and dormant volcano, avowing a resistance to rejoin the community: "I remain in possession here" (75)—a fantasy he enlists to support his psychic security— "I am keeping hold" (77). Heyst's isolation and ownership of the island provide him with an illusion of mastery no longer commensurate with his frame of mind.

Psychoanalysis has argued that the repetition of a symptom enables the subject to gain imaginary control over intolerable trauma: "*what cannot be remembered is repeated in behavior.*" [21] By analogy, Heyst may attempt to manage his crisis by projecting his internal collapse as an external drama. This apparent solution recalls Octave Mannoni's argument about the psychology of colonialism, in which the impulse to mastery and the subjection of others obstructs a difficulty that would otherwise surface on "home soil";[22] the subjection of others displaces a crisis in domestic culture and ontology by augmenting the colonial's power. However, Heyst's dilemma between public exposure and nomadic narcissism also confirms Davidson's earlier remark that his desire for invisibility reenacts a prior history of reclusion: "as in those earlier days when he used to make a bolt" (74). The logic of this solution is apparent only from its third and final displacement, when Heyst and Lena elope to Samburan. Although they reach reclusive safety and Heyst believes "the ghost of Morrison needn't haunt" them (218), the specter of the past returns in the figure of Mr. Jones: Jones recalls Schomberg, who reminds Heyst of Lena, who asks about Morrison, who resembles Heyst's father. The past recedes in a trace of unresolved questions that haunt every relationship from the outset.

In the ensuing dialogue between Heyst and Lena, Heyst Sr. resurfaces for Heyst as an ambivalent figure, his philosophy of spiritual detachment representing both an ascetic ideal and an impossible demand. During his adolescence, Heyst's father exhorted his son to emulate his renunciation of worldly desires. To consolidate his autonomy, Heyst tried to distance himself from this unappeasable command, though a conflict emerged over his father's insoluble proscription: copy me/become different, an injunction Tony Tanner has condensed still further as a twofold demand: "abstain/repeat." [23]

This crisis of desire and identification encodes *Victory*'s paternal metaphor, for Heyst's abstention from sexual contact with Morrison secures a tenuous identification with his father on condition that his desire is mimetic and emulative—that is, paternally faithful. In *Victory*, mimicry of the father must erase all trace of different, wayward desire; the son must reproduce the "same," thus rescinding any impulse toward contrary aims. [24] Despite Heyst's assumption that he embodies the "same" to his father, however, Heyst Sr. is always already an other, so the imperative to repeat and then replace the father—to emulate him by procreation—expresses desire for an object *other* than the one he chose (such is the strength of the oedipal taboo). Heyst's repetition of desire bears only a likeness to his father; identification with him creates a fantasy of homology that functions generically by demanding that Heyst discover a similar but nonidentical object. Heyst's difficulty in obeying this condition of masculine identification derives from the fact that his father forbids the expression of *all* desire. Heyst takes the command to "abstain/repeat" seriously and overliteralizes the paternal metaphor; [25] his father's precepts frustrate Heyst's social and sexual attachments, binding him to silent spectatorship by the twofold injunction: "look on—make no sound" (194), an injunction Heyst performs by long periods of abjection and aimless travel. [26]

These precepts derive from the philosophy of Arthur Schopenhauer, who extolled the "inward joy" and "pure contemplation" that "denial of the will to love" allegedly produces. Heyst Sr., captivated by this philosophy, believes that "will" ensnares the subject in a "bitter struggle . . . with desire, fear, envy [and anger]"—emotions that "drag us hither and thither in constant pain." [27] By his following Schopenhauer's advice and exercising "ardent strain," Heyst's own "will is silenced" and he is "as it were, freed from himself." He also gains a reflective—if tenuous—"purity" with which to "look back smiling and at rest on the delusions of this world." [28]

According to Schopenhauer, the subject wards off both intimacy's shattering effects and inaugurating desires by observing the delusions of a world in which it can take no real part. Despite Schopenhauer's promise, however, characters in *Victory* never entirely conquer this "bitter struggle"; the compromise between social abjection and alienation demands a vigilance that frustrates their peace of mind. Heyst, for instance, feels caught in a conflict between "need" and "will," in which he denies both with such vehemence that their repression—or, in Schopenhauer's words, "privation"—makes the threat of internal collapse and external invasion seem increasingly likely. Heyst's options are to submit to his father's will by erecting a defense against every desired object, or to resist his father's will by rejecting the impulse to desire altogether, which would cast him nearer to psychotic immolation. Both options fail: Heyst is unable to silence his will or deny his need; he binds both with such severity that he deems any manifestation of desire a betrayal of paternal Law.

Heyst temporarily adopts the second option by traveling aimlessly through the Malay Archipelago. His decision to "drift" (129) is characteristically partial; as Davidson remarks, "his detachment from the world was not complete. And *incompleteness* of any sort leads to trouble" (79; my emphasis). In *Victory*'s spatio-psychic topography, Heyst is a literal émigré and a figurative ex/patriate fueled by a desire to live beyond his father's spectral influence and at a remove from the national home. As we have seen, however, Heyst's effort to live without desire falters when he meets Morrison; here, in a text in which "consciousness" and "instinct" conflict, the impulse to connect resurfaces as an irrepressible demand.

Although the question of what Heyst wants of Morrison is always enigmatic in this text, Morrison's "rescue" seems to act out a prior agenda: his helplessness before a legislative authority (the Portuguese) repeats the intransigence that Heyst confronts in his father. Morrison's claim that he awaits a death sentence ("I am being murdered . . . I am to have my throat cut the day after tomorrow" [64]) seems to redouble Heyst's fear of punishment by a similarly hostile body. Heyst's "impulse" to rescue Morrison may also obtain from a fantasy of reparation in which he assuages internal fear by external action. Thus Davidson observes that "the Swede was as much distressed as Morrison, for he understood the other's feelings perfectly . . . and he felt acutely his defeat" (68). Yet Heyst can check his anxiety only for their relationship's duration; his perception of filial "disobedience" returns when Morrison dies, and in his guilt he anticipates punishment.

Years later, having brought Lena to the island of Samburan without the community's "official" permission—as if pleasure was so illicit and tied to "privation" in this text that Heyst must steal it—he is unable to answer Lena's question, "why are you here?" (211). Heyst wavers, preferring to talk about "the man in that picture you so often look at [who] is responsible for my existence" (212). The portrait is of his father, and Heyst's incongruous response is surely an oblique answer to her question. Moments later, when Heyst reiterates to Lena "your question is unanswerable," he makes a further connection and inadvertent disclosure: "One day I met a cornered man . . . [who] captivated my fancy" (213–14).

As home to the portrait of his father, and the place to which he (and his desire) return, Samburan is clearly allegorical—not in the sense of Edenic paradise, as many critics have argued, in which the couple represents biblical archetypes whose bliss shatters after the "Satanic" Jones arrives,[29] but as a cultural and psychological topography in which the ground represents a split within each character. In response to Lena's question and beneath his father's portrait, Heyst is able to "compose his face" (230) by reading one of his father's texts in a bid to become "the living vehicle of his father's precepts." [30] Heyst retains his father as an ideal whose "voice" supplants Heyst's inadequate response to life and its demands: "The rooms, filling with shadows, seemed haunted by a melancholy, uneasy presence which could not express itself. The young man got up with a strange sense of making way for *something impalpable* that claimed possession, went out of the house, and locked the door" (195; my emphasis).

Since the anxiety surrounding Morrison's death and the frantic drive to recover his loss persist in this text, it is important to consider the second of my earlier questions in greater detail—that is, the function of this guilt and its trace throughout Conrad's narrative. Recall that Heyst's "disenchantment" and sense of "failure" at Morrison's death made him feel "the gnawing pain of useless apostasy, a sort of shame before his own betrayed nature; and, in addition, he also suffered from plain, downright remorse. He deemed himself guilty of Morrison's death" (109). Like the critic Leavis, the narrator considers this guilt "a rather absurd feeling" (109) because Heyst was unable to prevent Morrison's impulsive departure for England or to predict the bleak weather that precipitated his death. However, the narrator fails to address the drives, fantasies, and resistances that surface among all of the book's characters—a point that emerges after his banal account of the deaths of Jones, Heyst, and Lena at the novel's end.

Heyst's self-accusations of "apostasy, shame, [and] guilt" (109) may be inappropriate for the loss of an acquaintance, but his sense of "useless apostasy" and "betray[al]" nonetheless invoke his father's legacy. After Heyst has explained Morrison's death to Lena, for instance, Lena informs him of Schomberg's rumor, and Heyst does not dispute it so much as disclose its internal significance: " 'It wasn't murder,' she insisted earnestly. 'I know. I understand. It was worse' " (224). Heyst compounds this remark's opacity in his attempt to draw a distinction between the referent to "it" and "the comparatively decent act of killing a man [in] the wilds" (224), where subjects occasionally revoke civilized meanings to survive. By leaving un-answered the question of what is both less—and more—than murder, Heyst invests "it" with a significance that seems to exceed this "decent act."

One response to this question may be a murder that Heyst devises and desires but finally forecloses because its idea provokes horror and dread. In *Civilization and Its Discontents* (1930), Freud considered fantasies of par-ricide as an axiomatic consequence of the dissolution of the Oedipus com-plex.[31] Irrespective of this fantasy's material realization, its recollection by the superego induces guilt. Freud also argued that the superego recognizes no distinction between an intended and a performed act, or fantasized and criminal practice, because the guilt attached to each is fundamentally the same: "Owing to the omniscience of the super-ego, the difference between an aggression intended and an aggression carried out lost its force. Hence-forward a sense of guilt could be produced not only by an act of violence that is actually carried out (as all the world knows), but also by one that is merely intended (as psychoanalysis has discovered). . . . [32] *Victory* elaborates this guilt with unusual prescience by virtually impounding Heyst's subjec-tivity. Heyst's remark to Lena about an outcome "worse" than murder may indicate that he attributes Morrison's death to his father's retribution, simply because Heyst disobeyed his prohibition of intimacy.[33]

This "murder" and the narrative's sequence of sexual and spectral fantasy also have affinity with psychoanalytic accounts of the primal scene.[34] Freud argued that the boy infers that his mother is "wounded" as punishment for her phallic dispossession. He also argued that this belief in loss inaugu-rates fantasies of castration, forcing the boy anxiously to identify with the father.[35] By analogy, Heyst's detachment from his father fails to allay his an-ticipation of violence; his father requires abstention from *all* object relations rather than a specific taboo against one: "I only know that he who forms a tie is lost. The germ of corruption has already entered his soul" (215).

In presenting this analogy between *Victory*'s account of intimacy and the primal scene, I intend to explore the text's metaphors of guilt and repara-tion in describing Morrison's death. These metaphors raise issues of splitting, antagonism, and self-division in *Victory* whenever characters become inti-mate. Heyst discounts this intimacy by suggesting that Morrison "beguiled [him] into action" (109), for instance, and he later informs Davidson that Lena "tempted him into action" (98). In this text desire is so fraught with anxiety and resistance that its protagonists must deny these factors altogether, pro-jecting them onto an object as their cause. The impulse too "beguile[s]"; it requires subterfuge to conceal a prior moment of horror. Although elliptical in the encounter with Morrison, this drive returns in an equivalent scene, when Heyst is "tempted" to befriend Lena.

Curiously, critics tend to overlook the context of their meeting and the speed of Heyst's and Lena's ensuing elopement. When critics do examine this meeting, they emphasize Heyst's distress, and the fascination and repugnance he feels toward the orchestra, without connecting the encounter to the scene that inspires it.[36] When Heyst overhears a visiting orchestra's tune at Schomberg's hotel, for instance, he displaces his "remorse" onto "the lamentations of string instruments," whose "plaintive . . . scraps of tunes" exteriorize and haunt his thoughts. To Heyst, the strings' "intrusi[ve] . . . rasping character" is "inexpressibly tedious" because they lead him to ruminate on his failed relationship with Morrison and the "hour of renunciation" that replaced it: "Nothing is more painful than the shock of sharp contradictions that lacerate our intelligence and our feelings" (110). The noise "pursues" Heyst with its ceaseless repetition until, "driven to desperation," he abandons all pretense of detachment and enters the music hall to confront its irritating source.

The orchestra is amateurish and comically relentless, but the scene that Heyst observes conveys more than the crude production of music: it orchestrates other, primal emotions by "a suggestion of brutality" (111). Fantasmatic meaning so overlays this scene, it causes its observer acute discomfort and dread: "The uproar in that small, barn-like structure . . . was simply stunning. An instrumental uproar, screaming, grunting, whining, sobbing, scraping, squealing some kind of lively air. . . . In the quick time of that music, in the varied, piercing clamour of the strings, in the movements of the bare arms, in the low dresses, the coarse faces, the stony eyes of the executants, there was a suggestion of brutality—something cruel, sensual, and repulsive" (111). The execution of music, which the narrator likens to the death of an animal or person, is shockingly comic. Although the fleshy violence of this scene disgusts Heyst, the narrator notes his response by the adjacency and confluence of the adjectives "cruel, sensual, and repulsive"; the scene is sensual *because* of its suggestion of cruelty, and repulsive as an effect of its sensuousness. Despite or because of this cruelty, Heyst stalls in "unholy fascination," "astonished at himself" (112) for his desire to continue watching "this rude exhibition of vigour, . . . [an] unnatural spectacle . . . [that] was simply murdering silence with a vulgar, ferocious energy. One felt as if witnessing a deed of violence" (112).

The impact of these sensations derives from Heyst's characterization of the scene's excess and from the narrative's shift of voice and perspective: the narrator moves imperceptibly from impersonal and "objective" anonymity to the flux and panic of Heyst's accompanying thoughts. This movement destabilizes the episode, demonstrating that in Heyst's fantasy, he is indeed witnessing a deed of sexual—not musical—violence. Heyst's association of the concert with a primal scene is palpable from the narrative's focus on disparate fantasies, its effort to suture Heyst's interiority to the orchestral event, and the points where his fantasy interrupts the concert by inflecting the external event with psychic meaning: the narrative emphasizes the bodies of the conductor and his "players," while it filters the audience and other objects from Heyst's vision. The narrative also abstracts and disfigures bodies, presenting them without identity or character; sound and vision lose congruency and unseam to provide sensory disjuncture.[37] Thus the grand piano is "operated upon by a bony, red-faced woman with bad-tempered nostrils" (111);[38] "shoulders" emerge from a platform filled with "white muslin dresses [and] bare arms [that] . . . sawed away without respite"; finally, when Zangiacomo "conducted . . . his longish, tousled hair and his great beard were purple-black. He was horrible. The heat was terrific" (111).

When the noise abates Heyst experiences a "relief . . . so great that he felt slightly dizzy," before he perceives the conductor as further reduced in feature and function: "The male creature with the hooked nose and purple-black beard disappeared somewhere" (112). The metonymic shift between "hooked nose" and penis—or "purple-black beard" and pubic coloration—is overdetermined, as is the frequent reference to each woman's flush. When the interval intervenes as "a chasm of silence [that] yawned at his feet" (112), the audience interrupts Heyst's fixation to "fraternise [in a] symbol of familiarity" and the musicians finally emerge with "worn cheeks [that] were slightly rouged" (112). The sexuality of the performance is of considerable relevance to Heyst's preceding and proceeding actions, and helps explain why critical interpreters have assiduously ignored it: The "gnawing pain . . . and remorse" (109) that Heyst experiences lead him to form a tie without paternal censure. In other words, while the concert encourages Heyst's grief for Morrison to wane, the interval of silence also enables—and even obliges—him to search for a substitute object.

By emphasizing the persistence of guilt and attempted reparation in the novel, I intend to demythologize the romance that many critics attribute to this encounter. The narrative's preoccupation with musical and sexual violence may demonstrate that Heyst's "impulse" to rescue Lena from Zangiacomo and the orchestra is neither altruistic nor romantic; it derives from identificatory anger at witnessing Lena's humiliation by the pianist, a woman whom Heyst later describes as "more disagreeable than any cannibal I have ever had to do with" (117). Lena's humiliation and rescue seem to repeat and displace Heyst's rescue of Morrison from the "murder[ous]" Portuguese authorities. Like Morrison, Lena suffers humiliation from external forces: Schomberg's repeated harassment and Zangiacomo's unjust punishment; the same adjective describes their humiliation: they are both "cornered" by a threatening body. Heyst explains to Lena: "he was . . . a good man cornered—a sight for the gods. . . . And you, who have been cornered too—did you think of offering a prayer?" (214).

If both acts of rescue derive from equivalent moments of crisis, they also quell Heyst's imminent sense of calamity. Since the interval of the concert signifies a psychological end to Heyst's relationship with Morrison, the paternal violence that Morrison formerly abated is able to return. Heyst's relationship with Morrison does not rehearse a replete and "sexual" relationship with Lena; as Lacan would corroborate, she answers a demand by supplanting a more cherished object. In this sense, Lena is the means by which Heyst can recover and forget both Morrison and all that he signifies.

This reading of *Victory* examines the text's radical concern with fantasy, sexual drive, and identification by arguing that the novel prioritizes a subject's impulse over the object at which it aims. By de-emphasizing Lena's gendered difference from Morrison, I suggest that the text demonstrates a significant proximity between Heyst's homo- and heterosexual interests.[39] By separating the cause and aim of desire from their effect, *Victory* effectively denatures heterosexual romance and represents the instability of its characters' sexual identifications and object choices.

Allegories of Homosexual Desire

> . . . plain Mr. Jones, his eyes fixed darkly on Schomberg, [told him] not to worry himself about things he did not understand; . . . "I don't understand?" grumbled Schomberg. "Oh yes, I understand perfectly well. I——" "You are frightened," interrupted Mr. Jones. "What *is* the matter?"
> —Joseph Conrad (144–45)

> It was unnatural, [Schomberg] thought somewhat peevishly. How was one to reckon up the unnatural? There were no rules for that.
> —Conrad (267–68)

In *Victory,* Schomberg's hypervirility has the significant function of warding off his emulative and sexual interest in Heyst; the narrative represents this interest as rivalry for Lena. If Schomberg oscillates, with considerable violence, between desiring Heyst as an object and repudiating him as a rival, the text also seems unable to sustain its emphasis on masculine difference; once again, we return to the turbulent scene of sexual proximity and partial differentiation.

Critics who allege *Victory*'s inferiority often define Schomberg as its principal weakness. They have described Schomberg's behavior as "bizarre," unrealistic, and responsible for the book's lamentable decline into melodrama.[40] Despite noting his obsessional behavior, criticism has failed to account for it, suggesting merely that his antipathy toward Heyst, and the charge of Morrison's murder, precipitates a revenge motif and the death of the principal characters. Thus the prominence of Schomberg's obsessions permit a number of assumptions to prevail, behind which pressing and difficult questions lie unasked.

When critics invoke *Victory*'s "failure," they read Schomberg and Jones as a melodramatic lapse in the novel's otherwise consistent allegory.[41] My interest in Schomberg derives from a similar shift between the text's literal and allegorical registers, but it hinges on the place where a conservative reading of *Victory* as a religious or moral-ethical allegory becomes impossible to sustain. Schomberg's influence on the narrative is curiously disproportionate to his marginal status in the text; through him most of the novel's enigmas find their most lucid expression. Schomberg's obsessive behavior is thus integral to this text because his obsessions represent—or make too evident— that which passes for enigma or symptom elsewhere. The vulgarity and the inadvertent slips that emerge unbidden from Schomberg's elaborate defenses make the narrative's resistance to commentary and denial of homosexuality immensely significant. Thus, the narrator consistently fails to interpret the desire that passes between Heyst and Morrison and its effect on their more assiduous observer, Schomberg.

Like Conrad's narrator Marlow in *Lord Jim* (1900), Schomberg performs an intertextual role: in *Lord Jim* he runs a hotel in Bangkok and represents the "irrepressible retailer of all [its] scandalous gossip"; in "Falk" (1902) he is "the proprietor of the smaller of two hotels" in Bangkok and remains a source of unreliable information.[42] When Schomberg resurfaces in *Victory,* he bears a reputation that, according to Conrad, performs "a still larger part, true to life (I hope), but also true to himself. Only, in this instance, his deeper passions come into play and thus his grotesque psychology is completed at last." [43] Schomberg may be "grotesque" because he joins incongruous qualities: an overbearing and repugnant virility with the malign pettiness and "ungovernable tongue" of a local gossip (69). *Victory's* association of masculinity with heroic detachment and verbal concision is so extensive, however, that the presence of these qualities in a scurrilous gossip appears curious and puzzling; in Schomberg these qualities jeopardize the meaning of his masculinity: his virility may compensate for sexual deficiency, or his gossip may be the social expression of an impermissible enthusiasm for others' conduct and passions. Though Schomberg retains both qualities, their balance proves astonishingly precarious.

From the outset, the narrator overstates Schomberg's virility. He first describes Schomberg as "a big, manly, bearded creature" (69), features echoing those in *Lord Jim:* "a hirsute Alsation of manly bearing" [44] that recur with slight variation and much tedium: "big, manly . . . portly style, and profusely bearded" (74); "keen manly . . . creature" (74); "squared his manly chest" (75); "lounged out, portly, deliberate" (83), et cetera. The recurrence of these adjectives—and the inability of the text to describe him without them—encourages the reader to suspect either caricature or the persistence of a problem that the narrator cannot address or resolve. Preoccupied with Schomberg's masculinity, the narrator seems to ask what it means to be, desire, or identify as a man, in an attempt to stabilize the meaning of masculinity at home and abroad. Other elements in *Victory* confirm this problem's repetition: the unusual resistance—even indifference—of *all* of its principal characters to marriage. To Jones, for instance, Schomberg's "marriage" is worthy of scorn; for Schomberg, marriage's ability to emasculate provokes rage and shame.[45] The representation of women in this text accompanies its narrative instability; women assume an importance to masculine identification that is both utterly predictable and strikingly unusual: Lena brings Heyst to an awareness of his sexual crisis in a way other fictions either displace or resolve by marriage.

Schomberg initiates discussion of masculine desire by inquiring into its meaning for others. Having assessed the behavior of Heyst, Morrison, and Jones, Schomberg's inquiry becomes more urgent and extensive as he enlists the response of others—hotel guests, Davidson, the expatriate community— to allay his palpable fear: he "invents" Morrison's murder, representing it as "calumny" (74); refuses to be impressed by Heyst's attempted recovery (74); feels such hatred toward Heyst that even the narrator finds it "gratuitous" (74); finally—returning to my reading of allotropes and masculine resemblance—he discloses an acute fear of being blinded by Heyst's charm and of losing his detachment: "gentlemen, . . . he can't throw any of his coal-dust in my eyes" (74).

Although unwarranted, Schomberg's rage persists and intensifies. Schomberg's names for Heyst chart the trajectory of his affective turbulence, from the "Enchanted" to the "Spider" (Morrison is his "Fly"), "the Enemy" (74), and "the deepest, the most dangerous, the most hateful of scoundrels" (132). With apparent sexual inflection, Schomberg twice remarks that Heyst "squeezes you dry" (72, 104), while his fantasy of Morrison's murder connects with Heyst's "long and tormented existence" (75) by anticipating *Heyst's* death: "I hope the fellow did not go and drown himself" (75). According to the confused narrator, Schomberg makes this comment both in "comic earnestness" and from the belief that his audience is so "superficial" it cannot "apprehend the psychology of this pious hope" (75).

The narrator explains neither this "hope" nor its surrounding "psychology"; like Conrad's reference to "deeper passions [that] come into play" (45), the reiteration of Schomberg's fixation seems designed to obscure clarification and provoke more inquiry. However, his delusion's clarity also allows the "passion" or "hope" that underwrites it to surface, precisely because Schomberg's delirium militates against understanding of its purpose or origin. Thus the comic repetition of his fixation works as a defense, allowing Schomberg to erupt with such rage at Heyst that Davidson is "inwardly startled at the savage tone" (85); to "gnash his teeth" in public (85, 103); to declare "unmotivated" abuse toward Heyst "with such vehemence that he actually choked himself" (92); and finally, at the thought of "squeezing" Morrison, to explode with fury: " 'Its disgusting—tfui,' he spat. He choked with rage— for he saw visions no doubt. He jumped up from his chair, and went away to flee from them—perhaps . . . [Mrs. Schomberg] could not have been very soothing to the sort of torment from which he was suffering" (104).

Numerous passages illustrate this preoccupation with Heyst's sexuality. My purpose here simply is to argue that each outburst illustrates a discrepancy between a nebulous event (Heyst's intimacy with Morrison) and its conscious and unconscious meanings for Schomberg. By declining to interpret points in the narrative, the narrator calls attention to Schomberg's delirium and then ignores it. While criticism of *Victory* alludes only to an analogy between Heyst and Schomberg, I suggest this analogy is more than coincidence; it may be central to the text's concerns, for Schomberg's delirium mirrors Heyst's dejection. If the origin of Schomberg's rumor appears "gratuitous," the reason for his "hatred" of Heyst—his "theft" of Lena—is not adequate or unrelated to his obsession with Heyst; the obsession actually begins before Schomberg has even met or seen Lena. Clearly, there is more to Schomberg's harassment of Lena than is first apparent.

Although Schomberg's harassment of Lena predates Heyst's elopement with her, it justifies Heyst's intervention and induces Schomberg's rage only after he has "stolen" her. I suggest not that Schomberg's harassment is entirely disingenuous but that it is conflated with humiliation by his arch rival, Heyst. If Schomberg's harassment of Lena alleviates any misgivings he might have about his potency and publicly avowed heterosexuality, the bathetic collapse of his planned seduction justifies his pathological jealousy and the pretext for a vendetta supporting a complex wish for revenge. As ever, Schomberg's declarative interiority explicates this "coincidence": "He ran off with a girl. What do I care for the girl? The girl is nothing to me" (92).

The bewildered narrator, often at a loss for explanation, rationalizes this outburst as concern for the hotel's reputation: the elopement jeopardizes the security of its female guests. However, Schomberg's desire for vengeance resumes a stubbornly familiar hatred for Heyst, so it is not enough to suggest that Lena is desirable to Schomberg only because she is "unavailable"; Lena precipitates an opportunity (a cause) for Schomberg to compete with Heyst, and a fantasy of supplanting—and even vicariously receiving—his desire. This, I suggest, constitutes an attraction equal to or greater than "winning" Lena. The narrator briefly corroborates: "The effect of [Schomberg's] outburst was augmented [by Ricardo] by the quiet lowering of the eyelids, by a reserved pause as though this had been a confession of another kind of love. Schomberg cudgelled his brains for a new topic, but he could not find one. His usual scandalous gossip would not serve this turn. . . . [He] was almost compelled to keep to the subject" (155). Although this scenario captures the suppressed homoeroticism of male bonding, Schomberg's declared fantasy and impulse indicate these bonds' internal dynamic by representing a drive that is closer to emulative and erotic identification with the other man's desire.[46]

My suggestion that Heyst does not simply "desire" Lena muddies the currency of desire in *Victory* still further: Heyst implicates Lena in repeated projections that defend against his own insoluble difficulties with masculinity and filial duty. An analogy between Heyst and Schomberg is useful here: each wards off actual and imaginary obstacles to identification by adopting a strategy of evasion—abstinence and retreat, denial and projection—that devolves the entire problem onto one woman. We might recall Lacan's dictum here: "*man's desire is the desire of the Other.*" [47]

Like Morrison, Lena is "cornered" by men—Zangiacomo ensnares her; Schomberg harasses her; Heyst approaches her. She also links Heyst and Schomberg (Schomberg did not represent Morrison so intensely as a contested object). If Lena is an envied object who "joins" Heyst's and Schomberg's convergent paths, she is also the means, as a vanishing mediator, by which that rivalry becomes possible. Though she supplements masculine rivalry, the drama of this exchange and substitution therefore operates with considerable complexity without her: it centers on the intrigue and unmentionable speculation that Heyst attracts, and the peripheral figures with whom he repeatedly collides and associates. His name, already a subject of inference and projection, attests to this difficulty. As Axel Heyst, he forms an axis linking commensurate terms: *Heissen* in German means "to name" and "denominate" as well as "to mean." Several critics use his proper name to support a religious and metaphysical interpretation of the text (Heyst-Christ, Lena-Magdalene),[48] invoking the obvious pun between his social title (Baron) and his socio-sexual topography (barren).[49] In keeping with this account of resemblance and equivalence, the reading that I propose invokes Heyst as *tryst*, the place where two or more variables meet: if Heyst is the figure in whom *Victory*'s conflict is "joined," he is also the topos on which these issues find their most volatile expression.

I suggest that relationships between male characters in *Victory* do not sustain a fundamental difference; the similarities joining one man to another generate a crisis of resemblance and proximity that surfaces in a terror of indistinction, and a need to separate otherwise similar and analogous aspects of culture and ontology into dramatically "dissimilar identi[ties]" (159). Since this text establishes meaning only by relation and difference, it attaches formidable reliance to the context supporting it; the same inquiry surely could not occur on "home soil." *Victory*'s geographical dislocation exacerbates this pressure by freeing referents from their usual context; the text requires considerable force to hold these (masculine) referents apart and thus prevent their implosion.

Heyst's struggle for skeptical detachment and ontological sufficiency is impossible without the narrative's exploration of the background from which he "drifts" and the expatriate community that fights over the security of its cultural meaning. In other Conrad texts, the ship's democratic ideal figures this desired, but rarely found, stability; the ship represents a body with limits that detach from the subaltern's "corruptive" influence. The ship explores uncharted waters, drifts unmoored, and casts perspective on the land that it leaves behind—the cultural *oikos* of Britain—without allowing an outside "alien" to overwhelm it. In *Victory* the boat cannot perform this function; it merely transports people from the peninsula to the island of Samburan. Thus, the narrative's interest lies less in the journey's adventure than the anxiety of departure and the fear of arrival. *Victory*'s outlying geography is also as "tired" and subdued as its inhabitants: the narrator describes Samburan repeatedly as suffused with "general desolation" (89), a "brood[ing] somnolence" (110), and "the silence . . . that seem[ed] pregnant with fatal issues" (229); this last metaphor manifests the turbulence of an apparently asexual narrative.

The fatigue circulating among colonial communities and subjects in *Victory* represents the stress that falls on community and subject alike. Commonly, the narrator illustrates this stress by the community's defense against invasion—the enemy to its traditions and values. The community expels this enemy to an actual or imaginary frontier from which it menaces a threatening return. In Kipling's texts, for instance, anxiety governs the impression that the colonized encroaches on the expatriates' cultural and administrative purity. In *Victory*, however, the "alien" does not intrude culturally or racially; the colonial community appears so confident of its superiority that it reduces the "indigenous" population to a shadow: "Both these white men [Schomberg and Ricardo] looked on native life as a mere play of shadows. A play of shadows the dominant race could walk through unaffected and disregarded in the pursuit of its incomprehensible aims and needs" (188). Since the cultural double of "native life" seems little threat to this community, we must ask what figure "shadows" this community, haunting its environment "with somnolence"?[50] In a narrative already riddled with references to "Shade" and "shadow," the menace of this "play of shadows" signifies a metonym for Evil as its unbidden, undesirable, and unnamable symptom.

Victory's colonial community fears that its "enemy" will structurally dismantle its identification and that "civilization" will coalesce with its underlying "savagery" when the colonialist and native lose their conceptual difference and the "gentleman" descends to the rank of "barbarian." One could also argue that *Victory*'s concern to expose the processes of identification, and to reduce colonial and racial signifiers to their point of greatest resistance, forcefully examines the empire's differential fault lines. Although this elaboration of difference and similarity is surely not the text's primary intention, it elicits this reading by the impossibility of sustaining an overriding principle of difference.

Tony Tanner has argued convincingly that *Victory* anticipates a loss of distinction among cultures and civilizations, though he interprets this loss as social and evolutionary dissolution.[51] Without disregarding Tanner's reading, I suggest that *Victory* illustrates less an exclusive conflict *between* cultural and evolutionary modalities than a conflict *within* the "Empire of the Selfsame's" real and imaginary boundaries. By indicating the number of times *Victory* repeats the word "gentleman," Tanner contends that the narrative depletes this word of lexical meaning.[52] He draws a useful analogy with Meredith's contemporaneous novel *The Egoist* (1915), arguing that the Egoist's vulgar self-interest threatened the gentleman's emphasis on refinement, virtue, and altruism. By exploiting a breach between refinement and barbarism, the Egoist created an unsettling link between social poles that previous historical periods managed to efface. If this interpretation of conflict within the nation is correct, the buccaneer would further deplete assumptions about the gentleman by illustrating a grasping demand for colonial power and wealth from the same pretext of refinement and civility. This point surfaces in the tryst between Heyst and Jones:

> Mr. Jones, taking violent offence, snorted like a savage skeleton.
> "Strange as it may seem to you, it is because of my origin, my breeding, my traditions, my early associations, and such-like trifles. Not everybody can divest himself of the prejudices of a gentleman as easily as you have done, Mr. Heyst." (362–63)[53]

I am arguing that the colonial "frame" encouraged the Egoist/buccaneer to exploit an already precarious cultural distinction: the geographical distance between nation and colony offered leeway to social custom and little resilience against undesirable and opportunistic intruders. Tanner contends that the Egoist threatened cultural lineage, not community resistance, by reminding the gentleman that his refinement was corruptible and imaginary. *Victory* foregrounds this proximity between the gentleman, egoist, and buccaneer by insisting on the cultural and evolutionary differences that emerge between Jones, Ricardo, and Pedro: Jones apparently is the pinnacle of this lineage while Pedro is its barbaric counterpart (see 138, 166, and 171): "A spectre, a cat, an ape—there was a pretty association from a mere man to remonstrate with" (172). A similar, unsustainable racial history informs Heyst's and Wang's actions and identifications (see 198–200). However, most critics agree that Mr. Jones, the "incurious spectre" (142), embodies this cultural and evolutionary faultline by representing the difficulty of masculine identification and colonial meaning with dramatic urgency.

"Every hero is a patricide" [54]

> [Heyst] was . . . very masculine and perplexed, enveloped in the atmosphere of femininity as in a cloud, suspecting pitfalls . . . afraid to move.
> —Joseph Conrad (232)

> If there is no longer a father, why tell stories?
> —Roland Barthes [55]

In the final section of this chapter, I interpret Jones's impact on *Victory*'s pattern of desire by arguing that he precipitates the retribution of all of the text's sexual and colonial dilemmas. The figure of Mr. Jones brings this anxious similarity into relief by engendering a twofold critique of masculinity: first, by embodying a form of effeminacy that enables homosexual desire to surface among male similarities; second, by embodying a form of colonial opportunism that jeopardizes the expatriate community's precarious culture and group stability in *Victory*. Jones joins this chapter's two concerns by associating masculine anxiety with a specific geography and colonial meaning.

Though Heyst and Morrison first meet on the island of Timor, the narrator later argues that Heyst's encounter with Lena at the concert generates a different response: "But this was another sort of plunge altogether, and likely to lead to a very different kind of partnership" (118). The narrator is characteristically wrong in this matter, but—the mistake notwithstanding—he argues that this difference derives from the look they exchange, and the way they internally recognize desire: "He looked at her anxiously, *as no man ever looks at another man;* and he positively forgot where he was" (113; my emphasis). This subclause is curious because the narrator constantly refers to Morrison as the forgotten object, and because Jones's arrival transforms the narrator's assertion into an immediate untruth: before Schomberg registers "the possessor of the handsome but emaciated face" (135) on an arriving ship, he experiences "a dark, sunken stare plunging down on him" (135). The exchange of looks between men carries an anxiety comparable to that which passes between men and women.[56]

This introduction to Jones, only three brief chapters after the narrator's disclaimer, is not even an exception to the rule: other people's thoughts and fears characterize Jones, for their perception of him is integral to his representation. The participle "plunging" echoes Heyst's pursuit of Morrison,[57] while Jones's "black, cavernous, mesmerising glance" (137) inspires horror in all who receive it (137)—especially Schomberg—because it is "darkly . . . fixed" (144) and "steady" (148). Jones's companions, Ricardo and Pedro, precipitate a similar anxiety in Schomberg, who adopts a transparent semiotics of masculinity directly corresponding to the narrator's perception of what is "ambiguous" (142), "equivocal" (143), and "inscrutably mysterious" (142) in them.

Contrary to the narrator's suggestion, Jones's recurring gaze at other men impounds and disempowers subjectivity: his look is sufficient "to dissolve the last grain of resolution in [Schomberg's] character" (145), while the presence of the trio fosters in him an "inwardly abject attitude" (153) and an eagerness to submit from "fear and resignation" (150).[58] In contrast with Heyst and Lena's visual exchanges, the intensity of Jones's gaze belies intention and significance; it projects only emptiness and death.

Despite the narrator's unwillingness to compare these looks, Heyst and Lena's visual exchanges are also difficult to interpret. Their gaze differs from Jones's only because Heyst and Lena *anticipate* mutual understanding; the truth of their encounter is equally disappointing, since *Victory* interrupts and denatures both heterosexuality and homosexuality. As I argued in chapter 3 over questions of asymmetry in Beerbohm's *The Happy Hypocrite,* Lacan's proposition that "there is no sexual relation" is invaluable here because it suggests that there is only the fantasy of a relation, while no relation can exist without sexuality.[59] *Victory* confirms this psychic breach between characters: though Lena finds Heyst "too wonderfully difficult to know" (252), she exists for him as a specular fantasy, "a sort of charming mirage in the barren aridity of his thoughts" (122) and a "phantom-like apparition" (123) who is "as unreadable as ever" (231). Lena's demand that Heyst de-etherealize her precipitates in him an ontological and sexual crisis.[60] Finally, Heyst and Lena's intractable problem of reading each other's intention disappoints the narrator's desire to signify their intimacy: Heyst considers Lena "like a script in an unknown language, or even more simply mysterious: like any writing to the illiterate" (233). Despite the pleasure that sexual drives promise, *Victory* seems compelled to show that its protagonists cannot fully know these drives. By representing desire only by its resemblance to a previous passion, the narrative demonstrates that full understanding of this desire is impossible. With its movement between impulse and gaze, longing and difficulty, Heyst and Lena's relationship appears no different in form and success from the opaque eroticism that in this text surfaces between men.

This pattern manifests less as a physical encounter than as a drama of fantasy and denial connecting each preceding character in a narrative trace. When Schomberg "put[s Jones] . . . on another track . . . the track of a man!" (178) to perform an actual and imaginary act of revenge, Schomberg's obsessions dissipate. The narrator confirms: "In his simplicity, he was not able to give up the idea which had entered his head. An idea must be driven out by another idea . . ." (185). Schomberg's vendetta against Heyst takes a geographical "track" that issues from the tortuous paths of Schomberg's obsession, while his fixation—and the meanings it supports and condenses—shifts from one object to another: from "hatred" for Heyst to the "theft" of Lena, and then to revenge by Jones. Schomberg's convenience in ridding himself of the "desperadoes" brings the added relief of using one fantasy to expiate another in order to annul both. Thus Jones answers to a need that he inaugurates by embodying the symptom of a desire that is always "put . . . on another track"; he clarifies needs without allowing their fulfillment, and precipitates desire by underscoring characters' homo/sexual metonymy.

Schomberg's displacement of Jones signals the return of a problem for Heyst: Jones not only "transports" one man's revenge to another but also reminds Heyst of a filial guilt he cannot escape. Having "explained" his relationship with Morrison to Lena in terms that are new and shocking to himself, Heyst wrongly imagines that "the shade of Morrison needn't haunt [him]" (218) on Samburan. His ongoing inability to explain his intimacy with Morrison creates an anxiety that Heyst at first flippantly disavows, "like a habit one has schooled oneself into" (218). Then he displays astonishment: "Strange that it should hurt me!" (221). Next despair: " 'What more do you want from me?' [asks Lena]. He made no sound for a time. 'The impossible, I suppose' " (223). Finally, he experiences abjection: "I feel a disgust at my own person, as if I had tumbled into some filth hole" (226). Heyst's disgust corresponds to his realization that he "had again lost control of himself" (226)—an issue that forces sexual, and perhaps even preoedipal, drives to surface as Jones gains real and imaginary access to Heyst through a figurative and topographical "hole," the island's backwater. In another sense, Jones's "entry" onto the island signifies the rupturing of an internal defense that Heyst represents in characteristically violent and sexual terms: "Nothing can break in on us here" (233).

Heyst and Wang spy Jones's boat immediately after this statement. Thus Jones's arrival on the island constitutes another form of "rescue" (Heyst feels compelled to give him and his crew water to prevent their death by dehydration) and the shattering of a dyadic idyll that Heyst and Lena tenuously forged. For many critics, this intrusion—or figural penetration—represents Satan's allegorical violation of Eden, and Conrad's representation of Jones as "an insolent spirit on leave from Hades" (148) certainly lends support to this reading.[61] If we accept this reading, however, we must also consider what constitutes, and for whom, the "temptation" of Eden—a question these critics never broach. Since Lena represents for Jones an object of horror—unlike Eve's allure for Satan—she never receives the "knowledge" of her biblical counterpart. Thus if Lena represents a figure of redemption whose "triumph" embodies the titular "victory" of the text, we should ask, From what or whom must Heyst be redeemed? The redemption is also illusory, because both Jones and Lena die—Lena is shot by Jones, who is shot, in turn, by Ricardo; the trope of revenge demonstrates that victory is never simply substantive—it is also victory *over* a defeated antagonist. As I argued before, Lena joins and partially binds these forces for Heyst; as her previous name (Alma) suggests, she amalgamates the narrative's disparate strains (126). Her attempted reparation fails because the narrative never incorporates this symbol of "temptation," leaving unanswered questions that are integral to the temptation.

By avoiding the novel's undermining psychic and colonial issues, the conservative reading of *Victory* as religious-metaphysical allegory breaks down: Jones cannot embody Evil or Satan, for the novel's account of negation is more complex; nor can he simply represent the repression and eventual return of a denied "homosexuality" that the text finally kills off; his actions relate tangentially to preceding issues and attachments.[62] I suggest that Jones's incongruity, and the multivalences surrounding his vendetta, give meaning to his "revenge"—if indeed it is properly his. Jones represents the anachronism of a dandy, the travesty of a gentleman, the immorality of a buccaneer, and the scorn of an avenger by configuring unmentionable elements of each. *Victory*'s uneasy absorption of fantasies and identifications across cultures, communities, and subjects gives its "repressed" components a potent meaning. While the terms and enactment of this revenge certainly appear "homosexual," it is necessary to interpret why the narrator attributes significance to Jones in this manner, without our considering his actions or desires as the single truth on which all narrative explanation hinges.

Certainly, Jones's vendetta releases Schomberg's burden of unexpressed desire and partly explains the enigma of Heyst's involvement with Morrison. Jones also repeats the text's unresolved paternal function in his resemblance to Heyst Sr., which resumes *Victory*'s interest in guilt and the death drive.[63] Contrary to critics who read the closing deaths as a metaphysical resolution, the revenge motif foregrounds the novel's difficulty with desire by proving that a coherent heterosexual closure is impossible: Jones interrupts Heyst's elopement with Lena by reintroducing his past sexual conflicts without permitting their resolution. *Victory* thus embarks on a radical critique of psychic drives, as the narrator isolates, interrogates, and metonymically conflates the novel's sexual "relations."

This disseveration of sexuality into its basic constituents resembles Freud's account of "Instincts and Their Vicissitudes," published the same year (1915). In that paper, as I have previously recounted, Freud distinguished psychic drives from biological impulses, and the object of desire from the subject's aim.[64] Mirroring Freud's intention, Jones configures the sexual meaning and violence to which each character feels drawn but is unable to entertain. Desire is violent in *Victory* because it destroys all psychic and thematic resolution by cutting across nebulous symbols. With the bodies of its principal characters strewn across the shoreline, the novel concludes with a remainder of desire, a surplus of meaning, and the problem of interpreting the shattering effect of sexuality on ontology when its meaning, as embodied in Jones, finally reaches Axel Heyst.

5

Maugham's

Of Human Bondage

and the

Anatomy of Desire

The Stammer of Desire

There must have been some strange morbidity in his nature
which made him take a grim pleasure in self-torture. . . . His
passion made him abject.
—W. Somerset Maugham [1]

None can, none may give Him utterance.
Oh, Word, Word, Word that I lack!
—Arnold Schoenburg [2]

W. Somerset Maugham's *Of Human Bondage* (1915) resembles Conrad's *Victory* in its preoccupation with masculine desire and identification. [3] Both
novels raise urgent questions about same-sex fantasy and intimacy that culminate in distress about their limit and possibility: Conrad's protagonist appeals
to Schopenhauer for sexual and ethical guidance while Maugham's protagonist, Philip Carey, reads the same philosopher to understand the vicissitudes
of his aberrant and unmanageable "will." Maugham attributes Carey's confusion to his resistance to marriage and domestic stability; however, the problem is not external to Carey—it stubbornly connects with antagonism and
recalcitrance toward his homosexual drives.

Since *Of Human Bondage* details several competitive relationships between men for women, my account owes much to René Girard's account of erotic rivalry and Eve Kosofsky Sedgwick's related critique of homosocial exchange and homosexual panic. In this chapter, I extend Girard's and Sedgwick's work by engaging the psychic terrain of jealousy in Maugham's novel and its related crises about fantasy, identification, and envy. To focus on this psychic configuration, this chapter briefly suspends discussion of the British Empire, though it elaborates on the domestic and intranational concerns that informed it. At the end of this interpretation, I return to colonial issues by focusing on Maugham's engagement with foreign travel and the role of the "homosexual" expatriate. I also introduce a reading of "structural misogyny," which examines the status of femininity in Maugham's writing and the meaning he attributes to masculine exploration.

Although *Of Human Bondage* is generally faithful to Maugham's life, its shift from autobiography to fictional narrative represents two significant displacements:[4] at the end of the novel, Carey resolves to travel abroad in an effort to detach from his past. Though Maugham pursued this course, Carey receives news of his fiancée's unwanted pregnancy, and finally balks at the idea of freedom from women, community, and Britain. Carey's handicap defines the other difference: while Maugham endured a stammer for most of his life, Carey is emotionally and physically "crippled" by a clubfoot.

Despite Maugham's concern to separate his stammer from Carey's clubfoot, they perform similar psychic and narrative functions in his novel. While stammers are often described by a psychic and physical difficulty — "a crippling stammer," "a stumbling tongue," "speech paralysis," et cetera[5] — both signify actual and metaphoric impediments to expression and movement. As a conventional hindrance to speech, the etymology of *stutter* gives *stotage,* "to falter and totter," and *stossen,* "to strike or stumble against."[6] Thus, the type of impediment may be immaterial in Maugham's novel because "the awareness of handicap matters far more than its nature."[7] All the same, Carey's clubfoot assumes immense internal significance to this novel, which represents his handicap as a trope for sexual and emotional distress. The narrator remarks, for instance, that Carey "accepted the deformity which had made life so hard for him; he knew that it had warped his character, but now he saw also that by reason of it he had acquired th[e] power of introspection . . ." (696).[8] The novel's obsession with Carey's "deformity" (258) consistently links his speech and desire with internal and external impediments.

By substituting physical problems of movement for psychic conflicts of torment and desire, the narrative tries to suppress discussion of Carey's distress; the ensuing conflict produces an intriguing tension. As one reviewer noted in 1915, "The author has so handicapped his hero as to remove him out of the category of the average." [9] By invoking the "average" of gender, other reviewers propose a model of heroism that requires an axiomatic mastery over women.[10] Thus Carey's "deficient" masculinity can "explain" why American readers disparaged the novel, appalled by the mawkish reticence of "futile Philip":[11] "The hero was a weakling, not for a moment to be tolerated by sound, right-thinking men." [12] Nevertheless, Carey's condition poses a question that the narrative tries to formulate and artfully conceal: What is the source of conflict that prefigures its manifestation in his body?

Maugham's transition from autobiography to fiction, and corresponding displacement from stammer to limp, represents part of this conflict. The displacement signifies an emotional effort that stymies whenever Carey contemplates the meaning of his desire. As with Melville's Billy Budd, whose stammer compounds his homoerotic fantasies with "organic hesitancy, in fact more or less of a stutter and even worse," [13] Maugham's novel impedes desire by a demand that it correspond to its subject's masculine ideal.

Following his perception of human nature, Maugham attributed his stammer to hereditary factors.[14] Although this explanation was current in his youth, the belief that a stammer's etiology was almost entirely psychological superseded it. Freud advanced a theory, still current and accepted today, that the stammer is a symptom for the partial condensation of incompatible drives,[15] representing "the influence of thoughts that lie outside the intended speech which determines the occurrence of the slip and provides an adequate explanation of the mistake." [16] Freud distinguished a stammer from the more common example of parapraxis by invoking the strength of the subject's resistance and the intrusion of thoughts that more fluent speakers pass over with only momentary embarrassment.

At the risk of pushing Freud's analogy between self-reproach and speech interruption to its extreme—an analogy that Maugham's novel repeatedly sustains—the fantasies impeding a subject's enunciation "can be represented by . . . losses of bodily equilibrium." [17] An involuntary stumble may reproduce an internal conflict by staging self-punishment as either the atonement of a crime or the doubt and guilt to which it constantly refers.[18] However, this analogy between speech and movement refers only to a spontaneous stumble or loss of balance. When applied to a sustained physical handicap, it would indicate a deliberate—albeit unconscious—choice of disability. As a psychic account of physical injury, this argument would be erroneous; clearly, there is no inevitable or axiomatic link between psychic and physical disability. I mean only to interpret the fantasmatic importance of Carey's clubfoot since Maugham consciously distanced it from his life; both handicap and distancing strategies surface repeatedly in the text.[19] For instance, characters comment on the clubfoot whenever they express desire for each other; Carey and Maugham's resistance may also obstruct the full meaning of the novel's "homosexual desire" by exemplifying Wittgenstein's pronouncement that "whereof one cannot speak, thereof one must remain silent." [20] In the reading that follows, I push this analogy to its limit by suggesting that we also can represent *Of Human Bondage*'s problematic as "whereof one cannot desire, thereof one must remain impotent." [21]

Jealousy and Immolation

Sensual pleasures are the most violent and the most exquisite. I am a man blessed with vivid senses, and I have indulged them with all my soul. I have to pay the penalty now, and I am ready to pay.
—W. Somerset Maugham (465)

The people were dull and pretentious; old ladies with elderly maiden daughters; funny old bachelors with mincing ways. . . .
—Maugham (533)

Like many turn-of-the-century narratives, *Of Human Bondage* contains few direct references to homosexual desire. The second epigraph is part of a description of Carey and Mildred's brief holiday in Brighton—a town already renowned for its sexual tolerance in the 1900s[22]—in which the "mincing" bachelors and aging spinsters who stay at the same rest house comment on the unmarried couple's use of a single room. Allusions to homosexual desire recur when Carey works in a department store in London and receives the attention of a flamboyant designer who "t[akes] a fancy to Philip" by rubbing his hands and winking at him. Later, the designer promises to look after Carey if he is conscientious at his job and avoids "larking about the girls like what some of them do" (605, 611). The designer never receives reciprocal interest, but he promotes Carey to design women's dresses; Carey's assiduous blindness over this promotion's cause and effect can only leave the reader with a wry smile.

The introduction of Mr. Simpson, the designer, follows Carey's visit to the British Museum, during which he comments on an "exquisite and . . .

very beautiful [carving], a bas-relief of two young men holding each other's hand" (601).[23] The narrator considers the sculptor's "genuine emotion" a pæan to "precious . . . friendship," and Carey is moved to tears at the thought of a close male friend in Paris. In a novel replete with tortuously wrought and unresolved feelings, no other incident provokes such *unsolicited* emotion. Even Mildred's "willful destruction" of Carey's apartment and art collection produces only a fleeting "anger" that leaves him "bewildered . . . astonished . . . [and stymied by] an overwhelming sense of boredom" (554, 556).

Every one of the book's references to homophilia is carefully ambiguous. The narrator insists that the carving's beauty lies as much in the skill of its sculptor as the friendship of its subjects. Though the desire to foster talent absorbs Mr. Simpson's "fancy," homophilia is a pretext for nonsexual "intimacy" (485) in earlier accounts of Carey's friendship with Mr. Athenly. The "funny old bachelors" also emphasize a dread of isolation that surfaces whenever the narrator extols the family as a promise of sanctuary. Thus, Carey remarks without irony: "It's rather jolly to come back and find some-one about the place. A woman and a baby make very good decoration in a room" (517). The bachelors have a distressing resemblance to Carey, how-ever, because the apparent peculiarity of a "mincing" walk in this novel seems indistinguishable from his slow hobble.

Of Human Bondage anticipates homosexuality by probing its char-acters' intentions; it resolves this problem only by erasing all desire from narrative and psychic consciousness. Nonetheless, homosexuality obtrudes as a fantasy when Carey fails to control his desire; his demand for masculine intimacy compels him to examine the precise terms of its composition before Carey can ruefully excise his aberrant impulses.[24] Although this paradigm is close to Eve Kosofsky Sedgwick's account of homosocial desire, the psychic constituents of Carey's desire prevent us from reading homosexuality as this novel's hidden drama or single panic.[25] The potential for homosexual desire is not inscrutable in *Of Human Bondage;* if Carey grasps at marriage to resolve his dilemma, the marriage occurs only after a seven-hundred-page exegesis on the shame of desiring at all.

At school, a fantasy of possessing the other man's desire mitigates Carey's general horror of desire: Carey's first consciousness of his "handi-cap" leads him to realize that "he would have given anything to change places with them . . . [even] the dullest boy in the school who was whole of limb" (78). This preoccupation with "deformity" does not stay with Carey's foot, however; his limp is synecdochic of an entire consciousness of difference that only envious pretense at being someone else can redeem: "He would imagine that he was some boy whom he had a particular fancy for; he would throw his soul, as it were, into the other's body, talk with his voice and laugh with his laugh; he would imagine himself doing all the things the other did. It was so vivid that he seemed for a moment really to be no longer himself. In this way he enjoyed many intervals of fantastic happiness" (78–79). This fantasy centers on Rose, a boy who shares Carey's study, and to whom he "had always looked . . . with envious admiration" (79). Rose's kindness gives Carey "a curious tremor in his heart" (79), which recurs whenever Carey tries to "throw himself into the other's skin, imagining what life would be like if he were [the other man]" (186).[26] Others note the "sudden intimacy" of Carey and Rose with alarm; Carey's demand for "a more exclusive attachment" makes Rose panic, while Carey founders over imaginary betrayal: "He watched jealously Rose's companionship with others" (80, 81). As the "abandonment" deepens, Carey—no longer "master of himself"—assumes the role of a dejected and abandoned lover; the "desire to wound . . . [and] revenge himself for the pain and humiliation he had endured" (85) overwhelms him. Carey stifles this desire by striking up "a violent friendship with a boy . . . whom he hated and despised" (84). In this way, he replaces envious identification with another boy (and later, other men) by emotional masochism that assuages the difficulty of his homosexual desire. As the narrator later remarks about Carey's relationship with Mildred, the alleged cause of his "bondage": "It delighted him to perform menial tasks . . ."; "he longed for an opportunity to gratify the desire for self-sacrifice which consumed him" (389, 403). However, masculine envy also intensifies the supposed "agony" of homosexual desire; the narrator observes of every imaginary substitution that "he would never be able to stand in that man's place" (183).[27]

Every scene of rivalry in *Of Human Bondage* illustrates this shift between "acceptable" competition between men and "unconscious" (though presiding) forms of rivalry. Consider the narrative effect of Carey's competition with women friends for their male partners: observing scenes of heterosexuality, Carey becomes anxious about his envy, enraged by his difference, and jealous of *both* parties. For instance, when Carey realizes that his friend Lawson is not only painting Ruth Chalice but actively seducing her, this "shock[ing] revelation" and the "kind of effluence surrounding them" disgust him, "as though the air were heavy with something strange" (256). From this moment on, Carey cannot look at Ruth through Lawson's eyes; he is angry not only that she desires but also that she welcomes desire from an envied friend. Later, though "[Carey] felt himself a fool not to see that she was attractive" (256), he soon forgets her, remembering only that "she was there, in his way" (256). Carey devotes all remaining attention to his troubled and indefinite relation with Lawson: "He was envious of Lawson, and he was jealous, not of the individual concerned, but of his love. He wished that he was standing in his shoes and feeling with his heart. He was troubled, and the fear seized him that love would pass him by. He wanted a passion to seize him, he wanted to be swept off his feet and borne powerless in a mighty rush he cared not whither" (256).

Although Carey attributes his "fear" to a conviction that he will never experience passion, this passion actually surfaces in the preceding sentence when Carey describes his "wish" to "stand in the shoes" of another man—a reference also to his clubfoot. Thus Carey's fantasy of desire without aim or object is disingenuous; the "fear" recurs less as a panic of never finding love than as one of endlessly discovering it. In an internal monologue, Carey chides himself for losing Ruth (the narrative records no other admission of this attraction) before acknowledging: "he suddenly felt quite different; he had no desire to take her in his arms, and he could not imagine himself kissing her. It was very curious. . . . He could not understand himself. Would he always love in absence. . . ?" (257–58). Once he rejects desire for Ruth, nothing can explain Carey's earlier remarks except as longing for Lawson; perhaps conscious of this residue of meaning, the narrative shifts to melodrama and a rhetorical question to impede further discussion.

This circuitous and substitutive logic governs *Of Human Bondage*. Carey scarcely asks himself, "Would he always love in absence. . . ?" before the narrative returns him an embodied "answer." A female friend introduces Carey to a Spanish model whose presence and features immediately attract him; Carey uses Miguel's body for an aesthetic purpose—sculpture—to mitigate this desire's crisis: "Philip's attention was attracted by the manner in which he held himself . . . with clenched hands, and with his head defiantly thrown forward, the attitude emphasized his fine figure. . . . His air of passionate energy excited Philip's romantic imagination" (262).

Since Carey can entertain only the attraction of representing Miguel's physique, the intimacy flounders and disappoints. However, the sculpture of Miguel—like his country of origin—signifies a fantasy of romance on which Carey endlessly ruminates when the mold of his desire and the shape of his future appear doubtful (264). I return to these fantasies at the end of this chapter; here we may note simply that Miguel—and the problem he represents—exceeds Carey's interest in sculpture, forcing him to consider what he may actually want of Miguel: his talent, vibrancy, and uninhibited passion. Although their friendship becomes flaccid after this confusion of interests, the narrative carries the burden of withheld intention as a punishment until Flanagan, Carey's next intimate friend, takes him dancing.

When Carey and Flanagan visit a ballroom, an anxiety overwhelms Carey for which the event is not fully responsible. Robust and exuberant, Flanagan "leap[s] over the barrier [to the dance floor] with a wild shout" (271), while Carey, unable to dance, observes the "sordid scene" with contempt. His response is so different from Flanagan's and the other dancers', and manifests itself internally with such vehemence, it indicates a more pervasive horror of desire. Differing slightly from the comparable scene in *Victory* I discussed in the previous chapter, women dancers bear the brunt of this disgust; the narrator dismisses them as "hussies . . . [of] notoriety, their eyes . . . heavy with black and their cheeks impudently scarlet" (272), while the men are never more than "faces [that] shone with sweat" or anonymous figures who "danced furiously . . . [having] thrown off the guard . . . of convention" (272). Pursuing the hysterical fixation of Carey's stream of consciousness, the narrative elaborates his projection of the dancers' sexual display: "In that moment of abandon they were strangely animal: some were foxy and some were wolf-like. . . . Their features were blunted by mean interests, and their little eyes were shifty and cunning. . . . [F]or all of them life was a long succession of petty concerns and sordid thoughts. The air was heavy with the musty smell of humanity. But they danced furiously as though impelled by some strange power . . . they were driven forward by a rage for enjoyment. They were seeking desperately to escape from a world of horror. The desire for pleasure, . . . the only motive of human action, urged them blindly on, and the very vehemence of the desire seemed to rob it of all pleasure" (272). Carey externalizes this scene, turning it into a display he feels compelled—without force or logic—to witness. His restless notation silences the event's noise; unease accompanies his perception of watching a dumb show: "Their silence was vaguely alarming. It was as if life terrified them and robbed them of power of speech so that the shriek which was in their hearts died at their throats" (273).

Like the "shriek" of the heart in this novel—and Heyst's relentless loneliness in *Victory*—the "terror" lives solely in Carey, the scene's troubled observer. If the "shriek" of desire emerges from the dancers' "heart," however, it also "die[s]" at this novel's "throat" from a stammer impeding most narrative desire. Though the narrative casts this shriek as the dancers' problem, not the protagonist's, it discloses Carey's impediment in the following observation: "Their eyes were haggard and grim [, . . .] notwithstanding the beastly lust that disfigured them" (273). Perceiving "lust" as a phenomenon responsible for "beastly" disfiguration returns us to the debilitating psychic and physical qualities of Carey's desire.

As in Conrad's novel, the "scene" in Maugham's text closes abruptly without explanation; rather than "dissect his feelings," Carey turns to medical research to "doctor" the human body: "dissection" provides a metonymic link between Carey's "feelings" and his body (Maugham also was a physician). As part of his training for surgery, Carey receives a human leg to dissect, though the text throws the reader a bone shorn of figurative meaning: the leg offers little besides the "acrid smell" of "emaciated . . . skin" (299, 300). The knowledge it might impart of the anatomy of desire stalls; Carey swiftly concludes, "Anatomy was a dreary science . . . dissection bored him" (305).

Throughout this period, the narrative characterizes Carey's relationship with Mildred by a similar resistance to "self-analysis": the "desire" motivating their relationship comprises cycles of deceit, self-punishment, and unsatisfied longing. Carey's attraction to Mildred is curious and irritating to the reader because she is not obviously responsible for it; the narrator notes repeatedly that "Philip did not find anything attractive in her" (306). If Carey's attraction is to a feminine ideal without body or sexual demand, it also relates to an unforeseen, homoerotic effect of Mildred's deficient "femininity": she is "tall and thin, with narrow hips and the chest of a boy" (306). Once Carey has dispelled her abstract allure, all that remains for him is contempt and aversion: "he devised a plan to show her that he despised her" (313).

Additional complications soon emerge: Carey meets Mildred in the company of another male friend, Dunsford, which event asks him to consider his discomfort with Dunsford's admiration—" 'She's got a ripping face,' said Dunsford. 'What *does* the face matter?' " (306; original emphasis)—to stabilize a "triangular" economy of desire: " 'All I want is a lead,' [Dunsford] said, 'and then I can manage for myself' " (307).

Since Dunsford's desire fascinates Carey, he fantasizes taking Dunsford's place on the pretext of enhancing his own "normalcy." Mildred is largely incidental to this drama because Carey juxtaposes her anemic and anorexic body with Dunsford's health and vitality: he has "jolly curling hair, a fresh complexion, and a beautiful smile. Philip thought of these advantages with envy" (311). Though several critics have commented on Carey's bizarre and unfathomable attraction to Mildred,[28] none has noticed the constant presence of a rival against whom Carey measures his potency and interest in her. This figure changes from Dunsford to the masculine "German" suitor, and from Griffiths to Mildred's eventual husband, Emil. The rival's presence is a constant spur to Carey's heterosexual complacency; it ensures devotion to Mildred to mitigate increasing interest in every new competitor. Carey's questions to Mildred convey curiosity from a jealous pretext—"Is he in love with you?" (320); "he was flirting with Mildred, and [Carey] was horribly jealous of him" (324); "I can't look at you now without thinking of Emil and Griffiths" (550). The earlier triangular configuration of Carey, Lawson, and Ruth Chalice intensifies when the narrative introduces Griffiths.[29]

Like Dunsford—and, indeed, all other men in the text—Carey notes Griffiths's robust health and exuberant virility. The reader easily could confuse Griffiths with his predecessor, for his features are almost identical to Carey's friends': he represents a comparable masculine imago. When Carey falls ill, for instance, the "healthy, strong, and cheerful" Griffiths (373) nurses him back to health; the "feminine tenderness of this strong young man," combined with "a humorous, motherly attitude," is sufficient to produce an immediate transference: "Philip worshipped him" (376).

Carey is so taken with Griffiths that, as before with Dunsford, he feels compelled to introduce him to Mildred. The narrator and Carey reappraise his physique and beauty, while Mildred's response, in pleasing Carey, reverses the more conventional display of a woman for masculine assessment: "He was a handsome creature, tall and thin; . . . his curly hair, his bold, friendly eyes, his red mouth, were charming. Philip saw Mildred look at him with appreciation, and he felt a curious satisfaction" (412). Whenever affection between men exceeds appropriate nomenclature in this text, the narrator describes it as "curious." Following the tradition of Rose, Hayward, Lawson, and Dunsford, masculine friendship is this novel's cherished intimacy since it fosters an exchange of ideas and jealously guards against the usurping relationship between women and men: heterosexuality interrupts homophilia as a form of shame, horror, and disgust; the "wholesome" Sally is the only exception.[30] As the alleged cause of ontological distress, heterosexuality also precipitates sexual confusion and masquerade: "He pretended to be much more passionate than he really was, and he succeeded in playing a part which looked very well in his own eyes" (163).[31]

Following an established pattern of rejection and despair, Mildred leaves Carey for Griffiths. Though Carey deems Mildred responsible for their separation, "What hurt him most was Griffiths's treachery; they had been such good friends, and Griffiths knew how passionately devoted he was to Mildred" (429). In this way, the narrator represents Mildred as an answer to Carey's emotion, not its cause; the erotic path of *Of Human Bondage* turns on a declaration of male affection whose value the narrator refuses to interpret.

Between 1910 and 1922, Freud wrote several accounts of male homosexuality that characterize a similar, partial recognition of homoeroticism. Five years before the publication of *Of Human Bondage,* Freud theorized "A Special Type of Choice of Object Made by Men" (1910), in which a man's heterosexual interest depends on two conditions. The first stipulates the presence of "an injured third party" (i.e., a man) so that the desired woman is never "disengaged . . . [or] unattached." [32] The second concerns men drawn exclusively to a "woman who is in some way or other of bad repute sexually, whose fidelity and reliability [are] open to some doubt" because a woman "whose reputation is irreproachable never exercise[s] an attraction." [33]

Freud did not discuss the woman's sexual interests; he assumed that men would have a clear understanding of the value and meaning of female "repute" and "chastity." [34] Instead, Freud devoted all remaining attention to the woman's exchange between two (or more) competing men: in the first "jealous" paradigm, the other man presents "an opportunity for gratifying impulses of rivalry and hostility directed at the man from whom the woman is wrested"; in the second, the woman's likeness to a "prostitute" is "connected with the experiencing of *jealousy.*" [35] These trajectories rapidly coalesce, however, because the man in the second scenario is jealous less of the *woman's* status than that of her suitors—the men "from whom she must be wrested" (Freud does not elaborate on this psychic imperative "must"). Thus, the woman's poor sexual repute *requires* other men's attention; it is not her principal attraction. This type of masculine "jealousy" aligns the second group of men (those attracted only to "fallen women") with the first, whose attraction requires an injured third party to whom they can "gratify . . . impulses of rivalry and hostility"; the difference between these groups is simply that the second stipulates the woman's "poor" sexual reputation while the first allows it to pass without comment.

Disregarding the proximity between masculine "jealousy" and the "urge to '*rescue*' [a] woman" [36] from other men, Freud quickly dispelled the rival's fantasmatic importance: the man's fixation on her "unimpeachable moral purity" [37] allegedly compels him to pursue a moral and sexual counterpart to his mother. Even here, though, the rival is a crucial element of the man's fantasy. As Freud observed: "What is strange is that it is not the lawful possessor of the loved one who becomes the target of this jealousy, but strangers, making their appearance for the first time, in relation to whom the loved one can be brought under suspicion. In glaring instances the lover shows no wish for exclusive possession of the woman and seems to be perfectly comfortable in the triangular situation. . . . In some cases this precondition proves so cogent that a woman can be ignored, or even rejected, so long as she does not belong to any man, but becomes the object of passionate feelings immediately she comes into one of these relationships with another man." [38]

Beyond this phenomenon lies a further component that troubles Freud's interpretation: the boy who later requires these extremes of female sexuality to sustain heterosexual interest seems to resist acknowledging his father as an obstacle to his mother's desire; instead, the boy establishes a tenuous paternal identification by fantasizing a "pure" mother without entirely renouncing her as sexually unavailable. The remarkable similarity between Freud's 1910 account of mother-son attachment and his contemporaneous description of male homosexuality has bearing on my reading of Maugham. A footnote to his *Three Essays on the Theory of Sexuality* (1905), added in 1910, makes this similarity explicit: "[W]e have established the fact that the future inverts, in the earliest years of their childhood, pass through a phase of very intense but short-lived fixation to a woman (usually their mother), and that, after leaving this behind, they identify themselves with a woman and take *themselves* as their sexual object." [39] Since the boy appears to resolve this scenario by "narcissistic" homosexuality, Freud does not mention the boy's problems in distinguishing between desire for the father and identification with him. Indeed, Freud did not consider the influence of "both parents" on male homosexuality until his now famous 1915 revision of the *Three Essays on the Theory of Sexuality*. Even here, he argued that "the absence of a strong father in childhood" combines with other factors — "a retention of the erotic significance of the anal zone," "accidental factors" such as "early deterrence, by fear, from sexual activity," "frustration," and the ongoing "operation of narcissistic object-choice." [40] Freud vacillated among various "causes" of male homosexual desire, prioritizing none of these determinants: six years later, he formally introduced the negative oedipal relation into discussion of male homosexuality in "A Seventeenth-Century Demonological Neurosis" (1923) and "Dostoevsky and Parricide" (1928); almost concurrently, he considered the influence of sibling rivalry in "Some Neurotic Mechanisms in Jealousy, Paranoia and Homosexuality" (1922).[41]

Though Freud's etiology of male homosexuality underwent considerable transformation, investing varying significance in each maternal, paternal, and fraternal imago, we can consider every shift as part of an ongoing difficulty in *representing* male homosexuality. Similar to Maugham's *Of Human Bondage* in its insistence on the value of a feminine mystique, Freud's 1910 paper on "A Special Type of Object Choice" enumerates and interprets intense rivalry and erotic cathexes between men. When Freud revised his earliest accounts of rivalrous "homosexuality" in a 1920 footnote to his *Three Essays,* for instance, he followed Sándor Ferenczi's decision to give this phenomenon "a better name, 'homo-eroticism.' "[42] This clarification between homoerotic and homosexual desire suggests that Freud would have written a very different account of "special object choice" in 1910, had he considered the degree to which homoeroticism devolves on the figure of the rival. Indeed, in later papers such as "Dostoevsky and Parricide" he considered the radical possibility that a woman—perhaps his mother—may represent a rival for the boy's "homosexual" attachment to his father.

This development alters psychoanalytic accounts of jealousy and turn-of-the-century symbolizations of male homosexuality: the other man "from whom the woman must be wrested" cannot *remain* merely an object of envy, competition, or hostility that the first man displaces or supplants because he carries an additional—and sometimes formative—erotic cathexis that unsettles the woman's primary status in every jealous scenario. Although Freud's later papers do not preclude the significance of his 1910 reading of "A Special Type of Choice of Object," his later work did consider this psychic proximity between ("heterosexual") jealousy and ("homosexual") envy.[43] The proposition that a woman can be both object and rival for a man introduces a small but critical difference into homosocial accounts of rivalry, in which a primary interest in a (female) object apparently masquerades for a subordinate, but more important, element of sexual rivalry (with other men).

This psychic reading takes us beyond the supposition that the woman is instrumental to a scenario that would otherwise be homosexual were the men prepared to be more direct or honest about their desire;[44] in Maugham's and many other narratives, concurrent interest in men and women does not always culminate in mutually exclusive hetero- or homosexual attachments. As Freud remarked in 1899 in a letter to Fliess, "Bisexuality! I am sure you are right about it. And I am accustoming myself to regarding every sexual act as an event between four individuals."[45] In Maugham's novel self-deceit renders homosexuality neither a hidden secret nor an unspeakable truth; it indicates a conceptual turbulence about the meaning of desire and masculine identification in which homosexuality acts as one of several sexual determinants. Thus, my account of Maugham engages different configurations of desire without consigning them to rigid sexual binaries (hetero/homo), distinctions of psychic "depth" (latent/declared), or cultural symbols (open/secret, etc.). It is also consistent with the combined reticence and epistemological indeterminacy of the text, which in turn is emblematic of late-Victorian and Edwardian British culture. The problem of sexual nomenclature with its attendant

anxiety of meaning — what name to give this sexual enigma, how to characterize its difference — is a question of deceit and denial that also points to
blind spots readable only with specific lexical and psychic distinctions.

Freud's later essays on sexuality assist this reading of Maugham
by implying that a man's identification with another man can be concurrent
with a masochistic desire for a woman without concluding that the "real"
or "underlying" problem is homosexual reticence. Freud's work is important precisely for the *indeterminate* meaning it gives to object choice and its
ability to interpret two or more trajectories of desire — for the man *and/or*
the woman — without compelling one to occlude the other. Thus if we read
Freud's 1910 paper alongside his 1899 letter to Fliess and his marginal re-
visions of *The Three Essays on the Theory of Sexuality,* Freud's remarks on
the coercive function of "normalcy" subsume, and even disband, resolution
about object choice. Indeed, this is the logical conclusion of a project that begins by assuming the definitional importance of sexual perversion, and ends
by acknowledging, "from the point of view of psycho-analysis the exclusive
sexual interest felt by men for women is also a problem that needs elucidating and is not a self-evident fact based upon an attraction that is ultimately
of a chemical nature." [46]

Although *Of Human Bondage* illustrates the horror of naming and acknowledging desires alternative to heterosexuality, it inadvertently addresses
Freud's inquiry: its "problems" and doubts about "exclusive sexual interest . . . for women" prevail with such anxiety that the narrative reorients
its putative homosexual desire toward an *emulative* interest in other men.[47]
Carey's pattern of intimacy (and sexual "rivalry") with Rose at school, Lawson in Paris, and Griffiths in London recurs whenever he expresses love for
Mildred; his fixation on the beauty and sexual power of his "competitors" increases and naturalizes his ardor for Mildred, as if a rival could easily usurp
this interest. In this way, the narrator can declare, "He understood Griffiths'
love well enough, for he put himself in Griffiths' place and saw with his eyes,
touched with his hands, he was able to think himself in Griffiths' body, and he
kissed her with his lips, smiled at her with his smiling blue eyes" (426–27).

Soon after this "confession" to the reader, Griffiths and Mildred
elope. This assures Griffiths's "normalcy" and confirms in Maugham's text
the impossibility of a *reciprocal* masculine desire; it also spares Carey further
embarrassment by forestalling his idealization of Griffiths. Although his relationship with Mildred never recovers — he passes between periods of acute
masochism and complete indifference toward her — this affective turbulence
surfaces not only because Griffiths and Mildred have breached a trust, but

also because Carey's competitive interest in his rival is no longer a pressing concern.

Carey's belief in masculine emulation allows him to postpone decisions by temporarily "inhabiting" another man's body and life. Since his self-loathing enlists each beloved—male or female—as a figure of sexual redemption, his vicarious pleasure relieves the agony of self-responsibility by encouraging him to limp toward self-development. However, the pleasure it brings is transitory and soon transformed into intolerable loneliness. Impelled toward future uncertainty by accepting his mediocrity as a painter, Carey deems himself "an explorer" who has yet to discover his real and imaginary terrains: "He felt himself like a traveller in unknown countries and as he pushed forward the enterprise fascinated him. . . . He was like an explorer now who has reasoned that certain natural features must present themselves" (294, 296).

This colonial metaphor corresponds precisely with the novel's account of its sexual indeterminacy and political context: the narrator attributes part of Carey's financial difficulties to the Boer War, for the clubfoot disqualifies Carey from military service, thus also impeding his passage to national heroism. Though this physical handicap obstructs masculine development, Carey's desire for travel ultimately collides with another "symptom"—involvement with a woman: Carey perceives women as an obstacle to freedom and self-development because they restrict his choices and blind him to alternatives.[48]

This association of masculine desire with colonial travel not only recalls Lacan's observations on the vagaries and "adventure" of psychic drives, cited in my introduction; it also introduces a fundamental link between discovery, loss, and nostalgia that hinges for Maugham on the pursuit and recovery of another "home." Given the ambivalent role that women perform for men in this domestic drama, we can appreciate why the affective turbulence of so many colonial protagonists in Maugham's writing has an intimate bearing on ontological lack and masculine castration. More generally, we can also see why colonial literature is lacerated and haunted by primary questions about national and sexual identification and the unfinished business of the "family romance." By paraphrasing Lacan's premise of "lack-in-being," for instance, Jane Gallop has argued that "desire can be married to a threat, or it can join a nostalgia instead. If the threat is understood as the male's castration anxiety, fear of losing what he has as the mother lost hers, then perhaps the nostalgia is the female's regret for what she does not have (any longer). Man's desire will henceforth be linked by law to a menace; but woman's desire will legally cohabit with nostalgia." [49]

Toward the end of this chapter, we will witness the pressure accompanying the enforced (and still only imaginary) resolution of this drama. Here, we may note simply that Carey's ability to "find himself" again with Mildred after a brief period alone is psychically expedient because material and psychic impediments block his external and internal exploration. Carey's obsession relieves the task of self-determination by obstructing the journey, though he resents Mildred for compromising his liberty. Reaching beyond the mundane and domestic, while remaining wholly attached to it, Carey rapidly projects his escape onto an empire of signs: "He wanted to go to the East; and his fancy was rich with pictures of Bangkok and Shanghai, and the ports of Japan: he pictured to himself palm-trees and skies blue and hot, and dark-skinned people, pagodas; the scents of the Orient intoxicated his nostrils. His heart beat with passionate desire for the beauty and the strangeness of the world" (537).

While the woman seems to displace every crisis about masculine identity and desire, I suggest that the Orient or Spain is synecdochic of imaginary intimacy with another man.[50] In other words, the foreign signifies a nebulous encounter between men that Carey cannot conceive *without* fantasy: he rhapsodizes Oriental and Mediterranean erotic signifiers—Miguel and El Greco—as an alluring terrain that is always beyond his grasp and only partially diffused of his homo/sexual fascination: "[H]e would go to Spain . . . the land which stood to him for romance; after that he would go to the East . . . [where] he could wander, for years if he chose, in unfrequented places, amid strange peoples, where life was led in strange ways. . . . [H]e had a feeling that he would gain some clue to the mystery that he had solved only to find more mysterious. And even if he found nothing he would allay the unrest which gnawed at his heart" (671).[51] Since Carey finally rejects his "passionate desire for the beauty and the strangeness of the world" at the novel's end, his fiancée Sally Athenly transforms Britain into an "exquisite homely naturalness" (690), and a "fair haven . . . again[st] the loneliness and the tempest" (699). Formerly, Britain's border signified to Carey an intractable demand for marriage, family, and sexual normativity from which he fled by adopting Paris and Heidelberg as "a place of exile" (561). When he returns to Britain, however, Carey considers himself "at home" though Britain cannot resolve his internal displacements and psychic dissociations (564). By stifling his restlessness, Carey's decision to marry upholds a corresponding shift in the narrative, in which Britain's once reviled tameness manifests as a saving grace and the Orient's formerly alluring secret now signifies an antagonistic and *unheimlich* enemy.[52] We could argue that Carey tries to resolve this conflict by marrying a female Athenly (or Athens), which combines both domestic security and a welcome legacy of homosexual desire from Ancient Greece.

This structural relation between travel and masculine identification recurs throughout Maugham's writing. To consider only his most contemporaneous work, his 1908 play, *The Explorer,* turns on its protagonist's choice between London and Kenya. As in *Of Human Bondage,* London connotes membership with friends, the company of a loyal male companion, and an incidental marriage to a respected (but not adored) woman;[53] the colony anticipates ontological pleasure, "masculine" fulfillment, and political recognition by imperial conquest:

> Dick: I wish to goodness you'd give up these horrible explorations.
> Alec: But they're the very breath of my life. You don't know the exhilaration of the daily dangers—the joy of treading where only wild beasts have trodden before. Oh, already I can hardly bear my impatience when I think of the boundless country and the enchanting freedom. Here one grows so small, so despicable, but in Africa everything is built to a nobler standard. There a man is really a man; there one knows what are will and strength and courage. . . . I love the sense of power and mastery. What do you think I care for the tinsel rewards of kings and peoples?[54]

Though clearly rhetorical, the question is no less significant for being asked. Later, in his *Writer's Notebook* (1949), Maugham considered the "type" most appropriate for the rugged needs of the British Empire and extolled the virtue of "the strong silent man" in a description replete with eroticism and quite devoid of irony: "He is the master of men. Such is the strong silent man who bears the white man's burden, the founder of our country's greatness, the Empire-builder, the support and mainstay of our power. He toils ceaselessly in remote and inaccessible places of the world. . . . No one can contemplate him without a thrill of pride. He is everywhere that is a long way off. It is that indeed which makes him endurable.[55] In other words, "the strong silent man" is everywhere and no place, a ubiquitous imago in Maugham's fiction that hovers between an ideal and an unequivocal sexualization of masculine power; we may recall Kipling's similar confusion over Torpenhow's representation in *The Light That Failed.* The dilemma between family commitment and artistic development also recurs in *The Moon and Sixpence* (1919), as if

Maugham were returning to—and vengefully rewriting—Carey's "mistake" in *Of Human Bondage* when he substitutes a woman for his artistic career. Consistent with the former novel, *The Moon and Sixpence* represents a notorious, and apparently structural, misogyny: unlike Philip Carey, the protagonist Charles Strickland redeems his abjection before women by violently rejecting them. Nonetheless, his contempt for women is remarkably similar to Carey's: "I can't overcome my desire, but I hate it; it imprisons my spirit. . . . Women are the instruments of my pleasure. I have no patience with their claim to be helpmates, partners, companions. . . . The soul of man wanders through the uttermost regions of the universe and she ["woman"] seeks to imprison it in the circle of her account book. . . ."[56] By repeating and reframing this paradigm, Maugham endorsed many misogynist suppositions of his time, whose literary advocates range from Kipling (*The Light That Failed* and *Stalky & Co.*) to D. H. Lawrence (*Aaron's Rod* and *The Plumed Serpent*). Whether the object is travel, art, or a nebulous idea of "independence," a woman's intractable opposition stymies this project's masculine drive.[57] Nina Baym has identified a similar phenomenon in North American literature: "In these stories, the encroaching, constricting, destroying society is represented with particular urgency in the figure of one or more women. [If a man] . . . is heterosexual—his lovers and spouses become the agents of a permanent socialization and domestication. Thus, although women are not the source of social power, they are experienced as such."[58] Maugham reproduces this mythology by ensuring that Carey's relationship with Sally Athenly resolves his ontological dilemma. Since the novel counterpoises marriage with exploration of foreign terrain and alternative sexuality, the paralyzing conformity of marriage expiates the risk of travel and the danger of alternative sexualities.[59]

Critics differ in their interpretation of this ending. Jerome Buckley argues that Carey's marriage to Sally is "idyllic,"[60] while Theodore Dreiser noted when the novel appeared, "All at once . . . the truth is forced upon you that there has been a series of intimacies which have not been accounted for. . . . [I]t strikes one as strange."[61] Recently, Walter Allen corroborated this complaint by suggesting that "the fault of the novel lies . . . in the ending. . . . *Of Human Bondage* ends in a fake idyll."[62] Thus on the one hand, Maugham's recognition of this text as an "autobiographical novel" (3) renders its closure necessarily imaginary. On the other, this artifice overemphasizes the difference between Carey's choice of marriage and Maugham's initial resistance to domestic stability.

Although literary theory has clarified the difference in narrative voice between author and protagonist, Maugham often disturbed this distinction in his novels by his pronouncements on marriage: "There was no one I particularly wanted to marry. It was a condition that attracted me. *It seemed a necessary motif* in the pattern of life that I had designed. . . . It offered peace from the disturbance of love affairs." [63] We might also consider Maugham's comments on the relation between marriage and masculine ascription in light of *Of Human Bondage*'s conclusion: "The pattern I had designed for myself insisted that I should take the utmost part I could in this fantastic affair of being a man." [64] Finally, the novel's tortuous denial of homosexual desire may now seem stubbornly familiar: "Mer-my greatest [mistake] was this. I tried to persuade myself that I was three-quarters normal and that only one quarter of me was queer—whereas really it was the other way round." [65] This last citation is notable for its sexual imperative, and the sense that Maugham's identity split to sustain the appearance of being at least "three-quarters normal."

Although *Of Human Bondage* concludes with a "fake idyll" that relates poorly to its preceding drama,[66] the novel—like its protagonist—could not envisage bachelorhood, celibacy, suicide, or love for another man as an alternative to marriage. By substituting questions of projection, censorship, and self-division for an intractable problem of autobiography and authorial influence, the novel is clearly unable to resolve its prior concerns. I have argued that much of this difficulty derives from drives and compulsions that are immanent to the novel's protagonist, whose ensuing conflict throws heterosexual desire and masculine identification awry. Although the text refuses to investigate the meaning of these drives, the novel's conclusion illuminates their resilience by suggesting that an alternative for the narrative and its protagonist is impossible. As the final words declare with breathless haste and a bewildering lack of irony:

> "I wonder if you'll marry me, Sally."
> She did not move and there was no flicker of emotion on her face, but she did not look at him when she answered:
> "If you like."
> "Don't you want to?"
> "Oh, of course I'd like to have a house of my own, and it's about time I was settling down."
> He smiled a little. . . . "But don't you want to marry *me?*"
> "There's no one else I would marry."
> "Then that settles it." (700; original italics)

6

Managing
"The White Man's Burden":
The Racial Imaginary
of Forster's
Colonial Narratives

The Struggle to Connect

Are the sexes really races, each with its own code of morality,
and their mutual love a mere device of Nature to keep things
going? Strip human intercourse of the proprieties, and is it
reduced to this?
— E. M. Forster [1]

There is no such thing as ordinary democratic intimacy in
India; the cooli and I both knew that we were specializing.
We watched one another down architectural vistas.
— Forster [2]

How can psychoanalytic and postcolonial theory engage with E. M. Forster's
accounts of interracial desire? In this chapter, I follow recent theorists in
interpreting the difficult, often treacherous, terrain of interracial desire in
colonial literature; my aim is to foreground the ambivalent sexual and unconscious fantasies that underpin relations between colonizer and colonized in
Forster's writing.

145

Forster's treatment of colonial and sexual relations is particularly significant because he professed a liberal-humanist commitment to interracial friendship that often falters in his fiction. The gap between his political maxim that we must "only connect the prose and the passion" (174) and his private fantasies about the pain and price of this connection clarify the precarious quality of interracial desire in his fiction. To interpret this real and often antagonistic gap between Forster's politics and fiction, and again between his "public" novels about friendship and his "private" and posthumous stories about sex between men of different races, I want to compare *A Passage to India* (1924) with the short stories "The Life to Come" (1922) and "The Other Boat" (1915–16), arguing that Forster's accounts of racial difference often build on his assumptions of an intractable "geographical" divide between men and women. Though Forster assumed that this divide could be bridged to bring men of different races and nationalities into closer proximity, the result is often startling in its ambivalence: far from resolving political distance into personal connection, interracial sexuality usually compels Forster's characters to disavow or redefine the precise meaning of their national and sexual identities.

If same-sex racial integration was Forster's ideal, his fiction repeatedly failed to realize it. Though "Live in fragments no longer" is the imperative governing *Howards End* (174–75), Forster's short stories are suffused by sexual indeterminacy and colonial ambivalence, not class harmony and interracial romance. The political and psychic constituents of this ambivalence surface when we examine Forster's accounts of homosexuality, homophilia, and homophobia. Forster's difficulty in representing homosexual and racial intimacy raises unconscious meanings that resonate beyond his writing; his stories' oscillation between racially "similar" and "different" objects yields a complex interpretive interest by its epistemological and sexual uncertainty.

I want to begin by comparing the violence and ambivalence of Forster's sexual fantasies in his posthumous collection, *The Life to Come and Other Stories* (1972), with the following, relatively benign proposition in *A Passage to India:* "Between people of distant climes there is always the possibility of romance. . . ." In the context of the repeated failure of this possibility in that novel and in *The Life to Come,* we should note that Forster completed the sentence as follows: "but the various branches of Indians know too much about each other to surmount the unknowable easily." [3] If we attribute this difficulty in overcoming the "unknowable" to Indians' generic differences from Europeans, as Forster seemed to intend, where does his statement place the European's apparently "knowable" concerns and desires? Part of my purpose in asking this question is to determine the meaning of sexual desire for Forster's white characters and the possibility of sustained homosexual intimacy for men of different races, classes, and nations; Forster's narratives consistently frustrate these encounters by wounding or destroying the protagonists who attempt to fulfill them.

In many accounts of British colonial relations, an intimate bond between colonizer and colonized underpins economic mastery and subordination. Several theorists have claimed that this bond exceeded, and even displaced, the intimacy British men and women professed for one another. Ashis Nandy, for example, has argued that "white women in India were generally more exclusive and racist because they unconsciously saw themselves as the sexual competitors of Indian men, with whom their men had established an unconscious homo-eroticized bonding. It was this bonding which the 'passive resisters' and 'non-cooperators' exploited, not merely the liberal political institutions. They were helped in this by the split that had emerged in the Victorian culture between two ideals of masculinity . . . [T]he lower classes were expected to act out their manliness by demonstrating their sexual prowess; the upper classes were expected to affirm their masculinity through sexual distance, abstinence and self-control." [4] Though Nandy does not elaborate on the significance of this unconscious competition and bonding, I suggest that both factors clarify a psychic difficulty about race that impedes Forster's imperative to "connect." Forster tends to repress this difficulty in his political essays, though it surfaces repeatedly in his fiction as a conflict between a representation of racially divided heterosexuality and an apparently racially integrated model of same-sex romance. To understand this difficulty in connection, we need to consider Forster's often troubled relation to his writing and the publication history that informed his literary and colonial canonization; this canonization has shaped the way we interpret Forster's accounts of race and homosexuality.

Once critics and friends affirmed Forster's homosexuality—long an "open secret"—after his death in 1971 and retrieved a series of short stories and the novel *Maurice* for publication, they began to consider his "homosexual" writings first as a supplement to and then as a revision of his preceding work. Forster's long awaited and long overdue "outing" seemed to require an immediate and wholesale revision of his earlier novels in light of a new sexual truth; it also intensified discussion about his relation to the literary canon, and to modernism more generally.

In the context of Britain's sexual conservatism, it is perhaps unsurprising that Forster's fiction was an embarrassment to friends and critics anxious to defend his fantasies from such a "tarnish," and to set his own canon of texts—*A Passage to India, Howards End, The Longest Journey,* and *Where Angels Fear to Tread*—apart from the influence of his unfortunate "homosexual pornography." [5] Both proponents and opponents of this rereading, however, saw in the discovery of Forster's homosexuality a challenge to the ostensible heterosexuality of his earlier novels that they either freely encouraged or fiercely resisted. No one, it seems, questioned the inevitability of this wholesale revision and the assumption behind it that Forster's fiction should fall conclusively on either side of a concrete sexual binary. Besides the assumptions of authorial intention and psychobiography that framed these debates, additional problems emerged for those who sought to reinterpret his earlier work within the field of sexual meaning.

The first debate expressed fear about homosexuality's specificity in Forster's short stories and *Maurice* and a concern that readers would glean this interest without appreciating the works' "broader" or "universal" thematic—that is, the story is about love; we shouldn't express too much interest in the fact that it involves two (or three) men.[6] The second concerned the representation of women in Forster's earlier fiction, arguing that heterosexuality masquerades in the place of Forster's primary or authentic homosexual interest; accordingly, his women are merely foils in a romance that Forster would have debunked had he the opportunity, or courage, to write otherwise. John Sayre Martin remarked that "Forster's homosexuality may help to account for his generally unconvincing portrayal of heterosexual feeling," a peculiar statement that Samuel Hynes endorsed from a position of unarguable truth: "Most obviously, Forster could not imagine any aspect of the range of experience between men and women—heterosexual attraction, heterosexual relations, and marriage were mysterious to him. No wonder he resented having to write 'marriage novels'—the subject was quite beyond his range." [7] According to this reading, not only are Forster's women distorted men, but Forster is wholly unconvincing when representing women because they are uninteresting to him and beyond his experience. The point of course assumes that lesbians and gay men have no knowledge of a sexual preference their parents, peers, and culture coerce them relentlessly to adopt, a presumption of ignorance and uninterest that never seems to apply to heterosexual writers, critics, and film directors, who represent homosexuality with whatever perspective and authority seem appropriate to them at the time. Apart from their specific relation to Forster, the naiveté and anxiety that inform these assumptions attest to homosexuality's strictures and the dearth of symbolic positions it can occupy in modern writing and culture.

Recall Forster's ambivalence about sexual representation and textual resolution, however, and it is possible to read the earlier novels for their sexual *indeterminacy,* in which various narrative impulses pursue different, and finally incommensurate, aims. The gap between the object and aim of Forster's texts would therefore mark the influence of drives that turn his representations awry. In this way, we can read an implicit and impalpable homosexuality in tension with the narrative's avowal of heterosexuality, in which the ensuing oscillation makes both and neither possible. Forster's own homosexuality cannot occlude, redeem, or substitute for the heterosexual interest of his characters; the faltering of this interest—and the narratives' failure to develop others—becomes a point of interpretation that cannot rewrite his literary project.[8] This approach disrupts the assumption that texts simply reproduce their author's history; yet we must still address the intertextual dialogue between Forster's novels and short stories, especially in the context of his interest in literary censorship.

Writing Homosexuality at Home and Abroad: Censorship and the Literary Taboo

What the public really loathes in homosexuality is not the thing itself, but having to think about it. . . .
—E. M. Forster[9]

Physical love means reaction, being panic in essence. . . .
—Forster[10]

Many critics have noted that despite his continuing production of essays, criticism, and biography, Forster published no fiction after *A Passage to India* in 1924.[11] His decision to write nonfiction thereafter, and to foreclose the publication of *Maurice* after its completion in 1913–14, suggests that the difficulty of sexual relations in texts before *A Passage to India* contributed to its geopolitical terrain. Although Forster wrote the earlier novels at close intervals between 1905 and 1914, and the public received them favorably, the choice of material for subsequent texts seemed to generate much experiential and literary anxiety.

Entries in Forster's diary and correspondence with friends confirm this difficulty. In 1911, Forster explained his "weariness of the only subject that I both can and may treat—the love of men for women and vice-versa."[12]

The remark shows the effect of external and internal constraints on his writing; censorship impeded both. However, Forster's statement acquires more significance when we connect it to the short stories, the earliest of which he produced alongside the novels; it illustrates a creative conflict over whether to write about one subject under the pretext of representing another (in this instance, heterosexuality for homosexuality) by suppressing the creative impulse, or whether to adopt a subject from internal choice and return censorship to the public notion of obscenity by risking social and legal humiliation. As his publication history testifies, Forster wavered between each option, first "distorting," not transforming, the initial material (the early novels), then establishing an "authentic" and private relation to it without the public crisis publication would generate (*Maurice*). However, Forster returned to an ambiguous compromise (*A Passage to India*) before disbanding the fictional project altogether as an unworkable procedure. It is interesting that his decision not to publish *Maurice* seemed to exacerbate, rather than relieve, this conflict between impulse and representation; the completion of this novel greatly unsettled Forster's production, leaving *Arctic Summer* and *Nottingham Lace* as unfinished and discarded fragments.[13]

Forster's defense of other homosexual texts of the period generally supported a demand for their representation, though he made no reference to his own writing, perhaps to avoid the risk of public opprobrium.[14] During the trial of Radclyffe Hall's *The Well of Loneliness* in 1928, Forster published an article in *Nation and Athenæum* that supported the text without mentioning the subject of controversy—its lesbianism. Instead, he stressed the importance of not curtailing "the creative impulses" or the literary exploration of "forbidden areas."[15] Though clearly at odds with his own diagnosis, this perspective on homosexuality comforted literary authorities because its heuristic aims were analogous to the colonial export of knowledge to "undisciplined" peoples. Thus for Forster, the topography on which colonialism exerted its influence conflated political inquiry with psychic anxiety.

The following year (1929), Forster published another article, "The 'Censorship' of Books," that was more direct in its challenge to censorship, and attentive to the cause of the controversy: "Finally, I must touch, though very reluctantly, on the subject of homosexuality . . . [I]t enters personally into very few lives, and is uninteresting or repellent to the majority; nevertheless it exists, and this being the case, I do not see why writers who desire to treat it should be debarred from doing so—always providing that there is nothing pornographic in their treatment."[16] This passage's "scientific" precision and tortuous reticence suggest "a decent man with a conscience look[ing] squarely at a distasteful subject." [17] According to Forster, those who avow their homosexuality cannot claim it simply as their volition; homosexuality, like censorship, falls on a hapless minority with regrettable bad luck. Notwithstanding his embarrassment, Forster was wrong to assume that the subject was "uninteresting . . . to the majority"; the fear that homosexuality was "contagious" lent some urgency to its attempted eradication from public consciousness in Britain and its colonies.[18]

Forster's impassive relation to homosexuality indicates more than political expediency; his allegiance wavered between scientific disinterest and dishonest respectability. Many years later, when T. S. Eliot and he were elected as literary representatives of the 1958 Select Committee on Obscene Publications—a forerunner to the British Act of Parliament the following year—Forster declared: "Some authors—I do not say Mr. Eliot or myself—are inhibited by the harsh and at present uncertain position of the law as regards obscenity, and I think many of them wish to introduce scenes or phrases and hesitate to do so in case they get into trouble." [19]

With the manuscript of *Maurice* secured under lock and key beneath the note "Publishable, but worth it?" [20] Forster's innocuous disclaimer about censorship's effects on his own writing was transparently untrue. His statement indicates the strength of Britain's literary taboo, and the internal and external pressure that led him to excise homosexual desire from much of his fiction. Thus, the reception of *Maurice* in 1971 as an "apologia" for homosexuality is understandable,[21] though it is unclear why Forster did not publish it as such—similar to J. Addington Symonds's *Sexual Inversion* (1897) or Edward Carpenter's "Homogenic Love" (1895)[22]—or why it was not a more passionate vindication of homosexuality (like Forster's later short stories), since he decided to leave it unpublished. *Maurice* suffered the effects of a double censorship: besides not giving the text public exposure, Forster privately excised much of its eroticism, as if the very fact of writing the novel signified an unbearable exposure and a need for its immediate erasure.[23] D. H. Lawrence alluded to this difficulty when he made the following interesting observation about Forster: "He tries to dodge himself—the sight is painful. . . . He knows that *self-realisation is not his ultimate desire.*" [24] Lawrence's remark asks us to consider the implications of a desire in Forster's writing that is not heuristic or epiphanic, but which deliberately impedes interpretation and representation: this is the task of the present chapter.

Forster's troubled relation between creativity and sexual representation suggests that he neither discarded nor directly addressed the issue of homosexuality; he allowed it to surface on another terrain. If we reconsider my citation from *A Passage to India*—"Between people of distant climes there is always the possibility of romance . . ." (264–65)—we might argue, following George Steiner, that *A Passage to India* partially fufilled *Maurice*'s idealistic closure by making Aziz and Fielding's interracial friendship displace the later novel's unresolved homosexual intimacy. Steiner observed: "The encounters between white and native, between emancipated rulers and 'advanced' Indians, in *A Passage to India,* are a brilliant projection of the confrontations between society and the homosexual in *Maurice.*" [25] Beyond the idea of creative possibility, this suggests that a shift in geography was the condition for homosexuality tangentially to reemerge in Forster's texts; he transposed the problem of homosexuality onto race and colonialism. This analogy pits travel against domestic constraints, representing exile as the condition through which an otherwise impossible homosexual drama could fleetingly emerge.[26]

Forster seemed to adopt this perspective about exile on several occasions: he wrote a series of fantasies that elaborate, manage, and compress an almost insoluble disjuncture in Britain between homosexuality's creative expression and its public representation. Forster's fantasies also mark the transition between his fictional and nonliterary writing, though their fictional terrain is significant because it describes a passage between Europe, Africa, or the Subaltern, and a mythical atopia. These fantasies rarely occur on British soil, and when they do, Forster represents their setting by either abstract or pastoral terms.[27] The following accounts of Forster's short stories frame this issue of setting through the lens of fantasy and physical intimacy. I want to underscore the terms permitting Forster's literal and conceptual relation between homosexuality and race, and the real and imaginary ground on which he was able and willing for it to occur.

Fantasy and the Difficulty of Difference

"I wish we were labelled," said Richie. He wished that all the confidence and mutual knowledge that is born in such a place as Cambridge could be organized. People went down into the world saying, "We know and we like each other; we shan't forget." But they did forget, for man is so made that he cannot remember long without a symbol.
—E. M. Forster [28]

The structure of a friendship is seldom submitted to analysis until it comes under pressure.
— Paul Scott [29]

Since Forster never intended his short stories for more than a discreet dissemination among close friends, they could avoid an antagonistic public reception. All the same, Forster held a characteristically ambivalent response toward them, writing at one moment to Edward Garnett, "I think them better than my long books" [30] and at another, without apparent explanation, deciding to "burn . . . my indecent writings or as many as the fire will take. Not a moral repentance, but [from] the belief that they clogged me artistically. They were written not to express myself but to excite myself . . . [and] they were a wrong channel for my pen." [31]

As I suggested earlier, the precise constituents of this "right" channel were, for Forster, an ongoing concern. On the one hand, "expression" and "excite[ment]" needed to converge for his writing to be fluid and inspiring; on the other, the shame that forced them apart ensured that his prose became unexciting — even in private he was afraid of saying too much, and of being unable to escape public censure. Though excitement rarely is responsible for internal "clogging," Forster's short stories are a residue of "acceptable" fantasy that he wrote before the First World War. Those fantasies that Forster excised of, or rendered merely allusive to, homosexual content he published individually and then as two collections, *The Celestial Omnibus* (1911) and *The Eternal Moment* (1928);[32] he deferred those stories that were obstinate in their sexual expression for posthumous publication under the title *The Life to Come and Other Stories* (1972).[33]

Since most Forster criticism has been evaluative rather than interpretive, appraising the short stories' relative merits or aesthetic "failure," it has generally proclaimed them as inferior to his novels. Critics usually note their "whimsy" and sentimentality before retelling their plot in a summary almost as long as the stories themselves.[34] Post–1972 criticism that has not ignored *The Life to Come* collection has often dismissed the stories as "puerile" and "guilt-ridden," [35] "tepid and ultimately joyless," [36] and a general cause for embarrassment. Donald Salter struck a characteristic note when he opined, "There is no doubt that one's unease regarding some of the relationships in the stories and novels derives from their disguised homosexual nature." [37]

In the earlier, "self-censored" collections (*The Celestial Omnibus* and *The Eternal Moment*), Forster actively inhibits the free movement of narrative, leading each fantasy to the brink of a development before forestalling and incongruously resolving it. In this respect, "whimsy" and "sentiment" perform a *peripeteic* function by tidying up the loose strands of sexual allusion through either a chance encounter or an intervening and abstract figure of myth. In the posthumous collection of short stories, Forster's elaboration of sexual fantasy tended to be freer; however—and this is my interest—the sexual tension that accompanied Forster's explicit accounts of homosexuality in *The Life to Come* tended to compress his anxiety, not diffuse it. In each collection, the management of sexual tension and violence is instructive; we must therefore consider their palpable and often unsuccessful suppression in the earlier stories and their inexplicable eruption in much of the posthumous collection.

Virginia Woolf, one of Forster's most perceptive early readers, drew attention to this tension when she wrote of his first collection, "The vein of fantasy is not deep enough or strong enough to fight single-handed against those impulses which are part of his endowment. We feel that he is an uneasy truant in fairyland." [38] For Woolf, fantasy was not an appropriate or "natural" form for Forster's stories but rather a device he chose for its displacement of idea and content. Since Forster was unable or unwilling to develop each narrative's impulse, he appeared to turn it away, protecting it by a strategic clinamen. Every story's deliberate confusion and atopia appear to obscure the narrative's intention by releasing the story from a demand to make sense.[39] As Woolf maintained, however, in its failure to hide the pressure behind each narrative impulse, Forster's displacement of content created a fight that was all the more obvious for his efforts to smother it. As she wrote of the earlier novel, *The Longest Journey,* with relevance to his short stories' conflict of form and content: "The neat surface is always being thrown into disarray by an outburst of lyric poetry." [40] Woolf's sentence deftly captures Forster's efforts to subdue with poetry this conflict; nothing but an overemphatic lyricism could salvage his stories from their recurrent, internal antagonisms.

Forster's fantasies often bog down in their attempt to impede the free association of ideas and to silence the outburst of desire with which fantasy repeatedly collides. Though Forster's caution over narrative desires inhibited his fantasies' artistic success, they are worthy of study precisely for this reason. David Shusterman claims they are weak because "The author . . . was not entirely sure what he wanted to show in them. Consequently, in most of them the thought and the symbol do not always meet and merge; the idea is often . . . ambiguous. . . ." [41] However, the ideas informing these narratives also confront an insurmountable resistance, as if Forster wanted fantasy to empty and disperse its contents before it could attach to a symbol.

Forster exemplifies this resistance in an obtuse chapter of *Aspects of the Novel* (1927).[42] Despite this text's expositional aims, Forster's definition of fantasy clarifies only his attempt to retain its unreliable mystery. Veiling fantasy by obscurity, Forster defines it as an elliptical investment, which "asks [the reader] to pay something extra [and to] compel us to an adjustment" (103). Forster displaces this "something" by another metaphor "that cuts across them [a novel's 'time or people or logic'] like a bar of light" (102). Thus the reader can understand fantasy only by what it requires—the suspension of narrative disbelief. In an oblique reference to "divings into and dividings of personality" (106), Forster then displaces this "something" in turn by "the *fantastic*"—a realm of fiction that he defines by its transcendence, ephemera, and textual improbability.

What comes out of Forster's account of fantasy are the qualities that realism resists, cannot explore, and consigns to the responsibility of "another world" (106). The title of Forster's later collection of stories, *The Life to Come,* is interesting in this regard because it refers to a future uncoupled from any direct or necessary relation to the present. Forster defers homosexuality as a narrative code in this collection because its immediate realization is perhaps unimaginable. In other words, the futurity is convenient for displacing the present difficulty of incorporating homosexuality in psychic and symbolic terms and for demonstrating the conflict and alienation this incorporation would entail for Forster's narrative.

If we examine the closing scene of *A Passage to India* in these terms, it clarifies some of the tension surrounding the novel's attempt at such an incorporation: the ending refuses to develop or curtail Aziz and Fielding's intimacy; geography intervenes, bringing their contact to a provisional halt without irreparable damage. The novel's closing sentences foreground a drama about the men's sexual intimacy and the abstract forces that keep them apart:

> "We shall drive every blasted Englishman into the sea, and then" —[Aziz] rode against him furiously—"and then," he concluded, half kissing him, "you and I shall be friends."
>
> "Why can't we be friends now?" said the other [Fielding], holding him affectionately. "It's what I want. It's what you want."
>
> But the horses didn't want it—they swerved apart; the earth didn't want it, sending up rocks through which riders must pass single file;

the temples, the tank, the jail, the palace, the birds, the carrion, the Guest House, that came into view as they issued from the gap and saw Mau beneath: they didn't want it, they said in their hundred voices: "No, not yet," and the sky said: "No, not there." (316)[43]

Forster's anxiety about fantasy's acceptable and controllable limits transformed his preoccupation with travel into a metaphor for psychic and symbolic exploration. His stress on the effort of the journey, and the mapping of points among what he anticipated, feared, and knew, clarifies a passage between external boundaries and internal constraints by using one set to elaborate the other. For example, "The Celestial Omnibus" charts a journey from imaginary to epistemological borders ("What is that out there? . . . What does it rest on, out at the other end?" [Collected, 49]), while "The Other Side of the Hedge" frames a boundary, and a space beyond, without clarifying whether each is a religious parable, a symbol of the unknown, or a sexual limit briefly transgressed. Passing to the other side of the hedge, the walker meets a man who "trace[s] . . . its moist margin," and he assures the first man that the road is the same as before—it only·"doubles so often that it is never far from our boundary and sometimes touches it" (38). At the story's close, the man is "gently lowered" into sleep, allowing Forster to imagine an intimacy that also "hedges" with words; the story concludes before he need take it any further.

At other moments in these stories, an external force that substitutes for the author's conventional explanation interrupts the urge to connect. In "Story of a Panic" (1904), Pan disbands an intimate friendship between two boys, Eustace and Gerrano, that is alarming to their adult overseers. They worry because Gerrano has a different nationality and class, though the boys' growing affection, which these differences support and even precipitate, seems to cause them more alarm. The panic that Forster recounts is also ambiguous: it may obtain from the sudden presence of Pan, who sweeps over Eustace, leaving him delirious, or from the horror of reciprocal passion between two boys that precedes—or finds its appropriate answer in—this mythological intrusion. In either case, panic does not derive from the boys who enjoy each other; it lies with the witnesses who consider "this habit of promiscuous intimacy . . . perfectly intolerable," "an affront to us all" (Collected, 22, 23). After the observing party sends Gerrano to the woods to find Eustace, they overhear "absurd cries of pleasure from the poor boy" (29). The adults later confine Eustace, who attempts to escape with Gerrano before fleeing to the woods alone in delirious laughter. The figure of Pan is clearly incidental to this drama—Pan is its symptom, not its cause—for the group's panic returns obsessively to the problem of the boys' affection rather than

Eustace's disappearance. Whether the panic is finally about masturbation or homosexuality is difficult to determine (consider, for instance, the general thematic proximity between "Eustace" and "ecstasy"); the drama pursues and then disbands this investigation.[44]

In many other texts by Forster, woodland ruptures the sexual and familial constraints of the city by promising freedom from conventional authority. *Maurice* ends with a retreat to the boathouse and beyond, for the novel requires a zone of imaginary sanctuary for Maurice and Scudder.[45] The same is true of "The Celestial Omnibus," "The Curate's Friend," and "The Other Kingdom," in which the narrator describes the purchase and upkeep of an almost metaphysical garden: "The bridge is built, the fence finished and Other Kingdom lies tethered by a ribbon of asphalt to our front door" (*Collected*, 80). By the time Forster came to envisage "The Life to Come," however, the African "greenwood" in which its male protagonists have sex is smaller, less able to shield them, and no longer detached from the community's prurience. Instead the community mines the greenwood for its value, an ecological crime that brings disease and famine to the village; the concomitant destruction of its homosexual assailants is first a vindication of their passion and then a symbol of its impossibility.

Forster wrote "The Life to Come" in 1922, two years before he published *A Passage to India*. The short story anticipates and exceeds the novel's ambiguous resolution of interracial friendship by detailing sexual intimacy between an English missionary and an African prince. The shame surrounding their intimacy, and the extent to which the Englishman denies its meaning, suggests a complex emotional and physical attachment. The story elaborates each man's relation to his desire: the missionary, Paul Pinmay, is so troubled by guilt, he can recognize homosexual desire only by disavowal; the prince, Vithobai, is eager for contact without a need for explanatory vocabulary. The story represents one stereotype of sexual guilt (the white man consumed by it, the black man indifferent toward it) by reversing another: the myth, still current in many postcolonial cultures today, that homosexuality was a white man's export whose imposition precipitated a twofold emasculation of African culture.[46]

This account of interracial desire does not date from this century's independence movements. Let me briefly explain why: In the 1880s and the years that led up to Forster's writing "The Life to Come," the colonial crisis over miscegenation and interracial desire intensified in a series of public scandals, most of them heterosexual. While the French and Portuguese empires often encouraged miscegenation to consolidate their cultural and linguistic influence, the British introduced a policy of racial and sexual separation to retain the "purity" — and the alleged moral and political "integrity" — of their colonial practice.[47] Critics have traced this policy to the Indian "Mutiny" in 1857; the ensuing British distrust contributed to a number of violent campaigns in other British colonies in the 1880s and 1890s, most notably in the East Africa Protectorate (now Uganda, Kenya, Burundi, and Tanzania) and Northern and Southern Rhodesia (now Zambia and Zimbabwe). Besides this colonial distrust, Britain introduced its own legacy of sexual anxiety from the Purity movement of the 1880s and 1890s by condemning prostitution, vagrancy, abortion, and homosexuality at home and across many parts of the globe.[48] At the turn of the century, as British officials boasted in a much-touted figure, Britain had administrative control over one-third of the world.

Britain's administrative power over international policy meant that London could disseminate orders for sexual restraint across Britain's colonies with relative ease, regulating local administrations by punitive measures and threats of dismissal. One of Britain's first legislative interventions into its colonies' sexual practice, the Crewe Circular of 1909 was a key instance of this pressure. Although not mentioned in the circular, homosexuality was a sufficient preoccupation to influence all public policy on sexuality. Previous examples of homosexual panic and legislation included the Dublin Castle officials scandal in 1884 and the Cleveland Street scandals in 1889–90, Britain's introduction of flogging for homosexual soliciting in 1889, Wilde's trials in 1895, and various other drives to check soliciting between 1901 and 1906.[49] To this extent, homosexuality was implicit in the circular's admonitions, just as the decision not to criminalize lesbianism in Britain in 1885 did not guarantee its freedom from juridical control, then or now.[50]

Although the Crewe Circular intensified the sexual prejudice of late-Victorian British culture, the factors that prompted it were entirely specific: a scandal in Kenya in which Hubert Silberrad, an Englishman, refused to pay the customary *lobola,* or bride-price, for a twelve- or thirteen-year-old Kenyan girl with whom he had had sex.[51] Silberrad had previously "adopted" two other girls of a similar age, and was finally reported to the local governor by his affronted neighbors, Mr. and Mrs. Routledge. Although British administrations tried to leave sexual relations a private concern unless the public brought them to attention, the colonial office was unable to ignore Silberrad's case and decided to condemn interracial affairs as an "injurious and dangerous" evil.[52] Their report became a significant intervention in private behavior and colonial authority; the Silberrad controversy was synecdochic of Britain's concern about its national reputation and moral purity abroad. Writing to the

London *Times* in January of the same year (1909), for instance, T. F. Victor Buxton deplored the absence of "a high moral standard" in the colonies. He went on to say: "If . . . we are to rise to our responsibilities as an Imperial race—if we are not to bring grievous discredit upon the Christianity we profess—it is essential that those who represent us abroad should be clean living men, whose conduct may command the respect of the peoples they govern." [53] Correspondence in the *Times* and *The Spectator* during this period amplified Buxton's opinion by conjoining debates on "women suffrage in India" with the need to maintain "the loyalty of the classes and the contentment of the masses." The British press also discussed "Indo-English Marriages" as a problem of twinning Christianity with Hinduism or Islam without losing the religious or cultural integrity of the former to either of the latter.[54] While the *Times*'s editorials about the Silberrad case insisted that "the honour of Britain was at stake," *The Spectator* went further in claiming: "It would mean nothing short of ruin to the Empire if we were once to allow the notion to get abroad that men charged with the duties of administration can be permitted to exercise the tremendous powers placed in their hands to gratify their animal passions. If we fail to punish with the utmost severity men who have used their official position for purposes such as the official in question is said to have used his, then the ruin of the Empire must be at hand." [55] Britain's press repeatedly implied a correlation between political domination and sexual self-mastery by assuming that the abandonment of sexual restraint would precipitate colonial insurrection. This threat helped to endorse the belief that sexual havoc was an immediate precursor to moral and political degeneration.

For an account of this imaginary threat and its culmination in the Crewe Circular, we need only turn to Richard Meinertzhagen's *Kenya Diary (1902–1906)*. Meinertzhagen was an official in Britain's East Africa Protectorate; his diary is riddled with accounts of presumed "infractions" and violently excessive punishments. On June 7, 1902, for instance, he recorded the following scenario:

> Last week I brought a man to orderly room for insubordination; he told his sergeant that his mother was a crocodile and his father a hyæna. Bailey sentenced him to 25 lashes. As his company officer I had to witness the flogging. The culprit was lashed to a triangle, his breeches were removed, and he was then flogged by a hefty Sudanese with a strip of hippopotamus hide; he was bleeding horribly when it was over and I was nearly sick. I hated and resented the punishment so furiously that I went off to the orderly room and

expressed my thorough disgust at such brutal punishment, which I thought should be ordered only in cases of violence or cruelty; and said that a flogging should always be automatically followed by discharge, for how can a man have any self-respect left after a brutal public flogging? Bailey and Mackay gaped in astonishment, told me I was squeamish, that I did not understand the African and that it was gross impertinence questioning an orderly room punishment.[56]

Two weeks later, Meinertzhagen substituted a new event resonating with comparable voyeurism and sexual disgust for the previous scene of punishment: "In the afternoon the natives gave us a treat. A large party of young men and girls danced together for many a hot hour. To my mind the dance was most suggestive and immoral, but that did not make it any the less interesting. I imagine the origin of all dancing is to incite or play on the sexual senses." [57] Just over one year later, Meinertzhagen reported excitedly on the thrills of "pig-sticking" and the emotional intensity of killing animals with other men;[58] by November 15, 1905, however, he had begun to rue Africa's influence on his psychic "deterioration," with remarks that Haggard's account of racial and psychic proximity endorsed in chapter 2. Meinertzhagen's regret is so detailed in its many displacements, it is worth quoting at length:

Normally I am healthy-minded, but the worries and conditions of the past few months have been too much for me. All men are not affected in the same way. Others with greater strength of character than myself might suffer little from moral and intellectual starvation. To others, natural history or some object of unceasing pursuit is an effective barrier against complete isolation. But my experience shows me that it is but a small percentage of white men whose characters do not in some way or another *undergo a subtle process of deterioration* when they are compelled to live for any length of time among savage races and under such conditions as exist in tropical climates. It is hard to resist the savagery of Africa when one falls under its spell. *One soon reverts to one's ancestral character, both mind and temperament becoming brutalised.* I have myself felt *the magnetic power* of the African climate drawing me lower and lower to the level of a savage. This is a condition which is accentuated by worry or mental depression, and which *has to be combated with all the force in one's power.* My love of home and my family, *the dread of being eventually overcome by savage Africa, the horror of losing one's veneer of western civilisation* and cutting adrift from all one holds good—these are the forces which help me to *fight the temptation to drift down to the temporary luxury of the civilisation of the savage.*[59]

What is perhaps most striking about Meinertzhagen's account is his ceaseless juxtaposition of temptation and restraint with longing and delight. As his diary recounts in minute detail, Meinertzhagen failed so often to refuse savagery's "temporary luxury" that the narrative appears to ritualize this failure by other, more palatable, forms of enjoyment. We might even suggest that the narrative's oscillation between guilt and pleasure manifests its own internal excuse for colonial seduction. In this respect, our difficulty lies in distinguishing Meinertzhagen's behavior and testimony from the practices of British administrations that he partly represented. As Forster would demonstrate in "The Life to Come," Meinertzhagen's hypocrisy was synecdochic not only of British administrative policy in eastern and southern African, but also the grain of this deceit at the precise level of sexual drives.

The Crewe Circular that dealt with comparable infractions and dilemmas was sent to all British colonies, with the exception of the Federated Malay States, Malta, Gibraltar, South Africa, and Northern and Southern Rhodesia. It warned that "concubinage with girls or women belonging to the native population . . . [would be considered an] instance . . . of misconduct . . . which would result . . . in scandal and grave discredit to the public service." [60] It urged established officials to "spare no effort to diminish these abuses," [61] and warned the new recruit that "such practices . . . lower . . . himself in the eyes of the natives, and diminish . . . his authority to an extent which will seriously impair his capacity for useful work . . . [by bringing] disgrace and official ruin . . . from any dereliction of duty. . . ." [62] Also relevant to establishing my reading of Forster is the *Church Missionary Review*'s ambivalence in an editorial conceding that though Routledge had served "the honour of the ruling race in Africa" by his complaint against Silberrad, its readers should remember the better side of the "white intrusion," such as the work of the medical missions.[63]

In 1886, several decades before the Silberrad controversy, a bitter public scandal involved the church when the king of Buganda executed converts to Catholicism and Protestantism in reaction to European evangelism and its fervent denunciation of homosexuality.[64] Before this massacre, British missionaries had warned their religious converts that they would not tolerate "crimes against nature" (i.e., sodomy) in the court of Mwanga. Thus I am arguing that Britain's fears about African homosexuality had considerable impact on the sensitivity of colonial officials in Kenya, and their precipitous treatment of Silberrad's pedophilia in 1908. While these issues raged throughout Britain's Parliament and across its empire between 1906 and 1929, for instance, British officials raised concern about the practice of polygyny in East Africa and female clitoridectomy in Kenya. These factors suggest that Britain's hostile response to African homo- and heterosexuality not only informed its Crewe Circular but also influenced sexual practices and beliefs in the British Empire, and shaped many of the sexual determinants of Forster's colonial writing.[65]

The death of almost one hundred Ugandans in the massacre of 1886 is arguably a powerful precursor to Forster's 1922 story "The Life to Come." Vithobai, with his rank as a prince and his unembarrassed homosexuality, shares an analogous plight to Mwanga.[66] Indeed, Forster's association of African homosexuality with the clandestine affairs of a white missionary reiterated the brutal effects of Christian hypocrisy in Africa in the 1910s and 1920s by implicating the church in a practice it repeatedly condemned.

Forster's disdain for religious zeal underpinned his general antipathy toward the church and men like Meinertzhagen; he criticized the missionary's belief that he or she exports a system of ethics quite different from or superior to native Africans. Besides its imposition of colonial values, evangelism works by scourging sexual pleasure: the missionary Paul Pinmay strenuously "sublimates" his homosexuality to punish the native for failing to repress his own. Forster elaborates on the hypocrisy of this scenario through Vithobai's ironic confusion between religious and homosexual conversion: in "The Life to Come" homosexuality is an act of sublime faith. Vithobai also scorns the missionary's demand for sexual askesis to comply with God's "Law"; both men find this injunction impossible to obey.

Once urged to "embrace" Christianity, Vithobai confuses the religion with its proponent and reintroduces a banished sexual component to religious worship. Though the narrative risks endorsing a stereotype about the intransigent native, Vithobai's naiveté draws out the spurious and dishonest aims of the missionary's faith. Vithobai's insistence, "God orders me to love you," finds no other response than Paul's confused retort, "He orders me to refrain." [67] In this tale, different ethical systems and notions of pleasure manipulate God's word; Vithobai's desire draws out the muddled precepts of a religion that encourages devotion to God while forbidding demonstrative love for another man. The missionary's hypocrisy transforms the words of St. Paul, and the ambiguous, biblical commands of Romans and Leviticus, into an anxiety about physical intimacy and a horror of the body's drives.[68] By redefining religious conflict as a drama about the interpretation of sexuality, Forster unravels the internal forms of control that religion tries to impose on each protagonist. Vithobai's indifference to any distinction between love for God and love for another man implies that he is a more successful Christian because phobia does not define or delimit his affection. While Paul suffers from a frantic demand for self-control, for instance, Vithobai—like the unconscious—recognizes few differences between homo- and heterosexual objects.[69]

This division between sexual and racial relations recurs throughout Forster's writing. As June Perry Levine argued recently, his fiction tends to construct a division between "tame" and "savage" elements of personality.[70] These elements do not coexist in each partner but define one or the other's exclusive property; a relatively simple schema aligns each character with a specific set of traits. To this structural division of tame and savage qualities, Forster adds other elements and values: the "tame" lover conventionally is moral, independently wealthy, well-educated, and white (Maurice, Paul in "The Life to Come," Fielding in *A Passage to India,* and Lionel in "The Other Boat" are obvious examples). Conversely, the "savage" man generally represents Forster's idealized notion of the working-class hero as self-educated, poor, and enticingly amoral. Insofar as each "savage" partner represents otherness, his marginal properties signify a virile rebellion against orthodox behavior. (This type includes Scudder in *Maurice,* Gerrano in "Story of a Panic," Vithobai in "The Life to Come," Cocoanut in "The Other Boat," and Aziz in *A Passage to India.*) As Perry Levine argues, if tame characters precariously retain "civilized" power, their "savage" counterpart displays greater integrity because he is considered at ease with the environment's "natural" authority.[71] This clarifies Forster's axiom that the "savage" lover is closer to nature and sexual freedom; civilized power emasculates the "tame" hero, leaving him vulnerable to the hostility of heterosexual culture.

Forster's "savage" characters demonstrate less commitment to homosexuality than do their "tame" lovers, so their relationship to homosexuality is less inhibited and reliable, due to their marginal relation to culture. Paradoxically, the "savage" man's relation to nature creates an assurance of masculinity, which his homosexuality does not compromise but enhances. Wrapped in tortuous self-interrogation and sexual guilt, the "tame" man's cerebral understanding of his desire defines him as both more and less homosexual than the man he chooses for a partner. While the anxiety of sexual self-definition emasculates the hero by robbing him of spontaneity and bisexual variance, the "savage" partner's physical confidence is defiantly independent of the social-symbolic order. Forster's well-known fantasy of an aggressive working-class lover is not unrelated to this scenario; it adds tension to that lover's sexual indeterminacy, as if the pleasure of a drifting hetero-sexual were more alluring and intriguing than sustainable intimacy with a committed homosexual.[72]

This idealization of sexual fluidity inverts the power relation in-forming each "tame" and "savage" partnership. Though the "savage" man is always at an economic and cultural disadvantage, the "tame" man's sexual and emotional dependence on his partner gives the latter enough psycho-logical power to redeem the former's sexual guilt. The "tame" man never possesses an independent sexual identity; he valorizes this element as the "savage" man's attractive—and threatening—quality. Since the "tame" man's projection onto his beloved also disinhibits his sexual anxiety, this produces a binding, and often violent, transference: in "The Life to Come" and "The Other Boat," both Vithobai and Cocoanut pay for this sexual guilt with their lives. This scenario of "tame" and "savage" qualities resonates in both these stories in sexual and racial terms, so it is worth considering Forster's premise about masculine friendship or homophilia more closely.

In *Maurice,* a scene in the British Museum usefully illustrates the in-version of Forster's ideal scenario: Alec Scudder interrupts Maurice's roman-tic allusion to Greek homophilia by threatening him with blackmail.[73] The scene jars with the bulk of the novel in which the men fall in love and elope to the boathouse: an imperative governs the text that their romance succeed; they must overcome all disequivalences between "civilized" and "savage" power. The fantasy of otherness that Alec represents for the novel is clearly at odds with the narrative's insistence that romantic love between two men can endure both external and internal opposition; the power differential between Alec and Maurice that is first a prerequisite to their desire must also vanish to sustain their intimacy. Forster's solution was to leave Maurice socially inse-cure, since his sexual and emotional happiness is incompatible with a "tame" desire for economic comfort. Rather than "emasculate" Alec by drawing him—and homosexual desire—into the social field, Forster disparaged the at-tempt, leaving the lovers to banish themselves before their community forced them to exile.

As an early reader of Forster's manuscript, Lytton Strachey disputed the permanence of Forster's characters' attachment, and their ability to live in virtual isolation did not convince him.[74] While *Maurice* draws on a mythology of romantic love as socially exclusive and self-sufficient, there is clearly an underside to this fantasy that *Maurice* and *A Passage to India* cannot permit—a relation that I would argue is one of profound dependency on, and ambivalence toward, the beloved. As Forster's literary and sexual ambivalence demonstrates, each novel elaborates this underside in a supplemental narrative.[75] "The Life to Come" arguably is to *A Passage to India* what "The Other Boat" is to *Maurice;* Forster could achieve the literary success of the novels only by substituting one fantasy (of difference, violence, and ambivalence) for another (of friendship, intimacy, and solidarity).

This distinction between homophilia and homosexuality allows us to read sexual antagonism in Forster's texts as responsible for much of their narrative violence. According to the logic of homophilia, one man claims to find his other unthreatening because he represents the other's difference as the basis of their attachment. However, homosexual desire in Forster appears to shatter this idealism because it represents the other's difference as violently at odds with the friendship that homophilia dictates. In the move from novel to short story, Forster oscillates between these familiar and unfamiliar accounts of friendship and sexual relations, though this movement always hinges on the violent management and final erasure of racial difference.

In his political writing, Forster's anti-imperialism often attests to this difficulty of neutralizing racial difference: the maxim "only connect" derives from his belief that humanity can surmount the diverse formations of culture and language of which it consists. Whatever ideal this expresses, its failure manifests as a displacement of colonial subjection and exploitation. I suggest that liberalism is inattentive to historical antagonisms because it ignores unconscious hostility, suspicion, and aversion toward the other. Forster is significant in this respect because he projects this antagonism onto the colonized at the precise moment that his colonizer denies responsibility for his cultural and economic advantage. Thus Forster's liberalism permits a conscious (and even conscientious) tolerance of diversity by repressing its accompanying structural ambivalence.[76] Since Forster requires certain ideas about class, race, and sexuality to stay at the margins of his novels, these ideas acquire immense significance in his literary fantasies. This may explain why he experienced such difficulty in making his fantasies available to an audience wider than his friends, and why the decision to represent fantasy added tension to an already acute ontological crisis. Forster usefully confirmed this problem in "What I Believe": "Psychology has split and shattered the idea of a 'Person,' and has shown us that there is something incalculable in each of us, which may at any moment rise to the surface and destroy our normal balance. We don't know what we are like. We can't know what other people are like. *How, then, can we put any trust in personal relationships, or cling to them in the gathering political storm? In theory we cannot. But in practice we can and do. . . .* For the purpose of living one has to assume that the personality is solid, and the "self" is an entity, and to ignore all contrary evidence.[77]

Insofar as they elaborate class and racial difference, then, *Maurice* and *A Passage to India* tell only one side of the story—the residue of ambivalence surfaces in their fictional supplements as a sign of Forster's limited tolerance. Here, benign difference transforms into a threatening antagonism in which the other wields an imaginary potency, which emerges from the discrepancy between the other's physical presence and the "tame" man's perception of his power. This discrepancy represents the "incalculable . . . something" that emerges between the "split and shattered . . . idea of a 'Person' " and the mistaken assumption that the "personality is solid." However, in Forster's terms, the other's potency is wholly unaccountable: the lovers of Paul ("The Life to Come") and Lionel ("The Other Boat") are affectionate and "supple" to a degree that would promote another fantasy of sexual malleability, were it not for the violence they finally enact. As the narrator of "The Life to Come" ironically explains by recounting Paul's troubled thoughts: "He had scarcely recognised the sardonic chief in this gracious and bare-limbed boy" (*Life*, 96).

In "The Life to Come," the narrative strives to understand the precise meaning of Paul and Vithobai's intimacy to recognize Paul's desire for Vithobai. Paul's mission splits between two incommensurate aims: to convert Vithobai to Catholicism and to accept his own sexual desire. The narrative implies that Paul's primary intention is Vithobai's sexual—not religious—conversion. This puts his missionary zeal in disrepute by emptying it of religious meaning and by disclosing its sexual ambition. Forster's willingness to combine a reluctant homosexual (Paul) with an influential homophobe (St. Paul) in his naming of the missionary is also astutely ironic: " 'Come to Christ!' he had cried, and Vithobai had said, 'Is that your name?' He explained No, his name was not Christ, although he had the fortune to be called Paul after a great apostle, and of course he was no god but a sinful man, chosen to call other sinners to the Mercy seat" (96). Neither Paul can judge Vithobai's repentance. As the narrator clarifies, however, this inability derives not from Vithobai's homosexual "sin" (which is ethically relative) but from the fact that Paul's self-deception projects all of his desire onto a reprehensible cause: "He confessed his defilement (the very name of which cannot be mentioned among Christians), he lamented that he had postponed, perhaps for a generation, the victory of the Church, and he condemned, with increasing severity, the arts of his seducer. On the last topic he became truly eloquent, he always found something more to say, and having begun by recommending the boy to mercy he ended by asking that he might be damned" (98). This shift from unmentionable "vice" to accusing those who do not resist it is carefully sardonic. Like the historic encounter in Buganda which it tropes, Vithobai succumbs to Christianity/Paul and renames himself "Barnabas," though his faith in sexual salvation mimics his "master's" failed religious ideals; Vithobai transforms religious service into a sexual demand.[78] In despair, Paul forbids all reference to their desire, destroys the hut in which they first have sex, and tries to persuade himself and Vithobai to marry women: Paul to counter fears for his respectability (the fear is entirely self-made); Vithobai to comply with his tribe's expectations. These constraints do not diminish homosexual desire; they give it an obsessional urgency that overcomes the impediment of marriage: Paul continues to "watch him furtively" (107) while urging Vithobai to atone and repent. Paul draws more heavily on projection (while Forster leans more heavily on Christian hypocrisy) by reconverting Vithobai in psychic terms into an abject figure, investing him with the severity of his own self-hatred: "Did God, in His mystery, demand from [Paul] that he should cleanse his brother's soul before his own could be accepted? The dark erotic perversion that the chief mistook for Christianity — who had implanted it? He had put this question from him in the press of his earlier dangers, but it intruded itself now that he was safe. Day after day he heard the cold voice of the somewhat scraggy and unattractive native inviting him to sin . . ." (106). Ironically, the rejection of homosexuality appears to *work* in Forster's narrative by "cleansing" Paul of desire and by recasting Vithobai as a sexual and rhetorical "bad object." In the process, Forster reactivates in Paul the mechanism he previously deplores;[79] the success of Paul's sexual redemption and projection leaves Vithobai vulnerable to racist accusation and violence.

This projection transforms Vithobai from a "boy wild with passion" into something "festering, equivocal, and perhaps acquiring some sinister power" (102, 108). Strangely, the narrative appears to endorse this change in perspective by moving from mockery of Paul's self-deception and hypocrisy to a palpable horror of Vithobai. This does not prevent contemporary readers from identifying fully with Vithobai's confusion and manifest betrayal; it simply means that the narrative fails to differentiate Paul's spiraling projection from its own. Though this perspective foregrounds the deceit of Paul's marriage, it judges Vithobai more harshly by failing to quell his sexual interest in Paul. When Vithobai avows this desire in a cart on their way to the forest, for instance, Paul's revulsion mirrors the narrator's alarm at Vithobai's indiscretion. By offering no response to Paul's hypocrisy, the narrative begins to rationalize his physical and psychic dread: "Without replying, Barnabas

handed him the reins, and then jerked himself out of the cart. It was a most uncanny movement, which seemed to proceed direct from the will. He scarcely
used his hands or rose to his feet before jumping. But his soul uncoiled
like a spring, and thrust the cart violently away from it against the ground.
Mr. Pinmay had heard of such contortions, but never witnessed them; they
were startling, they were disgusting. And the descent was equally sinister.
Barnabas lay helpless as if the evil uprush had suddenly failed" (105). After
Forster's previous indictment of Christian hypocrisy in "The Life to Come,"
the term "evil uprush" as a signifier for homosexual desire seems bizarre and
inexplicable. Besides the manner of his exit from the cart, Vithobai's reckless
expression — "which seemed to proceed direct from the will" — fuels the narrator's disdain, as if Vithobai's lack of restraint transforms Vithobai's desire
into something "startling . . . disgusting . . . sinister . . . [and] evil. . . ." This
fusing of racial difference and homosexual hostility is remarkably similar to
Aaron Sisson's contempt for the Indian doctor in D. H. Lawrence's *Aaron's
Rod,* also published in 1922: "He saw in the black, void, glistening eyes of the
Oriental only the same danger, the same menace which he saw in the land-
lady. Fair, wise, even benevolent words: always the human good speaking,
and always underneath, something hateful, something detestable and murderous. Wise speech, and good intentions — they were invariably *maggoty with
these secret lustful inclinations to destroy the man in a man.*" [80] The underside to Lawrence's "poisonous Indian viper" is a "secret lustful inclination";
Vithobai also apparently embodies a "dark erotic perversion" whose passion
is vulgar and unbearable because he cannot defer it until "the life to come"
(105). His demand for immediate gratification unleashes a monstrous, homosexual *jouissance* that resists the voice of Law and its punitive askesis. Ironically, the Lord's Prayer represents this conflict in the expression *Thy will be
done.* As Lacan quips in his commentary on this phrase, it implies: "[God]
is saying this to me, but what does he want?" [81] In Forster's story, "will" also
defines each character's psychic confusion: either to submit to a higher authority to ward off sexual distress, or to act on one's own will and experience
the terror and bliss of shattering each psychic and religious impediment. As
Vithobai admits to Paul in the throes of death, and in response to a plea that
he must finally surrender his will: "It was a deed . . . which now you call joy,
now sin" (109).

   With the scene of temptation briefly reversed, Paul offers religious
salvation by kissing Vithobai on the forehead: "Do not misunderstand me this
time . . . [it is] in perfect purity" (110). However, the act backfires because

the narrator represents Vithobai as the cause of Paul's seduction and downfall: "Mr. Pinmay feared to venture the kiss lest Satan took an advantage" (110). On the point of death, Vithobai corroborates this fear (at least for Paul and the narrator) by recovering a feverish energy, grabbing hold of a knife, and stabbing Paul in the heart. The act is so gratuitous and bathetic that the text hovers on the brink of farce. However, Vithobai's murder of Paul actually seems consistent with Forster's anxiety and the problem of managing colonial and sexual fantasy. As I suggested earlier in my account of "Story of a Panic," the closing frame of many Forster short stories interrupts and disbands what might otherwise spiral out of control. Although racial difference precipitates Paul and Vithobai's sexual encounter, difference is finally a horrifying trap from which Paul is unable to escape.

Since the narrative represents race as a violent problem, Forster appears to privilege restraint and discretion over the satisfaction of his characters' sexual desire. However, this caution (like Paul's anger) attributes each failure of sexual discretion to the colonized, whose lack of inhibition apparently represents psychic destruction and death. Thus the narrative aligns the colonized with the violent damage of *jouissance* by unmaking the subjective cohesion of its European lovers and Forster's fictional closure. The closing image of Vithobai signifies this horror of desire run amok as he mounts Paul's corpse in delirious passion before leaping to his death. This image not only forges a comparison between sexual desire and colonial insubordination, but also assumes, as its corollary, an analogy between the unconscious and a state of savagery (see my reading of this analogy in chapter 2).[82] Vithobai's (always anticipated) regression into "perversion," insanity, and barbarism confirms his inability to "sublimate" his homosexual drives: "Mounting on the corpse, he climbed higher, raised his arms over his head, sunlit, naked, victorious, leaving all disease and humiliation behind him, and he swooped like a falcon from the parapet in pursuit of the terrified shade" (111–12).

Judith Scherer Herz considers this ending "not gratuitous, and not merely poetic [but rather] a final spending of all the energies that have built up through the story."[83] Perry Levine by contrast seems oblivious to the characters on whom these "energies" are "spen[t]," going further than Herz in her claim that Forster's "art pays homage to the redemptive possibilities inherent in the love of the totally other, one who must be reached by stepping over the chasm of class or race."[84] But what "redemptive possibilities" inhere in the other in these stories? Since Forster does not step over, but consciously retains, this "chasm" of class or race, his claim of defending a friend over loyalty to one's country in "What I Believe" is idealist; in these stories, his loyalty to the nation prevails over each sexual transgression.[85]

We can assess the strength of Forster's fraternal idealism in "What I Believe" by noting how he struggled to conclude "The Life to Come" with redemptive happiness. Comparing the actual ending of "The Life to Come" — which details Pinmay's murder and Vithobai's suicide — with the following letter that Forster wrote to Siegfried Sassoon on July 21, 1923, allows us to measure the tension in Forster's writing between his imaginary and represented passions:

> I wish the story could have [had] another ending, but however much skill and passion I put into it, it would never have satisfied you. I tried another chapter, it is true, in the forests of the Underworld "where all the trees that have been cut down on earth take root again and grow for ever" and the hut has been rebuilt on an enormous scale. The dead come crashing down through the foliage in an internal embrace. Pinmay prays to his God who appears on high through a rift in the leaves and pities him but can do nothing. "It is very unfortunate," says God: "if he had died first you would have taken him to your heaven, but he has taken you to his instead. I am very sorry, oh good and faithful servant, but I cannot do anything." The leaves close, and Pinmay enters Eternity as a slave while Vithobai reigns with his peers. I hear rejoicing inside the hut, to which occasionally the slaves are summoned. I see them comes [sic] out again broken in spirit and crowd outside the entrance or lie like logs under the ice-cold flow of the stream. A gloomy prospect you see — except for Vithobai, who has won the odd trick. (277–78)

Perhaps what is most striking about this fascinating confession, with its anticipation of Tony Kushner's *Angels in America* (1993), is Forster's insistence that sexual inequality persists in Heaven. In his determination to retain Pinmay's and Vithobai's intimacy — a determination that went hopelessly awry in the narrative's execution — Forster could not conceive of homosexual desire without accompanying elements of violence, slavery, and distress. Thus we might argue that Forster's expectation of redemption precipitates an astonishing burden on his texts, forcing them to buckle under the strain of reconciling impossibly conflicted sexual and racial desires.

Altered States; or, The Antagonism of Desire

> There was a saying among young Indians that friendships made with
> white men seldom stood the strain of separation and never the acuter
> strain of reunion on the Indian's native soil.
> —Paul Scott [86]

> Nothing is more obdurate to artistic treatment than the carnal.
> —E. M. Forster [87]

Many of these tensions recur in "The Other Boat" (1915–16), a
novella written after *Maurice,* that Forster first abandoned and subsequently
published in 1948 as a fragment.[88] The text describes a relationship between
an English officer, Lionel, and an Indian naval secretary, Cocoanut, on a ship
bound for India. While the narrative elaborates on their furtive intimacy in
more detail than "The Life to Come," it presents an equally violent collision
of homophobia, sexual racism, and national prejudice. Forster's mythopoetic
account of travel adds a metaphoric significance to the boat, which is—like
the boat in Conrad's *Lord Jim* (1900)—representative of exile, expatriate
community, and other colonial problems.

The direction of travel is significant here because proximity to England exacerbates the racial constraints operating between Lionel and Cocoanut. Their sexual intimacy begins when they enter the Mediterranean, and
they consummate this intimacy when they reach the Red Sea. However, "The
Other Boat" cannot locate all racial and sexual prejudice outside the lovers.
While Lionel expresses his homosexuality only below deck in a locked cabin,
this desire connects defiantly to the rest of the ship. Unlike *Maurice* or "Story
of a Panic," there is no place to which Lionel and Cocoanut can happily retire
and escape. The proximity of homosexuality to the wider community—indeed, that it now inhabits it—renews Forster's problem of integrating desire
within his narrative; Lionel's confusion between desire for Cocoanut and
hatred of other Indians makes their relationship as fraught with antagonism
inside the cabin as it is without.

Critics often overlook this point by simplifying and idealizing
their attachment. For instance, Perry Levine describes the story as one of
"thwarted love," [89] while Norman Page argues: "Their mutual infatuation
overrides differences of race and social background, so that in the cabin they
inhabit a world different from that of the deck and the dining-room; as the

boat retraces in reverse the route of the earlier voyage, the two recapture the relationship of their boyhood, except that the tentative and half-realized sexuality of that time is now fully explicit.[90] However, Lionel and Cocoanut in fact are unable to "override" these differences. Although their intimacy largely derives from them, following "The Life to Come," it subsequently founders on them. The cabin is not, as Page claims, "a world different from that of the deck," as if culture and prejudice ended with a lock on the door; the fantasies that this locked door enable intensify the antagonism that surfaces behind it.

In the context of this story, the Forsterian maxim "only connect" confirms intractable points of resistance between conscious knowledge and unconscious antagonism. Stuart Hampshire touched on this problem when he argued about *A Passage to India:* "The connection that needs to be made is between the upper and literate reaches of the mind and the lower and unwashed, or proletarian, levels of consciousness, which can no longer be downtrodden and despised." [91] J. R. Ackerley, novelist and Forster's friend, went further down this path by characterizing the unconscious in palpably racist terms: "However honestly we may wish to examine ourselves we can do no more than scratch the surface. The golliwog that lies within and bobs up to dishonour us in our unguarded moments is too clever to be caught when we want him. . . ." [92]

For Ackerley, as perhaps for Forster, the ego is a white man as the unconscious is a black man. "The Other Boat" 's narrative is a palimpsest that positions Cocoanut within a cabin that is, in turn, inside the ship, as if to frame the potential insurrection of this racially "unwashed" whenever it "bobs up to dishonour us." [93] Lionel publicly disparages the occupant of his cabin, then returns to him in ritualized shame; the narrator explains: "his colour-prejudices were tribal rather than personal, and only worked when an observer was present" (211). Later, making what the narrator considers a "shrewd move," Lionel "brays": " 'I got a passage all right . . . but at the cost of sharing my cabin with a wog.' " The narrator continues: "All condoled, and Colonel Arbuthnot in the merriest of moods exclaimed, 'Let's hope the blacks don't come off on the sheets . . .' " (212). What comes off on the sheets—and emerges in the text—is Lionel's sexual guilt, which erupts when he strangles Cocoanut. Arbuthnot's "joke" symbolizes a murder that is, according to its narrator, "ecstasy hardened into agony" and a "sweet act of vengeance" (233). Within this tale's perverse logic, Cocoanut precipitates Lionel's disgust, rendering his gratuitous violence an inevitable and justifiable response to Cocoanut's provocation.

While Lionel moves between cabin and deck, resuming an identity among "The Ruling Race" that keeps his homosexuality under wraps, Cocoa-nut's desire is dangerously profuse. Since the narrator proclaims throughout that Cocoanut is part Indian, his indeterminate racial identity apparently ex-plains his sexual manipulation of Lionel. Thus the narrator juxtaposes the "decent and reliable" Lionel with a lover whom he describes as behaving "like a monkey," "almost like a vulture snatching," "no better than a mon-key," and "the little snake" because Cocoanut forgets to lock their cabin door (210, 216, 218, 228).[94] Cocoanut's proper name is also curious—it derives ap-parently from his head's disfiguration—for the narrator shortens it repeatedly to "Cocoa," a name that renders him both an embodiment of race and, by its proximity to two homonyms, representative of both their sexual "cocoon" (the cabin/closet) and the figurative "ca-ca," or excrement, that apparently warrants his death.

Following Vithobai's example, Cocoanut's transformation occurs over a substantial period of time. At the tale's beginning, the narrator de-scribes Cocoanut as a "subtle supple boy" (210), his disfigurement a feature of charm, and his character considerably more honest than that of his lover. Points of ambivalence later distort this image: the narrator indicates more than once that "[Cocoanut] had no scruples at perverting Lionel's instincts in order to gratify his own, or at endangering his prospects of paternity" (219).

Like Vithobai, Cocoanut assumes the role of precipitating his lover's downfall by drawing him into a conspiracy that will obviously ruin him. The narrator condemns Cocoanut for his conscious abuse of sexual intimacy and the way he permits himself to be desired; this renders him a symptom of Lionel's ardent and impossible longing. While Cocoanut and Vithobai hold an ambiguous relation to colonial law and Forster's ethics of sexual discre-tion, they are clearly at the mercy of an accompanying racial projection and its hate-ridden contents. By dwelling on what Lionel and Paul have to lose (colonial privilege) and, by implication, what Cocoanut and Vithobai have to gain (a vested interest in power), the narrator seems to merge sexual and racial projection into a wider colonial schema, aligning himself with the white lover by proposing that the black man is responsible for his and his lover's social and psychic collapse.

At these moments of narrative ambivalence, various conflations be-tween narrator and character make it almost impossible to distinguish Lionel's sudden hatred for Cocoanut from Forster's own version of sexual and racial hostility in *Hill of Devi and Other Indian Writings*. In "Kanaya" (1922), a fragment written in the same year as "The Life to Come," Forster describes his sexual relationship with an Indian boy in ways similar to the ill-fated relationship between Paul and Vithobai, and Lionel and Cocoanut. He begins by stating his resistance to Kanaya's effeminacy and compliance, and ends in exasperation: "What relation beyond carnality could one establish with such people?"[95] Nevertheless, Forster chose to heighten, not dissolve, this ambivalence, and so "resume . . . sexual intercourse, but it was now mixed with a desire to inflict pain. It didn't hurt him to speak of, but it was bad for me, and new in me, my temperament not being that way. I've never had the desire with anyone else, before or after, and I wasn't trying to punish him—I knew his silly little soul was incurable. I just felt that he was a slave, without rights, and I a despot whom no one could call to account."[96]

The assumption that Indians experience no pain prevails throughout "The Other Boat," in which the "sweet act of vengeance" of Cocoanut's murder is apparently "sweeter than ever for both of them" (233), as if strangulation were the sublime culmination of his implacable Indian masochism. With little to lose, and no apparent ego to speak of, Kanaya and Cocoanut confirm their status, each as a "silly . . . slave." By contrast, in murdering Cocoanut, the "Half Ganymede, half Goth" figure of *Lionel* reinscribes the masculinity that homosexual desire and its disclosure appear to destabilize (215). As in Forster's piece on Kanaya, Cocoanut's murder intensifies and reaffirms what was previously in doubt: the white man's authority and right to inflict pain. Forster was conscious of this dubious right when he described the response of the Indian coolies to his affair with Kanaya: "They weren't openly rude but there was an air of *rollicking equality:* 'You're no better than we are, after all' and probably a little racial vengeance."[97]

Rather than experience the shame of "rollicking equality," Lionel leaps to his death without a "racial" stain on his skin; however, he still bears traces of Cocoanut's sperm on his body. His corpse floats "northwards—contrary to the prevailing current" (234) before it is consumed by sharks. When the scandal breaks, other—human—sharks dis-seminate it, inducing such disgust in Lionel's mother that she resolves "never [to] mention . . . his name again" (234).[98] The public (and narrative) give little further attention to Cocoanut's death beyond the presumption that he instigated it, as if this projection absolves Lionel of guilt and homosexual desire by upholding the public's refusal to accept their intimacy.

The text ends this fantasy by repeating "The Life to Come" 's erasure of interracial desire. In both stories, the narrator replaces *peripeteia,* the trope that denotes abrupt and inexplicable change, with *preterition,* which silences the subject altogether. This substitution of hostility for desire apparently "resolves" an otherwise insoluble drama. This point contradicts the claim that love between men was unrepresentable at this time beyond a furtive encounter or fleeting intimacy; as fantasies, Forster could have inscribed these relationships more optimistically had he so chosen. I suggest that his continuation with such fantasies was impossible, given the sexual and racial politics they uncover, because it would have meant examining the racial inequalities that determine their structure.

In this respect, Forster's account of interracial friendship in *A Passage to India* appears idealist and distorted; to grasp this novel's political concerns, we need to consider the sexual and racial ambivalence that Forster foregrounds in *The Life to Come and Other Stories*. Although these fantasies are politically and psychically reactionary, they are nonetheless useful to contemporary criticism in elaborating aspects of colonial subjection that would otherwise never be mentioned.

7

Re/Orientations:

Firbank's "Anglophobia"

and the Sexual Nomad

And now this sudden change, this call to the East instead.
There had been no time, unfortunately, before setting out to
sit again in the picturesque "sombrero" of an explorer, but a
ready camera had performed miracles. . . .
— Ronald Firbank[1]

My mother bore me in the southern wild,
And I am black, but O! my soul is white;
White as an angel is the English child,
But I am black, as if bereav'd of light.
— William Blake[2]

In his collection of literary criticism *Abinger Harvest* (1936), E. M. Forster
extolled Ronald Firbank's fiction for qualities that are "impossible to anatomize."[3] This statement suggests both a fragility in Firbank's writing that
readers must protect from literary criticism's "surgical" procedures, and
Forster's concern to place fantasy beyond the realm of critical analysis: "It
makes them look so foolish," he writes, for "with quiet eyes . . . they pass
from point to point, . . . defin[ing] fantasy as 'the unserious treatment of the
unusual'— an impeccable definition, the only objection to it being that it defines."[4] Since Forster provided no reference to this "foolish . . . impeccable
definition," the reader could easily dismiss it as his characterization. However, many critics have considered Firbank's work unserious, as if his fiction's

176

frivolity supports a surface so slight it cannot withstand the rigor of critical reading.

Sarah Barnhill and Edward Martin Potoker have usefully challenged this assumption by arguing that an "honest desperation" and "unmitigated sadness" lie behind Firbank's banter and innuendo.[5] They also claim that Firbank's writing represents a voice of sexual and political exile from Britain and a sense of mourning for the devastation of postwar European culture. These are suggestions I support and wish to amplify here, though with caution about assumptions of loss behind or beneath his texts' "bizarre gaiety" because these assumptions introduce an argument about literary and psychic depth that Firbank was at pains to revoke.[6] This critical approach also represents the superficial innocence of Firbank's fantasies as a screen to a more difficult agony, leaving fantasy again free from attention. Ironically, this indifference to fantasy endorses Forster's complacency; his interest lay not in the frivolity or seriousness of Firbank's fantasy, but rather in ensuring that it remained without definition. To Forster, only the "higher animals"—that is, literary "greats"—could be "dissect[ed]" because "they are full of helpful secrets"; the frail "butterfly" of Firbank "become[s] meaningless as soon as you stretch [him] on this rack." [7]

Forster's position complies with his untheoretical arguments in *Aspects of the Novel,* whose humanism formulates criticism as a torture to art; accordingly, readers must protect and conserve their literary object. While critics like Norman Alford advance a similar argument about Firbank's burlesque, claiming that analytic reading spoils its intricacy and hilarity,[8] other critics like Susan Sontag and Robert Kiernan make this general point about the phenomenon of camp: the critic should record—but never betray—its studied ephemera.[9] Contrary to these arguments, I suggest that Firbank's literary fantasies present a racial and homosexual significance that is not "impossible to anatomize" since they yield to attentive interpretation. From this premise, fantasy is neither a superfluous barrier to more serious emotion nor a delicate film that is meaningless without its context; it is a form of representation through which Firbank expresses multiple meanings with varying degrees of intensity. Insofar as Firbank's fictional imagoes comprise stereotypes of Oriental and African-Caribbean sexualities, I argue that they are particularly instructive for modern criticism; they embody the projection of some of Britain's most intractable racial fantasies.

By associating (particularly male) homosexuality with irony, critics like Barnhill, Samuel Hynes, and Alan Hollinghurst emphasize the "amoral possibilities" and sexual fluidity of Firbank's writing.[10] Virtually all of Firbank's narratives engender this textual idiosyncrasy and lyricism by their preoccupation with "vice" and desire: priests display an unrequited passion for boys; dandies ignore marriage to pursue beauty; lesbians explore romantic possibilities through poetry and travel. Firbank ritualizes this aesthetic as a ceremonial "perversion" to counter the rigidity of his surrounding culture. His interest in travel and indigenous cultures provides another exit from the demand for a normative sexuality; his fantasies offer alternative positions and pursuits that fall under the sway of an effusive—though normally allusive— homosexuality. As Hollinghurst notes, "It is in this margin between naturalism and fantasy—between responsibility to observed life and to the imagination—that the subversive and unstable element of homosexual concealment flourishes." [11]

Hollinghurst later observes that women often express Firbank's allusions to homosexuality. This may illustrate an evasion of censorship due to greater public tolerance—or ignorance—of lesbianism; it may also signify the displacement of a hazardous and censorious desire that would otherwise surface between men. Firbank's lesbians generally conform to an aesthetic of the 1920s art deco movement,[12] though lesbian *desire* is also circumspect in his fiction. Thus, while Firbank defines few characters without nonfigurative and unequivocal signifiers of desire, dandyism and languid effeminacy constantly betray the orientation of his male protagonists'. In this manner, male homosexuality appears so ubiquitous, the reader can presume a man's "ruling passion" unless the narrator declares that he is otherwise engaged.

Although this strategy of partial equivocation substitutes alternative desires for male homosexuality, it does not silence or efface homosexuality; nor does this strategy transform homosexuality into an exclusive but impalpable concern, as if Firbank could imagine—or write of—no other subject. Rather, this proliferation of "perversions" helps vindicate Firbank's symbolization of homosexuality by normativizing an array of propensities that assuage the difficulty of intimacy and desire between men. Firbank's emphasis on the normalcy of male and female homosexuality inverts a cultural supposition by casting heterosexuality as an arduous social ritual that veers away from the "natural" Firbankian affection of each gender for its own. By adopting a Wildean principle of surface, Firbank brings heterosexuality into relief as an elaborate construction; he also aligns homosexuality with the deepest truth of personality—whatever depth the personality can sustain. As W. R. Irwin argues, "Ordinary heterosexuality is rare [in Firbank's writing], and when it does occur it is afflicted with an etiolation that renders it less than serious. There are few exceptions; Firbank is not the author for sexual passion treated straight." [13]

This displacement of cultural norms accompanies a shift in terrain; Firbank's geography is rarely specific and generally supports an imaginary significance. Thus he described his last novella, *The New Rythum* [*sic*] (1926): "Ah, the East . . . I propose to return there, some day, when I write about New York." [14] Firbank began this novella about "the *thought* of New York" in Cairo, where he "set up a parasol and 'a little French writing table' in the desert every morning and 'pictured the American scene in a mirage.' " [15] He also wrote to Aldous Huxley of his earlier novella *Prancing Nigger* (1924), claiming that he intended "to go to the West Indies to live among the Negroes so as to collect material for a novel about Mayfair," a wealthy neighborhood in the heart of London.[16] Thus, Firbank's interest in African-Caribbean, Islamic, and Oriental cultures permits a real and imaginary exploration that partially displaces his narrative focus on homosexuality. As this chapter will demonstrate, however, the ensuing literary and sexual fantasies are ambivalent and often difficult to assess.

As an Edwardian British writer, Firbank is unusual because his black characters are rarely peripheral to his narrative; generally, they are integral to his narrative procedure and prominent within his fictional communities. Although *Prancing Nigger* carries a troubling title whose history is important to consider,[17] the novella is striking because it hinges on the concerns of an African-Caribbean family for whom the novella's two white expatriates are an appendage and not—as usually occurs in Edwardian literature—the reverse. Firbank also foregrounds black characters in sexual terms; homosexual desire between black men is more "natural" and successful than the novella's equivalent and exploitative intimacy between a black woman and a white man.

Although Firbank tends to denature cultural expectations about sexual difference, he also retains an ambivalence about racial difference that we cannot ignore or analyze away. In an attempt to overlook the more disturbing elements of *Prancing Nigger,* Kiernan argued recently that Firbank was not racist because his exaggerated Caribbean dialect parodied only British cultural rigidity.[18] Brigid Brophy also sought to redeem the novella by arguing that Firbank shared an affinity with black people, projecting an image through them that dispelled misgivings he felt about his own.[19] Let us consider these points carefully; they imply that race functions as a metonym for cultural displacement and homosexuality in Firbank's work, without effacing or superseding either. If Firbank's analogy between blacks and homosexuals does not reduce both groups to the same phenomenon, it nonetheless implies that they share similarities as marginal and repressed components of colonial society. According to this reading, the fact that Mrs. Mouth chooses the name "prancing nigger" for her husband may represent the trope for a would-be prancing homosexual (the name is not a racial slur issuing from a white expatriate). The novella supports this point by frequently representing Charlie as a "prancing" black man who desires other (black) men.[20]

This analogy between race and homosexuality recalls George Steiner's observation that Forster's shift from England to colonial India alleviated his difficulties in writing about homosexual desire from home.[21] To this extent, Firbank's ambivalence toward Britain and its colonies surfaces in his writing because he temporarily assumed the perspective of a foreigner; distance and difference seemed to precipitate in him a national antipathy he could not assuage as an émigré.[22]

Valmouth: A Romantic Novel (1919) pronounces this situation, in which the sexual ambivalence of Captain Thoroughfare, an English naval officer in Jamaica, reflects the presence in Britain of a predominantly Tahitian—though racially "confused"—masseuse, Mrs. Yajñavalkya.[23] His absence precipitates a threefold commentary: on his intimacy with fellow crew members, on the masseuse's origins (which fascinate and concern the British community of Valmouth), and on the glaring deficiencies of British custom and sexual culture. In these terms, Mrs. Yajñavalkya's arrival assists the captain's departure and subsequent sexual activity. She is also the only character who correctly interprets the behavior of the novella's present and absent men; Firbank gives her the knowledge to read, in their resistance to marriage, an interest they conduct elsewhere. Mrs. Yajñavalkya carries the following message from the returned (though never visible) captain: "He has abjured, he says, de female sex" (456); she also receives the pressing claim of her apprentice, Carry Smith:

> ". . . Oh, Miss! . . . I know at last . . . I know *at last*—about the gentlemen."
> "About what gentlemen?"
> "I know all about them."
> "So do I—traitors."
> "Oh, miss!"
> "Don't be a fool, Carry Smith."
> "I know, miss, about them."

"You may think you do."

"Ah, but I *know*." (460–61)

Willfully misinterpreting the reason for his uninterest in her, Carry decides that the captain would have desired her had she not tried to present herself as white: "It exasperates me though to think of the trouble I gave myself over maquillage. Blanching my face and fingers . . . when all the while . . . he'd sooner have had me black!" (461). In this example race functions as a metonym for gendered and sexual interest; the captain bestows his attention only on his lieutenant, Jack Whorwood, whom the narrative introduces as his "middy-chum . . . who was not much over fifteen, and the youngest hand on board. 'That little lad,' he had said [to Miss Tooke], with a peculiar smile that revealed his regular pointed teeth, 'that little lad, upon a cruise, is, to me, what Patroclus was to Achilles, and even more' " (398). The meaning of this "even more" is a source of conjecture for the remainder of the novella; it leads Lady Parvula to ruminate: "[The captain] seems to *me* to be an unpublished type" (457). Captain Thoroughfare neglects his (clearly superfluous) bride on his return and devotes his attention to his "conciliatory hand Lieutenant Whorwood" (453). The narrator's description of the lieutenant gestures to his effeminacy and his intricate manipulation—or performance—of gender roles: "As he lagged along in the faint boreal light behind his friend *he resembled singularly some girl masquerading as a boy for reasons of romance*" (453; my emphasis). Insofar as the narrative twice manipulates the lieutenant's gender, Firbank suspends his discussion of race to inquire into his characters' sexual aims and preference.

If travel relieves the text (and its writer) of a paralyzing inhibition, it also assists the expression of homosexuality from another terrain—the Caribbean, or an actual or mythical "East." Firbank's diverse accounts of homosexuality in the colonial scene resemble Forster's in their ambivalence toward Britain and its expatriates. Though both writers vent the greater part of their ambivalence against Britain's repressive legislation, Firbank often extols the sexual nomad's atopic possibilities, allowing him to symbolize desires he cannot avow at home. While in Firbank's text the impulse to travel derives from profound Anglophobia, as Barnhill suggests, Britain still provides Firbank with his evaluation of cultural refinement and nostalgia for aesthetic elegance. This retention of nationalist bias may culminate in a restless and idealized Anglophilia, which Firbank nonetheless phobically directs at the émigré community to which he tenuously belonged. As Barnhill writes of *The Flower Beneath the Foot,* a text that dovetails the ennui and insularity of an imaginary expatriate community, the narrative cannot resolve its figurative rootlessness and "malaise of loss and exile."[24] For instance, the narrator always refers to one of the text's more obvious homosexual protagonists, "Eddy" Monteith, by quotation marks; "Eddy" also muses on the cultural difference of bees for a metonymic understanding of his alienation: "Closing his eyes he fell to considering whether the bee of one country would understand the remarks of that of another. The effect of the soil of a nation, had it consequences upon its flora? Were plants influenced at their roots? People sometimes spoke (and especially ladies) of the language of flowers . . . and a bee born and bred at home . . . would be at a loss to understand (it clearly followed) the conversation of one born and bred, here, abroad. A bee's idiom varied then, as did man's!" (537). This consideration raises questions on which each character reflects: the effeminate literary assistant to Count Cabinet, Peter Passer, "follow[s] the fallen statesman into exile" (565); Sir Somebody Something tries wistfully to re-create in Kairoulla the cultural and commercial experience of London. Only Mrs. Montgomery triumphs over estrangement; she adapts to life abroad by resolutely denying the fact of leaving England: "It was as if something of her native land had crept in through the doorway with her, so successfully had she inculcated its tendencies, or spiritual Ideals, upon everything around" (569).

Firbank's national ambivalence oscillates between Anglophilia and Anglophobia by converting his fantasy of the colony into either a welcome point of reprieve or a more parochial version of the cultural same. Since the colony provides only an inadequate copy of its "master" culture, Firbank's racism actually seems most prominent in moments of Anglophilia. However, in *Prancing Nigger,* Firbank seems intent on returning to Britain an image of its imperial decline. The Arcadian beauty of Mediaville combines social cohesion with sexual honesty—at least for its black homosexual men:

> . . . strolling towards the sea, two young men passed by with fingers intermingled.
>
> With a slight shrug, the lady [Mrs. Mouth] plied her fan.
>
> As the mother of a pair of oncoming girls, the number of ineligible young men or confirmed bachelors around the neighbourhood was a constant source of irritation to her. (594)

The narrative cannot sustain this Arcadian image; sexual division and homophobia soon corrupt it. When the Mouth family move to the city of Cuna-Cuna for social advancement, their class aspirations also appear woefully explicit and unsuccessful. At the close of the text, as the Mouth family disbands along its various axes, neither they nor their aspirations are secure. With Edna and Mimi unmarried, Mrs. Mouth is more restless than ever, while Charlie, her son, finds only a semblance of desperate and self-destructive happiness: "Charlie [was] fast going to pieces, having joined the Promenade of a notorious Bar with its bright particular galaxy of boys" (636). The narrator previously observed that the band comprises "youths of a certain life, known as bwam-wam bwam-wams . . . whose equivocal behaviour, indeed, was perhaps more shocking even than the shocks, [and] set the pent Park ahum" (625, 627). The dance troupe's alliterative name may mimic its equivocal sexual composition; more importantly, the distance between desire and its fulfillment in this novella foregrounds a drama of self-composition in which every character potentially can "go to pieces." Like the previous chapter's reading of Forster's "The Life to Come" and "The Other Boat," desire in Firbank's writing is often responsible for his characters' internal collapse, prevailing whenever they live beyond their psychic means.[25]

Several critics have argued that the Mouth family's ascendancy and decomposition mirror their movement from pastoral idyll to corrupt metropolis. This movement is a trope on which the morality of nineteenth-century fiction often hinges.[26] However, *Prancing Nigger*'s psychic drama indicts not only British culture as a form of colonial despair, but also colonial subjects: the narrator largely attributes the Mouth family's social decline to European culture and sexual hypocrisy. With racial conservatism, the text also implies that the Mouths would have been successful had they decided to remain in their "natural" sphere; their happiest environment is not the metropolis but rather the tranquil and unspoiled village of Mediaville. While the Mouths' bid for social improvement culminates in their ruin and despair, it also shatters the rural community's equanimity by engendering an "Occidental" materialism.

Ultimately, Firbank presents the disadvantages and benefits of Anglophilia and Anglophobia without endorsing either perspective; his myriad irony ensures that both are possible and neither is satisfactory. Clearly, we cannot ignore the profound racism that both positions embody: the first offers an account of Britain's decline by representing African-Caribbean society as its parodic "other" and lamentable failure. The second represents black people as "noble savages" whose endeavor to become "civilized" (i.e., white) precipitates their social and self-ruination. Although *Prancing Nigger* never makes this second position explicit, Firbank implies that the colonized are open to ridicule if their social ambition is too exorbitant; their failure seems ultimately to signify their tenuous hold on civilization.

Without ignoring these egregious assumptions about race and civilization, I suggest that Firbank affirmed the first position more frequently; he strove to promote Anglophobia and the absence of sexual prejudice in the colonies by returning to Britain an image of sexual and cultural freedom that prevailed over its relentless demand for repression. This myth of foreign freedom is clearly inseparable from idealizations of Afro-Caribbean sexual behavior, which veer toward a stereotype of "natural" —because less "civil" —desire. As Hollinghurst argues, more in celebration of Firbank's relaxed tolerance than from caution about the possibility of racial fetishism: "Their naturalness is their innocence, but part of their significance to Firbank is that they allow him more fully to sexualize his concept of innocence, to diminish his indirectness, and to describe the more overtly libidinous quality of his imagination." [27]

Firbank's oscillation between the for and against positions is generally more abstruse and indefinite than Hollinghurst implies. I suggest that Firbank chose to cast the society of Cuna-Cuna as a symptom of colonial repression by designating the Mouth family as its frustrated and dispirited stereotype. Firbank's white and black characters are thus intentionally never more than cardboard figures that haunt colonial and expatriate alike with ineluctable fears and assumptions about insurrection, savagery, and intimacy. While the black characters return to the colonizer all of his fears and assumptions, Firbank stands aside, unwilling to ratify this projection and often deliberately undermining it. The narrator describes the Mouth family without contempt or aversion, for instance; they elicit as much empathy from the reader as Firbank's characters ever achieve. In this regard, it is worth comparing the Mouths to the expatriates Madame Ruiz and her son, Vittorio, who are incidental to the narrative beyond their instigation of Edna's downfall: she too readily trusts in her attachment to Vittorio (he is twenty-six, she thirteen). In their social and sexual manipulations, both mother and son ratify a stock expatriate cliché.

Firbank's account of "natural" and "sexually innocent" elements of foreign culture clearly implicates his writing in an established tradition of primitivism. However, it may be counterproductive to dismiss his work simply because of this racial emphasis; Firbank also modified and troubled an obdurate frame of fantasy in Britain's colonial imaginary that criticism cannot ignore. His consciousness of stereotype binds his fiction to Britain's most intractable mythologies of race. Yet without presenting a fixed idea of race, as Britain's imperial propaganda strove to do, Firbank used irony and parody to transform these racial imagoes. He represented explicit and impalpable forms of prejudice by parodying less the *objects* or victims of colonialism than their overriding political *aims*. Unlike Forster, Firbank did not try to fix his fantasized colonies as irremediably other to Britain; like H. Rider Haggard, but from a radically different perspective, Firbank identified similarities between England and its colonies by eroding the myth that an irreducible difference separates the colonizer from the colonized. As Mrs. Yajñavalkya in *Valmouth* remarks with astute and troubling irony: "Ya Allah, but whenever I see a Market [here in England] I no longer feel Abroad. . . . And w'y, I wonder, is de reason ob dis? . . . Because human nature is de same ebberywhere" (432; original ellipses). If human nature fundamentally is the same in Mrs. Yajñavalkya's terms, England cannot maintain a fantasy of superiority over its colonized when it reproduces the "barbarism" it denounces in others. Though much of this joke falls at Mrs. Yajñavalkya's expense, her dialect and behavior puncture both England's assumptions about its imperial refinement and the belief that it adequately suppresses this "natural" aggression.[28]

Several of Firbank's white characters pointedly—and unsuccessfully—resist this argument about cultural and racial similarity, but their fantasies of race bring every resistance into relief because the narrative tirelessly documents them. These characters dissolve "race" of a colonially specific meaning and refigure it unsuccessfully as an absolute social division. Niri-Esther, Mrs. Yajñavalkya's cousin, whom the British extol for her beauty and deem an eligible wife for Dick Thoroughfare at the close of *Valmouth,* formerly is perceived as too "primitive" (i.e., naïve, unspoiled, *and* culturally inferior) for the captain:[29]

> "She needs debarbarising, of course."
> "She'd still be black, Eulalia!"
> "Black or no, she's certainly perfectly beautiful."
> "She may appeal to your epicurism, dear, although she mayn't to mine." [. . .]
> "I found her so interesting." (448)

In this equivocal response to the narrative's black characters, Firbank's white characters repeat the formal ambivalence I identified in several of Forster's texts. This oscillation suggests a promise of equivalent civilization between Britain and its colonies and an immediate recoil from an always potential barbarism. It also manifests Firbank's intractable ambivalence toward his culture and the unavoidable barbarism of Britain's imperialist policies. Despite his disdain for Britain, Firbank's allegiance to the culturally different was never absolute; Jean Genet came closer to this complete allegiance by his repeated denunciation and joyous betrayal of French colonialism. Firbank perhaps could not decide whether the advantage of sexual fluidity in the colonies outweighed their paucity as a cultural substitute for Britain. (Such was the extent of Genet's hatred of France that the question never arose—identification with the colonized was *axiomatic*.)[30] However, Firbank also derides the colonial project in its drive to establish a "home from home," by relating this practice to the mythical re-creation of a national home. As he demonstrates in *The Flower Beneath the Foot,* this myth stems from the denial of geopolitical displacement that allows an émigré to adopt—however temporarily—a precarious alternative.[31]

This national home is tenuous on foreign soil because the émigré cannot annul the differences that beset him or her. Regardless of the colony's mimetic ingenuity, it is always inadequate as a copy of its "origin." The émigré must acknowledge the colony's insular terrain whenever he or she breaches its boundaries and encounters the difference from which the colony temporarily "protects" him or her. While this alterity is specific to every colony, language and custom remind émigrés that any attempt to disband their status as foreigners, is a fantasy that obtains from trying to repress the difficulty of difference. In Firbank's work, expatriates must acknowledge that they inhabit a margin; they obtrude with foreign specularity on a culture to which they have no claim and over which they have no sovereignty.

Firbank's and Forster's infrequent claim that African-Caribbean and Near Eastern cultures engender this difficulty is arguably the most racist aspect of their work; the foreign assumes a plenitude that "civilizations" either have displaced or the West appears to lack. This scenario produces African-Caribbean and Near Eastern cultures by default; their civilizations allegedly begin at the moment of colonization, as if their precolonial communities never existed in their own right. However, Firbank's ambivalence never never existed in their own right. However, Firbank's ambivalence never carries the vehement, and often violent, hostility that erupts in Forster's short stories. Rather than imbuing his black characters with aggressive alterity, Firbank tends to invest them with laconic passivity. For all their ambition, the Mouth family never illustrate the same frantic manipulation and obsessional rage as do Vithobai in Forster's "The Life to Come" and Cocoanut in "The Other Boat." Firbank's *Santal* (1921) is replete with metaphors of fatigue, for instance, that signify dejection and despair rather than indolence and indifference:[32] Cherif, the protagonist, has "forlorn, profound eyes that had vision in them" (479) and "a great melancholy . . . in his face" (480); "disappoint[ment]" (481) exhausts other characters, who display "gaunt etiolated head[s]" (479) and suffer from an unremitting complaint of "inward groan[s]" (482). This weariness among *Santal*'s characters is not simply an ontological or racial characteristic: it bespeaks an analogous and structural fatigue that recurs throughout the novella. Consider the redolence of this fatigue and yearning in the following passage:

> Lounging like sprawling flowers before their doors men were arguing drowsily over small shell-shaped cups of Kahoua. The clamour of the Souk had ceased. Along white walls receptive to every shadow, Cherif meditatively advanced. In the streets of the Courtesans, behind a doorway mysteriously ajar, a woman with myrtle-leaves in her hair was waiting for a lover flattened listlessly against the wall. But it was not for the courtesans, but rather for the unfrequented garden of ben Chemoun, that at present his spirit craved. Wide sweeping steps that time had worn all away led up to it from the street. It was quite a beautiful garden, where often he had experienced before the heart serenity that comes with solitude. (491)

Despite the narrator's constant insistence to the contrary, solitude does not bring serenity in *Santal;* it raises the haunting specter of a demand for something more and something else—a future that Cherif cannot pull within the aegis of the present and a horizon that stubbornly recedes whenever he tries to reach it.

This novella's structural lassitude may obviously support another stereotype of loyal complicity, devotion, and subservience to Europe, which perniciously denies the colonized a right to opposition. However, Firbank's stereotypes supersede race by emptying this category of condensed anxiety and projection. Firbank also promotes exchange between colonizer and colonized by dissolving their difference; his imaginary topoi transform every scene of culture by suspending hierarchy and merging cultural difference. This process precipitates a colonial simulacrum, rather than a specific colonial terrain that manifests rigid discrepancies of power.

Earlier, I suggested that Firbank uses this fantasmatic register to elaborate homosexual possiblity. I would add that although we cannot restrict homosexual desire to his atopias, it often counters the fraught legal and social consequence of same-sex intimacy in late Victorian and Edwardian Britain. Clearly, it would be misleading to propose an authentic desire that one could express without—or beyond—inhibition and partial repression, but travel abroad may have generated symbols of desire that Firbank could distinguish from the intolerance prevailing in Britain at the turn of the last century. Writing in the aftermath of Wilde's 1895 trials, Firbank shares with him a principle of aesthetic rigor, an awareness of the price of decadence, and the cultural danger accompanying the interruption or transposition of sexual difference. As Lady Parvula exclaims in *Valmouth:*

> "Men, men! . . . 'They are always there,' dear, aren't they, as the Russians say?"
> Mrs. Hurstpierpoint repressed a grimace.
> "Nowadays," she murmured, "a man . . . to me . . . somehow . . . oh! he is something so wildly *strange.*"
> "Strange?"
> "Unglimpsable."
> "Still, some men are ultra-womanly, and they're the kind I love!" Mrs. Thoroughfare chirruped.
> "I suppose that none but those whose courage is unquestionable can venture to be effeminate." (406; original ellipses and italics)

In this allusion to fin de siècle decadence, and perhaps to Wilde (a writer and figure he certainly admired), Firbank pits one embodiment of masculinity—the "unglimpsable" and "wildly strange"—against the familiar comfort of the "ultra-womanly" and "effeminate." The latter, as criticism and biography attest, was closest to his own, leading Hollinghurst to argue that Firbank aligns an array of women—maternal spinsters, lesbians, wives, and débutantes—with the stay-at-home dandy and "confirmed bachelor," while other men are absent, abroad, or indifferent to the attractions of home.[33]

In this scenario, Hollinghurst identifies Firbank's profound attachment to his mother as an ambivalence toward home—an urgent bid to leave it and an endless yearning to return to it. Though provocative, this reading reduces the question of cultural symbolization and sexual identification to a psychobiographical drama; Firbank clearly engaged a wider problematic in his work. For instance, *Santal* would support Hollinghurst's reading because Cherif leaves his family and an unspecified Islamic community to search for a religious ideal he never finds. However, the novella also engages with Firbank's "even more" (398): despite the limitations of his community, Cherif also labors through the difficulty of establishing possession, roots, membership, and security. By the end of the text, he reaches a terrain that is bare and uninhabitable, a place where faith dissolves amid the aridity and cruelty of the surrounding landscape: "riding on and on, and leaving these [hills] behind, he came to country less clement. It was a country all of rock, a land of crags and boulders, over whose riven steeps circled restless flocks of birds" (497–98).

In stark contrast to the rural beauty and communal stability Cherif leaves behind, this new landscape appears to symbolize the difference between what he sought as reassurance and reward—the trophy of spiritual redemption—and what he found: desolation, anguish, and unanswerable longing. As the narrator continues:

> But as the country grew more, and still more, desolate, these birds, as well, he left behind. Beneath the pitiless sun all signs of life had vanished, and in the deep of noon the hills looked to ache with light. . . .
> "Allah show compassion to thy child Cherif," he implored. And there came a time when hope quite left him. (498)

Although critics have disparaged *Santal* for the sternness of its inquiry,[34] we cannot simply dismiss its thematic as another example of Oriental exoticism. The citations I include here demonstrate that Firbank counterpoised his fetishism of the Near East with a disdain for England. On an ontological level, *Santal* represents Cherif's aim and poignant failure to privilege his identity's nomadic elements over domestic constraints. In the context of this mythography of "the effulgent East" (496), where his aunts and companions fail to understand his restlessness, Cherif's search for a spiritual and masculine overseer leads him topographically across the desert and psychically toward askesis.

What is the object Cherif pursues and then endeavors to renounce? The literal and figurative aridity of his quest anticipates the parched land and rock of T. S. Eliot's wasteland by signifying Cherif's longing for a water to satisfy his thirst and rejuvenate the land with elements it lacks.[35] In another sense, Cherif's dilemma embodies the psychic (but not simply psychobiographical) difficulty that in the 1920s beset homosexuals as a result of their not receiving the comfort of circularity that derives from repeating, through matrimony and family, the drama of birth and upbringing. Refusing to marry or reproduce, Cherif ruminates on a series of profound ontological questions analogous to concerns about homo/sexual subjects' aims and objects, as well as the course they should pursue. As Firbank writes of Cherif, "sampling the sweet-grained fruit, he fell to thinking of the course best adapted for him to pursue" (492). These issues are as much psychic—in the sense that they repeat the infant's awkward trajectory from the mother's body to the Law of the Father—as they are political in the sense that they demand, but rarely receive, the appropriate weight of familial wisdom, historical precedent, and cultural support.[36] Hélène Cixous may therefore be too emphatic when she writes: "A boy's journey is the return to the native land, the *Heimweh* Freud speaks of, the nostalgia that makes man a being who tends to come back to the point of departure to appropriate it for himself and to die there. A girl's journey is farther—to the unknown, to invent." [37]

Placing my reading of *Santal* alongside Hollinghurst's interpretation of Firbank's maternal attachment prevents psychobiography from resolving the "problem" of Firbank's self-differentiation and the autonomy he failed to achieve. For Hollinghurst, as for many critics of Forster, interpretation reduces fiction to a therapeutic exercise that represents to these writers the difficulty of their desire;[38] fiction reproduces their effort to relinquish the mother as a primary object.[39] This is surely an important aspect of biographical interpretation of Forster's and Firbank's work, though it is also a mistake to formulate the relation between writer and text so schematically. What this account loses—or strives too quickly to resolve—are questions that Firbank's fiction posed to sexual difference and the symbolization of masculinity and race in Britain and its colonies at the turn of the last century.

In *Concerning the Eccentricities of Cardinal Pirelli* (1926), men's "wildness" and rootlessness return as palpable indictments:[40] "Men (eternal hunters, novelty seekers, insatiable beings), men in their natural lives, pursue the concrete no less than the ideal . . ." (696); "men with their selfishness, fickleness and lies!" (674); "Men are my raging disgust" (671). These remarks concern not only masculine drives but their expression through the project of colonialism, and the empire's organization of power in its rapacious demand for political subjection. If we counterpoise these hunters' selfishness with Firbank's description of the "courage[ous] . . . venture [of the] effeminate," colonial masculinity begins to resemble the "savagery" it sets out to master. By redefining the conventional regulation of gender, Firbank attributes greater courage to those men who stay home.

This critique of colonial masculinity endorses Firbank's other accounts of masculine identification, in which the problems that beset the homosexual trouble the entire spectrum of his male characters. This qualitative insufficiency of masculinity is ubiquitous in his writing; it is not the specific "deficit" of male homosexuals. While the homosexual embodies questions confronting every man, the surrounding culture misrecognizes these questions by finding in him a disorder it denies elsewhere.[41]

Firbank's writing elaborates on this sexual denial and gendered insufficiency by locating the problem in culture and terrain rather than in the homo/sexual subject. This explains, in part, the restlessness of his characters, who reflect more on their impossible relation to the community than on their specific sexual "failing" of it. Since homosexual desire tends to be allusive or elsewhere in his fiction, it can resist the "strange[ness]" of colonial masculinity. Thus homosexuality haunts the home and colony without belonging to either because Firbank never assigns it an identifiable role or position. By invoking the dystopic elements of British culture, Firbank represents travel as a metonym for homosexual desire. As she ponders a friend's grave, for instance, Mrs. Tooke considers: "Here lay Balty Vincent Wise, having lived and died—*unmarried*. Oh what a funny fellow! Oh what a curious man! . . . What did he mean going off like that? Was no woman good enough for him then? Oh but he should have settled; ranged himself as every bachelor should! Improper naughty thing! He should be exorcised and whipped; or had he loved? Loved perchance *elsewhere. . . ?* " (437; original ellipses and italics). *Valmouth* leaves these questions unanswered, though the ellipses mark the assumptions that are unavowable to Mrs. Tooke and unrepresentable in the text. By posing these questions, the text returns the work of inference to the reader, asking him or her to supply Mrs. Tooke's missing knowledge. In this citation, the imperatives that regulate sexual conduct—the repeated *should*s—haunt the narrative by gesturing to an absence that the narrative cannot answer or elide.

This citation is one of Firbank's most poignant references to homosexuality; by drawing attention to what his homosexual characters cannot specify, enunciate, or locate of their desire, the ellipses illustrate what the narrative also cannot signify. Since Firbank avoids direct references to homosexuality, this term's vanishing point represents a nomenclature of desire by default—Firbank encodes homosexuality metaleptically, at the furthest possible limit of legibility. He therefore censors himself before the reader without excising references to homosexuality; their partial absence intensifies whatever significance they can generate in the text. In this oblique and partial way, Firbank represents desire by drawing attention to the impossibility of nonfigurative writing. The pastiche of tropes that partially compose his style— metonymy, metalepsis, and periphrasis—pronounce an endless conflict between expression and silence, declaration and opacity. Besides his dialogue's frequent malapropisms and lacunae, every breach of conventional grammar and syntax constitutes a "moral nonconformity" by signifying the unmentionable.[42] As Jocelyn Brooke argues about Firbank's "Sternian" punctuation, "Those . . . dots imply the whole of Krafft-Ebing and Havelock Ellis—and even (as Firbank might have added) more." [43] They also represent a modernist principle of parataxis and juxtaposition by demonstrating the inadequacy of realism with the psychic work of analogy, association, and substitution that Firbank strove to portray.

I have argued that Firbank deployed this rhetorical procedure in the substance and representation of his literary fantasies. By adopting a narrative clinamen, Firbank was able to suggest—and then swerve from—his fiction's impossible terrain. The imaginary communities, inflections of race, and array of sexual pursuits that surface in his writing—lesbianism, masochism, pedophilia, and miscegenation—displace much of the condensed difficulty of male homosexual desire. Like the exchange between Captain Thoroughfare and Mrs. Yajñavalkya, whose arrival assists the captain's departure and sexual activity, Firbank's emphasis on racial and sexual differences accentuates the absence of direct references to male homosexuality, leaving a surplus of non-referential desire for the reader to interpret. In the process, Firbank brilliantly averted the danger of censorship, and challenged the project of controlling what could enter—or fall out of—symbolization. He wrote a symbol of desire in the residue of what he demonstrated was still unsaid.

8

In Defense of the Realm: Sassoon's Memoirs and "Other Opaque Arenas of War"[1]

It was a sad story, but I make no apology for dragging it from its decent oblivion. All squalid, abject, and inglorious elements in war should be remembered. The intimate mental history of any man who went to the War would make unheroic reading.
—Siegfried Sassoon[2]

Do I want death? I don't know yet. Anyhow the war is outside of life, and I'm in the war.
—Sassoon[3]

There is only the fight to recover what has been lost
And found and lost again and again: and now, under
    conditions
That seem unpropitious. But perhaps neither gain nor loss.
For us, there is only the trying.
—T. S. Eliot[4]

There is a way of referring to the generation of First World War poets that is still popular in Britain today. According to this myth, a group of men set out to chronicle the nation's experience of combat for those back home oblivious of its meaning. By capturing the elegiac testament of a "lost generation," their poetry allegedly records a nation's suffering.

In line with all myth, we cannot ignore this reading's elements of truth: many soldiers assumed the task of writing the war in a spirit of grief and protest; the discrepancy between their suffering and Britain's rhetorical denial of horror exacerbated their military experience. This was a war in which several million people died, a war that continues to illustrate its historical pointlessness.

Although we cannot discount the large number killed and maimed in the war, I propose that we also cannot reduce the meaning of war to a set of political or social determinants. While the conflict ended over seventy years ago, its legacy is still palpable as an image of global carnage, patriotic fervor, and national shattering that has haunted European—and especially British— memory ever since.[5] The task of separating the real from the mythological aspects of war may therefore be impossible because it confronts our continued belief that every military event is an empirical and coherent certainty.[6] Britain's First World War poetry illustrates how cultural meaning invests in and projects onto history; we cannot isolate this poetry from the work of Britain's national memory and mourning, for Britain has repeatedly framed the war as a *literary* event.[7] As Virginia Woolf's narrator observes in *To the Lighthouse* (1927): "[Mr. Carmichael brought out a volume of poems that spring, which had an unexpected success. The war, people said, had revived their interest in poetry.]"[8] The conventional wisdom that Sassoon, Owen, Thomas, Graves, and Brooke produced only elegiac accounts of the war also generates a single reading of their work by assuming their allegiance to a mythology that is all but indifferent to their ontological resistance.

Rather than argue that Britain has wrongly appropriated this reading, I suggest that there are elements of these writers' work that endorse it, and a resonance to their writing that criticism often ignores. Since Sassoon's writing is emblematic of this link between subjectivity, desire, and loss for British culture, his grief and disorientation appear to mirror the collapse of Britain's imperial power.[9] Similar to an obsessional fantasy, Britain repeats to itself with unfailing fascination the image of its international decline: it assumes that Sassoon's dream of a bygone era is the poetic expression of this waning power. In line with all forms of nostalgia, this reading of the war poets signals a commemorative appeal for what the war shattered: the apparent pastoral beauty and metropolitan elegance of Edwardian Britain. Each account of this period ushers in a fantasy of national stability by an alarming "refurbishment of the Empire's tarnished image." [10]

Contrary to the presumption that these poets shared an identical response to the First World War, this chapter focuses on elements of Sassoon's work that question national allegiance and military combat. These elements are central to the war, and to the reflexive and interrogative modernity to which it contributed. I suggest that two aspects of these questions require examination: the notion that the iconography of the "war poets" rescinds their ambivalence to Britain's military policies, and the assumption that an excision of same-sex desire from this ideal grants a specific reliability to Britain's wartime allegory.

In terms of the first proposition, Sassoon, Owen, Brooke, and Graves publicly redefined their support for the war, and changed from ardent patriotism at its beginning to prominent criticism by its end. Their trajectory is significant in encouraging a shift in public consciousness that did not jeopardize the alleged integrity of British masculinity: these poets tried to end the war by downplaying the idea of surrender as national emasculation. In terms of the second proposition, and despite the relative invisibility of homosexual desire in Sassoon's poetry, I contend that it is influenced by a tradition of homophilia that encompasses a yearning passion for camaraderie and intimacy. Although many critics interpret this yearning as a desire for fraternal bonding, or a generic defense by European allies against the terror of the German enemy, they rely on a select reading of Sassoon's poetry that ignores his memoirs and diaries.

Sassoon's broadly intermediary period of protest between unquestioning patriotism and repudiation of violence connects with Britain's wartime allegory of masculinity and the difficulty of encoding same-sex desire; he directed most of his anger at the British public's cowardice and the incompetence of its political representatives. [11] The title of one of his collections, *Counter-Attack,* suggests this embittered reversal as a resistance to combat and a suggestion that he might take up arms against an enemy he identified at home. Thus Sassoon reframed cowardice as the vindictive aims of a public intent on killing its citizens, not the classic "effeminacy" of those who uphold principles of pacifism.

The authorities' response to Sassoon's "willful defiance" was one of bewildered reproach, followed by silencing strategies, accusations of treachery and, finally, an order for his detention for the treatment of a psychiatric disorder—"war-shock." Literary criticism of his *Counter-Attack* has paradoxically endorsed this prognosis by suggesting that a tone of "adolescent" rage "bludgeons" the reader into acquiescence by focusing relentlessly on the mutilation and decomposition of men's bodies.[12] In other words, what is unappealing or "unpoetic" about these poems is their refusal to adopt an aesthetic of death as heroic, and their insistently naturalist transposition of the sublime into corporeal abjection.[13]

Sassoon was not the only poet to describe this transposition, but his later writing is significant in representing the war as a constitutive influence on European modernity; his memoirs foreground the impossibility of the sublime as one of their principal effects.[14] I contend that this representation was largely inadvert, that Sassoon's resistance to modernism in his early memoirs and poetry sought to reverse Europe's shift toward cubism, futurism, and vorticism, as well as dada's absurdist response to the war, by reinvoking the previous century's romantic aesthetic. This may explain why the war poets remain so enduringly popular, and why their aesthetic seems central to Britain's disavowal of its imperial dissolution and economic turbulence at the war's end. While numerous examples attest to a contrary social history, Edwardian Britain is thus *recalled* as a period of untroubled peace and harmony.

One example of this retroactive collation of British culture is the opening volume to Sassoon's autobiography, *Memoirs of a Fox-Hunting Man* (1928). Sassoon began writing this account after the war had ended, as if the danger of forgetting was his principal concern. However, the task of rewriting the war expanded into a lifetime's project, as Sassoon devoted his remaining years to revising texts whose sole preoccupation was the anticipated, lived, or protracted experience of combat. While periods overlap in these texts, Sassoon orients chronology toward psychic time; his diaries return to, amend, and rechronicle an experience already detailed by his testimonial poetry—and again by memoir—as if to work through what was clearly the central inspiration of his life.

This reworking of temporality and constant rebinding of the war's signification drew Sassoon closer to the conceptual and stylistic procedures of European modernism. As part of his reminiscence, and contrary to his desire to return to an ideal subjectivity, however, Sassoon never reached the mythic tranquillity of prewar culture; he could define it only against the turbulence of the present. Thus his project defeated itself because the drive to envisage life before the war endlessly devolved on a catastrophe he could never forget. Since Sassoon never gave up trying, the actual war recedes in his fiction, and the fantasy that outlasts it hones the event down to an increasingly diffuse recollection.

Besides his textual accounts of violence, Sassoon's writing is notable because the war configures issues to which it holds no necessary relation. The questions of his childhood, choice of career, literary friendships, and homosexual desire appear to cohere around this event because it organizes their meaning. The war encouraged Sassoon to revise the narrative of his childhood, for instance, and to associate the absence of war with domestic and psychic plenitude. Military and personal conflict also coalesce in his *Memoirs* and *Diaries,* for Sassoon seemed unable or unwilling to distinguish between historical and psychic issues. Thus war stands in as a metaphor for his childhood breaks and transitions by substituting writing for the ontological crises that precede it: the conflicts of desire and violence that shatter him into a chaotic order of military symbols.

It would be easy for criticism to adopt a similar procedure and exchange war for unresolved psychic conflict thus reducing literature to psychobiography. This is not my suggestion; yet the reverse supposition that war and subjectivity are distinct also is unsatisfactory.[15] The problem with Sassoon's writing is that war repeats *and* interprets moments of immense psychic resonance: since military recollection is not fortuitous in his writing, we cannot consign its prevalence to incorrect or idealistic fantasy.

Memoirs of a Fox-Hunting Man supports this association between psychic violence and cultural nostalgia by constituting the past as a time of mythical happiness. Sassoon isolates and spins events into a narrative so overlaid with sentiment that it almost excludes the traumatic events of 1914. Chapters comprise the description of memorable hunts or rounds of golf; by adopting the archaisms—now clichés—of romanticism, Sassoon virtually suspends the influence of the modern by reverting to scenes of pastoral tranquillity.[16] In writing of his childhood home, Sassoon so overwrites his account that the prose almost balks from the weight of allusion:

> Looking back across the years I listen to the summer afternoon cooing of my aunt's white pigeons, and the soft clatter of their wings as they flutter upward from the lawn at the approach of one of the well-nourished cats. I remember, too, the smell of strawberry jam being made; and Aunt Evelyn with a green bee-veil over her head . . . The large rambling garden, with its Irish yews and sloping paths and wind-buffeted rose arches, remains to haunt my sleep. The quince tree which grew beside the little pond was the only quince

tree in the world. With a sense of abiding strangeness, I see my-self looking down from an upper window on a confusion of green branches shaken by the summer breeze. In an endless variety of dream-distorted versions the garden persists as the background of my unconscious existence. (24–25; original ellipsis)

Despite his opening caution ("In this brightly visualised world of simplicities and misapprehensions"), Sassoon's prose resists the post-Edenic bathos of war because his irony extends only to childhood fragility, not historical crisis. Sassoon's aesthetic is so successful that his frequent digressions into other episodes bolster this ideal instead of puncturing the very drive to recreate it. This counters John Onions's suggestion that Sassoon's memoirs are an "ironic prefiguration" of the war;[17] his narratives strive to displace military conflict, and return to themselves in a strategic hope of forgetting.

Toward the end of this text, Sassoon absolves the war of crisis and refigures it as an extension of Britain's idyll: "For me, so far, the War had been a mounted infantry picnic in perfect weather. The inaugural excitement had died down, and I was agreeably relieved of all sense of personal responsibility" (244). Sassoon writes, with an irony modern readers may appreciate, that being in the army is "very much like being back at school" (244) because its disciplinary structures encourage heroism and male camaraderie, and—one might add—infantilism. This emphasis on order and intimacy protects Sassoon from violence, while the health of outdoor living and "homely smells" recreate lost pleasure: "there was something almost idyllic about those early weeks of the War" (245). As the narrative moves listlessly toward the war, the convolution of figurative language becomes more intense, resisting the incipience of conflict by dwelling on each renunciation of pleasure. The struggle for amnesia is impossible, however, because violence surfaces from the place that Sassoon formerly denied it: "Everything I had known before the War seemed to be withering and falling to pieces" (294).

Sassoon often describes "the spellbound serenity" of Edwardian Britain by metaphorizing a seasonal transition from late summer to bleak winter to emphasize why the "cloudless weather of that August and September [of 1914] need not be dwelt on; it is a hard fact in history" (248). However, the figurative cannot occlude *the Fall* as a "hard fact" of history because it fetishizes "the peaceful past" (24) as a security that is no longer tenable. Analogous to the body of a soldier he confronts whose "whole spurious edifice fell to bits" (266), Sassoon's military experience shatters his illusion of "spellbound serenity" when the figurative fails to supplant this violent intensity. This metaphor parallels his allusion to British pastoralism; *Memoirs of a Fox-Hunting Man* endeavors to replace the empty space of death and the traumatic *real* of war.

Insofar as he returned to his childhood fourteen years later, Sassoon's first memoir failed to memorialize his past. Sassoon produced two other volumes that chart his youth from the perspective of his literary career, though their remarkable avoidance of death only intensifies the urgency of his lyricism.[18] Sassoon tints *The Weald of Youth* (1942) with such nostalgia that it is closer to Thomas Hardy's late-Victorian poetics than the retributive and almost contemporaneous anger of John Osborne, Joe Orton, or Graham Greene:[19] "Some way back I have defined this book as an attempt to compose an outline of my mental history. That sounds safe and comfortable enough, and can be kept modestly plausible while the said history is unfolding itself through actual episodes . . ." (27). The episode in question is not the Second World War, as we might suppose from its historical proximity, or even Sassoon's preoccupation with the First; it is the story of how he came to publish his first book of poetry. Even "this impulsive holocaust" is an exorbitant reference to his destruction of juvenilia in a text otherwise obsessed with the "gentle revisitation of the days that are no more" (41). It later transpires that this "revisitation" consists of piecing his childhood together from mnemonic fragments of bicycle rides, tennis games, and resplendent sunsets: "Out on the lawn the Eden freshness was like something never breathed before. In a purified ecstasy I inhaled the smell of dew-soaked grass, and all the goodness of being alive now met me in a moment, as I stood on the door-step outside the drawing-room. . . . Somehow the sound [of an . . .] exultant chorus of birds . . . gave me a comfortable feeling of the world remaining pleasantly unchanged and peaceful. . . . In the Arcadian cherry orchard across the road a bird-scaring boy had begun his shouting cries and clattering of pans . . ." (39–40; last two sets of ellipses in original). The reference to Arcadia in post-Holocaust Europe apparently is no irony for Sassoon; it indicates the preoccupation of a man whose present exists with almost no other referent than the legacy of unresolved violence. Thus history and the present converge as Sassoon meanders wistfully from past simple to present continuous—"Meanwhile I am still overhearing . . ." (44)—and from present simple to a future conditional, a syntactical clause in which Sassoon reframes history by imaginary projection: "Revisiting some such house I should go there in summer—preferably on a dozy July morning. I should find myself in an upstairs room . . . It is an unfrequented room, seeming to contain vibrations of vanished life" (44–45).

Since he conflates adolescence with middle-aged nostalgia, and psychoanàlysis also insists that psychic time relates to its subject's erratic self-narrativization, it is not surprising that Sassoon's version of the war—at the end of this now supplemental memoir—erases all record of violence and renders the war a vanishing point of his imaginary. Despite its *post*war fantasies of *pre*war pleasure, *The Weald of Youth* ceaselessly enumerates the war's psychic resonance in Sassoon. Accompanying the rage and bitterness of many of his poems, he remarks: "I should have been quite put out if someone had told me that there might not be a war after all, for the war had become so much my own affair that it was—temporarily and to the exclusion of all other considerations—merely me!" (272). Sassoon's overidentification with the war suggests that it produced the right conditions for him to bind otherwise disparate elements of his personality. I suggest that it also encouraged him to realize and partially resolve a tension between ambition and desire by bringing each diffuse element of his character to the fore: "It was possible, I found, to divide myself—as I had existed during the past year [1913]—into three fairly distinct parts; the hunting man; the person who had spent ten weeks in Raymond Buildings [the London aesthete]; and the invisible being who shadowed the other two with his lordly ambition to produce original poetry" (266–67). If the "hunting man" was restless with inactivity and the aesthete dispirited by the loneliness of city life, "the invisible" third[20]—according to Sassoon—"was mainly responsible for the ineffectiveness of the whole affair" (267). He tried immediately to interpret this self-impediment: "The actual Me who had the management of these ingredients sat worrying about them at Weirleigh, unable to see any way out of the dismal and irresolute situation to which he—and they—had reduced himself" (268). The war seemed to dispel this anxiety and ennui by "tak[ing] the trivial personal problem off his hands" (268), providing a symbol for each component of his personality: the "sportsman" developed into a soldier, the aesthete into an officer, the writer into a poet overwhelmed by creative incentive. However, the war cut across these symbolic constituents because it embodied, rationalized, and finally legitimized physical intimacy with other men.

Rather than claim that we can restrict desire and military ambition to biographical interest, I interpret Sassoon's experiential investment in war as synecdochic of a generic reorientation of sexuality at the time.[21] Although Sassoon gave the "invisible being" that immobilized his existence in London the attributes of a poet, this persona's influence surfaces at the beginning of *Memoirs of a Fox-Hunting Man* as the missing half of his character: "As a consequence of my loneliness I created in my childish day-dreams an ideal companion who became much more of a reality than such unfriendly boys as I encountered at Christmas parties [when . . .] I was so glad to escape from the horrors of my own hospitality. . . . The 'ideal companion' probably originated in my desire for an elder brother" (11). Since this volume curtails Sassoon's discussion of childhood, the plenitude of rural life soon displaces his "ideal companion." Sassoon's passion for horses and their masculine care-takers briefly supplants the need for "an elder brother" before memory restores it as a burning demand: "[He] has cropped up with an odd effect of importance which makes me feel he must be worth a passing mention. The fact is that, as soon as I began to picture in my mind the house and garden where I spent so much of my early life, I caught sight of my small, vanished self with this other non-existent boy standing beside him. And though it sounds silly enough, I felt queerly touched by the recollection of that forgotten companionship" (11). Sassoon's division of his character into specific interests arguably connects with his management of memory — "the actual Me" who tries to unify this fraction — for he claims later that Sherston, his memoirs' fictional protagonist, "is only one-fifth of myself," [22] a figure curious for its mathematical precision and the suggestion of a remainder that his memoirs excise. Sassoon's interest in poetry is the most obvious omission from this fraction,[23] though the remainder actually expands in later accounts from "one third" to "one half," to finally "four-fifths" of his missing identity. As Bernard Knox remarks without substantiation: "The persona of Sherston dictated the exclusion of poetry from the trilogy. . . . Poetry, however, was not the only side of Sassoon that was suppressed in Sherston; the war diaries reveal clearly enough that the poet's tenderest feelings were for those of his own sex." [24]

Sassoon's *Diaries* clarify these fractions without rendering him whole.[25] The testimony of his private word explicates, but never redeems, his artistic disseveration because the fantasy that we can read Sassoon entire rests on a premise that language and desire form an adequate relation. Instead of searching for this fraction, or paradoxically extolling the critical possibilities of its absence, I suggest that Sassoon's struggle with sexual representation surfaces throughout his preceding narratives. The intrusion of this desire — indeed, the demand that it now be heard — suggests more than an assumption that Sassoon formerly denied it; Sassoon attributes the entire conflict to war's psychological damage. Rather than accept this self-prognosis, we we might consider that his diary's interrogative style pronounces this conflict a misrecognition, demonstrating consistently that cohesion is an ontological impossibility:

Writing the last words of a book, more than four years ago, I left a man—young for his age, though nearly thirty-four—standing in Trafalgar Square, vaguely conscious that his career had reached a point where he must begin it all over again. That man was, of course, myself. I had conducted him as far as August 1920 with a fair amount of confidence in my ability to get back into his skin and describe his state of mind. He was remote, but *unamenable to the process of reconstruction.* Since leaving him, I have often tried to get in touch with him again. But the distance between us has widened in more than years, and I have found myself complaining that *we are now scarcely on speaking terms*—that he has dropped out of my life, and that if I were to meet him I should not know what to say to him. It seems that *I, his successor, have outlived our former intimacy.* And I am not sure that I want to revive my relationship with one so inexperienced, uninformed, and self-dramatising as he then was. (15; my emphases)

Sassoon adopts many personal pronouns in his diary because each one infers, and immediately questions, the adequacy of self-reference: "I . . . myself . . . I . . . him . . . my . . . he . . . us . . . I . . . myself . . . we . . . ," and so on. Although the idea of imagining oneself as the other of one's speech is a convention of journal writing, Sassoon also interrogates the adequacy of each reflexive pronoun: "myself . . . my . . . our." What does "our" incorporate that "he" cannot, and what does "myself" mean in its radical disservation from "us"? In their respective ways, poststructuralist and psychoanalytic criticism represent the breach between the "I" and "my" of linguistic utterance as a sign of the insoluble difference between the place from which one speaks and the position from which one is spoken. Sassoon never ceases to probe and confound the fictional unity of the subject as it speaks from the place it has been. To put this another way, Sassoon demonstrates that the desire to solidify the present, and represent oneself *as* "self-present," is possible only by projecting oneself from an imaginary reconstitution of the past. As Lacan corroborated more recently, we can apprehend subjectivity in the future anterior only because this tense collates the present from a fantasy of what will have been.[26] Sassoon seemed to imply this when he wrote: "I doubt whether this book is giving anything like a chart of what is really going on inside me. Anyhow it is as near as I can get" (33). The signifier can approximate only the profuse web of fantasy that underlies and disturbs it.

Beyond this general difficulty of language and expression, Sassoon compounds the drama of self-presence by the meaning he attributes to each personal register. His "I" confers an authority on a "self" that looks with misgiving and frequent disgust on the parts of a "he" it would rather disown. As his diary testifies, this split occurs whenever Sassoon broaches the question of sexuality; his desire seems to separate from consciousness and represent a painful incursion on friendship and intimacy: "It was a very lovely and peaceful affair [with the painter Gabriel Atkin] and made us both feel better . . . because I felt the existence of a bond which is untroubled by animalism" (31). When Sassoon ruminates on Gabriel as a "distraction," however, he comments: "I seem to suffer from a poisoned mind; an unwholesome unhappiness pervades my healthy body. Is it pride — conceited pride — that makes me crave to alienate everyone?" (77–78). An answer seems to surface the following week as a more extreme self-accusation: "What is wrong with me? Is it this cursed complication of sex that afflicts me?" (81). The question persists throughout the journal, and soon represents the entirety of his discontent: "Attractive faces in streets. Cursed nuisance of sex . . . Rome doesn't disappoint me. *It is myself that fails.* Why am I so dreary and unreceptive, incapable of imaginative enthusiasm and romantic youthfulness? . . . Is it my own fault that I am under this cursed obsession of sex-cravings[?] . . . My mind is somehow diseased and distorted. I live in myself — seek freedom in myself — self-poisoned, self-imprisoned. . . . If I had my heart's desire I should be happy; but not for long" (86–87; my emphasis). Although Sassoon's self-loathing and recrimination are poignantly elaborate, they also are contrary to his writing's ongoing announcement of homosexual desire: he oscillates between periods of insanity, "morosity," and "a sort of self-lacerating irritability . . . that . . . is not unconnected with my animal passions" (88–89). This characterization of desire — and his vigilant wish to control it — exacerbates his self-recrimination by leading him to the brink of suicide at the end of this year (1921). As its etymology (*sui-cædere*) reminds, suicide is an annihilation of the self that relates intimately to Sassoon's impossibly proscribed tasks, values, and behaviors.

It may be reductive and superfluous to speculate on the relation between Sassoon's homosexual defense and his postwar illness. What is more certain and interesting is the way he enjoined on himself a ferocious command to sublimate, excise, and expel this set of impulses. The command not only failed (the demand would not go away), but Sassoon later attributed this sexual persistence to his dearth of creative success. He associated with such writers as Hardy and Forster, and frantically emulated them in the hope of producing "another *Madame Bovary* dealing with sexual inversion, a book that the world must recognise and learn to understand! O, that unwritten book! Its difficulties are overwhelming" (53).[27] Later, stymied by exhaustion and self-censorship, he impulsively dissolved the project altogether: "Now I am no longer in the mood to reveal the workings of my thought-processes for the benefit of unbeggoten generations of psychopathic subjects. I cannot put down more than a fraction of what was in my head" (53). Since this "curse" of fractions and desires besets all of Sassoon's writing, we must consider the labor and impossible ambition involved in his attempt to write his "entire" life story; something always stalls or goes awry at the level of narrative, memory, and consciousness.

Recognizing all of the dangers of prognosis—and psychobiography is not my interest here—I suggest that Sassoon's inability to write had little or nothing to do with artistic ability, which clearly was considerable. Writing led him to an impasse that seized over the use of acceptable symbols—acceptable, that is, to both its writer and public readers. We risk taking Sassoon at his (frequently unreliable) word if we accept that the residue of the unwritten was little more "than a fraction of what was in my head"; the "cursed" supplement of sexual "obsession" had already emerged, and been displaced, elsewhere. Recall that in chapter 6, Forster expressed similar discomfort and disingenuous confession when he decided to "burn . . . my indecent writings or as many as the fire will take. Not a moral repentance, but [from] the belief that they clogged me artistically." [28]

I suggest that Sassoon's 1920–1922 *Diaries* illustrate a complex literary displacement that represents the compression *and* release of his desire in the trenches. This substitution of "cursed" desires is more successful in a military context because combat, struggle, and tension already function as metaphors in his writing. Thus Sassoon frequently counterpoises the antagonism of his desire ("and is there anything in life which can be *disconnected* from this curse of sex?" [103; my emphasis]) with the threat of its disappearance ("but I must have feelings toward *something!*" [103]), which precipitates a crisis over his desire's coherence and persistence: "The question now arises—which of myselves is the most worthy of survival? Which of myselves is writing this excorium? And, having written it, how can it be responsible for what future selves may reveal?" (104).

Sassoon's questions force us to consider his choice of genre and narrative style: if the *Memoirs* are—by his conscious division—"only one-fifth of myself," the problem remains where and how to deposit the remainder. Writing is central to this difficulty because it supports a belief that Sassoon can project internal war as a conflict among competing nations. Though the question of self-survival is largely unanswerable to Sassoon, the assumption that it corresponds to political hatred suggests a reprieve from self-accusation. As Sassoon poignantly explained: "In retrospection we see ourselves as we never existed. So I am keeping a journal in order to record my daily and essential inconsistency and constitutional silliness. From this jungle of misinterpretations of my ever-changing and never-steadfast selves, some future fool may, perhaps, derive instruction and amusement" (104). Although this analogy between national and psychic war offers a fleeting resolution, it poses questions about the relation between this "jungle of misinterpretations" and the battlefield on which so many millions of lives were destroyed. As many critics have argued, the war also engaged critical questions about meaning and validation,[29] and the point is worth reiterating to revoke the simple assumption that military conflict is entirely responsible for mental illness. I suggest that it may actually have *disinhibited* Sassoon's psychic distress before intensifying it later with the prominence of visible devastation.

The argument that military conflict alleviates *and* compounds distress is worth considering because critics usually consider only the latter proposition: they interpret war's effect on a generation or series of individuals without asking to what "needs" a war answers or responds. Eric Leed's work is interesting in this regard because he argues that the First World War marked a paradigm shift from "offensive" military strategies to "defensive" personal appeals against national violence. It may be misleading to suggest that this war inaugurated an era of alienation, as if alienation were a new phenomenon; Leed suggests only that the war shattered a notion of heroic valor and patriotism that Wordsworth's "Happy Warrior" hitherto exemplified.[30] The extent to which British troops "fraternized" with the Germans may have eroded a corresponding projection of the enemy as a bad object; the war's vacillating levels of hatred also meant that the soldier could neither retreat (for fear of punishment by "desertion"), nor move into enemy lines (since this required an extension into increasingly intolerable terrain). Thus it is surely no accident that the phrase "No Man's Land" acquired much resonance at the time, and that the soldier (or *solderer*) generated figurative importance as the emblem of several liminal frontiers: between the home culture and its "other-alien," the military unit and its various subjects, and the subject and its psychic composition. For this reason, Lacan has argued about the dissolution of the Oedipus complex and the ties of kinship: "This is what is designated as the field of culture—somewhat inadequately, because this field is supposed to be based on a *no man's land* in which genitality as such subsists, whereas it is in fact dissolved, not re-assembled." [31] Leed has also commented on this trope's modernist implications: "Modern battle is the fragmentation of spatial and temporal unities. It is the creation of a system with no center and no periphery in which men, both attackers and defenders, are lost." [32]

Sassoon's second volume of autobiography, *Memoirs of an Infantry Officer* (1930), demonstrates ambivalence about these conflicts' political inflections. His memoir also details a conflict of defending one realm (Britain's national borders) over the interests of another (his internal and psychic safety).[33]

Primal Scenes: Desire, Disfiguration, and "The Spirit of the Bayonet"

Love of his country begins in a man's house.
—Francis Bacon [34]

. . . I had done what I could to tidy up the mess in no-man's land.
—Siegfried Sassoon, *Memoirs of an Infantry Officer* (29)

By the time Sassoon wrote *Memoirs of an Infantry Officer* (1930), the war it described had receded into popular mythology, and another of greater magnitude loomed on the political horizon—the consolidation of National Socialism in Germany was underway. Although Sassoon's perception of the Second World War displaced the terms of its historical truth, he no longer could produce a companion volume that "would lead [him] along pleasant associative lanes connected with the English counties" (10); the creation of "one of those peaceful war pictures" was impossible because they have "vanished for ever and are rarely recovered in imaginative retrospect" (10–11).

With its emphasis on greater fidelity to historical drama, *Memoirs of an Infantry Officer* describes the civilian's substitution by its military counterpart. Leed has described the psychic consequence of this transformation by paraphrasing a prominent military strategist: "The purpose of training is to get the soldier to 'pattern himself after his persecutors (his officers)'; if successful, this causes the trainee to undergo a 'psychological regression during which his character is restructured into a combat personality.' " [35]

The psychological regression that military training entails demands nothing less than a return to the place of Law—the moment when the infant first apprehends the threat of violence and the alterity of language, prohibition, and sexual difference shatters its imaginary. Additionally, the prerequisite unraveling of the civilian into a "combat personality" offers the soldier a fantasy of mastering the bad object (the enemy) by submitting to orders that are closer to home. Sassoon's narrative is significant, however, because his defense against this regression unmakes each order, setting up a challenge through irony, illness, and defiance. In other words, the command, and the identification on which it relies, constantly *fails*. By his resistance to full participation, Sassoon empties the command of meaning, assessing its effect on his subjectivity by bringing the personal and military into profound conflict. Thus he writes of his "spectral presences": "Such hauntings might be as inadequate as those which now absorb my mental energy. For trench life was an existence saturated by the external senses; and although our actions were domineered over by military discipline, our animal instincts were always uppermost. While I stood there then, I had no desire to diagnose my environment. Freedom from its oppressiveness was what I longed for" (33).

Memoirs of an Infantry Officer juxtaposes Sassoon's precarious loyalty to Britain with his corresponding desire to defy its authority. When Sassoon involuntarily listens to a lecture on "The Spirit of the Bayonet," for instance, he judges the "homicidal eloquence" of the officer with critical disdain. As the officer cites the *Manual of Bayonet Training* — "The bullet and the bayonet are brother and sister"; "if you don't kill him, he'll kill you"; "stick him between the eyes, in the throat, in the chest" (12) — Sassoon's response is one of understandable revulsion. The officer also develops a penetrative fantasy — "Don't waste good steel. Six inches are enough. . . . Three inches will do for him; when he coughs, go and look for another. . . . Remember . . . [the] importance of a 'quick withdrawal' " (12) — in which the bayonet's castrating power invites the soldier sexually to usurp the enemy. The soldier must invest the bayonet with a spirit that absolves him of responsibility by conflating his territorial incursion with imaginary insemination: "We will force open the closed door and enter by force into the forbidden land. And for us who have for so long been forced to accumulate in desolate fields of shell holes, the idea of this thrust into the depths holds a compelling fascination." [36]

To the extent that almost all military rhetoric elaborates this "homosexual" fantasy, it is significant that Sassoon's irony inveighs only against the lecturer's brusque and ruthless manner. This may indicate Sassoon's blindness to what might otherwise have been a sexual critique of both the war and Britain's colonial appropriation of "forbidden land." [37] Instead of this critique, *Memoirs of an Infantry Officer* describes Sassoon's shifting relation to the enemy at home and abroad: his position wavered between a loyalty that subsumed him beneath the camaraderie of his unit (32) and a counterimpulse to detach from its contaminating influence (34). By domesticating the war to the level of a schoolboy "escapade" (51), which develops from an adolescent "prank" (73) into "a form of outdoor sports" (66), the narrative never unifies this oscillation. Sassoon later describes the war with the disdain of an aesthete who pursues beauty to redeem his surrounding violence.

This fantasy of wartime "escapades" recurs in many Edwardian narratives as a lineage from British public schools to the empire's contested frontiers: both represent "an adventure" (16) fought by team spirit, stolid endurance, and an obligatory "stiff upper-lip." [38] It is no accident that many of the narratives aimed at upper-class boys and young men at the end of the nineteenth century begin at these schools; they often close with the same group of friends reunited in a trench or a subaltern outpost. Kipling's *Stalky & Co.* (1899) is a notable example:

> "Now all together—takin' time from your Uncle Stalky:
> "It's a way we have in the Army,
> "It's a way we have in the Navy,
> "It's a way we have in the Public Schools
> "Which nobody can deny!" [39]

Kipling implies in *Stalky & Co.* that pedagogical hierarchies of discipline and subordination regulate the empire and its wars; we might also consider his accounts of the 1899 Boer War. Sassoon also notes that the army's hierarchy resembles "some fortunate colony" (10), while he addresses his helpmate, Flook, in the trenches rather as a prefect would speak to a junior in a public-school context of "fagging" (14, 16, 29, 40). As another example of this synecdoche, Thomas Hughes's popular *Tom Brown's Schooldays* (1857) is similar with structural homoeroticism, representing school as a preparation for war and war as a schoolboy venture its participants have never outgrown: "It was not at all unusual in those days for two School-house boys to have a fight. . . . After all, what would life be like without fighting? From the cradle to the grave, fighting, rightly understood, is the business, the real, highest, honestest [sic] business of every son of man. Every one who is worth his salt has his enemies, who must be beaten, be they evil thoughts and habits in himself, or spiritual wickedness in high places, or Russians, or Border-ruffians, or Bill, Tom, or Harry, who will not let him live his life in quiet till he has thrashed them." [40]

This proximity between Britain's public schools and empire suggests that the first was synecdochic of the second because its values flourished in national policy and global management. The allegedly successful economies of "sublimation" and "purity" that ranged from Britain's public-school system to its empire were integral to both sexes' management in Britain's colonies.[41] Thus J. B. Priestley's description of the emotional training of all-male public schools is unsurprising in its reference to the "relief . . . of [living] a wholly masculine way of life uncomplicated by Woman";[42] as my opening section on Kipling's contemporaries demonstrated, almost all forms of government at the time portrayed this masculine investment.

Sassoon's focus on a love object tended to stabilize this tradition's oscillations, however, by encouraging him to grasp the unstable ground between group immolation and solitary detachment. By expanding on the passionate friendships in *Memoirs of a Fox-Hunting Man,* Sassoon "betrayed" a deep affection for two men, Stephen Colwood and David Cromlech, that released him from London's sexual impediments. Thus the war offered a context for same-sex intimacy by representing a generic body to which Sassoon could attribute it. In *Memoirs of an Infantry Officer,* Sassoon represented this intimacy as if it falls under the banner of fraternal—or "nonsexual"—concern since his "*indefinite* pang of affection" (76; my emphasis) for Cromlech intercedes between solitude, the allies, and the enemy.

If affection is "indefinite" in this memoir, it is largely because Sassoon characterizes it as a diffuse and nonexclusive quality. However, the love object is not amorphous in this memoir but entirely specific; Sassoon and Cromlech's relationship allows them to anticipate the end of war and to speculate on their continued intimacy after it (77). Since Cromlech occupies in fantasy the place of his missing "half"—the absent brother/lover[43]—he repeats Sassoon's childhood fantasy of an "ideal companion." As Sassoon's memoir fails to distinguish between psychic and military registers, it conflates the war with a psychological drama that compels him to fight and recoil as if from an equivalent scene of violence.

The first half of *Memoirs of an Infantry Officer* anticipates this violence because the enemy is formless and ubiquitous, not recognizable in the narrative. The memoir begins with Sassoon's preparing for conflict, though it later elaborates his dread that the unit will stumble on a fantasmatically comparable battle zone. As Sassoon considers the imminence of this attack, he interprets who and what the enemy is, and why he invests it with such a capacity for psychic retribution: "Then I rushed at the bank, vaguely expecting some sort of scuffle with my imagined enemy" (66). In each projection, Sassoon patterns the enemy after a model of internal conflict; his external encounter with the Germans is *unheimlich* when he discovers them maimed and disfigured: their bodies are sufficiently similar (as men) to endorse his private antagonism, and dissimilar (as enemies in a different uniform) to render the corpse a brutal encounter with the *real.*

Since *Memoirs of an Infantry Officer* struggles to resolve two competing aims, it splits between supporting Britain by converting the "enemy" into a "fiend" (96), and confronting death by associating the German corpses with the military and psychic abject.[44] The liminal border between these aims separates Sassoon's passionate interest in David Cromlech from the German bodies by upholding a precarious distinction between friend and foe on which Sassoon's perception of the war relies. This oscillation is largely inevitable because the line between loyalty and desertion for Sassoon—and the army and nation at large—is particularly fragile.

It would appear that Sassoon had trouble reconciling this tension, for it haunted him long after the war had receded as historical fact. The difference between national friend and foreign enemy turns on the strength of Sassoon's identification with the group and his submission to contrary demands. However, the problem is more urgent when Sassoon considers the idea of brotherhood because it forces him to recognize what is desirable in and "other" to the brother, and then to separate the beloved of David Cromlech from the enemy that finally kills him. Although this recognition seems quite obvious in national and political rhetoric, its psychic distinction is more arbitrary. The difference between these registers poses an ontological dilemma for Sassoon that asks him to examine what it means to identify with a nation, the military commands of the "father," and the land that Sassoon claimed and violated in the name of his real and imaginary authority.

I suggest that Sassoon failed to resolve these questions because they surface in each memoir as a troubled relation to national service. Britain's demand that Sassoon identify with and fight for its people runs counter to his individualism and desire for a "brother," for instance, because it requires him to renounce these drives in the service of a collective aim. Thus Sassoon received the nation's call-up with fervor (244–45); his officers later rewarded him with a medal for courage: "I wanted to make the World War serve a similar purpose . . . of demonstrating my equality with my contemporaries . . . for if only I could get a Military Cross *I should feel comparatively safe* and confident" (18; my emphasis).

As I earlier described, however, Sassoon reversed this strategy by attacking the home front with a petition he described as "an act of willful defiance" (204). The question of what he needed to be safe from, and to whom he directed his defiance, asks us to consider the terms of his identification because Sassoon repeatedly signified each military representative as an imago of Law: he condemned the surrounding genocide by these "fathers" and continued to fight with a ferocious will to victory. As several members of his unit have commented, it is difficult to reconcile the outraged poet who "had just . . . published . . . a volume full of bitter indignation at the hideous cruelty of modern warfare" with the man who was "also . . . a first-rate soldier and a most aggressive company commander." [45]

During his temporary absence from the war, Sassoon was riven by such guilt that the relief of escape without physical injury seemed to recall memories of an earlier psychological battle: "It was nice to think that I'd been fighting with them, though exactly what I'd done to help them was difficult to define. An elderly man, cycling along a dusty road in a dark blue suit and a straw hat, removed one hand from the handle-bars to wave comprehensive gratitude. Everything seemed happy and homely. I was delivered from the idea of death, and that other thing which had haunted me, the dread of being blinded" (90–91). The guilt of avoiding some of the conflict may have been responsible for Sassoon's precipitous return to it; the war renewed his desire to fight and reaffiliate: "willfully . . . in 1918 after his protest, . . . [Sassoon] patroll[ed] to the German trenches as exuberantly as Julian Grenfell ever did in 1914–15." [46] Every transition between support and antagonism, submission and defiance, seemed to amalgamate diffuse constituents of his identity that the "opaque arenas of war" (37) formerly had struggled to bind. As he remarked with an inadvertently modernist consciousness: "Our inconsistencies are often what make us most interesting, and it is possible that, in my zeal to construct these memoirs carefully, I have eliminated many of my own self-contradictions." [47]

The zeal of Sassoon's elimination, and the prominence of self-contradiction, ask us to consider the fine line between passionate devotion to the nation and hostile defiance against it. These inconsistencies surface whenever Sassoon interprets heroic commitment, sacrifice to duty, and altruistic virtue, on the one hand, and annihilation, grief, and devastation on the other. Though Sassoon never resolved this dilemma, his "indefinite pang of affection" (76) for other men occupied the middle ground—or battleground—between these poles of military rhetoric because he was unable to locate desire outside, or beyond, the field of war. In his concern to inhabit this critical terrain, Sassoon identified with neither the sublime nor the abject, but rather with the bleak and precarious "No Man's Land" that intercedes between them as their vanishing mediator.

9

Saki/Munro:

"Savage Propensities";

or, The "Jungle-boy

in the Drawing-room"[1]

Man was a being with myriad lives and myriad sensations, a
complete multiform creature that bore within itself strange
legacies of thought and passion, and whose very soul was
tainted with the monstrous maladies of the dead.
—Saki[2]

Yeovil . . . broke into the conversation with an inspired flash
of malicious untruthfulness. . . . It was a poor substitute for
physical violence, but it was all that civilization allowed him
in the way of relieving his feelings; it had, moreover, the
effect of making Plarsey profoundly miserable.
—Saki (764)

. . . there are limits beyond which repressed emotions become
dangerous.
—Saki (117)

H. H. Munro often detailed the relation between militarism and homosexuality as impossibly conflicted. His writing seems to circulate around two
structural and conceptual frontiers: the first lies between the nation and its
enemies and generates a crisis of political allegiance; the second falls be-

tween masculine identification and homosexual desire as a conflict between the subject and its drives. The oscillation between these antagonisms is the subject of this chapter, which argues that they guide the reader toward the precarious status of the "he" that desires in Munro's writing.

Munro (pseudonym "Saki") expressed fierce loyalty to Britain's empire throughout his life in combat, though his homosexuality appeared to precipitate a conflict between his desire for full inclusion in Britain's military activities and the possibility of representing his homosexuality in fiction. It may not surprise us that Munro's problem of binding literature and patriotism into a coherent identity repeated a dilemma that beset other men and women during this period (Siegfried Sassoon and Wilfred Owen are notable examples). Frequently, these writers confronted a conflict between the military sublime of colonial heroism and the abjection of ontological crisis, a conflict that may have stalled and displaced the intermediary difficulty of homo/sexual desire.

In Saki's writing, two scenes recur with startling familiarity that clarify the tension informing his narratives' domestic and social relations: the drama in the Edwardian drawing room and the mannered artifice at a summer garden party. Saki shares with Henry James and Ronald Firbank an emphasis on decorum that his characters refine to its most subtle, delicate, and even violent nuance. In analogous ways to James's *The Awkward Age* (1899), Firbank's *Vainglory* (1915), and Wharton's *The House of Mirth* (1905), Saki conveys meaning through dialogue and gesture rather than an overarching narrative.[3] He also shares with Firbank a levity that devolves on ephemeral and frivolous aspects of social interaction. The short story is an appropriate genre for Saki's social dramas because they often build on a single scene and consist of light banter and arch quips that culminate in hilarious—and frequently macabre—conclusions.

Oscar Wilde and Max Beerbohm appear to have influenced Saki in this respect because his writing does not veil a deeper truth about interpersonal relations. Instead, his narratives rescind depth and spin out laterally across a taut and brilliantly condensed semiotic of Edwardian etiquette. Firbank often interrupted this tradition by representing himself as the urbane overseer of his drama, but Saki is an active participant in each scene, embroiling himself in each of his fictional personifications. Reginald, Clovis, and Comus form an array of dandies whose delicate taste and asinine wit display their author's cruel dispassion and nervous unease.

I do not mean to suggest that each dandy corresponds to Saki, or that there is even an authoritative and uncomplicated relation between them; the performative basis of Saki's writing disbands his identity's permanence and consistency.[4] Every impersonation casts doubt on the authority behind or beneath its utterance. This discontinuity draws attention to what is fictional and fractured about "Saki" by designating his characters as a composite of shifting and diffuse identifications. As Peter Sherringham observes about Miriam Rooth's character in James's *The Tragic Muse:* (1890) "These things were the fictions and shadows; *the representation was the deep substance.*"[5]

The complex signification of Munro's name illustrates this point: "Saki" is the nom de plume H. H. Munro adopted at the beginning of his literary career. It corresponds to a fictional character in Omar Khayyam's poem, "The Rubaiyat" whose "Sákí" was an Oriental Ganymede.[6] However, Munro applied the signature "Saki" only to fiction; he chose to write under his own name as a political journalist in Russia and Eastern Europe and, later, when he enrolled for military service in Britain. Saki's biographer A. J. Langguth describes the pen name as a "self-baptism [that] makes a man for the moment his own father" because it offers both a "concealment" and an inadvertent "reve[lation of] character."[7] In Munro's case, however, the precise terms of this character seem impossible to establish. Is "Munro"—and the attributes that accompany that name—the authentic character underwriting "Saki," or does each name project a composite of conflicting aims and identifications that resist cohesion? If the second proposition captures the shifts and inflections of Munro's writing, as I contend, it implies that "Saki" is less a character than an example of identity's generic difficulty. In this respect, Munro's name stands in for a missing alternative.

The refined control of "Saki" and the effete languor of his literary personifications appear quite irreconcilable with the militarism and reactionary prejudice of the journalist and soldier who enlisted to fight as "Munro." Indeed, the radical inconsistency between these identifications and the disparity of their final aims manifests in Saki's writing as a general scission between military identification and homosexual desire in Britain at the turn of the century. Accordingly, Saki/Munro's disseveration reveals not only a breach between two discrete identities, but also a symbolic and political antinomy. Though he is not simply symptomatic of this period, Saki may "stand in" for a time when this dissociation was a common strategy for the survival of war, and for the intense cultural and ontological difficulty that beset many of his contemporaries about homosexual desire. Saki may also illustrate a divide across eras, as well as the liminal difficulties that emerged between the decadence and symbolist movements of the 1890s and the incipience of pre- and postwar European modernism; the conflict he enacted between different and antagonistic components of his identity resonates with the rhetorical and sexual turbulence of this time.

My reading of Saki begins from the psychoanalytic premise that there is always a remainder to desire that identity cannot incorporate; subjectivity and language resist mastery and completion. Many psychoanalytic theorists have argued that this remainder fails at the level of language, though it persists as an unconscious influence on the subject.[8] When the restrictive categories of militarism and colonialism define the various roles the subject can adopt, they bring to bear a specific pressure on the organization of desire and the available symbols a subject can enunciate. In this respect, Munro's militarism engages with an interesting set of questions about his management of aggressivity and prejudice, and his alarming valorization of violence in his wartime journalism. Why, for instance, did he later repudiate the fictional coalescence of aesthetics and effeminacy in the interests of fascism, anti-Semitism, and colonial "virility"? Langguth observes, "It was Hector who would write the best of the stories; it was Munro who would go off to war. But the name of Saki could stand for the both of them. . . ."[9] This, however, does not account for Munro's shift in identification; Langguth's biography of Munro seems less an account of one man's life than the impossible task of drawing so many components within the aegis of a single, masterable subject. The claim that a pen name must "stand for both of them" suggests that allegory bound the displaced and antagonistic elements of Munro's identity and homosexuality into a temporary coherence around his proper name; my reading demonstrates that in Munro's case—as for all of the writers I have examined in this book—this allegorical principle failed in significant and interesting ways.

In its title and thematic, Saki's short story "Gabriel-Ernest" (c. 1910) captures this tension between binding and diffusion. Strictly speaking, this story's title does not correspond to an eponymous character; one character gives this name to another without precise reason or denomination: "Gabriel-Ernest," already split and never simply one, is the name the protagonist's aunt gives to a boy whom she finds naked in their woods:

> "We must call him something till we know who he really is," she said. "Gabriel-Ernest, I think; those are nice suitable names."
> Van Cheele agreed, but he privately doubted whether they were *being grafted on to* a nice suitable child. (67; my emphasis)

By the end of the narrative, neither character is any wiser about "who he really is"; the name is an empty signifier they graft to his identity (or their fantasy of it) because they lack verifiable detail. "Gabriel-Ernest" also captures the boy's observers' desire to encode certain qualities that would otherwise defy description.[10]

The tale echoes many conceptual and thematic concerns that Wilde represented several years earlier: the christening of Ernest, a child found in a handbag in Victoria Station, in *The Importance of Being Ernest* (1899), and the "discovery" and painting of Dorian Gray by two admiring men in *The Picture of Dorian Gray* (1891) (see chapter 3).[11] However, Gabriel-Ernest resists the simple designation of orphan or Narcissus; he is a boy with "savage propensities" (67), a "wild, nude animal" whom Van Cheele brings into his "primly ordered house" (65) with disastrous consequence. Unlike Dorian Gray, who possesses elegant poise and whose "savagery" derives from his mentors' wish to discern his character's unrepresentable qualities, Gabriel-Ernest arrives naked, and with an appetite for flesh: "rabbits, wild-fowl, hares, poultry, lambs in their season, children when I can get any" (64). Gabriel-Ernest's uncanny response troubles Van Cheele; the boy's appetite is unmistakably sexual: "On a shelf of smooth stone overhanging a deep pool in the hollow of an oak coppice a boy of about sixteen lay asprawl, drying his wet brown limbs luxuriously in the sun. His wet hair, parted by a recent dive, lay close to his head, and his light-brown eyes, so light that there was a tigerish gleam in them, were turned towards Van Cheele with a certain lazy watchfulness. It was an unexpected apparition, and Van Cheele found himself engaged in the novel process of thinking before he spoke. Where on earth could the wild-looking boy hail from?" (64). A similar enigma shrouds the appearance of a "bronze figure of a youthful Pan" (163), who gores a woman to death in Saki's later story, "The Music on the Hill," before vanishing with "the echo of a boy's laughter, golden and equivocal" (166). Yet "Gabriel-Ernest" disallows this mythical reading because the narrative constantly undermines the boy's resemblance to a "wild animal" (64–67). Saki foregrounds the havoc that Gabriel-Ernest wreaks on the "civilized" properties of Van Cheele's home by transforming Cunningham's remark, "There is a wild beast in your woods" (63, 65) into a comment on the proximity between "tame" and "savage" elements of domestic and psychic life. In particular, the comment refigures the domestic as a resilient defense against the disordering and haunting "wildness" that surrounds it. The decision to bring Gabriel-Ernest into the home—or, as Hélène Cixous has put it, "the Realm of the Proper" [12]—is significant because the home is unable to assimilate the sexual force that Gabriel-Ernest embodies; Van Cheele quickly casts the boy out to his former nomadic wild(er)ness.

With its similarity to E. M. Forster's short story "Story of a Panic" (see chapter 6), the tale is unusually graphic in its homo/sexualization of Saki's aesthetic dramas.[13] Since Saki defines the domestic by its ability to rescind sexual influence, desire can never inhabit the home's "proper" boundary. That the boy is "brown," or "bronzed" like Pan, recalls other characters in Saki's writing—for instance, the "naked brown Nubian" houseboy in "Laura" (245) and the African boys in *The Unbearable Bassington* (680–81)—whose entry into the home demands that they be shorn of "wildness"; the narrative fetishizes their sexuality as "exotic."

Although a figural *metalepsis* represents the erasure of his sexuality, Gabriel-Ernest does not disappear. His expulsion from Van Cheele's home does not damage the house; it throws its surrounding habitat awry. Similar to Fleet's "snarling like a wolf" at the end of Kipling's "The Mark of the Beast" (1891), the narrative transforms the boy into a werewolf that unleashes his "repressed" drives: "On the open hillside where the boy had been standing a second ago, stood a large wolf, blackish in colour, with gleaming fangs and cruel, yellow eyes" (68). That "Gabriel-Ernest is now a werewolf" (68) who kills Van Cheele's animals confirms what we knew from the outset about his predatory tendencies and barely concealed savagery. By representing the ravenous and racially marked appetite of a prowling enemy, Gabriel-Ernest foregrounds an irreconcilable scission between "tame" and "savage" propensities. Van Cheele's efforts to ward off the "unwelcome guest" (65) convert the boy into a demonic power that tips the "prim order" of the bourgeois home into chaotic disarray.

My interest in Saki's fiction stems from its inability to sustain this antinomy between tame and savage: "Savage propensities" coexist with their "civilized" counterparts, when the macabre vengeance and infantile cruelty of the dandy surfaces as the refined equivalent of "barbarism." In "The Lumber-Room," for instance, a disgraced little boy locks his aunt in a rainwater tank and releases her only on condition that she give him jam for tea (371–77). Another boy hunts a tabby cat to death and ransacks a local candy store ("The Penance," 422–27), while an angry ten-year-old gets his revenge on his bossy guardian by setting his pet polecat-ferret on her; he ponders her savage death as he chews on some long denied toast ("Sredni Vashtar," 136–40).

Wild animals, which appear with striking regularity in Saki's writing, fulfill the private dreams of cruelty that his "civilized" protagonists must repress: wolves appear in "The Wolves of Cernogratz" when a human foregoes retribution; they also haunt a traveling baroness (410–14) before eating two squabbling neighbors at the end of "The Interlopers" (452). A hyena escapes from Lord Pabham's private park in "Esmé" (101–5) only to surface as a "wild beast" that roams the leafy glades of southern England, mauling unwatched babies ("The Quest," 147–51). Only Mrs. Packletide gets her revenge on "nature": her trip to India satisfies her desire to own a tiger skin, though the hunt backfires when the tiger dies from a heart attack after she mistakenly shoots her own goat ("Mrs. Packletide's Tiger," 115–18).[14]

The angelic purity that Gabriel-Ernest first assumes contaminates his surroundings by provoking and inducing a violent—almost demonic— response in others. In comparable ways, the aesthetic dignity of Saki may connect with the fascistic fantasies and military violence that Munro—his nonliterary counterpart—actively embraced. As one of his characters astutely observes, "There is always a see-saw with us between repression and violence" (45). It may be no accident that Saki wrote "Gabriel-Ernest," in which a hyphen uneasily sutures the name of its eponymous protagonist, before a tale he titled "The Goblin and the Saint," which pronounces this breach of personality more clearly; each figure competes for influence and mastery inside a cathedral. At the story's end, the Saint gains ascendancy over the Goblin, but the antinomy breaks down because the Saint allows himself to develop "the conscience of a goblin" (72). In other words, the Saint sustains an image of purity only by incorporating his corollary's most alluring and seductive tendencies.

In this pattern of asserting and dissolving defined antinomies, the intermediary ground between each pole seems impossible to define or inhabit. This impasse reiterates the notion with which I began this chapter (and indeed the "paradox" of my book's title): that homosexual desire can be either a sublime and de-eroticized hyperaesthesia that dandies exhibit, or a deculturalizing force that shatters social cohesion by reducing it to its "savage" constitutents. This dilemma contributed to Wilde's personal and literary decline, from decadent cultural icon in 1891 to captive prisoner and figure of national loathing in 1895. Freud graphically reproduced this antagonism in *Group Psychology and the Analysis of the Ego* (1921), in which "homosexuality" functions as an intermediate category between the Primal Horde's sexual barbarism and the bonded group's "sublimated" success. As I argued in chapter 1 about Kipling's interpretive difficulties over male symbolization and bonding, Freud argued that the Horde's barbarism can produce "sensual" friendship only when it bypasses the possibility of homosexual intimacy and pathology.

Though significant traces of Saki's aesthetic rigidity and stylized self-mastery recur in the figure of Munro, the political journalism and militarism that he produced under his own name sought to redeem through (hyper)masculinity the effeminate and urbane excess of his nom de plume. Munro signed up eagerly for military service and denounced the antiwar lethargy of those who, only months before, were similar to himself. His contempt was most vehement and persistent when he spoke of actors who later became soldiers, or "comrades of the stage"; their war effort seemed to him not only frivolous and equivocal, but also the extension of theater into the military field: "the 'Boys of the Lap-dog breed' remain trilling their songs, capering their dances, speaking their lines as complacently as though no war was in progress. . . . They have set themselves as something apart; something human and decorative and amusing; but *something not altogether British, not exactly masculine, something that one does not treat as equal."* [15] Here, the personal pronoun "one" invokes the imaginary consensus of a national group. Munro presumes that he is part of this "one" critiquing the actors' performance; they spoil the integrity of his wartime scene. Considering this attack, it is curious that Munro chose to sign the article " 'Saki,' 'A' Company"; the single quotation marks around his pen name designate it as "something . . . decorative" and visibly "apart" (i.e., *as* a part). It is also ironic that he described his conscription to his sister by an almost commensurate parapraxis, "Enroled"; [16] the missing '*l*' renders his service the extension of an already assumed role. What meaning and status can we give to this "one" that was never less than several, and in his own words, potentially a "myriad" of others?

Munro described periods of reprieve from his fervent patriotism, but the emotion that replaced it—most usually at the front—alternated between profound despair and nostalgia. While he prefaced "The Square Egg" (1924) as a meditation on "all the thousand and one horrors of civilization" (539), he declined to write it as critique, and subtitled it "A Badger's-Eye View on the Western Front." Another pastoral fragment, "Birds on the Western Front," follows in this tradition, noting war's effect on its surrounding habitat without criticizing its war-torn context: "Whatever else German frightfulness may have done it has not frightened the rook of North-Eastern France . . ." (546). Similar comments describe the barn owl, buzzard, and skylark, all of whose stoic resilience demonstrate that "Nature" can outlive human devastation.

Although Munro regretted the continuation of war, he never indicted its function or apparent inevitability. The wistful tone of those wartime fragments indicates their curious relation to the surrounding violence; they uphold a mythical pastoralism and simultaneously propose the enemy's complete devastation. The full implications of this nationalism and burgeoning masculine identification emerge in *When William Came* (1913), which represents a fantasy that Germany successfully invades and usurps Britain's government. Subtitled *A Story of London under the Hohenzollerns,* the novella depicts a division of the German army ruling London and southern England. To the chagrin of Britain's populace, this army dictates policy, controls behavior, and renames streets (e.g., "Regentstrasse"). While many Britons "take the thing in a tragical fashion, and clear off to the Colonies, or shut themselves up in their country houses, as though there was a sort of moral leprosy infecting London" (695), Munro berates the military incompetence of Britain's generals for allowing the invasion to occur, and the moral fatalism of its people for acceding to their political subordination.[17] The novel clarifies that the sovereignty of Britain and its empire is at stake; since the Germans deny British citizens the right to exercise power over others, they experience the corollary shame and "impotence" of becoming "a subject race" (708). Without considering the Fanonian implications of this reversal beyond its effect on national pride, Munro aligns colonization with emasculation, insisting that Britain overthrow its enemy to regain masculine authority. The following passage contains no hint of irony: "But surely—a nation such as ours, a virile, highly-civilized nation with an age-long tradition of mastery behind it, cannot be held under for ever by a few thousand bayonets and machine guns. We must surely rise up one day and drive them out" (708).

In its striking anticipation of war and the disintegration of Britain's empire, Munro's text leaves no part of British society exempt from recrimination: he blames politicians for not maintaining Britain's navy,[18] the upper classes for their apathy and indolent luxury, and the remainder of the population for its national disaffection and physical weakness. Munro also indicts Britain's treachery for refusing to control London's growing Jewish population,[19] and invokes the widespread debility in national health—which first caught the public eye during the 1899 Boer War—as an example of Britain's moral and sexual decline.[20]

Considering these complaints, it is less surprising that Munro emphasized robust virility as a restorative for national strength and purpose; he called on men to take up arms in a Lawrentian fantasy of dignity and service [21] and joined William James's refrain in "The Moral Equivalent of War" (1910) by associating masculinity with both the cause of and the solution to Britain's crisis:[22] "I have come across lads who were really drifting to the bad through the good qualities in them. A clean combative strain in their blood, and a natural turn for adventure, made the ordinary anemic routine of shop or warehouse or factory almost unbearable for them. What splendid little soldiers they would have made, and how grandly the discipline of a military training would have steadied them in after-life when steadiness was wanted. The only adventure that their surroundings offered them has been the adventure of practising mildly criminal misdeeds without getting landed in reformatories and prisons . . ." (760).

According to Munro, crime occurs when alternatives to effeminacy are missing. Conversely, the idea of full citizenship strengthens national identification by encouraging the citizen to renounce misdeeds for higher spiritual ideals. The militarism Munro first associated with personal salvation appears socially redemptive in this version by restoring the nation to the imperial glory with which it was formerly and "naturally" endowed: the "age-long tradition of mastery behind it." Munro also advanced the tradition of war's resplendent heroism in Wordsworth's "The Happy Warrior" (1807) by recreating in the "romance" of the military group an intimacy otherwise denied to men:

> Nearly every red-blooded human boy has had war, in some shape or form, for his first love; if his blood has remained red and he has kept some of his boyishness in after life, that first love will never have been forgotten. No one could really forget those wonderful leaden cavalry soldiers. . . . There were other unforgettable memories for those who had brothers to play with and fight with, of sieges and ambushes and pitched encounters, of the slaying of an entire garrison without quarter, or of chivalrous, punctilious courtesy to a defeated enemy. Then there was the slow unfolding of the long romance of actual war, particularly of European war, ghastly, devastating, heartrending in its effect, and yet somehow captivating to the imagination. . . . The thrill that those far-off things call forth in us may be ethically indefensible, but it comes in the first place from something too deep to be driven out; the magic region of the Low Countries is beckoning to us again, as it beckoned to our forefathers, who went campaigning there almost from force of habit.[23]

Since the "long romance of actual war" is almost a habit here, Munro can portray it as an "ethically" *defensible* inheritance of patrilinear descent; the dream of national salvation apparently lies deep within the hearts of men. Toward the end of *When William Came,* Munro's personal investment in this "romance" surfaces as an erotic demand; its palpable homoeroticism leads him perilously close to the "comrades of the stage" he earlier disparaged: "A group of lads from the tea-shop clustered on the pavement and watched the troops go by, staring at a phase of life in which they had no share. The martial trappings, the swaggering joy of life, the comradeship of camp and barracks, the hard discipline of drill yard and fatigue duty, the long sentry watches, the trench digging, forced marches, wounds, cold, hunger, makeshift hospitals, and the blood-wet laurels—these were not for them" (762). In this passage, Munro valorizes every aspect of the military by transforming the call of duty into men's devoted submission. Given the erotic attention that Munro bestows on these aspects, suffering might almost be sexual here, were it not so clearly substituted for the contact and intimacy that he berated elsewhere.[24]

This fascistic version of masculinity is notable not only for clarifying the trajectory of many European countries in the 1930s, but also for exchanging the effeminacy of Munro's assiduous dandies—Reginald, Clovis, and Comus—for the "glory" of military combat. Munro offset this paradigm's ineluctable trace of homosexual desire by the army's *hommosexuelle* character: since the army could not disband the persistent "romance" of war, it diffused and redefined this theme.[25] Accordingly, the *père-version* of Munro's national group redeems the specific "perversion" of Saki's dandy:[26] Munro recasts the homosexual as an icon of hypervirility rather than a lamentable example of masculine failure. For instance, Herr von Kwarl, the "heavily built" and "mature" official of the invading German army, allows Munro to extol resilience and self-sufficiency and thus paradoxically to identify against the dandy's solitary antics and the British public's risible effeminacy: "He was a bachelor of the type that is called confirmed, and which might better be labelled consecrated; from his early youth onward to his present age he had never had the faintest flickering intention of marriage. Children and animals he adored, women and plants he accounted somewhat of a nuisance . . ." (724).

This gratuitous elevation of masculinity encouraged Munro's misogyny to surface with sudden—if not unpredictable—force. Under the name Saki, Munro derided the suffragette movement in "Herman the Irascible—A Story of the Great Weep" (124–27) and "The Brogue" (250–54), though he otherwise maintained a Firbankian affection for women and often used femininity to elaborate much of his social discontent.[27] However, Munro's desire to promote a new order compelled his "ruling passion" (813) to spurn deviant, weak, and "perverse" elements of the social and to ratify absolute sexual difference as the organizing principle of a rigid and violent hierarchy. Despite or perhaps because of his earlier accounts of this binary's failure in "Gabriel-Ernest" and "The Goblin and the Saint," Munro's shift toward absolutism could temporarily suspend the anxiety that sexual indeterminacy and national ambivalence produced: "A new generation will spring up, a weaker memory of old glories will survive, the *éclat* of the ruling race will capture young imaginations" (775).

This prophecy's saddest irony was its historical realization. As many accounts have shown, much of Europe and parts of Britain in the 1920s and 1930s valorized these qualities as symbolic constituents of a new order of fascism whose contempt for "weak," or simply heterogeneous, social elements saturated its imagination. Munro's celebration of masculinity was consistent with the rigid division of gender advanced by the vorticist movement in Britain, whose proponents included Wyndham Lewis, Ezra Pound, and later, D. H. Lawrence and T. S. Eliot. Lewis, whose virulent conservatism is perhaps closest to Munro's in the 1910s, wrote several papers on the immediate postwar dynamic and sexual "imbalance," and strove to redress this gender crisis by adopting antifeminist and homophobic rhetoric. Chapters from *The Art of Being Ruled* (1926) titled "The Meaning of the 'Sex War' " and "The Matriarchate and Feminine Ascendancy" jostle alongside others describing "The Rôle of Inversion in the War on the Intellect" and "The 'Homo' the Child of the 'Suffragette.' " [28]

Notwithstanding Munro's fascination with fascism, my interest in his writing stems from his concern to map out arduous strategies that substitute the "effeminacy" of the decadence movement for the military—and psychic—defense of vorticism; a transition that mirrors the expulsion and punishment of the dandy in his fiction. For instance, Munro wrote *The Unbearable Bassington* in 1911–12, just before he published *When William Came,* and it captures most of the narrative and conceptual dilemmas of Munro's literary and political affiliations. The novella concerns the fate of Comus Bassington—the last in a line of urbane and capricious aesthetes—whose dissolute lifestyle leads his exasperated mother to try to marry him to an affluent débutante. With a pagan lineage already present in his name,[29] Comus shares with his predecessors Reginald and Clovis the spirit of an adolescent prankster that Munro idealized when it tips into disdain and cruelty: "boys are Nature's raw material" (579). Though Comus vents the greater part of this disdainful charm on his mother, on whom he is contemptuously dependent, her insistence that he marry and leave home generates a sense of urgency that leaves Comus forlorn and bereft of family.

From the outset, Comus assumes that his marriage to Elaine de Frey is certain; nonetheless, his fascination with his rival, Courtenay Youghal, vastly surpasses his interest in Elaine. Courtenay is a flamboyant politician whose only desire is to promote his career. A triangle rapidly develops, though each man's interest in Elaine is purely formal—"Courtenay Youghal had not been designed by Nature to fulfill the *rôle* of an ardent or devoted lover, and he scrupulously respected the limits which Nature had laid down" (597)—while Comus engages Courtenay in "an unsought intimacy [that] would probably fall to pieces the moment [Courtenay] tried seriously to take up the *rôle* of mentor" (593). This repetition of "role" recalls the fluid performance of Saki's actors, and the obvious character of Courtenay's sexual deceit. Courtenay's eventual honeymoon with Elaine coincides, not insignificantly, with a Viennese masquerade ball, and it elicits her "dismay [that he] did not necessarily expect her to be markedly affectionate in private. Some one had described him, after their marriage, as one of Nature's bachelors, and she began to see how aptly the description fitted him" (670).

The suggestion that Courtenay is playing a "role" puts his integrity in doubt, and renders his commitment to marriage "quite unreliable" (672); it allows a "harlequin spirit" to surface "as an undercurrent in his nature" (674). However, the disguise that he assumes at the masquerade ball is not the truth of his personality, but rather the symbolic realization of an impulse that is closer to his will; closer, that is, by suggesting a facade that he assumes more readily than the "role" of husband.[30] As the narrator archly explains: "The intimacy existing between the two young men had suffered no immediate dislocation from the circumstance that they were tacitly paying court to the same lady. It was an intimacy founded not in the least on friendship or community of tastes and ideas, but owed its existence to the fact that each was amused and interested by the other. Youghal found Comus, for the time being at any rate, just as amusing and interesting as a rival for Elaine's favour as he had been in the *rôle* of scapegrace boy-about-town" (602).

This reiterated intimacy performs a complicit drama among Comus, Courtenay, the narrator, and the reader in such a way that the hitherto elliptical secret of homosexual desire renders *heterosexuality* the novella's closet drama. The narrative implies that other characters—especially Elaine and Comus's mother—willfully disregard the "real" secret of this rivalrous courtship: that Courtenay and Comus intend to marry Elaine for effect rather than passion. With its official (hetero) and unofficial (homo) configurations in constant collision, the novel renders women blind participants in a drama they cannot hope to win. Indeed, in its egregious deception of women, the unofficial drama of intimacy between men recalls Firbank's contempt for men "with their selfishness, fickleness and lies!"[31] Elaine secures in Courtenay only the trappings of a husband, though it is clear she would have gained little more with Comus, who plays out a desire to desire—or a desire to supersede (and receive) the desire of his object (Courtenay). Since the text never symbolizes the two men's intimacy by a shift to mentorship, their affection indicates a possibility in the spectrum between mentor and rival that the text is unable to explore: the realm of the lover.[32] When Mrs. Bassington expresses alarm at her son's dissolute interest, for instance, her alarm concerns not the wrong woman but rather the wrong man:

> "And to think she should be captured by Courtenay Youghal," said Francesca [Bassington] bitterly; "I've always deplored your intimacy with that young man."
>
> "It's hardly my intimacy with him that's made Elaine accept him," said Comus. (651)

This artful symbolization of Comus's claim renders it immediately doubtful, and similar in manner to many other examples of Munro's writing. While Elaine's acceptance of Courtenay appears related to Comus's lack of interest in her, Courtenay's offer of marriage seems partially motivated by his desire to impede further intimacy between Comus and himself.

Since the different fates of Courtenay and Comus hinge on the success or failure of their marital ambition, one could attribute their ambition, in turn, to respectively diffident and successful performances of heterosexual intent. While both men participate in the same performance, sharing similar aims and ostensibly the same object, "each [is] amused and interested by the other" (602). In the marital stakes, Comus's "failure" seems related to his presumption of success, which demonstrates that he is either unable or unwilling to read the complex semiotics of courtship. As the narrator explains, "Comus, marching carelessly through unknown country, to effect what seemed already an assured victory, made the mistake of disregarding the existence of an unbeaten army on his flank" (628).

If both men's doubtful reading of courtship renders heterosexuality mysterious, the text also insists on the social predicates of courtship's goal. All the same, the narrative represents marriage as a ridiculous and desperate institution and a battleground on which characters must find and "win" masculine identity. While this pressure reduces love to others' superficial approval, the demand for this public satisfaction transforms the marital into the *martial;* male characters seek women solely for capture and possession. Much like Comus, Munro seems concerned less with outright victory than with the "war" itself, and specifically the strength of the competitor whom Comus carelessly overlooks, or regards quite differently from a conventional rival.

In this respect, the novella's presiding concern is the geography of desire between competitors, not the division of their (female) spoils.

Although the text outlines the semiotic nature of heterosexual courtship, it continues to stress its sociological and ontological significance; Munro does not consider performance as a form of political or psychic voluntarism. Comus's matrimonial defeat leads to his immediate expulsion from the home and then the nation in his shipment to a land set aside for the unwanted: a colony in West Africa that he presumes is "a convenient depository for tiresome people" (652). As he later remarks from domestic exile, the colony is "a sort of modern substitute for the old-fashioned *oubliette*. . . . Dear Uncle Henry may talk lugubriously about the burden of Empire, but he evidently recognizes its uses as a refuse consumer" (652).

Comus's disappointment and failure bring his battle's consequence with Courtenay into relief; Courtenay and Elaine's matrimonial masquerade in Vienna occurs while Comus ruefully assesses his "insurmountable folly and perverseness" (683) in West Africa. The thematic connection between his indecisive "marching . . . through unknown country" (628) when engaged in heterosexual competition and his "unutterable loneliness" in "another country" (to invoke Julian Mitchell's 1982 play about homosexuality in British Public Schools and James Baldwin's 1962 novel about life in Harlem, N.Y.)[33] signifies Comus's inescapable exile *within Britain,* had he continued to live there as a "confirmed bachelor." Thus Comus's final epitaph for his loss seems apposite and poignant as an epigraph for this novella: "If it was love that was to bring him back he must be an exile for ever" (682).

The epitaph represents an unavoidable truth in this novella: Comus finally dies in the colony in torment and solitude while his family lingers over dinner in Britain. This displacement indicates the price of his "insurmountable . . . perverseness," and the condition on which his return to England hinges: Comus's exile and his resistance to sanctioned forms of intimacy are central and related problems for this text. The colony foregrounds these problems by tormenting Comus with a lifestyle that will always exclude him.[34] He dies an "outsider, the lonely alien," who had "scanned with hungry intentness . . . the romance [he] could never have commanded" (680).

In this novella, the colony plays an especially cynical function; it is either a place to exploit natives in assisting a Western career or a useful depository for undesirable elements of British society. As Anne McClintock has argued, "In the public and political debates of the late nineteenth century, the relentless superfluity of women and men was represented as a malady and contagion in the national body politic which could best be countered by leeching off the bad fluid and depositing it in the colonies." [35] The colony nonetheless teems with its own life—with communities that govern themselves and an environment so energetic that it deprives the white man of significance by shattering his residual fantasies of power and relevance:

> In the life he had come from Comus had been accustomed to think of individuals as definite masterful personalities, making their several marks on the circumstances that revolved around them; they did well or ill, or in most cases indifferently, and were criticized, praised, blamed, thwarted, or tolerated, or given way to. In any case, humdrum or outstanding, they had their spheres of importance, little or big. . . . Here [in Africa] a man simply made a unit in an unnumbered population, an inconsequential dot in a loosely-compiled death-roll. Even his own position as a white man exalted conspicuously above a horde of black natives did not save Comus from the depressing sense of nothingness which his first experience of fever had thrown over him. He was a lost, soulless body in this great uncaring land; if he died another would take his place. . . . (679–80)

Similar to Firbank's subtle undermining of Eurocentrism in *The Flower Beneath the Foot, Santal,* and *Prancing Nigger,* Munro uses the domestic, national, and "masculine" dispossession of Comus to bring into relief the impossible subjection of others and his own sexual misery. Comus's expectation of racial power cannot assuage the difficulty of his sexual identity because his assumption of racial superiority accentuates his superfluous relation to a self-sufficient country. His thoughts highlight the sexual abjection of the forgotten and displaced expatriate while emptying the colonial project of its pompous and brutal self-justification. By elucidating Comus's impossible relation to the home culture, Munro/Saki also derides Britain's fantasies of exporting mastery. The drama of colonial dispossession reveals the tenuous and foreign status of homosexual desire by belying Britain's remorseless expectations of colonial power and authority.

The Unbearable Bassington's somber conclusion allows us to argue that Munro used the novella to excise and destroy his residual identification with the decadent movement as "Saki." Rather than encouraging a twofold critique of Britain's imperialist and homophobic rhetoric, this excision promoted a shift toward the redemptive militarism that brought Munro, Saki, and Comus into violent collision. The tension that inheres in the Saki/Munro virgule elucidates what is so unbearable about Bassington both for Munro and his culture and what character or propensity renders Bassington's exile politically expedient.[36]

I have argued that Munro's concern to bind diffuse aspects of his political and sexual identity beleaguered his life and writing. Since this problem of dispossession underpinned the procedural, conceptual, and imaginary government of the British Empire—we began precisely with this problem in Kipling—Munro's dilemma appears synecdochic of British colonialism. I suggest that the empire promoted a fantasy of (self-)mastery that relied on specific and frequently brutal identifications, and that Munro's writing often represents this fantasy by a structural antinomy between two possible "roles": the dandy and the soldier. To ruin this fantasy, I have emphasized points in Munro's writing where the idea of a complete, and fully masterable subjectivity, falls apart—that is, it falls into a part. Despite this fantasy's fragility and obvious faultlines, it continues to haunt Britain and exercise influence on many postcolonial societies. The resilience of this fantasy makes its critical interruption all the more urgent; we can never disband the colonial project without disengaging the imaginary dimension of imperialism.

E pilogue:

Britain's Disavowal
and the Mourning
of Empire

> A minute later I burnt off my adrenalin leaping down the
> stairs — which were bleakly concrete, like the long exit
> stairways at the back of cinemas. There was a smell of urine,
> and lines down the wall drawn by running hands. At the turn
> of each flight "NF" had been scrawled, with a pendant
> saying "Kill the Niggers" or "Wogs Out." I thought with
> yearning of the Hopes, whom I did not know, forced to
> contain their anger, contempt and hurt in such a world.
> —Alan Hollinghurst [1]

William Beckwith is the narrator and protagonist of Alan Hollinghurst's first novel, *The Swimming-Pool Library* (1988). The abbreviation "NF" in this passage signifies the National Front, Britain's neo-Nazi political party, which is committed to enforced repatriation for all of Britain's nonwhite residents; Arthur Hope, one of Beckwith's lovers, is embroiled in family conflicts about his homosexuality and the murder of his brother's friend over drug-related money. The name of Arthur's family is pointedly ironic in this novel—Beckwith laughs "mirthlessly" (170) at the coincidence—not because the novel aims to separate a black family from any hopeful role in Britain's future, but because the idea that hope resides in, and is delimited to, a poor and racist council estate in East London seems bleak and unimaginable. After Beckwith ruminates on Britain's national despair and difficulties with racial integration, several National Front supporters assault him for being both gay and a "fuckin' nigger-fucker" (173).

Since *The Swimming-Pool Library* is a complex account of inter-racial, cross-class, gay desire in Britain, I can only allude to a few of the issues it raises tentatively to conclude *The Ruling Passion*. In juxtaposing nine chapters on different literary accounts of disruptions in masculine symbolization with a brief interpretation of a contemporary novel, my purpose is simply to demonstrate how intractable the material and psychic issues I have written about have become in Britain. At the heart of Hollinghurst's novel is a profound crisis about Britain's present and future identity, which hinges urgently and violenty on the objects and ideas with which its citizens identify. It would be difficult to label these objects and ideas "postnational" or "postcolonial," though they are clearly many miles from a conception of the "multicultural." Beckwith's sexual excursions into different racial communities represent an adventurous departure from his own yuppie network of lords, barons, and stockbrokers, though his sexual interest in black men is the exception to this novel's peculiarly immobile urban topography. As partial endorsements of this immobility, Beckwith and his older gay friend, Lord Charles Nantwich, represent avatars of historically different but complementary attitudes toward race and empire. While Beckwith's consciousness of race is clearly more advanced than Nantwich's, both men tend to live by rigid sexual stereotypes. By invoking these stereotypes, they also capture the despair of Britain's national stagnation. Nantwich admits:

> "There are times when I can't think of my country without a kind of despairing shame. Something literally inexpressible, so I won't bother to try and speechify about it."
>
> "I know what you mean."
>
> "Only last year out at Stepney [East London] there were hateful scenes — precisely hateful. Oh — National Front and their like, spraying their slogans all over the Boys' Club, where, as you know, a lot of . . . non-whites go. Every day there were leaflets, just full of mindless hatred — I'm sorry to keep saying it. The horrific thing was that several of those boys were boys who used to come to the Club themselves." (244–45)

The subtlety and strength of Hollinghurst's novel lies in its ability to implicate every character in this invidious economy of racism without banalizing the complexity (and often the simplicity) of their sexual encounters or drawing pious conclusions about the need to transform or eradicate their thoughts. While Beckwith reproduces some of this racism in his relationship with Hope, he also interprets its underlying history when it surfaces, in Nantwich's diary, as an intricate testimonial of colonial desire. The diary presents a lineage of gay affairs throughout the twentieth century; it also interrupts every contemporary relationship by foregrounding the resilience of interracial turbulence and ambivalence. By representing his characters' fantasies as part of a vast confluence of racial and national difficulty, Hollinghurst demonstrates that Britain has become mired in a renewed vision of colonial splendor and global influence, a paralyzing conviction about its imminent global rejuvenation that Salman Rushdie has usefully derided as "the phantom twitchings of an amputated limb." [2] Rushdie elaborates: "Britain is in danger of entering a condition of cultural psychosis, in which it begins once again to strut and posture like a great power while in fact its power diminishes every year. The jewel in the crown is made, these days, of paste." [3]

How does this cultural psychosis implicate same-sex desire? As Hollinghurst demonstrates, fantasies of national expansion and colonial splendor are inseparable from homosexuality.[4] More recently, David Leavitt argued that his novel *While England Sleeps* (1993) is "among other things . . . about the hypocrisy of English attitudes toward homosexuality. In this regard its writing prophesied the crisis its publication would precipitate. Homophobia is global; what is unique about English homophobia is that it is part and parcel of a national fervor for gay sex in comparison to which the national fervor for accusing writers of plagiarism seems tame." [5] Leavitt's legal battle with Stephen Spender over his alleged plagiarism of Spender's autobiography *World Within World* (1951) is notable for its accompanying fantasies of treachery and retribution. Leavitt remarks: "I was rapidly finding myself being transformed from an Anglophile into an Anglophobe, as I became increasingly aware of the extent to which a strain of brutality, even barbarism, underlay the factitious veneer of English 'gentility,' particularly where homosexuality was concerned." [6]

Corroborating both Hollinghurst and Leavitt, I have interpreted the immense diversity of meaning that several fictional accounts of British colonialism attribute to homosexual desire. This interpretation has attempted to move beyond the "repressive hypothesis," which represents homosexuality as a secret, homogeneous, and unnamable phenomenon whose discovery yields a key to all textual enigma, clarifying what the writer intended—but failed—to express.[7] Instead, I have argued that the process of encoding desire illustrates a profound difficulty and variance of signification and a generic resistance to subjectivity's meaning. Considering these obstacles, we cannot critique a single phenomenon called "colonial homosexuality"; homosexuality is also impossible fully to represent, unify, or avoid because it pushes the texts I have examined toward a definitional crisis.

Although homosexual desire may appear without influence or significance in some of the texts I have interpreted, heterosexuality also confronts a hiatus, or limit point, whose uncertainty cannot prevent a concomitant crisis of desire and identification. Many critics such as Jeffrey Meyers have argued that modernism represented a profound epistemological crisis over various registers of subjectivity's meaning. I have not tried to claim or demonstrate that modernism—however we understand the term—was the productive site of undeclared homosexuality on which all meaning relating to subjectivity hinged or floundered.[8] Rather, I have established points where narratives required homosexuality to fall out of representation to allow other meanings to prevail; I also have suggested that these moments surface in allegorical forms. Thus, I have tried to read the signifier of each text—rather than assume the literary stability of the signified—by emphasizing the vital role of language and rhetorical figures in shaping colonial fantasies and desires.

Although this book has not occluded historical detail, it has attempted to interpret history through the lens of literary texts and figures, adding a dimension to colonialism that empirical studies often ignore. Accordingly, *The Ruling Passion* has argued that the nonobservable and unconscious exerted a profound influence on the twin histories of homosexuality and the empire, whose significance the largely untheorized field of biography has often recognized but poorly interpreted. I have described this phenomenon quite broadly as an "internal dynamic" within colonialism, a "colonial will to power," "colonial *jouissance*," and "the underside" to the empire to stress what has, until recently, received only cursory attention: the wide variety of drives, fantasies, displacements, and identifications that are integral to every set of imperialist beliefs.

Finally, as my brief account of *The Swimming-Pool Library* attests, addressing Britain's colonial past has acquired considerable urgency in light of that country's refusal to relinquish its historical and psychic investment in its empire. At present, Britain appears to have suspended this issue; it is neither forgotten nor entirely regretted. In Freud's rather schematic account of grief, Britain's situation would appear closer to melancholia than mourning, because it has yet to record the empire as a lost and irretrievable object; Britain's repetition of commemorative nostalgia signifies conservative blockage, not cultural process.[9] Freud elaborated on the terms of this resistance as follows: "Reality-testing has shown that the loved object no longer exists, and it proceeds to demand that all libido shall be withdrawn from its attachments to that object. This demand arouses considerable opposition—it is a matter of general observation that people never willingly abandon a libidinal position, not even, indeed, when a substitute is already beckoning to them. This opposition can be so intense that a turning away from reality takes place and a clinging to the object through the medium of a hallucinatory wishful psychosis." [10] A recurrent faith that Britain can and should return to a position of international dominance inaugurates this national melancholy. While fascism and the National Front keep this dream alive by fantasizing the expulsion of all "uninvited guests" from Britain, many less reactionary Britons secretly cherish and harbor this dream of imperial splendor.

This postcolonial dilemma is surely as urgent for Britain today as it was in the years I have addressed in this book. When Rushdie argued that a recent wave of Raj revivalism in modern film and public media precipitated "the refurbishment of the Empire's tarnished image," [11] he amplified what is at stake for Britain in continuing this fantasy. Following Rushdie, I suggest that this fantasy concerns not only political sovereignty but also rhetorical authority. In other words, I would endorse the claim that Britain has yet to accept the days of empire *as* past and to take responsibility for the brutal and perhaps irreparable damage it inflicted on cultures and communities across the world. Besides this historical disavowal, as Danny/Victoria explains in Stephen Frears and Hanif Kureishi's powerful account of London's inner-city riots in the 1980s, *Sammy and Rosie Get Laid* (1987), Britain has yet to address "the kind of domestic colonialism" under which so many of its inhabitants now live.[12] Britain will finally have begun this examination when its writers, film directors, and politicians can represent the issue without despair or nostalgia. With all of the paradoxes of this book's title and thematic, I place *The Ruling Passion* in the service of this aim to encourage the cultural and national mourning of an empire that for too long has been delayed.

Notes

Preface

1. John Addington Symonds, preface to *Sexual Inversion* (1897), New York: Bell, 1984, 6.

Introduction: Theorizing "The Empire of the Selfsame"

1. Hélène Cixous, "Sorties," in Cixous and Catherine Clément, *The Newly Born Woman,* trans. Betsy Wing, Minneapolis: U of Minnesota P, 1986, 78. It is important to note variations in translation of Cixous's phrase *"l'Empire du propre."* In *Sexual/Textual Politics: Feminist Literary Theory* (New York and London: Methuen, 1985), Toril Moi translates this phrase as "the Realm of the Proper" (111). With the exception of the final chapter of this book, in which I follow Moi's translation of *propre* as "proper," "appropriate," and "clean," I have adopted Wing's translation of this term as "Selfsame."

2. *The Concise Oxford Dictionary of English Eytomology,* ed. T. F. Hoad, Oxford: Clarendon, 1986, 339.

3. T. E. Lawrence, *Seven Pillars of Wisdom: A Triumph* (1926), Harmondsworth: Penguin, 1962, 422.

4. Ronald Hyam, *Britain's Imperial Century 1815–1914: A Study of Empire and Expansion,* London: Batsford, 1976, 135. Hyam's position has shifted in his recent work, though it still assumes that sublimation is productive, successful, and amenable to imperial expansion. Mark T. Berger provides a valuable critique of Hyam's revised argument in "Imperialism and Sexual Exploitation: A Response to Ronald Hyam's 'Empire and Sexual Opportunity,'" *Journal of Imperial and Commonwealth History* 17.1, 1988, 83–89. See also Hyam's counterresponse in the same issue (90–98), in which he maintains "my exposure of the viscera of empire was essentially subversive" (90).

5. Joseph Conrad, *Nostromo* (1904), Harmondsworth: Penguin, 1990, 351.

6. " 'Allegory.' (Gk. "speaking otherwise than one seems to speak") 1. Description of a subject under the guise of some other subject of aptly suggestive resemblance. 2. An instance of such description; a figurative sentence, discourse, or narrative; an extended or continued metaphor" (*The Oxford English Dictionary,* vol. 1, prepared by J. A. Simpson and E. S. C. Weiner, Oxford: Clarendon, 1989, 333). My use of

the term "allegory" follows Joel Fineman's excellent essay "The Structure of Allegorical Desire," *October: The First Decade,* ed. Annette Michelson, Rosalind Kraus, Douglas Crimp, and Joan Copjec, Cambridge, Mass.: MIT P, 1987, 373–92, in which he argues: "On the one hand, I am concerned with . . . a temporal issue regarding the way allegories linearly unfold, but also, as has often been pointed out, a symbolic progress that lends itself to spatial projection. . . . On the other hand, I am concerned with a specifically allegorical desire, a desire *for* allegory, that is implicit in the idea of structure itself, and explicit in criticism that directs itself towards the structurality of literature" (373). See also Angus Fletcher, "Psychoanalytic Analogues: Obsession and Compulsion," *Allegory: The Theory of a Symbolic Mode,* Ithaca: Cornell UP, 1964, 279–303.

7. See Lawrence Stone, *The Family, Sex, and Marriage in England 1500–1800,* London: Weidenfeld and Nicolson, 1977, 52–54, 379–80; Wayland Young, *Eros Denied,* London: Corgi, 1969, 190–91; Hyam, "Empire and Sexual Opportunity," *Journal of Imperial and Commonwealth History,* 14.2, 1986, 34–89. Stone has argued that a violent society of "bachelors took out their sexual frustration in military aggression"; Young, that the "British Empire was not acquired in a fit of absence of mind, it was acquired in a fit of absence of women."

8. Jacques Lacan, *The Four Fundamental Concepts of Psycho-Analysis,* ed. Jacques-Alain Miller, trans. Alan Sheridan, New York: Norton, 1978, 204. Subsequent references give pagination in main text.

9. For critical purposes, this strategy involves widening the gap between sexuality and identity so that the two can no longer simply appear commensurate. For elaboration on this point, see Diana Fuss, "Inside/Out," *Inside/Out: Lesbian Theories, Gay Theories,* ed. Fuss, New York: Routledge, 1991, 3, and my essay, "Is There a Homosexual in This Text?: Identity, Opacity, and the Elaboration of Desire," *GLQ: A Journal of Lesbian and Gay Studies,* forthcoming.

10. Herman Melville, "Benito Cereno" (1855), *Billy Budd, Sailor and Other Stories,* Harmondsworth: Penguin, 1983, 254.

11. Hyam repeats this assumption throughout *Empire and Sexuality: The British Experience,* Manchester: Manchester UP, 1990.

12. An example would be Eve Kosofsky Sedgwick's recent work on "homosexual panic." See especially "The Beast in the Closet: James and the Writing of Homosexual Panic," *Epistemology of the Closet,* Berkeley: U of California P, 1990, 182–212.

13. Examples of this form of literary criticism include Jeffrey Meyers, *Homosexuality and Literature 1890–1930,* London: Athlone, 1977; Georges-Michel Sarotte, *Like a Lover, Like a Brother: Male Homosexuality in the American Novel and Theater from Herman Melville to James Baldwin,* trans. Richard Miller, New York: Doubleday-Anchor, 1978; Rupert Croft-Cooke, *Feasting with Panthers: A New Consideration of Some Late Victorian Writers,* London: W. H. Allen, 1967. More obvious difficulties emerge from biographies of such figures as Rhodes, Kipling, and James.

14. T. S. Eliot, "The Hollow Men" (1925), *The Complete Poems and Plays of T. S. Eliot,* London: Faber, 1982, 85.

15. Michel Foucault, *The History of Sexuality,* vol. 1 (1976), trans. Robert Hurley, Harmondsworth: Penguin, 1984, 17.

16. My approach to colonialism owes much to the work of Abdul R. JanMohamed, especially "The Economy of Manichean Allegory: The Function of Racial Difference in Colonialist Literature," *Critical Inquiry* 12, 1985, 59–87, and "Sexuality on/of the Racial Border: Foucault, Wright, and the Articulation of 'Racialized Sexuality,' " *Discourses of Sexuality: From Aristotle to AIDS,* ed. Donma C. Stanton, Ann Arbor: U of Michigan P, 1992, 94–116. For an excellent set of readings of sexuality in contradistinction with nationalism, see also Andrew Parker, Mary Russo, Doris Summer, and Patricia Yaeger, eds., *Nationalisms and Sexualities,* New York: Routledge, 1992.

17. Foucault, *The History of Sexuality,* 72. Foucault's comments on psychoanalysis's contribution to *"le dispositif de sexualité"* are less consistent and critical than most Foucauldians have acknowledged. In section 1 of his introduction to *The History of Sexuality,* Foucault was careful to release—not attribute—the entire "repression hypothesis" to psychoanalysis (81); in section 4, he emphasized the antirepressive character of certain psychoanalytic paths (i.e., aspects of Freud, Reich, and Marcuse): "It is very well to look back from our vantage point and remark upon the normalizing impulse in Freud; one can go on to denounce the role played for many years by the psychoanalytic institution; but the fact remains that in the great family of technologies of sex, which goes so far back into the history of the Christian West, of all those institutions that set out in the nineteenth century to medicalize sex, it was the one that, up to the decade of the forties, rigorously opposed the political and institutional effects of the perversion-hereditary-degenerescence system" (119).

18. Jacques-Alain Miller, "Michel Foucault and Psychoanalysis," *Michel Foucault: Philosopher,* trans. Timothy J. Armstrong, New York: Routledge, 1992, 64.

19. Lacan, *The Four Fundamental Concepts of Psycho-Analysis*: "Is the reality that determines the awakening the slight noise against which the empire of the dream and of desire is maintained?" (68).

20. This procedure is set out with admirable rigor by Lee Edelman, "Homographesis," *Yale Journal of Criticism* 3.1, 1989, 189–207, and Leo Bersani, "Sexuality and Aesthetics," *October* 28, 1984, 27–42.

21. Meyers, *Homosexuality and Literature 1890–1930,* 3: "The emancipation of the homosexual has led, paradoxically, to the decline of his [*sic*] art."

22. Joseph Bristow has since published an account of imperial relations and masculine desire during this period—*Empire Boys: Adventures in a Man's World,* London: HarperCollins, 1991—though he focuses on adolescent and children's fiction, and is largely concerned with the cultural production of sexual meaning rather than its difficult relation to those who performed and inhabited it. Sara Suleri also has published an excellent account of the rhetoric of colonialism—*The Rhetoric of English India,* Chicago: U of Chicago P, 1992—though male homosexuality is largely tangential to her account. Finally, for an example of subtle work interpreting both male homosexuality and European colonialism, see Joseph A. Boone, "Mappings of Male Desire in Durrell's *Alexandria Quartet,*" *Displacing Homophobia: Gay Male Perspectives in Literature and Culture,* ed. Ronald R. Butters, John M. Clum, and Michael

Moon, Durham: Duke UP, 1989, 73–106, and Boone, "Vacation Cruises; or, The Homoerotics of Orientalism," *PMLA* 110.1, 1995, 89–107.

23. Jeffrey Weeks, *Coming Out: Homosexual Politics in Britain, from the Nineteenth-Century to the Present,* New York: Quartet Books, 1977, 26.

24. Sedgwick, "A Poem Is Being Written," *Representations* 17, 1987, 129–30.

25. Sedgwick, *Epistemology of the Closet,* 205.

26. See George L. Mosse, *Nationalism and Sexuality: Middle-Class Morality and Sexual Norms in Modern Europe,* Madison: U of Wisconsin P, 1985; Hyam, *Britain's Imperial Century 1815–1914: A Study of Empire and Expansion,* and *Empire and Sexuality: The British Experience;* and Kathryn Tidrick, *Empire and the English Character,* London: Tauris, 1992. Sedgwick has also argued for analyses of these institutions and their inaugurating fanaticism in *Between Men: English Literature and Male Homosocial Desire,* New York: Columbia UP, 1985, 19.

27. Adam Phillips, "Looking at Obstacles," *On Kissing, Tickling, and Being Bored: Psychoanalytic Essays on the Unexamined Life,* Cambridge, Mass.: Harvard UP, 1993, 83.

28. Ibid., 82–83.

29. Ibid., 86. This argument is central to my reading of Maugham's *Of Human Bondage* in chapter 5.

30. Freud, "Instincts and Their Vicissitudes" (1915), *Standard Edition* 14, 122–23. See also Slavoj Žižek, "The Real and Its Vicissitudes," *Newsletter of the Freudian Field* 3.1–2, 1989, 80–101, for an excellent account of this argument.

31. Freud, qtd. in Herman Nunberg and Ernst Federn, *Minutes of the Vienna Psychoanalytic Society,* vol. 1: *1906–1908,* trans. M. Nunberg, New York: International UP, 1962, 237, and interpreted by Edelman in "Plasticity, Paternity, Perversity: Freud's *Falcon,* Huston's *Freud,*" *American Imago* 51.1, 1994, 69–104. I am indebted to Edelman's essay for its rigorous account of the way that "homosexuality" is culturally and psychically "demonized . . . [for its alleged] involvement in the wastefulness of its representational economy" (69).

32. See also Lacan, *The Four Fundamental Concepts of Psycho-Analysis:* "The *objet a* is something from which the subject, in order to constitute itself, has separated itself off as organ. This serves as a symbol of the lack, that is to say, of the phallus, not as such, but in so far as it is lacking. It must, therefore, be an object that is, firstly, separable and, secondly, that has some relation to the lack" (103).

33. Freud, "On Narcissism: An Introduction" (1914), *Standard Edition,* vol. 14, 91 n.1.

34. According to Lacan, "The whole question is to discover how [the] love object may come to fulfill a role analogous with the object of desire—upon what equivocations does the possibility for the love object of becoming an object of desire rest?" (*The Four Fundamental Concepts of Psycho-Analysis,* 186).

1. The Incursions of Purity: Kipling's Legislators and the Anxiety of Psychic Demand

1. Rudyard Kipling, "A Song of the White Men," *Rudyard Kipling's Verse: Definitive Edition,* London: Hodder and Stoughton, 1943, 282.

2. Kipling, epigraph to "In the House of Suddhoo," *Plain Tales from the Hills* (1890), Harmondsworth: Penguin, 1987, 143. Subsequent references give pagination in main text.

3. Kipling, private correspondence to R. A. Duckworth Ford, September 16, 1907, qtd. in Lewis D. Wurgaft, *The Imperial Imagination: Myth and Magic in Kipling's India,* Middleton, Conn.: Wesleyan UP, 1983, 151. In this chapter, I am most indebted to Wurgaft's book for its thorough and astute research on Britain's imperialist relation to India.

4. Bosworth Smith, biographer of John Nicholson, the notorious colonialist of India, described Nicholson as driven by an "ungovernable restiveness." See R. Bosworth Smith, *Life of Lord Lawrence,* vol. 2, New York: Scribner's, 1885, 194.

5. Kipling, qtd. in Wurgaft, *The Imperial Imagination,* 169.

6. For examples, see Ronald Hyam, *Britain's Imperial Century 1815–1914: A Study of Empire and Expansion,* London: Batsford, 1976; Hyam, "Empire and Sexual Opportunity," *Journal of Imperial and Commonwealth History,* 14.2, 1986, 34–89; Hyam, *Empire and Sexuality: The British Experience,* Manchester: Manchester UP, 1990; Kathryn Tidrick, *Empire and the English Character,* London: Tauris, 1992; Lawrence Stone, *The Family, Sex, and Marriage in England 1500–1800,* London: Weidenfeld and Nicolson, 1977, 52–54, 379–80; and Wayland Young, *Eros Denied,* London: Corgi, 1969, 190–91. For a critique of these historians' assumptions about sexuality and sublimation, see notes 4 and 7 of my introduction.

7. Lord Horatio Kitchener, qtd. in Wurgaft, *The Imperial Imagination,* 10–11.

8. T. Rice Holmes described the British gratuitous assault on villages in India after the "Mutiny" in 1857 as "the infliction of punishment [that] was not a delight, but an awful duty" (Holmes, *A History of the Indian Mutiny,* London: Macmillan, 1904, 221). For further discussion of their model of chastity and askesis, see E. Joseph Bristow, "Against the Double Standard: From the Contagious Diseases Acts to White Slavery," *Vice and Vigilance: Purity Movements in Britain since 1700,* Dublin: Gill and Macmillan, 1977, 75–93.

9. Robert Needham Cust, *Pictures of Indian Life; Sketched with the Pen from 1852–1881,* London: Trubner, 1881, 101.

10. Henry Lawrence, qtd. in Sir Herbert Edwardes and Herman Merivale, *Life of Sir Henry Lawrence,* vol. 2, London: Smith, Elder, 1872, 219. His equally fanatical brother, Walter, spoke of the delusion surrounding this self-aggrandizement and the danger of its coercive practices: "Our life in India, our very work more or less, rests on illusion. I had the illusion, wherever I was, that I was infallible and invulnerable in my dealing with Indians. How else could I have dealt with angry mobs, with cholera-stricken masses, and with processions of religious fanatics? It was not conceit, Heaven knows: it was not the prestige of the British Raj, but it was the illusion which is in the very air of India. . . . They, the millions, made us believe we had a

divine mission. We made them believe we were right" (Walter Lawrence, *The India We Served*, Boston: Houghton, Mifflin, 1929, 42–43).

11. James Fitzjames Stephen, qtd. in Wurgaft, *The Imperial Imagination*, 71.

12. The term refers to drives that are ineffable, but still palpable, in these texts because they are ontologically satisfying but subjectively destructive. My use of the term obtains from Jacques Lacan's designation for the combined un/pleasures of the drive and *objet a*. See Lacan, *Four Fundamental Concepts of Psycho-Analysis*, ed. Jacques-Alain Miller and trans. Alan Sheridan, New York: Norton, 1978, 174–200.

13. Stephen, *Liberty, Equality, Fraternity*, London: Smith, Elder, 1874, 237.

14. Kipling, qtd. in *Kipling: Interviews and Recollections*, vol. 2, ed. H. Orel, Totowa: Barnes and Noble, 1982, 256–57.

15. Jacques Derrida refers to this term in *Of Grammatology*, trans. Gayatri Chakravorty Spivak, Baltimore: Johns Hopkins UP, 1974, 10–18, in this instance the term would refer to Law, Nature, "King and Country," and God.

16. Kipling, "Working-Tools," *Something of Myself* (1936), Harmondsworth: Penguin, 1988, 156.

17. Richard Holmes, introduction to *Something of Myself*, 10. See also David Lodge, " 'Mrs Bathurst': Indeterminacy in Modern Narrative," *Kipling Considered*, ed. Phillip Mallett, London: Macmillan, 1989, 71–84.

18. Kipling, *Kim* (1901), Harmondsworth: Penguin, 1989, 327–28. Subsequent references give pagination in main text.

19. Kipling, "Working-Tools," *Something of Myself*, 154.

20. Benita Parry, "The Content and Discontent of Kipling's Imperialism," *New Formations* 6, 1988, 58.

21. Zohreh T. Sullivan, "Memory and the Colonial Self in Kipling's Autobiography," *Prose Studies* 12.1, 1989, 83.

22. Kipling, *The Light That Failed* (1891), Harmondsworth: Penguin, 1988, 141. Subsequent references give pagination in main text.

23. Kipling, *Kim*, 321.

24. Heldar's model, Bessie, is drawn to Torpenhow, though he does not reciprocate the interest; it causes him considerable discomfort. He later follows Heldar's advice and flees from her, only later returning to ignore her entirely: "He went to the mantelpiece, buried his head on his arms, and groaned like a wounded bull. . . . 'Out you go immediately. Never resist the devil. . . . Fly from him. Pack your things and go.' 'I believe you are right. Where shall I go?' 'Pack first and inquire afterwards' " (121).

25. For a comparable reading of failure, which resonates with the passage I cited from T. E. Lawrence's *Seven Pillars of Wisdom: A Triumph* as my introduction's epigraph, and which unfortunately I discovered only in revising this chapter, see Robert L. Caserio, "Kipling in the Light of Failure," *Grand Street* 5.4, 1986, 179–212.

26. See Adam Phillips, "Plotting for Kisses," *On Kissing, Tickling, and Being Bored:*

Psychoanalytic Essays on the Unexamined Life, Cambridge, Mass.: Harvard UP, 1993, esp. 96–97.

27. Kipling, "With the Main Guard," *Soldiers Three: A Story of the Godslys in Black and White,* London: Macmillan, 1899, 72.

28. Kipling, "Love-o'-Women" (1893), *A Choice of Kipling Prose,* ed. Craig Raine, London: Faber, 1987, 178. Subsequent references give pagination in main text.

29. For an elaboration of the concept of friendship as philia and its distinction from "eros," see Derrida, "The Politics of Friendship," *The Journal of Philosophy* 85.11, 1988, 632–48.

30. Ibid., 633–34. I discuss this argument in Freud's *Group Psychology and the Analysis of the Ego* (1921), *Standard Edition,* vol. 18, 124n, in "Sublimation, Male Homosexuality, Esprit de Corps: Shattering the Dream of a Common Culture," *Homosexuality and Psychoanalysis,* ed. Tim Dean, London: Macmillan, 1996.

31. John M. Lyon correctly observes in his introduction to the Penguin edition that the passage is "mawkish"—indeed all physical intimacy, and any formulation of sexuality by Kipling, shares this quality—though Lyon is strangely adamant that the relationship between Heldar and Torpenhow is "not homoerotic" (xxiii). The passage, however, speaks for itself. Other Kipling critics, such as Mark Kinead-Weekes ("Vision in Kipling's Novels," *Kipling's Mind and Art,* ed. Andrew Rutherford, London: Oliver and Boyd, 1964, 197–234) and Martin Seymour-Smith in his recent biography (*Rudyard Kipling,* London: Queen Anne, 1989, 163–90), are less reluctant to consider its influence. Kinead-Weekes argues: "In that most significant eighth chapter, male friendship and the life of action are directly opposed to the love of Maisie and the hope of marriage" (206).

32. See Emmanuel Cooper, *The Sexual Perspective: Homosexuality and Art in the Last 100 Years in the West,* New York: Routledge, 1986, 63–111.

33. Lord Alfred Douglas, "Two Loves," *The Penguin Book of Homosexual Verse,* ed. Stephen Coote, Harmondsworth: Penguin, 1983, 262–64.

34. For an exposition of these codes, see Martha Vicinus, "Distance and Desire: English Boarding School Friendships, 1870–1920," *Hidden from History: Reclaiming the Gay and Lesbian Past,* ed. Martin B. Duberman, Martha Vicinus, and George Chauncey Jr., Harmondsworth: Penguin, 1991, 212–29; Carol Christ, "Victorian Masculinity and the Angel in the House," *A Widening Sphere: Changing Roles of Victorian Women,* Bloomington: Indiana UP, 1977, 146–62; and Jeffrey Richards, "Passing the Love of Women: Manly Love and Victorian Society," *Manliness and Morality: Middle-Class Masculinity in Britain and America, 1800–1940,* ed. J. A. Mangan and J. Walvin, Manchester: Manchester UP, 1987, 92–122.

35. Kinead-Weekes argues in "Vision in Kipling's Novels": "Kipling is making this male love a substitute and haven, and the very overtness of his worry over homosexuality shows the pressure that insists on risking it" (208). See also David M. Halperin, "Heroes and Their Pals," *One Hundred Years of Homosexuality, and Other Essays on Greek Love,* New York: Routledge, 1990, 75–87, and Dorothy Hammond and Alta Jablow, "Gilgamesh and the Sundance Kid: The Myth of Male Friendship," *The Making of Masculinities: The New Men's Studies,* ed. Harry Brod, Boston: Allen and Unwin, 1987, 241–58.

36. Seymour-Smith, *Rudyard Kipling,* 188.

37. Though it is abhorrent to consider that Kipling's readers identified with their mirth, Robert Buchanan's famous indictment of Kipling shows that there was dissent and reproach toward this violence at the time. See Robert Buchanan, "The Voice of the Hooligan," *Contemporary Review* 76, 1899, 775–89.

38. Kipling, *Kim,* 327–28.

39. Kipling, "In Partibus," *Early Verse by Rudyard Kipling, 1879–1889,* ed. Andrew Rutherford, Oxford: Clarendon, 1986, 472.

40. Rudyard Kipling, "The Man Who Would Be King" (1890), *A Choice of Kipling Prose,* 78. Subsequent references give pagination in main text.

41. Cecil Rhodes, "Confession of Faith" (1877), qtd. in S. G. Millin, *Rhodes,* London: Chatto, 1933, 138. See also Miles F. Shore, "Cecil Rhodes and the Ego Ideal," *Journal of Interdisciplinary History* 10.2, 1979, 249–65.

42. The word "Kafiristan," derived from the perjorative term "Kaffir," exploits the inflection of this second word's Arabic meaning as "infidel."

43. The British obviated the problem of a two-tier language system in Rhodesia by inventing an intermediary dialect—Chilapalapa—that absolved them of the "indignity" of speaking SiShona, SiNdebele, or SiSwana while still providing a language suitable for command: Chilapalapa was a vulgarized form of Zulu, English, and Afrikaans, emptied of all but formal inflection, and consisting almost entirely of directives in the second person and imperative voice.

44. See Lacan, "The Signification of the Phallus," *Écrits: A Selection,* trans. Alan Sheridan, New York: Norton, 1977, 281–91, and Slavoj Žižek, *The Sublime Object of Ideology,* New York: Verso, 1989, 155–58.

45. Freud, "The Dissection of the Psychical Personality" (1933), *Standard Edition,* vol. 22, 80.

46. Freud, *Inhibitions, Symptoms and Anxiety* (1926 [1925]), *Standard Edition,* vol. 20, 99. Freud is punning here on the German word *"Besetzung"* which can mean both "cathexis" and "garrison."

47. Ibid., 98.

48. Ibid., 92.

49. See Norman Etherington, "Rider Haggard, Imperialism, and the Layered Personality," *Victorian Studies* 22.1, 1978, 71–72.

50. Freud, *The Interpretation of Dreams* (1900), *Standard Edition,* vol. 5, 452.

51. Kipling, "Arithmetic on the Frontier," *Rudyard Kipling: Selected Verse,* ed. James Cochrane, Harmondsworth: Penguin, 1977, 13.

52. Freud, *The Ego and the Id* (1923), *Standard Edition,* vol. 19, 25. See also "The Dissection of the Psychical Personality," *Standard Edition,* vol. 22, 77.

53. For further discussion of the real, see Žižek, *The Sublime Object of Ideology,* 69–84, and Dean, "The Psychoanalysis of AIDS," *October* 63, 1993, 97 n. 31.

54. According to Lacan, this distinction is spurious because the "outside" is already "inside," and vice versa. See Jacques-Alain Miller, "Extimité," *Prose Studies* 11.3, 1988, 121–31, for elaboration of this argument.

55. Kipling, "The Strange Ride of Morrowbie Jukes," *Wee Willie Winkie and Other Stories,* (1895) London: Macmillan, 1918, 168. Subsequent references give pagination to the 1918 edition in main text.

56. This point endorses much of the reading of British culture that Peter Stallybrass and Allon White undertake in *The Politics and Poetics of Transgression,* London: Methuen, 1986. However, my emphasis falls on the psychic constituents of colonial authority and anxiety, and is therefore closer to the field of abjection and fantasy that Julia Kristeva interprets in *Powers of Horror: An Essay in Abjection,* trans. Leon S. Roudiez, New York: Columbia UP, 1982. See also Klaus Theweleit, *Male Fantasies,* vol. 1: *Women, Floods, Bodies, History,* trans. Stephen Conway in collaboration with Erica Carter and Chris Turner, Minneapolis: U of Minnesota P, 1987.

57. Joseph Conrad, *Victory: An Island Tale,* Harmondsworth: Penguin, 1989, 226.

58. Freud made this distinction in "Instincts and Their Vicissitudes" (1915), *Standard Edition,* vol. 14, 109–40. See also "Anaclisis," J. Laplanche and J.-B. Pontalis, *The Language of Psychoanalysis,* London: Karnac, 1988, 29–31.

59. Kipling, "Beyond the Pale" (1888), *A Choice of Kipling's Prose,* 43. Subsequent references give pagination in main text. Kipling's opening statement notably proceeds his choice of a Hindu Proverb as the story's epigraph: "Love heeds not caste nor sleep a broken bed. I went in search of love and lost myself" (43). For a critique of Kipling's racial binaries, see Satya P. Mohanty, "Drawing the Color Line: Kipling and the Culture of Colonial Rule," *The Bounds of Race: Perspectives on Hegemony and Resistance,* ed. Dominick LaCapra, Ithaca: Cornell UP, 1991, 311–43.

60. Kipling, "Dray Wara Yow Dee," *Soldiers Three,* 238, 240, and 242–43. Consider also Ortheris's reported remarks in "With the Main Guard": "A man behind me sez beseechful an' in a whisper:— 'Let me get at thim! For the love of Mary give me room beside ye, ye tall man!' " (*Soldiers Three,* 64).

61. Kipling, "The Mark of the Beast," *Life's Handicap: Being Stories of Mine Own People* (1891), Harmondsworth: Penguin, 1988, 196–97. Subsequent references give pagination in main text.

62. Kipling, "His Chance in Life" (1890), *Plain Tales from the Hills,* 91–96. Subsequent references give pagination in main text.

63. See Joseph Bristow, *Empire Boys: Adventures in a Man's World,* London: Harper-Collins, 1991; Hugh Brogan, *Mowgli's Sons: Kipling and Baden-Powell's Scouts,* London: Cape, 1987; Michael Roesenthal, *The Character Factory: Baden-Powell and the Origins of the Boy Scout Movement,* London: Collins, 1986.

64. Perhaps the most notorious example is Rhodes's decision to introduce gas chambers in the Boer War. See John Flint, *Cecil Rhodes,* London: Hutchinson, 1976, and S. B. Spies, *Methods of Barbarism?: Roberts and Kitchener and Civilians in the Boer War Republics, January 1900–May 1902,* Cape Town: Human and Rousseau, 1977.

65. Kipling, "The Law of the Jungle," *Rudyard Kipling: Selected Verse,* 252.

66. Kipling, "Follow Me 'Ome," *Rudyard Kipling: Selected Verse,* 199–200.

67. Virginia Woolf, *A Room of One's Own* (1929), London: Panther, 1984, 97.

68. Kipling, "Recessional" (1897), *Rudyard Kipling: Selected Verse,* 130.

69. Kipling, "The Islanders" (1902) and "The White Man's Burden" (1899), ibid., 116–19 and 128–29.

70. Benita Parry, "The Content and Discontent of Kipling's Imperialism," 55; Edward W. Said, "*Kim:* The Pleasures of Imperialism," *Raritan* 7.2, 1987, 42–43.

71. Kipling, "The Conversion of Aurelian McGoggin," *Plain Tales from the Hills* (1890), Harmondsworth: Penguin, 1990, 118. See also Kipling, "The Enlightenment of Pagett, M.P.": "If there were any political analogy between India and England, if the thousand races of this Empire were one; if there were any chance even of their learning to speak one language . . . this kind of talk might be worth listening to" (qtd. in Alan Sandison, "Rudyard Kipling: The Imperial Simulacrum," *The Wheel of Empire: A Study of the Imperial Idea in Some Late Nineteenth and Early Twentieth Century Fiction,* New York: St Martin's, 1967, 68).

72. As further illustration of this ambivalence and opportunism, Kipling commented in personal correspondence: "It is my fortune to have been born and to a large extent brought up among those whom white men call 'heathen'; and while I recognize the paramount duty of every white man to follow the teaching of his creed and con- science as 'a debtor to the whole law,' it seems to me cruel that white men, whose governments are armed with the most murderous weapons known to science, should amaze and confound their fellow creatures with a doctrine of salvation imperfectly understood by themselves and a code of ethics foreign to the climate and instincts of those races whose most cherished customs they outrage and whose gods they insult" (private correspondence, qtd. in Charles E. Carrington, *Rudyard Kipling: His Life and Work,* London: Macmillan, 1955, 361).

73. See Said, "*Kim:* The Pleasures of Imperialism," 32; Bristow, *Empire Boys: Ad- ventures in a Man's World,* 213; Patrick Williams, "*Kim* and Orientalism," *Kipling Considered,* ed. Phillip Mallett, London: Macmillan, 1989, 45–47.

74. Kipling wrote: "[T]he idea of our Empire as a community of men of allied race and identical aims, united in comradeship, comprehension, and sympathy, is no new thing. It grew up in the hearts of all our people with their national growth as the peoples in the Empire grew to the stature of distinct nations. None can say where it was born, but we all know the one man who in our time gave present life to that grand conception . . . Joseph Chamberlain" ("Imperial Relations," *A Book of Words: Selections from Speeches and Addresses Delivered Between 1906 and 1927,* London: Macmillan, 1928, 25–26).

75. Kipling, *Debits and Credits* (1918), qtd. in Joyce M. S. Tompkins, *The Art of Rudyard Kipling,* Lincoln: U of Nebraska P, 1965, 26.

76. Kipling, "As Easy as A.B.C." (1912), *A Diversity of Creatures* (1917), Harmonds- worth: Penguin, 1987, 27–56. For further discussion of Kipling's Masonic past and its inherited traditions, see M. Karim, "Rudyard Kipling and the Lodge Hope and Perseverance," *Kipling Journal* 189, 1974, 4–12.

77. For examples of recent theoretical inquiry, see Abdul JanMohamed, "The Econ- omy of Manichean Allegory: The Function of Racial Difference in Colonialist Literature," *Critical Inquiry* 12, 1985, 59–87; B. J. Moore-Gilbert, "Rudyard Kipling: Writing and Control," *Literature and Imperialism,* conference papers at Roehampton

Institute, ed. Moore-Gilbert, Guilford: U of Surrey P, 1983, 93–117, and Moore-Gilbert, *Kipling and "Orientalism,"* London: Croom Helm, 1986.

78. Kipling, "A Song of the English" (1893), *Rudyard Kipling: Selected Verse,* 76.

2. The Fate of the Pioneer: Mason, Haggard, and the Colonial Frame of Homophilia

1. Sir Jacob Epstein, engraving on Oscar Wilde's tomb, *Epstein: An Autobiography,* New York: Dutton, 1955, 51–54. As if to confirm this inscription, the authorities covered Wilde's tomb with a tarpaulin before Epstein was able to complete it; later, they forbade Epstein from exhibiting it in public. Artists and writers of the time organized a protest, but the courts still demanded that Epstein alter and remodel the monument. Even this did not satisfy the courts: they insisted that a tarpaulin cover the monument until the outbreak of the First World War.

2. A. E. W. Mason, *The Four Feathers,* London: Hodder and Stoughton, 1924, 66. Subsequent references give pagination in main text.

3. The difference between the current (December 1994) "Don't ask, don't tell" option and the previous policy of outright discrimination lies in the stipulation that "homosexual conduct," not "homosexuality," is incompatible with military service. For an explication of this debate, see Marc Wolinsky and Kenneth Sherrill, eds., *Gays and the Military: Joseph Steffan versus the United States,* Princeton: Princeton UP, 1993.

4. See Dennis Porter, *Haunted Journeys: Desire and Transgression in European Travel Writing,* Princeton: Princeton UP, 1991, 9–12. I interpret this argument in the second part of this chapter.

5. Oscar Wilde, *The Picture of Dorian Gray* (1891), Harmondsworth: Penguin, 1982, 157–58.

6. Wilde and others, *Teleny; or, The Reverse of the Medal* (1893), ed. John McRae, London: Gay Men's, 1986, 134.

7. In his biography of Mason, Roger Lancelyn Green writes, "Most early novels, as [Mason] himself remarked, are self-conscious autobiographies, either of complaint or of wish-fulfillment" (Green, *A. E. W. Mason,* London: Max Parrish, 1952, 63).

8. Other men of importance to Mason—aside from Warrender, Barrie, and Quiller-Couch—included Campbell Colquhoun, Charles Cannan, William Butler Yeats, and John Chayter Brinton, whom Mason described as "the most beautiful-looking man he had ever seen" (qtd. in Green, *A. E. W. Mason,* 34).

9. Ibid., 104.

10. J. M. Barrie, qtd. in ibid., 104. In contrast to his obtuse treatment of Mason's relationships with women, Green devotes the first third of his biography to Mason's close and affectionate ties with other men at Oxford. The following passage is indicative: "Mason's friendship with [Anthony Hope] Hawkins was but slight at Oxford, though it developed in later years into a close affection; but Quiller-Couch seems to have been his earliest Trinity friend, despite their two years' difference in age, and their close friendship increased greatly when in 1886 "Q" became his tutor. . . ." (30–31). Eve Kosofsky Sedgwick provides an interesting account of Barrie's bache-

lor fiction in *Epistemology of the Closet,* Berkeley: U of California P, 1990, 182–83 and 193–99.

11. Green, *A. E. W. Mason,* 106.

12. Ibid., 90.

13. Green describes Mason's literary affairs "outside" his texts in a comparable way: "A pleasanter, and more lasting affair, began in March 1889 when Mason was at Edinburgh and Glasgow with the Compton Comedy Company and met the actress Kate Cutler who was playing in one of these towns with another tour. . . . Yet another love affair occurred in 1901 or 1902 with Elspeth Cambell (to whom *The Four Feathers* is dedicated). . . . But the real love of his life was Edna May, the beautiful American singer who came to England in 1898 and made one of the greatest names ever achieved in light opera by her performance in *The Belle of New York.* There is no record of when Mason met Edna May, nor of how his wooing fared. It seems certain that he would have married her if she had been willing, but his love was not returned. . . . But her friendship with Mason continued, and they met from time to time until her death a year or so before his own [in 1948]" (*A. E. W. Mason,* 105–6). The nonreciprocal pattern of these relationships renders imprecise such descriptions as "a more lasting affair," "another love affair," and "the one real love of his life" (105).

14. Ibid., 89.

15. Wilde, *The Picture of Dorian Gray,* 187. Writing later of the "purifying" quality of punishment, Wilde notes of Dorian: "It was his duty to confess to suffer public shame, and to make public atonement" to "kill this monstrous soul-life" (246–47).

16. Green, *A. E. W. Mason,* 170–71.

17. See Jacques Lacan, *The Seminar of Jacques Lacan, Book VII: The Ethics of Psychoanalysis, 1959–1960,* ed. Jacques-Alain Miller, trans. Dennis Porter, New York: Norton, 1992, 186–87.

18. Feversham's name is interesting in this regard; it conjoins him to—and compels him to embody—"cowardice": "Feather-sham." (In these terms, we should also consider the implications of "Father-sham" and "Fever-sham.") Other names in this text are equally and crassly overdetermined: "Ethne" represents a people and its land. As the narrator remarks: "Dermod [her father] for once did an appropriate thing when he gave her that name. For she is of her country and more, of her county. She has the love of it in her bones" (26). Lieutenant Sutch's rank is more interesting in this regard because it demonstrates that his position (or "tenancy") also stands "in lieu" of Feversham's and may therefore foreclose on Feversham's humiliation. This idea emerges more succinctly in the text because Sutch is Feversham's mentor, having asked him in that opening scene in the hallway: "If ever you want to talk over a difficult question with an older man, I am at your service" (20). Sutch also leaves Britain to rescue Feversham from his imprisonment in the Sudan, and (like Mason) uses the idea of unrequited love to explain why he never married. The narrator explains: "The passage of the years had not diminished his great regard for Harry, he cared for him indeed with a woman's concentration of love, and he could not endure that his memory should be slighted" (252).

19. Ethne urges Feversham to sustain their public dissimulation of passion: "We

must show brave faces until daylight" (53). The narrator corroborates: "Habit assisted them. . . . Harry Feversham watched Ethne laugh and talk as though she never had a care, and was perpetually surprised, taking no thought that he wore the like mask of gaiety himself" (54).

20. Freud, "Instincts and Their Vicissitudes" (1915), *Standard Edition,* vol. 14, 122–23.

21. Compare the following citation about Feversham Sr. with the passage I quoted in note 19: "at the mere mention of his son's name the old General's face set like plaster. It became void of expression and inattentive *as a mask*" (85; my emphasis). Since *The Four Feathers* repeatedly conjoins passion with dissimulation, the general's masklike response intensifies his son's semiotic crisis of masculinity.

22. See Wilde, *The Picture of Dorian Gray,* 157–58.

23. Feversham is successful only insofar as he survives a life-threatening situation. Perversely, the task he appoints himself fails because the letters of General Gordon he rescues from "enemy hands" are all but worthless:

> "They were hardly worth risking a life for," said Mather.
> "Perhaps not," replied Durrance, a little doubtfully. "But, after all, one is glad they have been recovered." (111)

In ways that mirror the narrative, Feversham's task splits between an aim that is successful (redeeming his honor) and an object that is not (completing a task of recognized value). What is striking about the second half of this text is the ease with which its characters, who were formerly so punitive, are willing to overlook this failure to satisfy the urgency that Feversham succeed. If this disavowal—which Durrance's bland remark captures: "But, after all, one is glad they have been recovered" —was common during the period of Britain's empire, it recalls a practice of selective homophobia today: that is, "I don't like what lesbians or gay men do in bed, but I'm prepared to forego my disgust for the sake of their tolerable qualities, cultural achievements, etc." In relation to this text, and its initial antipathy to colonial constraints, several questions remain: What meaning can Feversham's act signify when the letters are valueless; Why is "courage" able to demonstrate itself independently of the act that conveys it; finally, Is Feversham's act not close to the male "simplicity" and "stupid[ity]" that the text initially derides?

24. John le Carré, *Tinker, Tailor, Soldier, Spy,* New York: Knopf, 1974, 328. For an antihomophobic account of this isolation, see Christopher Isherwood, *A Single Man,* New York: Simon and Schuster, 1964.

25. Mason, *The Broken Road,* London: Smith, Elder and Co., 1907. Subsequent references give pagination in main text.

26. Frantz Fanon, *Black Skin, White Masks* (1952), trans. Charles Lam Markmann, New York: Grove, 1967, esp. 63–82.

27. Mason, *The Philanderers* (1897), London: Hodder and Stoughton, 1926, 80.

28. H. Rider Haggard, *Nada the Lily,* London: Longmans, Green, 1892, 72. Subsequent references give pagination in main text.

29. See Anne McClintock, "Maidens, Maps and Mines: *King Solomon's Mines* and the Reinvention of Patriarchy in Colonial South Africa," *Women and Gender in*

Southern Africa to 1945, ed. Cheryl Walker, Cape Town: David Philip, 1990, 97–124; David Bunn, "Embodying Africa: Woman and Romance in Colonial Fiction," *English in Africa* 15.1, 1966, 1–26; Laura Chrisman, "The Imperial Unconscious?: Representations of Imperial Discourse," *Critical Quarterly* 32.3, 1990, 38–58; Claudia Crawford, "She," *SubStance* 29, 1981, 83–96; and Rebecca Stott, "The Dark Continent: Africa as Female Body in Haggard's Adventure Fiction," *Feminist Review* 32, 1989, 69–89.

30. As I suggest below, *Nada the Lily* describes a similar sexual adventure. One passage is worth citing here because it bears such resemblance to *King Solomon's Mines:* "Now I was on the breast of the mountain, and wandered to and fro awhile between great heaps of stone. At length, I found, as it were, a crack in the stone thrice as wide as a man can jump. . . . I looked down into the crack—it was very deep, and green with moss, and tall ferns grew about in it, for the damp gathered there. There was nothing else. I had dreamed a lying dream" (109).

31. Barbara Johnson, "Is Male to Female as Land Is to Figure?" *Feminism and Psychoanalysis,* ed. Richard Feldstein and Judith Roof, Ithaca: Cornell UP, 1989, 255–68.

32. For an acute and subtle interpretation of this conflation, see McClintock, "Maidens, Maps and Mines," 99–102, and Sandra M. Gilbert and Susan Gubar, "Heart of Darkness: The Agon of the Femme Fatale," *No Man's Land: The Place of the Woman Writer in the Twentieth Century,* vol. 2, *Sexchanges,* New Haven: Yale UP, 1989, 3–46.

33. See McClintock, "Maidens, Maps and Mines," 97–124; Bunn, "Embodying Africa: Woman and Romance in Colonial Fiction," 1–26; Brian V. Street, *The Savage in Literature: Representations of "Primitive" Society in English Fiction, 1858–1920,* London, Boston: Routledge and Kegan Paul, 1975.

34. Carl Vogt, *Lectures on Man: His Place in Creation, and in the History of the Earth,* ed. James Hunt, London: Longman, Green, 1864; Max Nordau, *Degeneration* (1894), New York: H. Fertig, 1968; E. S. Talbot, *Degeneracy: Its Causes, Signs and Results,* London: Walter Scott, 1898. For more recent criticism of these accounts, see Richard D. Walter, "What Became of the Degenerate?: A Brief History of the Concept," *Journal of the History of Medicine and the Allied Sciences* 11, 1956, 422–29, and Sander L. Gilman, *Difference and Pathology: Stereotypes of Sexuality, Race, and Madness,* Ithaca: Cornell UP, 1985.

35. Haggard, "About Fiction," *Contemporary Review* 2, February 1887, 176.

36. Haggard, *Allan Quartermain,* London: Longmans, Green, 1887, 4–6. Although Haggard appeared to share this opinion, Quartermain is speaking here.

37. Besides Freud's now infamous remarks on the "dark continent" of femininity, Carl Jung described Freud's "passion for knowledge which was to lay open a dark continent to his gaze" (Jung, "In Memory of Sigmund Freud" [1939], *The Collected Works of C. G. Jung,* vol. 15, ed. Sir Herbert Read, Michael Fordham, Gerhard Adler, and William McGuire, London: Routledge, 1979, 48).

38. Freud, *The Interpretation of Dreams* (1900), *Standard Edition,* vol. 5, 452.

39. Ibid., 453.

40. Ibid., 452.

41. Ibid., 453.

42. Jung, *The Collected Works of C. G. Jung,* vol. 9, i, 60, 516, and 518n. See also vol. 7, 298–99 and 375.

43. Norman Etherington, "Rider Haggard, Imperialism, and the Layered Personality," *Victorian Studies* 22.1, 1978, 81.

44. Wendy Katz supports this reading in *Rider Haggard and the Fiction of Empire,* Cambridge: Cambridge UP, 1987, 143–44.

45. Etherington, "Rider Haggard, Imperialism, and the Layered Personality," 83–84.

46. Haggard, *King Solomon's Mines* (1885), Oxford: Oxford UP, 1989, 226.

47. Consider the following "confession" by a white warrior in *Eric Brighteyes:* "My axe hung on the wainscot. I snatched it thence, and of what befell I know this alone, that when the madness passed, eight men lay stretched out before me, and all the place was but a gore of blood" (London: Longmans, Green, 1891, 73).

48. Haggard, *She: A History of Adventure* (1887), Oxford: Oxford UP, 1991. Subsequent references give pagination in main text.

49. Haggard intended his readers to receive *Nada the Lily, King Solomon's Mines,* and *She* as romances, a point that amply satisfied his readers (*King Solomon's Mines* alone was reprinted four times in the first three months, sold thirty-one thousand copies in the first year, and has never been out of print since its publication). When Haggard decided to write political history, however, his readers immediately grew alarmed and critical.

50. Porter, *Haunted Journeys: Desire and Transgression in European Travel Writing,* 11. Freud's essay on "The 'Uncanny' " (1919) is central to this discussion of repetition, familiarity, and haunting. Freud writes, "The uncanny is that class of the frightening which leads back to what is known of old and long familiar" (*Standard Edition,* vol. 17, 220).

51. L. P. Hartley, *The Go-Between,* London: Hamish Hamilton, 1953, 9.

52. Haggard, *King Solomon's Mines,* 198.

53. The possibility that the "woman" is incidental to a homoerotic scenario emerges in William J. Scheick's essay, "Adolescent Pornography and Imperialism in Haggard's *King Solomon's Mines,* " *English Literature in Transition* 34.1, 1991, 19–30. Scheick, however, does not interpret the homoerotic possibilities of Haggard's dedication of *King Solomon's Mines,* "To all the big and little boys who read it."

54. Kaja Silverman, "White Skin, Brown Masks: The Double Mimesis; or, With Lawrence in Arabia," *differences* 1.3, 1989, 3–54.

55. Haggard, *King Solomon's Mines,* 306, 246.

56. Ibid., 300.

57. "Oh! my father," [Umslopogaas] said, "I thought that you were dead with the others, and now you have come back to me, and I, I would have lifted the axe against you in my folly" (192).

58. Freud, *Totem and Taboo, Standard Edition,* vol. 13, 144.

59. Jacqueline Rose represents this tension as an asymmetrical relation between sexuality and identity by arguing that "men and women take up positions of symbolic and polarised oppositions against the grain of a multifarious and bisexual disposition. . . . The lines of that division are fragile in exact proportion to the rigid insistence with which our culture lays them down; they constantly converge and threaten to coalesce" (*Sexuality in the Field of Vision,* London: Verso, 1986, 226–27).

60. See Nina Baym, "Melodramas of Beset Manhood: How Theories of American Fiction Exclude Women Authors," *American Quarterly* 33.2, 1981, 123–39.

61. This lengthy passage from Haggard's novel strongly resembles Milton's account in *Paradise Lost* (1667), bk. 2, of the canine progeny of Sin and Death (the "son" who brutally rapes her immediately after "he" is born), which crawl back into Sin's womb to eat her innards. For Milton, this literal enactment of oedipal fantasy and aggressivity between Satan and Sin (his "daughter") and Sin and Death (her "son") apophatically defines the virtuous asexuality of God and his angels. In *Nada,* however, Haggard's account of monstrous sexuality appears to confirm a relation of horror between mothers and sons that develops into his male characters' apparently "natural" suspicion and dread of women.

62. Juliet Flower MacCannell interprets the complex stakes of this argument in *The Regime of the Brother: After the Patriarchy,* New York: Routledge, 1991.

63. Haggard, *Allan Quartermain,* 4.

64. *Oxford English Dictionary* vol. 11, 2d. ed., prepared by J. A. Simpson and E. S. C. Weiner, Oxford: Clarendon, 1989, 883.

65. Pierre Macherey, *A Theory of Literary Production,* trans. Geoffrey Wall, London, Boston: Routledge and Kegan Paul, 1978, 189.

66. Ibid.

3. Framing Fears, Reading Designs: The Homosexual Art of Painting in James, Wilde, and Beerbohm

In this chapter, all references to truth, lies, and secrets should be read ironically, symptomatically, as if accompanied by quotation marks.

1. Oscar Wilde, *The Portrait of Mr. W. H.* (1889), E. Hubler et al., *The Riddle of Shakespeare's Sonnets,* New York: Basic, 1962, 242.

2. Jacques Derrida, *The Truth in Painting,* trans. Geoff Bennington and Ian McLeod, Chicago: U of Chicago P, 1987, 5.

3. Jacques Lacan, *The Four Fundamental Concepts of Psycho-Analysis,* ed. Jacques-Alain Miller, trans. Alan Sheridan, New York: Norton, 1978, vii.

4. For a brilliant reading of this interest, see Shoshana Felman, "Turning the Screw of Interpretation," *Literature and Psychoanalysis: The Question of Reading — Otherwise,* ed. Felman, Baltimore: Johns Hopkins UP, 1977, 94–208.

5. Henry James, "The Liar" (1888), *The Complete Tales of Henry James,* vol. 6 (*1884–1888*), ed. Leon Edel, London: Hart-Davis, 1963, 383–441. Subsequent references give pagination in main text.

6. Leo Bersani, "The Jamesian Lie," *A Future for Astyanax: Character and Desire*

in Literature, Boston: Little, Brown, 1976, 128–55, and Allon White, "Vulgarity and Obscurity in James," *The Uses of Obscurity: The Fiction of Early Modernism,* London, Boston: Routledge and Kegan Paul, 1981, 144–47.

7. James, "The Art of Fiction" (1884), *Henry James: Selected Literary Criticism,* ed. Morris Shapira, New York: Horizon, 1981, 50.

8. Sharon Cameron, *Thinking in Henry James,* Chicago: U of Chicago P, 1989, 43. This is largely the phenomenon her book sets out to establish and interpret.

9. Writing more specifically on cubism, Georges Monnet has argued: "The painting is no longer either the equivalent or the direct cause of what is seen because there is more to the picture than what is offered on the canvas" ("Picasso and Cubism," trans. Dominic Faccini, *October* 60, 1992, 51).

10. Wilde, *The Portrait of Mr. W. H.,* 218.

11. See, for example, Eve Kosofsky Sedgwick's reading of "The Beast in the Jungle," an essay notable for its belief that homosexuality inheres in the protagonist Marcher as a visible decision, rather than as a propensity the text inevitably encounters from its obsession with Marcher's inability to sustain any object choice. Sedgwick, "The Beast in the Closet: James and the Writing of Homosexual Panic," *Epistemology of the Closet,* Berkeley: U of California P, 1990, 182–212.

12. Sigmund Freud, "Psychoanalytic Notes on an Autobiographical Account of a Case of Paranoia (Dementia Paranoides) (1911)," *The Standard Edition of the Complete Psychological Works of Sigmund Freud,* vol. 12, ed. and trans. James Strachey, London: Hogarth, 1957–74, 9.

13. Ibid.

14. For related interpretations of this tale, see Judith E. Funston, "James's Portrait of the Artist as Liar," *Studies in Short Fiction* 26.4, 1989, 431–38; Thomas H. Getz, "The Self-Portrait in the Portrait: John Ashbery's 'Self-Portrait in a Convex Mirror' and James's 'The Liar,' " *Studies in the Humanities* 13.1, 1986, 42–51; and Moshe Ron, "The Art of the Portrait According to James," *Yale French Studies* 69, 1985, 222–37.

15. For a comparable account of the analyst's role, see Lacan, *The Four Fundamental Concepts,* 246.

16. I should emphasize that the entire tale urgently postpones the inevitable death of its most obvious subject, Sir David. This suggests that Lyon's desire to capture the character of Sir David on canvas already implies an analogy between representation and death.

17. "Hypocrisy": Gk. *hupokrisis*— "acting, feigning" (*Krínein*— "decide, judge"), *The Concise Oxford Dictionary of English Etymology,* ed. T. F. Hoad, Oxford: Clarendon, 1986, 224.

18. John Addington Symonds, preface to *Sexual Inversion* (1897), rpt. New York: Bell, 1984, 107.

19. William James, "The Hidden Self," *Scribner's Magazine* 7, January–June 1890, 361.

20. Wilde, *The Picture of Dorian Gray* (1891), Harmondsworth: Penguin, 1982, 8, 129. Subsequent references give pagination in main text.

21. This argument differs from the more conventional charge of narcissism that critics of Wilde often level against Dorian. This claim argues that Dorian's self-obsession removes him from all object relations except with himself. It is interesting that many critical accounts of the tale of Narcissus similarly ignore or excise Ganymede's attempted "homosexual" seduction of Narcissus. By taking himself as his own object, Narcissus therefore rejects *both* heterosexual and homosexual relations. Similarly, while Dorian's final rejection of Sibyl Vane suggests his resistance to heterosexuality, Wilde maintains an obvious silence over the second (homosexual) possibility. To this extent, the charge of narcissism is misplaced, and may be used to elide the oblique difficulty of homosexual seduction, which, I am suggesting, is marked elliptically on the painting.

22. Freud, "A Note upon the 'Mystic Writing-Pad' " (1924), *The Standard Edition,* vol. 19, 227–34.

23. Lacan likened the structure of unconscious fantasy to a "scar" (Lacan, *The Four Fundamental Concepts,* 22).

24. For more specific accounts of masculinity and pleasure in this period, see Ed Cohen, "Writing Gone Wilde: Homoerotic Desire in the Closet of Representation," *PMLA* 102.5, 1987, 801–13; William A. Cohen, "Willie and Wilde: Reading *The Portrait of Mr. W. H.,* " *Displacing Homophobia: Gay Male Perspectives in Literature and Culture,* ed. Ronald R. Butters, John M. Clum, and Michael Moon, Durham: Duke UP, 1989, 207–33; and Sedgwick, "Wilde, Nietzsche, and the Sentimental Relations of the Male Body," *Epistemology of the Closet,* 131–81.

25. Consider Wilde's comment on the relation between the arts and self-realization: "Strange, that we [know] so little about ourselves, and that our most intimate personality [is] concealed from us. . . . [It is through Art that we] suddenly . . . become aware that we have passions of which we have never dreamed, thoughts that make us afraid, pleasures whose secret has been denied to us, sorrows that have been hidden from our tears" (*The Portrait of Mr. W. H.,* 242–45).

26. Wilde, "Pen, Pencil and Poison" (1891), *The Complete Works of Oscar Wilde,* London: Collins, 1966, 1008.

27. "The only way to get rid of a temptation is to yield to it" (*Dorian,* 25).

28. Jeffrey Weeks, *Coming Out: Homosexual Politics in Britain, from the Nineteenth Century to the Present,* London and New York: Quartet, 1977, 14.

29. Ibid., 13. For a more detailed analysis of the legal implications of this amendment, see F. B. Smith, "Labouchère's Amendment to the Criminal Law Amendment Bill," *Historical Studies* 17, 1976, 165–73.

30. Lawrence Danson, *Max Beerbohm and the Act of Writing,* New York: Oxford UP, 1989, 38–42.

31. Wilde writes: "Dorian . . . used to wonder at the shallow psychology of those who conceive the Ego in man as a thing simple, permanent, reliable, and of one essence. To him, man was a being with myriad lives and myriad sensations, a complex multiform creature that bore within itself strange legacies of thought and passion" (*Dorian,* 169). Consider also my first epigraph to Chapter 9.

32. See *Dorian Gray,* in which the necessity of maintaining one secret (hiding the

murdered painter's clothes and bag) leads metonymically to the reader's discovery of another: "They must be hidden away somewhere. He unlocked a secret press that was in the wainscoting, a press in which he kept his own curious disguises, and put them into it" (178). As signs of his identity, Hallward's clothes are incorporated into Dorian's already prominent secrecy. This further indicates the guilt he retains without visible effect.

33. See Paul de Man, "Autobiography as De-Facement," *MLN* 94, 1979, 919–30, and Ned Lukacher, "Prosopopoeia," *Primal Scenes: Literature, Philosophy, Psychoanalysis,* Ithaca: Cornell UP, 1986, 68–96.

34. For a modern counterpart to Wilde, see Jane Gallop's assertion that "Identity must be continually assumed and immediately called into question" (*The Daughter's Seduction: Feminism and Psychoanalysis,* Ithaca: Cornell UP, 1982, xii). Perhaps the reverse is a more realistic procedure for Wilde: only when identity is questioned can it then be assumed. Yet even here, the danger is that Wilde's insight could be recuperated for a conservative reading; that is, as a demand for better acting rather than an indictment of the dearth of roles available.

35. For James, this absence seemed more expedient because it veiled the symbol altogether without encouraging a critique of its limited reference. On this point, one might consider the linguistic indeterminacy of the question raised by certain groups to determine a man's sexual preference in the 1890s: "Is he *so?*" The absence of a specific referent ensured an ambiguity that offers a relative safety for the questioner, the object, and the topic itself. (See Noël Annan, "The Cult of Homosexuality in England, 1850–1950," *Biography: An Interdisciplinary Quarterly* 13.3, 1990, 189–202.)

36. "Excoriate": L. *corium*— "hide." "To shed, remove the skin from" (*The Concise Oxford Dictionary of English Etymology,* 159). The word is also a surgical term whose violence to the trope *prosopopoeia* seems particularly apposite.

37. Percy Bysshe Shelley, "The Triumph of Life" (1822), *The Complete Poetical Works of Percy Bysshe Shelley,* ed. Thomas Hutchinson, London: Oxford UP, 1929, 516.

38. Wilde, "Pen, Pencil and Poison," 995.

39. Martin Heidegger, *What Is Called Thinking?* trans. J. Glenn Gray, New York: Harper and Row, 1968, 62.

40. Max Beerbohm, *The Happy Hypocrite: A Fairy Tale for Tired Men* (1896), London: John Lane, 1920. Subsequent references give pagination in main text.

41. Danson, *Max Beerbohm and the Act of Writing,* 10, 39, 68–71, and especially 76: "Wilde's homosexuality seems not to have bothered Beerbohm so much as the flamboyance of the sexuality itself; not, that is to say, the object of Wilde's lust but the fact that he visibly lusted"; and David Cecil, *Max,* Boston: Houghton Mifflin, 1965, qtd. in Malcolm Muggeridge, "A Survivor," *New York Review of Books* 8, November 25, 1965, 33.

42. Muggeridge, "A Survivor," 33.

43. Danson, *Max Beerbohm and the Act of Writing,* 7.

44. For conjecture about Beerbohm's sexual preference, see Muggeridge: "The im-

pression that Beerbohm left on me was of someone in whom the instinct to run for cover had become second nature. But what was he scared of? Beerbohm . . . was in panic flight through most of his life from two things—his Jewishness and his homosexuality" ("A Survivor," 33). See also Frank Kermode, who describes the relationship between Beerbohm and Turner as one of "unusual intimacy," and who interprets Beerbohm's attachments to women as potentially "part of a delicate private joke between the two" ("Whom the Gods Loathe," *Encounter* 24, March 1965, 74). Kermode also comments generally on Beerbohm: "It is hard not to see in these letters a man for whom life was acceptable only if one could remain at a distance from it, yet in touch with something that stressed the appearance of life" (74–75). Danson, also citing Kermode's interpretation of the letters between Beerbohm and Turner during this period (1893–95), goes on to describe Beerbohm's "adoration" of women as a "part in the fiction-making process" (78) immediately after describing his antipathy to Wilde's homosexuality (see my note 41), apparently without being aware of a possible relation between the two attitudes, and while rejecting Muggeridge's conjecture on Beerbohm's putative homosexuality as "unique bad taste" and an "assertion . . . beyond the outrageous" (*Max Beerbohm and the Act of Writing,* 10 and 10n).

45. Letter from Max Beerbohm to John Middleton Murray, August 7, 1920, *Letters of Max Beerbohm 1892–1956,* ed. Rupert Hart-Davis, London: John Murray, 1988, 118.

46. Beerbohm, "A Peep into the Past," *A Peep into the Past, and Other Prose Pieces,* ed. Rupert Hart-Davis, Battleboro, Vt.: Stephen Greene, 1972, 4.

47. Ibid., 5, 6–7.

48. Muggeridge writes of Beerbohm's attitude toward Reggie Turner: "It was, as I see it, Turner's courageous acceptance of these two, in Beerbohm's eyes, appalling disabilities [Turner's Jewishness and homosexuality] which induced him to be so devoted to Turner, almost to the point of hero-worship . . ." ("A Survivor," 32).

49. Robert Scott, comp., *Greek-English Lexicon,* 9th ed., Oxford: Oxford UP, 1983.

50. On this point, Lacan has argued: "the *transference effect* . . . is love. It is clear that, like all love, it can be mapped, as Freud shows, only in the field of narcissism. To love is, essentially, to wish to be loved" (*The Four Fundamental Concepts,* 253).

51. See Lacan, "L'étourdit," *Scilicet* 4, 1973, 11–13, where Lacan's proposition, "*il n'y a pas de rapport sexuel,*" is elaborated in more detail.

52. In Milton's *Paradise Lost* (1674), Sin is described thus: "The one seemed woman to the waist, and fair,/But ended foul in many a scaly fold" (*Paradise Lost, Milton: Poetical Works,* ed. Douglas Bush, Oxford: Oxford UP, 1966, bk. 2, 650–51, 246). This seesaw equivocation between "fair" and "foul" also invokes the witches' properties in Shakespeare's *Macbeth* (1606). Finally, one might draw an analogy between La Gambogi and Lacan's conception of the woman's masquerade: "The fact that femininity takes refuge in this mask, because of the *Verdrängung* inherent to the phallic mark of desire, has the strange consequence that, in the human being, virile display itself appears as feminine" (Lacan, "The Meaning of the Phallus," *Feminine Sexuality: Jacques Lacan and the école freudienne,* ed. Juliet Mitchell and Jacqueline Rose, trans. Rose, New York: Norton, 1982, 85).

53. With relevance to homosexuality, though with different emphasis, see D. A. Miller, "Secret Subjects, Open Secrets," *The Novel and the Police,* Berkeley: U of California P, 1988, 195.

54. Friedrich Nietzsche, *Beyond Good and Evil* (1886), trans. R. J. Hollingdale, Harmondsworth: Penguin, 1984, 51.

55. See also Beerbohm, "The Pervasion of Rouge" (1894), *Works and More,* London: John Lane, 1930, 86–110; "Pretending" (1898), *More,* London: John Lane, 1907, 55–61; "A Pathetic Imposture" (1900), *Yet Again,* New York: Alfred A. Knopf, 1923, 77.

56. Beerbohm, *Works and More,* 107–8.

4. Fostering Subjection: Masculine Identification and Homosexual Allegory in Conrad's *Victory*

1. Joseph Conrad, qtd. in G. Jean-Aubry, *Joseph Conrad: Life and Letters,* vol. 1, Garden City: Doubleday, Page, 1927, 186.

2. Conrad, *Victory: An Island Tale* (1915), Harmondsworth: Penguin, 1989, 122. Subsequent references give pagination in main text.

3. See Freud, *Civilization and Its Discontents* (1930 [1929]), *Standard Edition,* vol. 21: "It is impossible to overlook the extent to which civilization is built up upon a renunciation of instinct, how much it presupposes precisely the non-satisfaction . . . of powerful instincts" (97). See also Leo Bersani, "Erotic Assumptions: Narcissism and Sublimation in Freud," *The Culture of Redemption,* Cambridge, Mass.: Harvard UP, 1990, 86.

4. See Tony Tanner, "Joseph Conrad and the Last Gentleman," *Critical Quarterly* 28.1–2, 1986, 109–42; Allen Hunter, *Joseph Conrad and the Ethics of Darwinism: The Challenges of Science,* London: Croom Helm, 1983; André Guillaume, "The Psychological Approach in *Victory,*" *L'époque conradienne,* Limoges: Société conradienne française, 1981, 119–54.

5. See Adam Gillon, "Betrayal and Redemption in Joseph Conrad," *Polish Review* 5, 1960, 18–35; Paul Kirschner, *Conrad: The Psychologist as Artist,* Edinburgh: Oliver and Boyd, 1968, 155–66; Douglas B. Park, "Conrad's *Victory:* The Anatomy of a Pose," *Nineteenth-Century Studies* 31, 1976, 150–69; Albert Guerard, *Conrad the Novelist,* Cambridge: Cambridge UP, 1958, 257; and Thomas Moser, *Joseph Conrad: Achievement and Decline,* Cambridge, Mass.: Harvard UP, 1957.

6. See Cedric Watts, *The Deceptive Text: An Introduction to Covert Plots,* Brighton: Harvester, 1984, 109, and John A. Palmer, *Joseph Conrad's Fiction: A Study in Literary Growth,* Ithaca: Cornell UP, 1968, 168.

7. Virginia Woolf, *To the Lighthouse* (1927), New York: Harcourt Brace Jovanovich, 1981, 187.

8. Park, "Conrad's *Victory:* The Anatomy of a Pose," 156.

9. Ted E. Boyle, *Symbol and Meaning in the Fiction of Joseph Conrad,* The Hague: Mouton, 1965, 221.

10. See Suresh Raval, "Conrad's *Victory:* Skepticism and Experience," *Nineteenth-Century Fiction* 34.4, 1980, 423.

11. Further indication of this doubt and the role of conjecture in the text surface much later at Lena's muted response to Heyst's explanation of events:

> "One day I met a 'cornered' man. I use the word because it expresses the man's situation exactly, and because you just used it yourself. You know what that means?"
>
> "What do you say?" she whispered, astounded. "A man!"
>
> Heyst laughed at her wondering eyes.
>
> "No! No! I mean in his own way."
>
> "I knew very well it couldn't be anything like that," she observed under her breath. (213)

12. For analysis of this liminality, see David M. Halperin, "Heroes and Their Pals," *One Hundred Years of Homosexuality, and Other Essays on Greek Love,* New York: Routledge, 1990, 75–87, and Dorothy Hammond and Alta Jablow, "Gilgamesh and the Sundance Kid: The Myth of Male Friendship," *The Making of Masculinities: The New Men's Studies,* ed. Harry Brod, Boston: Allen and Unwin, 1987, 241–58.

13. F. R. Leavis, *The Great Tradition: George Eliot, Henry James, Joseph Conrad* (1948), Harmondsworth: Peregrine, 1983, 233.

14. Jocelyn Baines, *Joseph Conrad: A Critical Biography,* New York: McGraw-Hill, 1960, 395.

15. Janet Butler Haugaard, "Conrad's *Victory:* Another Look at Axel Heyst," *Literature and Psychology* 31.3, 1981, 38.

16. Ibid.

17. Ibid., 42.

18. Freud made this distinction in "Mourning and Melancholia" (1917), *Standard Edition,* vol. 14, 243–44.

19. For an account of the compulsion to repeat, see Slavoj Žižek, *The Sublime Object of Ideology,* New York: Verso, 1989, 136–42.

20. For elaboration of the psychoanalytic concept of fading as *aphanisis,* see Jacques Lacan, *The Four Fundamental Concepts of Psycho-Analysis,* ed. Jacques-Alain Miller, trans. Alan Sheridan, New York: Norton, 1978, 209–15, and Kaja Silverman, *The Subject of Semiotics,* New York: Oxford UP, 1983, 168–73.

21. Lacan, *The Four Fundamental Concepts of Psycho-Analysis,* 129; original emphasis. Freud made this argument in "Remembering, Repeating and Working-Through (Further Recommendations on the Technique of Psycho-Analysis II)" (1914), *Standard Edition,* vol. 12, 145–56; Lacan revised some of this paper's guiding precepts in *The Four Fundamental Concepts of Psycho-Analysis,* 48–51.

22. Octave Mannoni, *Prospero and Caliban: The Psychology of Colonization,* trans. Pamela Powesland, New York: Praeger, 1956, 110–14.

23. Tanner, "Joseph Conrad and the Last Gentleman," 133: "Obey me and 'shrink' away from full sexual manhood: imitate me and go forth and copulate and multiply. Do not presume to be like me and take my place, my son: only by being like me will you become a proper man." Tanner is paraphrasing Freud's account of masculine identification, outlined in *Group Psychology and the Analysis of the Ego* (1921), *Standard Edition,* vol. 18, 105–10.

24. For elaboration of this point, see ibid., 106: "It is easy to state in a formula the distinction between an identification with the father and the choice of the father as an object. In the first case one's father is what one would like to *be,* and in the second he is what one would like to *have.*" The argument about "contrary desire" refers to Freud's discussion of the boy's "feminine attitude," or negative oedipal relation, in which the boy identifies with the mother and takes the father as an object of desire. See also Freud, "A Seventeenth-Century Demonological Neurosis" (1923 [1922]), *Standard Edition,* vol. 19, 67–105, and Silverman, "A Woman's Soul Enclosed in a Man's Body: Femininity in Male Homosexuality," *Male Subjectivity at the Margins,* New York: Routledge, 1992, 356–73.

25. In *Group Psychology and the Analysis of the Ego,* Freud argued that the masculine subject resolves this impossible demand by incorporating the paternal imago as its ego-ideal. Within, but also set apart from, the subject, the ego-ideal constrains the subject's behavior, punishing it with the guilt deriving from its repressed hostility toward the father. The boy aligns himself with his father only by converting hatred for him into an avowal of love, and by returning a modified form of this hatred onto itself as guilt. See *Standard Edition,* vol. 18, 105–6.

26. Although risking an overliteral reading, we could put this in comparable psycho-analytic terms by arguing that Heyst's identification fails to "proceed" to identifi-cation with the group and stymies in a "narcissistic" confusion between loss of the primary object and acceptance of paternal law. Freud's trajectory for the boy is more troubled and less schematic than this argument implies; however, my interest lies in thinking through Heyst's *resistance* to "full" masculine identification because it appears to represent his betrayal of a prior paternal injunction. For elaboration of this argument, see Richard Conn Davis, "Critical Introduction: The Discourse of the Father," *The Fictional Father: Lacanian Readings of the Text,* Amherst: U of Massachusetts P, 1981, 1–25.

27. Arthur Schopenhauer, *The World as Will and Idea* (1883), qtd. in Tanner, "Joseph Conrad and the Last Gentleman," 127. See also William W. Bonney, " 'Eastern Logic under My Western Eyes': Conrad, Schopenhauer, and the Orient," *Thorns and Arabesques: Contexts for Conrad's Fiction,* Baltimore: Johns Hopkins UP, 1980, 3–30.

28. Schopenhauer, *The World as Will and Idea,* qtd. in Tanner, "Joseph Conrad and the Last Gentleman," 127.

29. See Seymour L. Gross, "The Devil in Samburan: Jones and Ricardo in *Victory,*" *Nineteenth-Century Fiction* 16.1, 1961, 81–85; John F. Lewis, "Plain Mr. Jones and the Final Chapter of *Victory,*" *Conradian* 9.1, 1984, 4–14; and R. J. Lordi, "The Three Emissaries of Evil: Their Psychological Relationship in Conrad's *Victory,*" *College English* 23, 1961, 136–40.

30. Butler Haugaard, "Conrad's *Victory:* Another Look at Axel Heyst," 43.

31. Freud, *Civilization and Its Discontents, Standard Edition,* vol. 21, 137.

32. Ibid.

33. For discussion of askesis and paternal chastisement see Edward Said, *Begin-nings: Intention and Method,* New York: Columbia UP, 1985, 40–41; Harold Bloom, "*Askesis* or Purgation and Solipsism," *The Anxiety of Influence: A Theory of Poetry,*

Oxford: Oxford UP, 1973, 115–36; and Roland Barthes, "Askesis," *A Lover's Discourse: Fragments,* trans. Richard Howard, New York: Hill and Wang, 1978, 33.

34. See Freud, "From the History of an Infantile Neurosis" (1918 [1914]), *Standard Edition,* vol. 17, 19–28. For an adroit reading of the "Wolf Man" and Freud's discussion of masculine castration, see Silverman, "Too Early/Too Late: Subjectivity and the Primal Scene in Henry James," *Novel* 21.2–3, 1988, 147–73.

35. See Ralph R. Greenson, "Dis-identifying From the Mother—Its Special Importance for the Boy," *International Journal of Psychoanalysis* 49, 1968, 370–74; Prado de Oliveria, "La libération des hommes ou la création de la pathogénèse," *Cahiers confrontation,* Paris: Aubier-Montagne 6, 1981, 187–95; and Marie-Hélène Brousse, "L'homosexualité masculine dans les structures cliniques," *Traits de perversion,* ed. Fondation du champ freudien, Paris: Navarin, 1990, 162–71.

36. Gillon, "Betrayal and Redemption in Joseph Conrad," 18; Watts, *The Deceptive Text: An Introduction to Covert Plots,* 109.

37. See Roman Jakobson, "On the Linguistic Approach to the Problem of Consciousness and Unconsciousness," *The Framework of Meaning,* Ann Arbor: U of Michigan P, 1980, 113–30.

38. The "Wolf Man's" terror of horses as a displacement of their sexual counterpart perhaps is analogous to Heyst's horror of the woman's alleged equestrian qualities. See Freud, "From the History of an Infantile Neurosis," *Standard Edition,* vol. 17, 16.

39. See Freud, *Three Essays on the Theory of Sexuality* (1905), *Standard Edition,* vol. 7, 141–47.

40. Raval, "Conrad's *Victory:* Skepticism and Experience," 419; Leavis, *The Great Tradition: George Eliot, Henry James, Joseph Conrad,* 226; Jeffrey Meyers, *Homosexuality and Literature, 1890–1930,* London: Athlone, 1977, 79.

41. A notable exception to this criticism is Soo Young Chon, "Conrad's *Victory:* An Elusive Allegory," *English Language and Literature* 35.1, 1989, 83–101.

42. Conrad, "Falk," *Typhoon and Other Stories,* New York: Doubleday, Doran and Co., 1902, 155. Jones makes this intertext function by referring to the hotel in "Falk" as the source of his introduction to Schomberg.

43. Conrad, "Note to the First Edition of *Victory,*" 45.

44. Conrad, *Lord Jim* (1900), London: Dent, 1923, 198.

45. Consider Jones's remarks to Schomberg:

> "Tut, tut! You have a tolerable business. You are perfectly tame; you—"
> He paused, then added in a tone of disgust: "You have a wife."
> Schomberg tapped the floor angrily with his foot and uttered an indistinct, laughing curse.
> "What do you mean by flinging that damned trouble at my head?" he cried. "I wish you would carry her off with you somewhere to the devil! I wouldn't run after you."
> The unexpected outburst affected Mr. Jones strangely. He had a horrified recoil, chair and all, as if Schomberg had thrust a wriggling viper in his face. (147)

46. In a remarkable section of narrative that Conrad originally put at the end of chapter 5, the manuscript of *Victory* clarifies this homoerotic dynamic. Excised from *Victory*'s final version, this section contains an intimate conversation between Ricardo (occasionally named Ricard in the MS) and Jones (previously John Smith). One could speculate that Conrad was dissatisfied with this section because its suggestion of intimacy between Ricardo and Jones diminished some of the horror and mystery surrounding their relationship in the final version. Conrad's excision of its graphic racism is also consistent with *Victory*'s remainder and my reading of its racial accounts in the following section and in note 50 below. Volume 4 of the manuscript, held at the Harry Ransom Humanities Research Center, University of Texas at Austin, contains the following significant exchange:

> "You can do what you like with people," continued Ricardo with cautiously suppressed enthusiasm. "You have hypnotised him [Schomberg]."
>
> "Have I?," murmured John Smith absently.
>
> " 'Xactly as you have done them all along: Dago's, Portuguese's, Chinamen, niggers of every kind when it suited you. You are better than tha [*sic*] fellow we saw in that music-hall in Lima who used to stiffen people hard as iron on the stage. Not that you stiffen them—you make people soft all over when you like. You are a wonder."
>
> He paused. There had been a suggestion of obsequiosity in his deadened utterance. A cold murmur of "You think so" acknowledged it.
>
> "I know it. All I ask is that you should not try any of it on me. I couldn't stand it. As it is you make me sometimes feel queer all over without meaning it, I suppose; and perhaps I would draw on you if I thought you were really trying."
>
> "Would you really?," Mr. Smith asked with a low hollow chuckle, not at all mirthful, which Ricardo joined with a stiffened half-deferential, half-ferocious laugh.
>
> "No use," he said. "I couldn't pull the trigger on you. What would I do without you. I would be lost like a lost kid on this job." (4:300)

Three pages later, Jones and Ricardo return to Schomberg's obsession:

> "Sssh," hissed Smith.
>
> "He's been thinking you over, I bet," joined Ricard. (4:303)

47. Lacan, *The Four Fundamental Concepts of Psycho-Analysis,* 38.

48. Murial C. Bradbrook, "The Hollow Men," *Joseph Conrad: Poland's English Genius,* Cambridge: Cambridge UP, 1941, 41–67.

49. Arnold E. Davidson, *Conrad's Endings: A Study of the Five Major Novels,* Ann Arbor: UMI Research, 1984, 98–99.

50. This effacement often seems the result of the indigenous population's inability to undermine European hegemony, rather than the result of Conrad silencing race altogether. See Jones's remarks on 362: "What I was going to say is that Martin [Pedro] is much cleverer than a Chinaman [Wang]. Do you believe in racial superiority, Mr. Heyst? I do, firmly." And 198: "The couple lived at the edge of the forest, and she [Wang's unnamed partner] could sometimes be seen gazing towards the bungalow shading her eyes with her hand. Even from a distance she appeared to

be a shy, wild creature, and Heyst, anxious not to try her primitive nerves unduly, scrupulously avoided that side of the clearing in his strolls."

51. Tanner, "Joseph Conrad and the Last Gentleman," 116–18.

52. Ibid., 109. The word "gentleman" recurs 79 times in the novel; "gentlemen," 28 times. See James W. Parins, Robert J. Dilligan, and Todd K. Bender, *A Concordance to Conrad's Victory,* New York: Garland, 1979, for illustration of *Victory's* preoccupation with the meaning of "man" (293), "men" (81), "manly" (10), "manliness" (2), "masculine" (3), "masculinity" (2), and "mankind" (11). Figures in parentheses indicate the total number of times a word appears in the novel (ed. Heinemann, 1921). Also notable is the frequency of the words "no" (519), "never" (155), and "nothing" (160).

53. For an account of this proximity, see Marialuisa Bignami, "Joseph Conrad, the Malay Archipelago, and the Decadent Hero," *The Review of English Studies* 38.150, 1987, 199–210, and B. R. Burg, "Buccaneer Sexuality," *Sodomy and the Pirate Tradition: English Sea Rovers in the Seventeenth-Century Caribbean,* New York: New York UP, 1984, 107–38.

54. Julia Kristeva, *Powers of Horror: An Essay on Abjection,* trans. Leon S. Roudiez, New York: Columbia UP, 1982, 181.

55. Barthes, *The Pleasure of the Text,* trans. Richard Miller, New York: Hill and Wang, 1975, 47.

56. As illustration of the narrator who lies, forgets, or fails to connect one incident with another, consider Davidson's remarks about Heyst's and Morrison's specular interest in each other: "There was at once a great transformation act: Morrison raising his diminished head and sticking the glass in his eye to look affectionately at Heyst, a bottle being uncorked, and so on" (69), and earlier: "They were gazing earnestly into each other's eyes" (65).

57. "He was the same man who had plunged after the submerged Morrison . . . [b]ut this was another sort of plunge altogether, and likely to lead to a very different kind of partnership" (118). As ever, Davidson's pronouncement is unreliable here—consider also Lena's response, qtd. in note 11.

58. Jones is repeatedly aligned with the violence of retribution, decay, and death. See *Victory,* 145, 147–48, 172–73, and 239: "[Jones] was sitting up, silent, rigid, and very much like a corpse. His eyes were but two black patches, and his teeth glistened with a death's head grin between his retracted lips, no thicker than blackish parchment glued over the gums."

59. Lacan, "L'étourdit," *Scilicet* 4, 1973, 13: "*il n'y a pas de rapport sexuel.*"

60. Consider the anxiety that accompanies his final, impulsive intimacy with Lena (227)—one that Butler Haugaard considers the "release [of] his pent up shame and rage in a sexual aggression that is virtually a rape" ("Conrad's *Victory:* Another Look at Axel Heyst," 42).

61. Bradbrook, *Joseph Conrad: Poland's English Genius,* 41–67. According to Bradbrook, "Davy Jones" is sailors' slang for death; "Davy Jones's locker" also refers to the ocean floor.

62. See Kirschner, *Conrad: The Psychologist as Artist,* 161.

63. Jones wears a blue silk dressing gown on his death that is similar to the one Heyst Sr. is reported to have worn. For an account of these repetitions, see Butler Haugaard, "Conrad's *Victory:* Another Look at Axel Heyst," 44, and Park, "Conrad's *Victory:* The Anatomy of a Pose," 162.

64. Freud, "Instincts and Their Vicissitudes" (1915), *Standard Edition,* vol. 14, 122–23.

5. Maugham's *Of Human Bondage* and the Anatomy of Desire

1. W. Somerset Maugham, *Of Human Bondage* (1915), London: Mandarin, 1990, 330–32. Subsequent references give pagination in main text.

2. Arnold Schoenburg, *Moses and Aron,* vol. 2, London: Friends of Covent Garden, 1965, 35.

3. Maugham titled the unpublished 1897 manuscript *The Artistic Temperament of Stephen Carey* and then *Beauty for Ashes,* before he decided on *Of Human Bondage* as an adapted version of Spinoza's *Ethics,* "Of Human Bondage or the Strength of the Emotions."

4. See Maugham's foreword to *Of Human Bondage,* in which he describes the text as an "autobiographical novel." Maugham later avowed: "I suppose . . . the damned thing was more . . . autobiographical than I'd ever been willing to admit," qtd. in Forrest D. Burt, "William Somerset Maugham: An Adlerian Interpretation," *Journal of Individual Psychology* 26, 1970, 66. For an important reading of the relation between fiction and autobiography, see Paul de Man, "Autobiography as De-Facement," *MLN* 94, 1979, 919–30.

5. Philip French, "The Stammerer as Hero," *Encounter* 27, 1966, 71.

6. *The Concise Oxford Dictionary of English Etymology,* ed. T. F. Hoad, Oxford: Clarendon, 1986, 468. (*Stotage* derives from Middle English; *Stossen* from ancient Greek.) Thus *The Oxford English Dictionary* defines the verb *to stammer* as "to falter or stumble in one's speech"; to stutter is "to involuntarily repeat parts, especially initial consonants, of words in an effort to articulate" (J. A. Simpson and E. S. C. Weiner, *The Oxford English Dictionary,* vol. 16, 2d ed., Oxford: Clarendon, 1989, 479, 1005).

7. Jerome Hamilton Buckley, "Of Bondage and Freedom: Later Novels of Youth," *Season of Youth: The Bildungsroman from Dickens to Golding,* Cambridge, Mass.: Harvard UP, 1974, 249. See also Carl Van Doren, "Tom Jones and Philip Carey: Heroes of Two Centuries," *The Century Magazine* 110, 1925, 115–20.

8. This trope was significant for many other writers beside Maugham. In Forster's *The Longest Journey* (1907), Rickie Elliot is handicapped by his leg; by a commensurate Forsterian analogy, he also is emotionally and (homo)sexually crippled: Rickie "discover[s] that Mr. Elliot dubbed him Rickie because he was rickety, that he took pleasure in alluding to his son's deformity, and was sorry that it was not more serious than his own" (Harmondsworth: Penguin, 1989, 23). Forster's ally, G. Lowes Dickinson, also characterized his homosexuality as a "defect": "I am like a man born crippled; will and character may make more of such a life, through the very stimulus of the defect, than many normal men make of theirs" (qtd. in *The*

Autobiography of G. Lowes Dickinson and Other Unpublished Writings, ed. Dennis Proctor, London: Duckworth, 1973, 11). The trope of sexual "deviance" as psychic disfiguration extends perhaps to Aristophanes and the wandering feet of the once ambisexual body in Plato's *Symposium.* Plato's text had a strong significance for all the above readers, their contribution to the "Cambridge Apostles," and to Britain's neo-Hellenist movement at the end of the last century.

9. Unsigned review in *Nation and Athenæum* 1915, rpt. in *W. Somerset Maugham: The Critical Heritage,* ed. Anthony Curtis and John Whitehead, London, Boston: Routledge and Kegan Paul, 1987, 129.

10. It is also necessary to consider the importance the text gives to perceptions of sexual and physical normativity: "he saw that the normal was the rarest thing in the world. Everyone had some defect, of body or of mind" (696).

11. Review in *Philadelphia Press,* qtd. in *W. Somerset Maugham: The Critical Heritage,* 132.

12. Theodore Dreiser, "As a Realist Sees It," *New Republic,* December 25, 1915, 204.

13. Herman Melville, *Billy Budd, Sailor* (1891), *Billy Budd, Sailor and Other Stories,* Harmondsworth: Penguin, 1983, 331. See Eve Kosofsky Sedgwick, "Some Binarisms (I): *Billy Budd:* After the Homosexual," *Epistemology of the Closet,* Berkeley: U of California P, 1990, 92.

14. Maugham's belief in managing personal characteristics was strictly essentialist. This position conveniently displaced his attention from psychic resistance and egoic transformation: "We're the product of our genes and chromosomes. And there's nothing whatever we can do about it . . . no one can. Because we can't change the essential nature we're born with. . . . All we can do is to try and supplement our deficiencies" (qtd. in Robin Maugham, *Somerset and All the Maughams,* London: Longman, 1966, 42).

15. Freud, *The Psychopathology of Everyday Life* (1901), *Standard Edition,* vol. 6, 101.

16. Ibid., 80.

17. Ibid., 175.

18. Ibid., 184, 259.

19. See Susan Sontag, *Illness as Metaphor,* Harmondsworth: Penguin, 1983, 8, and the more contentious *AIDS and Its Metaphors,* London: Allen Lane, 1989. Sontag overlooks this fantasmatic significance in her concern to rule out all metaphoric significance to illness.

20. Ludwig Wittgenstein, *Tractatus Logico-Philosophicus,* London: Kegan Paul, Trench, Trubner, and Co., 1922, 189.

21. I am alluding to numerous contemporaneous links in literature between decadence, effeminacy, and the stammer—a trope that appears to detail an absence of mastery over language and sexual difference. See Bertie Wooster in P. G. Wodehouse, *The Clicking of Cuthbert,* London: Jenkins, 1922, and Anthony Blanche in Evelyn Waugh's *Brideshead Revisited: The Sacred and Profane Memories of Captain Charles Ryder—A Novel* (1945), London: Methuen, 1985.

22. See Brighton Ourstory Project, *Daring Hearts: Lesbian and Gay Lives of Brighton,* Brighton: QueenSpark Books, 1992.

23. This moment is particularly close to the scene of blackmail, also in the British Museum, between Maurice and Scudder in Forster's *Maurice* (1913–14), chapter 43.

24. See Sedgwick, "The Beast in the Closet: James and the Writing of Homosexual Panic," *Epistemology of the Closet,* 182–212, for an account of the sexual panic that derives from the erotic potential of same-sex friendships.

25. For an account and critique of the "repressive hypothesis," see Jeffrey Weeks, *Sexuality and Its Discontents: Meanings, Myths and Modern Sexualities,* London, Boston: Routledge, 1985, 91–108, 248–51.

26. The Victorian novelist A. C. Benson described how his idealized protagonist Arthur Hamilton "formed, in his last year at school, a very devoted friendship with a younger boy; such friendships like [*eispelas*] and the [*aitas*] of Sparta, when they are truly chivalrous and absolutely pure, are above all other loves, noble, refining, true; passion as white heat without taint, confidence of so intimate a kind as cannot even exist between husband and wife, trust such as cannot be shadowed, are its characteristics" (A. C. Benson, *Memoirs of Arthur Hamilton BA of Trinity College, Cambridge, Extracted from His Letters and Diaries by His Friend Christopher Carr of the Same College,* London: Kegan Paul, Trench, 1886, 23). For a discussion of Maugham's and Benson's context of neo-Hellenism and ephebophilia, see Tariq Rahman, "E. M. Forster and the Break Away from the Ephebophilic Tradition," *Études anglaises* 40.3, 1987, 267–78.

27. For different interpretations of jealousy and rivalry, see Ernest Jones, "La jalousie," *Revue française de psychanalyse* 3.2, 1929, 228–42; Daniel Lagache, "Contribution à l'étude des idées d'infidelité homosexuelle dans la jalousie," *Revue française de psychanalyse* 10.1, 1938, 709–19; René Girard, " 'Triangular' Desire," *Deceit, Desire, and the Novel: Self and Other in Literary Structure,* trans. Yvonne Freccero, Baltimore: Johns Hopkins UP, 1988, 1–52; Roland Barthes, "Jealousy," *A Lover's Discourse: Fragments,* trans. Richard Howard, New York: Hill and Wang, 1985, 144–47; and F. Gonzalez-Crussi, "On Male Jealousy," *On the Nature of Things Erotic,* New York: Harcourt Brace Jovanovich, 1988, 25–45.

28. Walter Allen described Mildred as "one of the most unpleasant women in fiction" (*The English Novel: A Short Critical History,* London: Phoenix House, 1954, 314). See also Joseph Dobrinsky, "The Dialectics of Art and Life in *Of Human Bondage,*" *Cahiers victoriens et édouardiens* 22, 1985, 42, 47, and Gerald Gould's review in *The New Statesman,* September 25, 1915, 594.

29. This erotic configuration recurs in Noël Coward, *Design for Living* (1933), a play that resolves a romantic triangle by two men's agreeing to live with one woman.

30. An extraordinary account of this masquerade is given below. For my purposes, the passage is notable because it details Philip's response to Mildred's first indication of desire for him:

> She put her face against his and rubbed his cheek with hers. To Philip her smile was an abominable leer, and the suggestive glitter of her eyes filled him with horror. He drew back instinctively.

"I won't," he said.

But she would not let him go. She sought his mouth with her lips. He took her hands and tore them roughly apart and pushed her away.

"You disgust me," he said. (551)

31. See also *Of Human Bondage,* 151, 153, 159, and 163.

32. Freud, "A Special Type of Choice of Object Made by Men (Contributions to the Psychology of Love I)" (1910), *Standard Edition,* vol. 11, 166.

33. Ibid.

34. For related inquiry, see Jane Gallop, "Why Does Freud Giggle When the Women Leave the Room?" *Thinking through the Body,* New York: Columbia UP, 1988, 33–37.

35. Freud, "A Special Type of Choice of Object Made by Men," *Standard Edition,* vol. 11, 166–67; original emphasis.

36. Ibid., 168.

37. Ibid., 170. See also *Of Human Bondage,* in which the narrator remarks: "There seemed to Philip to be in [Mildred] something of the Madonna" (402), a comment that part acknowledges the discrepancy between the existence of the quality in Mildred and her admirer's expectation—or projection—of that quality.

38. Freud, "A Special Type of Choice of Object Made by Men," *Standard Edition,* vol. 11, 167, 166.

39. Freud, *Three Essays on the Theory of Sexuality* (1905), *Standard Edition,* vol. 7, 145n.

40. Ibid., 146n.

41. Freud, "A Seventeenth-Century Demonological Neurosis" (1923 [1922]), *Standard Edition,* vol. 19, 67–105; "Dostoevsky and Parricide" (1928 [1927]), *Standard Edition,* vol. 21, 173–96; "Some Neurotic Mechanisms in Jealousy, Paranoia and Homosexuality" (1922), *Standard Edition,* vol. 18, 221–32.

42. Freud, *Three Essays on the Theory of Sexuality, Standard Edition,* vol. 7, 147n. See also Sándor Ferenczi, "On the Part Played by Homosexuality in the Pathogenesis of Paranoia," *Sex in Psycho-Analysis: Contributions to Psycho-Analysis,* Boston: Gorham, 1916, 154–84.

43. See Freud, "Some Neurotic Mechanisms in Jealousy, Paranoia and Homosexuality," *Standard Edition,* vol. 18, 231–32.

44. I have interpreted this narrative and theoretical presumption in "Is There a Homosexual in This Text?: Identity, Opacity, and the Elaboration of Desire," *GLQ,* forthcoming.

45. Freud, letter 113 to Fliess, August 1, 1899, rpt. in *The Ego and the Id* (1923), *Standard Edition,* vol. 19, 33 n.1.

46. Freud, *Three Essays on the Theory of Sexuality, Standard Edition,* vol. 7, 146n.

47. As Mikkel Borch-Jacobsen has observed, emulation between men maintains a warring, competitive, and fundamentally sexual rivalry. See *The Freudian Subject,* trans. Catherine Porter, Stanford: Stanford UP, 1988, 80–94.

48. Stanley Archer has argued that the text's principal theme is "the necessity for each man to free himself from the bondage of passion" — and thus, one could infer, from the influence of women ("Artists and Paintings in Maugham's *Of Human Bondage*," *English Literature in Transition* 14, 1971, 182).

49. Gallop, *Reading Lacan,* Ithaca: Cornell UP, 1985, 146. Gallop is paraphrasing and reorienting Lacan's question, "why must [men (*Mensch,* the human being)] take on the attributes [of his or her sex] only by means of a threat or even under the aspect of a deprivation?" (Lacan, "The Signification of the Phallus," *Écrits: A Selection,* New York: Norton, 1977, 281). Gallop elaborates: "As the context makes clear, Lacan is here talking about 'the castration complex in the masculine unconscious [and] *penisneid* [penis envy] in the woman's unconscious' " (*Écrits: A Selection,* 281, qtd. in *Reading Lacan,* 146).

50. Although oblique in the text, this meaning is redolent for the intensity of interest it refuses to express. Carey's identification with Miguel, like Maugham's with El Greco, suggests the conflation of Maugham (who did visit Toledo) and Carey (who only imagined doing so). Besides Miguel, El Greco is an erotic trope for Carey in proportion to his "secret's" mystification. Thus Maugham wrote in a 1917 entry to *A Writer's Notebook* (1949), London: Pan, 1978, in a comparison between El Greco and Dostoevsky: "Both had the same faculty for making the unseen visible; both had the same violence of emotion, the same passion. Both give the effect of having walked in unknown ways of the spirit. Both are tortured by the desire to express some tremendous secret, which they divine with some sense other than our five senses and which they struggle in vain to convey by use of them" (154). Later, in a 1929 entry in *A Writer's Notebook,* Maugham reassessed his fascination with El Greco: "I know vaguely what the men are in those cities of mystics [in his painting of Toledo], the manner of them and the peace they offer to the tortured heart; but what kind of men they are in this city of mine and why it is that all those others on the road so passionately seek it, I do not know. I only know that it imports me urgently to go there, and that when at last I slip through its gates, happiness awaits me" (220). Happiness, that is, in the shape of an awaiting man? In an almost singular reference to homosexuality — significant because someone else overheard and published it — Beverley Nichols recounts a conversation in which Maugham avowed: "I think that El Greco was probably a homosexual" (qtd. in Nichols, *A Case of Human Bondage,* London: Secker, 1966, 144). Notwithstanding its caution, the remark is one of the few occasions on which Maugham enunciated a desire with which perhaps to compare his own.

51. See Robert Aldrich, *The Seduction of the Mediterranean: Writing, Art and Homosexual Fantasy,* New York: Routledge, 1993. Aldrich's study concerns primarily Italy and Greece, but of Spain he writes: "Other destinations were less popular than Italy, or attracted only the more adventurous. Spain and Portugal lay off the beaten track and the Iberian countries were considered to have a stagnant culture, backward government, primitive economic conditions and few classical ruins or Renaissance art collections" (165).

52. In "The 'Uncanny' " (1919), Freud argued that the *unheimlich* relates to questions of the aesthetic, repetition, the unfamiliar, psychic dread, and death (*Standard Edition,* vol. 17, 220). Except for the last factor, Mildred seems to occupy this

unheimlich position by the end of Maugham's novel. (See note 30 above.) In the original film version of *Of Human Bondage* (Cromwell, 1934), Mildred, played by Bette Davis, does die.

53. This thematic recurs throughout Maugham's fiction, especially the ironically titled one-act play, *Marriages Are Made in Heaven* (1903). See Maugham, *A Traveller in Romance: Uncollected Writings 1901-1964,* ed. John Whitehead, London: Anthony Blond, 1984, 2–12.

54. Maugham, *The Explorer: A Melodrama in Four Acts,* London: Heineman, 1912, 138, 139.

55. Maugham, 1917 entry in *A Writer's Notebook,* 165–66.

56. Maugham, *The Moon and Sixpence* (1919), London: Mandarin, 1990, 140–41. Katherine Mansfield's retort made Strickland's repudiation gender-specific: "his contempt for women is fathomless" ("Inarticulations," *Nation and Athenæum,* May 9, 1919, 302).

57. Regarding this, see Bonnie Hoover Braendlin, "The Prostitute as Scapegoat: Mildred Rogers in Somerset Maugham's *Of Human Bondage," The Image of the Prostitute in Modern Literature,* ed. Pierre L. Horn and Mary Beth Pringle, New York: Frederick Ungar, 1984, 9–18. She argues that Mildred "incurs the blame for impeding Philip's progress" (12), a condition that allows him to "castigate her as culpable [for his failure]" (9) because she "personifies the very weakness of character that Philip himself displays" (13). In "Molly's 'Yes': The Transvaluation of Sex in Modern Fiction" (*Texas Studies in Literature and Language* 10, 1968–69), Wendell V. Harris also argues that *Of Human Bondage*'s misogyny closes with the demand that Mildred rescue the fallen man and so redeem Carey from the agony of meaninglessness (111). On this, consider my reading, in chapter 4, of the emotional and homo/sexual redemption Lena provides Heyst in Conrad's *Victory.*

58. Nina Baym, "Melodramas of Beset Manhood: How Theories of American Fiction Exclude Women Authors," *American Quarterly* 33.2, 1981, 133. Baym continues: "for a homosexual male, the demands of society that he link himself for life to a woman make for a particularly misogynist version of this aspect of the American myth, for the hero is propelled not by a rejected attraction but by true revulsion" (134). This point seems entirely in keeping with my reading of Maugham, though it warrants references and a certain caution, if only for the problematic inference that male homosexuality—rather than heterosexism—is the most rarefied form of misogyny, and that homosexual men are not simply the most egregious, but also the most emblematic, misogynists.

59. For illustration of this point, see Maugham, "A Traveller in Romance" (1909), *A Traveller in Romance: Uncollected Writings 1901-1964,* 156–59.

60. Buckley, *Season of Youth: The Bildungsroman from Dickens to Golding,* 253.

61. Dreiser, "As a Realist Sees It," *New Republic,* 203.

62. Allen, *The English Novel: A Short Critical History,* 314.

63. Maugham, *The Summing Up* (1938), New York: New American Library, 1964, 121; my emphasis.

64. Ibid., 88–89. While the exact relation between this "fantastic affair of being a

man" and marriage is cause for conjecture, it is clear that for Maugham, the second was a precondition to the first's success. Maugham did marry, therefore, and maintained—at least initially—some semblance of happiness and fidelity to Syrie Maugham, in addition to several passionate, and apparently sexual, affairs with men. It seems that his wife was able to tolerate these affairs, but not Maugham's later disregard of and increasing hostility toward her. (For an account of their increasing acrimony, which outlasted Maugham in a controversy of inheritance, see Nichols, *A Case of Human Bondage*.) Forrest D. Burt also cites a letter from Maugham to Syrie that provides some idea of their relationship's basis: "[Y]ou should be very well satisfied if you get from your husband courtesy and consideration, kindness and affection; but really you cannot expect passionate love" (Burt, "William Somerset Maugham: An Adlerian Interpretation," 79). Of course, my recourse to biography is not sufficient as an interpretation of the novel; instead it offers an indication of the difficulty of pursuing one "pattern of life" in marriage against the propensity to explore and inhabit another. I suggest that this disparity registers in *Of Human Bondage* as a qualitative insufficiency for happiness in marriage and a palpable resentment toward women for being, somehow, the cause of an ensuing masculine abjection.

65. Maugham, qtd. in Robin Maugham, *Somerset Maugham and All the Maughams*, 201.

66. Burt, "William Somerset Maugham: An Adlerian Interpretation," 66.

6. Managing the "White Man's Burden":
The Racial Imaginary of Forster's Colonial Narratives

1. E. M. Forster, *Howards End* (1910), Harmondsworth: Penguin, 1954, 224. Subsequent references give pagination in main text.

2. Forster, "Kanaya" (c. 1922), *Hill of Devi and Other Indian Writings,* ed. Elizabeth Heine, London: Edward Arnold, 1983, 312.

3. Forster, *A Passage to India* (1924), Harmondsworth: Penguin, 1984, 264–65. Subsequent references give pagination in main text.

4. Ashis Nandy, *The Intimate Enemy: Loss and Recovery of Self Under Colonialism,* Oxford: Oxford UP, 1983, 9–10. For other theorizations of this phenomenon, see Octave Mannoni, *Prospero and Caliban: The Psychology of Colonization,* trans. Pamela Powesland, New York: Praeger, 1956; Frantz Fanon, *Black Skin, White Masks,* trans. Charles Lam Markmann, New York: Grove, 1967; and A. P. A. Busia, "Miscegenation as Metonymy: Sexuality and Power in the Colonial Novel," *Ethnic and Racial Studies* 9, 1986, 360–72.

5. Donald Salter, "That Is My Ticket: The Homosexual Writings of E. M. Forster," *London Magazine* 14.6, 1975, 5–53. Wilfred Stone also pathologizes Forster's fiction by considering it a vehicle for recording "despair and . . . utter[ing] via fictional indirection his cry for help" ("Overleaping Class: Forster's Problem in Connection," *Modern Language Quarterly* 39, 1978, 389).

6. Eudora Welty, "The Life to Come," *New York Times Book Review,* May 13, 1973, 30: "Here, Forster is writing about all human desire." In "Forster's Love Story," *Observer,* October 10, 1971, Philip Toynbee argues: "Certainly I can detect nothing particularly homosexual about *Maurice* except that it happens to be about homo-

sexuals[!] . . . [A]ll the high sentiments—both of love and of passion—could as easily have been inspired by the most heterosexual of romances" (32).

7. See John Sayre Martin, *E. M. Forster: The Endless Journey,* Cambridge: Cambridge UP, 1976, 10, and Samuel Hynes, "A Chalice for Youth," *Times Literary Supplement* 3, 632, October 8, 1971, 1215. Hynes considers the obstacle of heterosexuality the source of all Forster's textual incoherence: "One must conclude that Forster was incapable of recording deep currents of feeling—sexual feeling most obviously, but other deep feeling as well [. . . .] *Ordinary emotional states were beyond Forster . . .*" (1216; my emphasis).

8. See Jeffrey Meyers, *Homosexuality and Literature 1890–1930,* London: Athlone, 1977, 93, 95, 107, and 113. For equivalent readings, see David Shusterman, *The Quest for Certitude in E. M. Forster's Fiction,* New York: Haskell House, 1973, 37–38, and Judith Scherer Herz, who argues that these representations of homosexuality "play out a psychomachia," as if they are palpable efforts at authorial self-analysis (*The Short Narratives of E. M. Forster,* New York: St. Martin's, 1988, 39).

9. Forster, qtd. in Noël Annan, "Love Story," *New York Review of Books* 17.6, October 21, 1971, 18.

10. Forster, *Maurice: A Romance* (1913–14), Harmondsworth: Penguin, 1987, 198.

11. See Annan, "Love Story," 12; Samuel Hynes, "A Chalice for Youth," 1215; George Steiner, "Under the Greenwood Tree," *The New Yorker* 47, October 9, 1971, 164; Norman Page, *E. M. Forster's Posthumous Fiction,* Victoria, B.C.: U of Victoria P, 1977, 12.

12. Forster, diary entry, June 16, 1911, unpublished manuscript held at King's College, Cambridge.

13. See Forster, *Arctic Summer and Other Fiction,* London: Edward Arnold, 1980.

14. Forster publicly defended James Hanley's *Boy* (1929); James Joyce's *Ulysses* (1922); D. H. Lawrence's *The Rainbow* (1915) and, famously, *Lady Chatterley's Lover* (1928). For further details, see Page, *E. M. Forster's Posthumous Fiction,* 7–20.

15. Forster, "The New Censorship," *Nation and Athenæum* 43, 1928, 696.

16. Forster, "The 'Censorship' of Books," *The Nineteenth Century and After* 105, 1929, 445.

17. Page, *E. M. Forster's Posthumous Fiction,* 13.

18. This argument reproduced the prevailing theory about prostitution only a decade earlier. See Judith Walkowitz, *Prostitution and Victorian Society: Women, Class, and the State,* Cambridge: Cambridge UP, 1980.

19. "Minutes of Evidence," *Report of the Select Committee on Obscene Publications,* London: HMSO, 1958, 15–18.

20. See Hynes, "A Chalice for Youth," 1216.

21. See Steiner, "Under the Greenwood Tree," 164; Annan, "Love Story," 18; Meyers, *Homosexuality and Literature,* 101–2.

22. See John Addington Symonds, *Sexual Inversion* (1897), New York: Bell, 1984; Edward Carpenter, *The Intermediate Sex: A Study of Some Transitional Types of Men*

and Women, London: Allen and Unwin, 1908; and Carpenter, "Homogenic Love and Its Place in a Free Society" (1895), London: Redundancy, n. d.

23. Forster excised much of the text's sexual material and metaphor. For details and analysis, see June Perry Levine, "The Tame in Pursuit of the Savage: The Posthumous Fiction of E. M. Forster," *PMLA* 99.1, 1984, 76–77.

24. D. H. Lawrence, letter to Barbara Low and Bertrand Russell, February 12, 1915, *The Letters of D. H. Lawrence,* vol. 2, ed. George J. Zytaruk and James T. Boulton, Cambridge: Cambridge UP, 1981, 283; my emphasis.

25. Steiner, "Under the Greenwood Tree," 166.

26. See Forster, "Kanaya," *Hill of Devi and Other Indian Writings;* J. R. Ackerley, *Hindoo Holiday: An Indian Journal* (1932), Harmondsworth: Penguin Travel, 1988; André Gide, *Travels in the Congo* (1927–28), trans. Dorothy Bussy, Harmondsworth: Penguin Travel, 1986; and Jean Genet, *Prisoner of Love* (1986), trans. Barbara Bray, London: Picador, 1989. For interpretation of this phenomenon, see Jonathan Dollimore, "Different Desires: Subjectivity and Transgression in Wilde and Gide," *Textual Practice* 1.1, 1987, 48–67.

27. Examples of pastoral fantasies include "Story of a Panic," "The Other Side of the Hedge," "Other Kingdom," and "Ansell." Notable dystopic fantasies are "The Celestial Omnibus," "The Machine Stops," "The Point of It," and "The Torque."

28. Forster, *The Longest Journey* (1907), Harmondsworth: Penguin, 1989, 64.

29. Paul Scott, *The Jewel in the Crown* (1966), New York: Avon, 1979, 261.

30. Forster, letter to Edward Garnett, November 12, 1910, *Selected Letters of E. M. Forster,* vol. 1: *1879–1920,* ed. Mary Lago and P. N. Furbank, London: Collins, 1983, 117.

31. Forster, diary entry, April 8, 1922, unpublished manuscript held at King's College, Cambridge.

32. Publishers have reprinted *The Celestial Omnibus* (1911) and *The Eternal Moment* (1928) under the erroneous title, *Collected Short Stories* (1947), Harmondsworth: Penguin, 1954. Subsequent references give pagination in main text.

33. The exception here was "The Other Boat," which previously appeared in fragment form as "Entrance to an Unwritten Novel," *The Listener,* December 23, 1948, and as "Cocoanut and Co.: Exit from an Abandoned Novel," *New York Times,* February 6, 1949.

34. Herz, *The Short Narratives of E. M. Forster,* 24.

35. Meyers, *Homosexuality and Literature,* 108.

36. Salter, "That Is My Ticket," 22.

37. Ibid., 7. My earlier point about Salter's presumption of readership is, I think, confirmed by his arrogant use of the personal pronoun "one," as if the reader shared the heterosexuality and thus the apparently axiomatic "unease" of the critic concerned. The "problem" seems to be rather that Forster did not disguise, but openly affirmed, homosexual fantasy in the *Life to Come* collection; Salter describes his "sadness" that such fantasies were "necessary sexual anodynes to a man of Forster's wisdom" ("That Is My Ticket," 22), as if wisdom requires a corollary uninterest in

sex and a calculated sublimation when that interest is homosexual. Those who are "wise," it seems, turn their interest elsewhere or have the decency to write about it with careful circumlocution.

Salter's comments are relevant to this discussion because they represent a conservative criticism that considers the avowal of homosexuality as an immediate loss of aesthetic appeal. Thus—clarifying a point I raised in this book's introduction and notes—Meyers complains about the "puerile" substance of Forster's fantasy, and the vulgarity of explicit homosexuality in contemporary writing, as if its partial decriminalization in Britain were the reason for an axiomatic decline in homosexuals' literary achievement: "When the laws of obscenity were changed and homosexuality became legal, apologies seemed inappropriate [!], the theme surfaced defiantly and sexual acts were grossly described. The emancipation of the homosexual has led, paradoxically, to the decline of his [sic] art" (Homosexuality and Literature, 3). As Forster ironically made clear in an earlier citation on homosexuality and censorship, however, the word "explicit," when used with a referent such as "homosexuality," is always in danger of assuming a "pornographic" significance. This suggests that homosexuality is "interesting" for these critics only on condition that writers not represent it but render it oblique and allusive, while the liberation of homosexuals is also detrimental to the quality of literature they produce. Wilde's imprisonment and premature death, we may infer, is a small price to pay for the poignant beauty of De Profundis . . .

38. Virginia Woolf, The Death of the Moth and Other Essays, New York: Harcourt, Brace and World, 1938, 70–77.

39. Forster's closest readers often asked him the purpose of many of his stories. Strachey's comment on "The Point of It" was "What is the point of it?" (qtd. in Page, E. M. Forster's Posthumous Fiction, 32). Herz has usefully interpreted this demand for narrative order as an "emptying" of sexual meaning in the short stories (The Short Narratives of E. M. Forster, 19). See also John Fletcher, "Forster's Self-erasure: Maurice and the Scene of Masculine Love," Sexual Sameness: Textual Differences in Lesbian and Gay Writing, ed. Joseph Bristow, New York: Routledge, 1992, 90.

40. Woolf, Collected Essays, vol. 1, ed. Leonard Woolf, London: Chatto and Windus, 1967, 344.

41. David Shusterman, The Quest for Certitude in E. M. Forster's Fiction, 36–59—a "quest" at which he assumes Forster to arrive. My title for this text would have been Forster's Repression of Incertitude.

42. Forster, "Fantasy," Aspects of the Novel (1927), Harmondsworth: Penguin, 1990, 101–15. Subsequent references give pagination in main text.

43. Sara Suleri gives this passage—and its wider resonance—an interesting reading in The Rhetoric of English India, Chicago: U of Chicago P, 1992, 132–48.

44. Turn-of-the-century literature frequently represented Pan as a figure of sexual disturbance and unaccountable force. As half-man and half-goat, Pan appeared to symbolize masculine drives that stay in check only by tenuous self-control. Thus Samuel Hynes claims that "Forster's Pan is the deity of a homosexual world, or a world in which homosexuality is natural. He is necessary to the stories and novels

simply because, in Forster's Sawston-and-Cambridge world, homosexual love could not be a force in itself; it was only by supernatural intervention that direct emotion could find expression" ("A Chalice for Youth," 1215). See also Patricia Merivale, *Pan the Goat-God: His Myth in Modern Times,* Cambridge, Mass.: Harvard UP, 1969.

45. In the terminal note to *Maurice,* Forster wrote: "A happy ending is imperative. I shouldn't have bothered to write otherwise. I was determined that in fiction anyway two men should fall in love and remain in it for the ever and ever that fiction allows . . ." (218).

46. By "twofold" I mean to distinguish between empirical and fantasmatic colonization. For an interpretation of both forms of "emasculation," see Chris Dunton, "Wheyting Be Dat?: The Treatment of Homosexuality in African Literature," *Research in African Literatures* 20.3, 1989, 422–48, and Moodie T. Dunbar, "Migrancy and Male Sexuality on the South African Gold Mines," *Journal of Southern African Studies* 14, 1988, 228–56.

47. See John Rex, "Racism and the Structure of Colonial Societies," *Racism and Colonialism: Essays on Ideology and Social Structure,* ed. Robert Ross, The Hague: Martinus Nijhoff, 1982, 200–1; P. D. Curtin, *The Image of Africa: British Ideas and Action, 1780–1850,* Madison: U of Wisconsin P, 1964; and P. Fryer, *Black People in the British Empire: An Introduction,* London: Pluto, 1988.

48. Jeffrey Weeks, " 'Sins and Diseases': Some Notes on Homosexuality in the Nineteenth Century," *History Workshop* 1, 1976, 211–19; Frank Mort, *Dangerous Sexualities: Medico-Moral Politics in England since 1830,* New York: Routledge, 1987.

49. Ronald Hyam, *Empire and Sexuality: The British Experience,* Manchester: Manchester UP, 1990, 157–81, and E. Joseph Bristow, *Vice and Vigilance: Purity Movements in Britain since 1700,* Dublin: Gill and Macmillan, 1977.

50. See Sheila Jeffreys, *The Spinster and Her Enemies: Feminism and Sexuality 1880–1930,* London, Boston: Pandora, 1985, and L. Coveney et al., eds., *The Sexuality Papers: Male Sexuality and the Social Control of Women,* London: Hutchinson, 1984.

51. Hyam, "Concubinage and the Colonial Service: The Crewe Connection (1909)," *Journal of Imperial and Commonwealth History* 14, 1986, 170–86.

52. Ibid., 171.

53. *Times,* Letters, January 9, 1909, 16. To enforce this idea of sexual purity, colonizers often projected their desire onto the colonized—a point that Fanon and Joel Kovel repeatedly emphasize. See especially Kovel, "The Fantasies of Race," *White Racism: A Psychohistory,* New York: Columbia UP, 1984, 51–92. In Forster's *A Passage to India,* McBryde's accusation of Aziz clearly upheld a powerful Anglo-Indian consensus at the turn of the century: "Mr. McBryde paused. He wanted to keep the proceedings as clean as possible, but Oriental Pathology, his favourite theme, lay all around him, and he could not resist it. Taking off his spectacles, as was his habit before enunciating a general truth, he looked into them sadly, and remarked that the darker races are physically attracted by the fairer, but not vice versa—not a matter for bitterness this, nor a matter for abuse, but just a fact which any scientific

observer will confirm" (*Passage,* 222). Gide also refers to the "savage ecstasy" of villagers in the Congo as one reason the French continually distrusted them (*Travels in the Congo,* 249).

54. *Times,* Letters, January 8, 1909, 15.

55. "A Canker in Imperial Administration," *The Spectator,* editorial, December 12, 1908, 980–81. This editorial is so emblematic of colonial opinion that it is worth quoting at length: "We fully recognise that in an Empire as great as ours there must often be cases in which men living under the very trying conditions that result from isolation, from the absence of a healthy public opinion, and from the special temptations which surround the possessors of unlimited power over a naturally slavish population, yield to those temptations. As a rule, however, these are exceptional, and are best dealt with by the authorities on the spot. They are in no sense symptomatic, and it would be the greatest mistake to exaggerate their significance" (980). The editorial later suggests that "The man who uses the forces of the Empire in order to gratify his lust one day may use them for the purposes of illicit gain the next, or, if he does not do so himself, may set an example in misdoing" (980), and so concludes: "A canker is at work there [in East Africa] which, if not eradicated by drastic treatment, may do incalculable harm. . . . It is to be feared . . . that the accepted standard of administration is far lower [there] than that of the Empire as a whole, and has, indeed, reached a point of peril" (980) . . . [We must therefore] remov[e] a canker from the body politic before it is too late" (981).

56. Richard Meinertzhagen, *Kenya Diary (1902–1906),* (1957), New York: Hippocrene, 1983, 11.

57. Ibid., 22.

58. Ibid., 96.

59. Ibid., 218; my emphasis.

60. Hyam, "Concubinage and the Colonial Service," 182.

61. Ibid., 183.

62. Ibid., 184.

63. Ibid., 181.

64. See J. P. Thoopen, *Black Martyrs,* London: Sheed and Ward, 1941; C. C. Wrigley, "Christian Revolution in Buganda," *Comparative Studies in Society and History* 2, 1959–60, 33–48; and J. A. Rowe, "The Purge of Christians at Mwanga's Court," *Journal of African History* 5, 1964, 55–71.

65. Hyam, *Empire and Sexuality,* 67–68.

66. For accounts of the wide popularity of homosexuality among Catholic priests and laity during this period, see David Hilliard, "UnEnglish and Unmanly: Anglo-Catholicism and Homosexuality," *Victorian Studies* 25.2, 1982, 181–210; and Noël Annan, "The Cult of Homosexuality in England, 1850–1950," *Biography* 13.3, 1990, 189–202.

67. Forster, *The Life to Come and Other Stories* (1972), Harmondsworth: Penguin, 1989, 101. Subsequent references give pagination in main text.

68. See Derrick Sherwin Bailey, *Homosexuality and the Western Christian Tradition,*

Hamden, Conn.: Archon, 1975, and John Boswell, *Christianity, Social Tolerance, and Homosexuality,* Chicago: U of Chicago P, 1980, for classic rereadings of the biblical story of Sodom and Gomorrah.

69. I examine Forster's problematic association between the unconscious and the indigenous more closely in the following section.

70. Perry Levine, "The Tame in Pursuit of the Savage," 72–88.

71. Ibid., 72–88.

72. Stephen Adams, *The Homosexual as Hero in Contemporary Fiction,* London: Vision, 1980, 106–30.

73. Forster, *Maurice,* 192–99.

74. Lytton Strachey, letter to Forster, March 12, 1915, *Forster: The Critical Heritage,* ed. Philip Gardner, London, Boston: Routledge and Kegan Paul, 1973, 430–31.

75. For theorization of the supplement, see Jacques Derrida, "The Double Session," *Dissemination,* trans. Barbara Johnson, Chicago: U of Chicago P, 1981, 173–287.

76. Scott usefully observed of the interracial friendship between his protagonists, Edwina Crane and Mr. Chaudhuri: "there had been between [them] right from the beginning what Miss Crane thought of as an almost classical reserve—classical in the sense that she felt they each suspected the other of hypocrisy, of unrevealed motives, *of hiding under the thinnest of liberal skins deeply conservative natures . . ."* (*The Jewel in the Crown,* 42; my emphasis).

77. Forster, "What I Believe," *Two Cheers for Democracy,* London: Edward Arnold, 1951, 68; my emphasis.

78. Homi Bhabha, "Of Mimicry and Man: The Ambivalence of Colonial Discourse," *October* 28, 1984, 125–33, and Pascal Bruckner, "The Ambivalence of Exotic Taste," *The Tears of the White Man: Compassion as Contempt,* trans. William R. Beer, New York: Free, 1986, 167–69.

79. Forster, "The Menace to Freedom" (1935), "Jew-Consciousness" (1939), "Racial Exercise" (1939), "Tolerance" (1941), and "A Letter to Madan Blanchard" (1931), *Two Cheers for Democracy,* 9–14, 17–20, 43–46, 305–14.

80. D. H. Lawrence, *Aaron's Rod* (1922), Harmondsworth: Penguin, 1976, 34; my emphasis.

81. Lacan, *The Four Fundamental Concepts of Psycho-Analysis,* ed. Jacques-Alain Miller, trans. Alan Sheridan, New York: Norton, 1978, 214, 38.

82. Freud offered a similar representation in "The Dissection of the Psychical Personality" (1933), *Standard Edition,* vol. 22: "We approach the id with analogies: we call it chaos, a cauldron full of seething excitations" (73), an analogy Lacan later clarified as a structural relation: "[T]he Freudian unconscious is situated at that point, where, between cause and that which it affects, there is always something wrong. . . . For what the unconscious does is to show us the gap through which neurosis re-creates a harmony with a real—a real that may well not be determined" (*The Four Fundamental Concepts of Psycho-Analysis,* 22). I interpret Freud's and Lacan's accounts of the unconscious in "Philosophy of the Unconscious: Vacillating on the Scene of Writing in Freud's *Project,*" *Prose Studies* 17.2, 1995, 98–129.

83. Herz, *The Short Narratives of E. M. Forster,* 46.

84. Perry Levine, "The Tame in Pursuit of the Savage," 87.

85. Forster, "What I Believe," *Two Cheers for Democracy,* 66.

86. Scott, *The Jewel in the Crown,* 267.

87. Forster, letter to Siegfried Sassoon, October 11, 1920, *Selected Letters of E. M. Forster,* vol. 1, 316.

88. Forster, "The Other Boat" (1915–16), *The Life to Come and Other Stories,* 202–34. Subsequent references give pagination in main text. See note 33 above for details of this novella's publication history.

89. Perry Levine, "The Tame in Pursuit of the Savage," 84. Perry Levine concludes that "Lionel's revulsion is not homophobic but against the bigotry of his class. When he finally does throw himself into the sea, it is not because he is disgusted with what has happened between Cocoa and himself but because 'if he forfeited [his caste's] companionship he would become nobody and nothing' " (86). This explains only his suicide, not his prior recoil from Cocoa. Perry Levine ignores both homo- and negrophobia in this story by acknowledging only Lionel's *conscious* "pursuit" of the other. Rather than suggest that "The story makes the violence he commits inevitable" (86), I would argue that it nonetheless makes that violence justifiable *within its own terms* as a necessary removal of the racial burden that the failure of its *psychic* management precipitates.

90. Page, *E. M. Forster's Posthumous Fiction,* 57. Meyers claims that also "these men overcome racial, social and sexual prejudices, and achieve temporary liberation by sodomizing . . . before lapsing back into their 'apparatus of decay' or plunging to a violent death" (*Homosexuality and Literature* 108). This statement assumes that their sexuality can be detached from both the prejudice that surrounds them and their internal drive toward death. My reading argues that sexuality inheres in the prejudice and death drive of both narrative and character.

91. Stuart Hampshire, "*The Cave and the Mountain: A Study of E. M. Forster* by W. Stone," *The New York Review of Books,* VI.8 May 12, 1966, 14–16.

92. J. R. Ackerley, *My Father and Myself* (1968), qtd. in Salter, "That Is My Ticket," 31.

93. For detailed examination of this point, see Sander Gilman and J. Edward Chamberlain, eds., *Degeneration: The Dark Side of Progress,* New York: Columbia UP, 1985; Kovel, *White Racism: A Psychohistory,* 51–92; and Daniel Pick, *Faces of Degeneration: A European Disorder, c. 1848–1918,* Cambridge: Cambridge UP, 1989.

94. For elaboration on this point, see Henry Louis Gates Jr., "The Blackness of Blackness: A Critique of the Sign and the Signifying Monkey," *Figures in Black: Words, Signs, and the "Racial" Self,* New York: Oxford UP, 1987, 235–76. Freud made an instructive—and unfortunate—link between racial and psychic topography when he wrote of the outcomes of instinctual impulses: "Their origin is what decides their fate. We may compare them with individuals of mixed race who, taken all round, resemble white men, but who betray their coloured descent by some striking feature or other, and on that account are excluded from society and enjoy none of the privileges of white people" ("The Unconscious" [1915], *Standard Edition,* vol. 14, 191).

95. Forster, *Hill of Devi and Other Indian Writings,* 323. See also T. Hammond, *"Paidikion:* A Pederastic Manuscript," *International Journal of Greek Love* 1, 1966, 28–37, and Forster, "Reflections in India I: Too Late?" *Nation and Athenæum* 30.17, 1922, 614b.

96. Forster, *Hill of Devi and Other Indian Writings,* 324.

97. Ibid., 321; my emphasis. See Gide, *Travels in the Congo,* for a similar account of the European's "degraded" status when the colonized discovers his homosexuality.

98. The mother's influence is important to consider because Lionel consciously associates his choice of an Indian lover with his father's abandonment of his mother for a Burmese woman, an act Lionel remembers with pain. The narrator mentions Lionel's mother several times as a figure of influence—particularly in her hatred of Cocoanut as an "unmanly" child (*Life,* 217). What is credible—and perhaps "Freudian"—in this story is the *mother's* projection of hatred for her husband's mistress onto Cocoanut as a child because of their ostensible racial equivalence.

7. Re/Orientations: Firbank's "Anglophobia" and the Sexual Nomad

1. Ronald Firbank, *The Flower Beneath the Foot* (1923), *The Complete Firbank,* London: Duckworth, 1961, 535. Subsequent references (excepting note 14) give pagination in main text.

2. William Blake, "The Little Black Boy," *Songs of Innocence, The Poems of William Blake,* ed. John Sampson, London: Chatto and Windus, 1921, 80–81. The combination of racial and oedipal determinants in the last stanza of Blake's poem recurs throughout Firbank's writing. In fact, Mrs. Yajñavalkya cites the poem's first two lines in *Valmouth* (scc *The Complete Firbank,* 415).

3. E. M. Forster, "Ronald Firbank" (1929) *Abinger Harvest* (1936), Harmondsworth: Penguin, 1967, 129.

4. Ibid., 129–30.

5. See Sarah Barnhill, "Method in Madness: Ronald Firbank's *The Flower Beneath the Foot,*" *English Literature in Transition* 32.3, 1989, 291, and Edward Martin Potoker, *Ronald Firbank,* New York: Columbia UP, 1969, 46.

6. Alan Hollinghurst, "The Creative Uses of Homosexuality in the Novels of E. M. Forster, Ronald Firbank, and L. P. Hartley," unpublished M.Litt thesis, Oxford: Bodleian Library, 1980, 112.

7. Forster, "Ronald Firbank," 129.

8. Norman W. Alford, "Seven Notebooks of Ronald Firbank," *Library Chronicle of the University of Texas, Austin* 8.3, 1967, 33.

9. Susan Sontag, "Notes on Camp," *Against Interpretation and Other Essays,* London: André Deutsch, 1964, 275: "To talk about camp is therefore to betray it." For analyses of camp in Firbank's writing see Robert F. Kiernan, *Frivolity Unbound: Six Masters of the Camp Novel: Thomas Peacock, Max Beerbohm, Ronald Firbank, E. F. Benson, P. G. Wodehouse, Ivy Compton-Burnett,* New York: Continuum, 1990, 49–65, and Robert Murray Davis, "Hyperaesthesia with Complications: The World of Ronald Firbank," *Rendezvous: Journal of Arts and Letters* 3.1, 1968, 5–15.

10. See Samuel Hynes, "A Chalice for Youth," *Times Literary Supplement* 3,632,

October 8, 1971, 1216, and Barnhill, "Method in Madness: Ronald Firbank's *The Flower Beneath the Foot*," 291. Susan Sontag also describes camp as "a solvent of morality," suggesting this as the reason "why homosexuals have pinned their integration into society on promoting the aesthetic sense" ("Notes on Camp," 290). Hollinghurst argues that society's characteristic tolerance of camp "also keep[s] sacrosanct the actual sexual subject, express[ing] itself in the frequent substitution of one form of abnormality for another" ("The Creative Uses of Homosexuality," 114). He also claims that the tradition of camp produces a respect for difference, even encouraging its proliferation; a contentious point, because camp is ironic and derisive about the very difference with which it is obsessed. For discussion of this point, see Andrew Ross, "Uses of Camp," *No Respect: Intellectuals and Popular Culture*, New York: Routledge, 1989, 135–70.

11. Hollinghurst, "The Creative Uses of Homosexuality," 9. W. R. Irwin usefully describes fantasy as "a story based on and controlled by an overt *violation* of what is generally accepted as possibility; it is the narrative result of transforming the condition contrary to fact into 'fact' itself" (*The Game of the Impossible: A Rhetoric of Fantasy*, Urbana: U of Illinois P, 1976, 4; my emphasis).

12. See Emmanuel Cooper, "Sexual Aesthetes" and "The Soul Identified with the Flesh," *The Sexual Perspective: Homosexuality and Art in the Last 100 Years in the West*, New York: Routledge, 1986, 63–111.

13. Irwin, *The Game of the Impossible: A Rhetoric of Fantasy*, 119.

14. Firbank, *The Flower Beneath the Foot*, New York: 1924, vii.

15. Firbank, qtd. in Miriam J. Benkovitz, *A Bibliography of Ronald Firbank*, London: Hart-Davis, 1963, 70.

16. Firbank, qtd. in Ifan Kyrle Fletcher, *Ronald Firbank: A Memoir*, London: Duckworth, 1930, 73.

17. Firbank, *Prancing Nigger* (1924), *The Complete Firbank*, 593–643. Subsequent references give pagination in main text. Firbank's first title for the novella was *Drama in Sunlight*, followed by *Sorrow in Sunlight*—choices that suggest the sadness and mourning the text represents. Carl Van Vechten subsequently titled the novella *Prancing Nigger* from the nickname Mrs. Mouth gives to her husband. Van Vechten, Firbank's literary adviser, altered the title with its final, more racist, form for the benefit of an American readership—it was a decision to which Firbank only later agreed. By describing it simply as a "Caribbean fiesta," Neville Braybrooke misses this novella's ambivalence, sadness, and theme of failure (see Braybrooke, "Thorns and Vanities: Ronald Firbank Revisited," *Encounter* 31.3, 1968, 71).

18. Kiernan, "Aestheticism Empurpled: Ronald Firbank," *Frivolity Unbound*, 57. Kiernan continues: "If the mix flirts with racial offensiveness, it does so shamelessly, with no attempt to render the native patois as anything other than a racist convention" (57). The point is significant, though I think it is also impossible to state unambiguously. My intention is rather to stress the ambivalence of Firbank's position, which he demonstrates contentiously is undecided about racial identification.

19. Brigid Brophy argues: "Firbank was a violently racially prejudiced man: in favour of the black races." It appears that this affirmative prejudice is "a passion for the exotic," an "erotic pursuit," and a "self-identification" (*Prancing Novelist: A*

Defence of Fiction in the Form of a Critical Biography in Praise of Ronald Firbank,
London: Macmillan, 1973, 174). I suggest that we should distinguish this form of
racial comparison from conscious political alignment on the grounds of a shared
social disaffiliation.

20. Hollinghurst, "The Creative Uses of Homosexuality," 138.

21. George Steiner, "Under the Greenwood Tree," *New Yorker* 47, October 9,
1971, 164.

22. See Terry Eagleton, Introduction to *Exiles and Émigrés: Studies in Modern Literature,* New York: Schocken, 1970, 9–19. Michael Seidel argues that "An exile is
someone who inhabits one place and remembers or *projects the reality of another"*
(*Exile and the Narrative Imagination,* New Haven: Yale UP, 1986, ix; my emphasis); Barnhill endorses this in her reading of Firbank: "[His] suggestion [is] that
home is often a state of mind, powerfully evocative and perpetually desirable, but no
more discernable on a map than is the Kingdom of Pisuerga" ("Method in Madness:
Ronald Firbank's *The Flower Beneath the Foot,"* 296).

23. Firbank, *Valmouth: A Romantic Novel* (1919), *The Complete Firbank,* 387–477.
Subsequent references give pagination in main text.

24. Barnhill, "Method in Madness: Ronald Firbank's *The Flower Beneath the
Foot,"* 295.

25. The reference is to Freud's "Thoughts for the Times on War and Death" (1915),
Standard Edition, vol. 14, 284, though the essays " 'Civilized' Sexual Morality and
Modern Nervous Illness" (1908), *Standard Edition,* vol. 9, 181–204, and *Civilization
and Its Discontents* (1930 [1929]), *Standard Edition,* vol. 21, 59–145, are also relevant
to this issue.

26. Jane Austen's *Sense and Sensibility* (1811) is an appropriate example. Kiernan
writes in *Frivolity Unbound:* "What especially distinguishes *Prancing Nigger* among
the author's novels is its superimposition of this ethereal, homosexual, mock-
religious, mock-bigoted, *Firbankian* world upon the socially circumstanced world
of Jane Austen. . . . When [Mr. and Mrs. Mouth] discuss the possibility of Vittorio's
marrying their Edna, they might be Mr. and Mrs. Bennet [from Austen's *Pride and
Prejudice*] discussing Elizabeth's chances with Mr. Darcy—*except, of course, for the
minstrel-show blackface*" (59; my emphasis). Establishing the price of this "except"
is the problem here. As it stands, Kiernan's point, while pertinent, is phrased to
make race gratuitous—an "indifference" that is racist precisely *because* he considers
it as gratuitous.

27. Hollinghurst, "The Creative Uses of Homosexuality," 49.

28. On the question of speech and mimicry, see Homi Bhabha, "Of Mimicry and
Man: The Ambivalence of Colonial Discourse," *October* 28, 1984, 125–33. Consider also the words of the countess of Tolga to the queen of Pisuerga in *The Flower
Beneath the Foot:* "Like their beagles and deer-hounds, that their Landseer so
loved to paint, I fear the British character is, at bottom, *nothing* if not rapacious!"
(*The Complete Firbank,* 583; original emphasis); or the mock-elegiac exclamation of the singing sailor in the same text: " 'London has robbed me of my throat,
sir!! It has deprived me of my voice' " (527); or, finally, the pompous ceremony
of " 'representatives of English Culture' . . . the ensemble the very apotheosis of

worn-out *cliché*" (592). See also Forster's "Notes on the English Character" (1920), *Abinger Harvest,* 13–26.

29. The relation between primitive culture and sexual naiveté is a powerful and over-determined trope whose legacy extends at least to the eighteenth century in Britain. See Brian V. Street, *The Savage in Literature: Representations of "Primitive" Society in English Fiction 1858–1920,* London, Boston: Routledge and Kegan Paul, 1975.

30. See Jean Genet, *Les Nègres* and "Pour jouer *Les Nègres,*" Paris: L'Arbalète, 1958, and *Un captif amoureux,* Paris: Gallimard, 1986, *Prisoner of Love,* trans. Barbara Bray, London: Picador, 1989. See also Alec G. Hargreaves, *The Colonial Experience in French Fiction,* London: Macmillan, 1981, for a study of comparable questions in writing by Pierre Loti, Ernest Psichari, and Pierre Mille.

31. Charles Baudelaire illustrated this anxiety in the role and conduct of the dandy when he advised: "[He must] be away from home and yet . . . feel . . . everywhere at home [in order] to see the world, *to be at the center of the world,* and yet to remain *hidden from the world . . .*" (*The Painter of Modern Life and Other Essays,* ed. and trans. Jonathan Mayne, New York: Da Capo, 1964, 28; my emphasis). On the question of the un/familiar and homeless, see Freud, "The 'Uncanny' " (1919), *Standard Edition,* vol. 17, 217–56, and Otto Rank's study, *The Double: A Psychoanalytic Study,* ed. and trans. Harry Tucker Jr., Chapel Hill: U of North Carolina P, 1971.

32. Firbank, *Santal* (1921), *The Complete Firbank,* 479–98. Subsequent references give pagination in main text.

33. Hollinghurst, "The Creative Uses of Homosexuality," 130.

34. See James Douglas Merritt, *Ronald Firbank,* New York: Twayne, 1969, 75–78; Potoker, *Ronald Firbank,* 17–19; and Jocelyn Brooke, *Ronald Firbank,* New York: Roy, 1951, 76.

35. T. S. Eliot, *The Waste Land* (1922), 5, *The Complete Poems and Plays of T. S. Eliot,* London: Faber, 1969, 72.

36. In a notebook for *Prancing Nigger,* Hollinghurst discovered that Firbank had copied the following quotation by George Sand: "*La société ne doit rien exiger de celui qui n'attend rien d'elle*" [Society ought to demand nothing from those who can expect nothing from it] (qtd. in Hollinghurst, "The Creative Uses of Homosexuality," 115). On this question of social margins and sexual exclusion, Braybrooke made the incongruous remark: "Firbank was a homosexual, and such men are often condemned to rigors of loneliness far surpassing the austerities of the cell. To them, others beckon . . . but seldom touch, if Claude Harvester may be paraphrased" ("Thorns and Vanities: Ronald Firbank Revisited," 71).

37. Hélène Cixous, "Sorties," *The Newly Born Woman,* with Catherine Clément, trans. Betsy Wing, Minneapolis: U of Minnesota P, 1986, 93.

38. See Jeffrey Meyers, *Homosexuality and Literature 1890–1930,* London: Athlone, 1977: "Despite its lack of conviction, *Maurice* was a *therapeutic* success, for Forster had to exorcise the homosexual themes that moved so threateningly within his early works so that he could complete his final masterpiece [*A Passage to India*]" (107).

39. Hollinghurst argues that Firbank's relationship with his mother "required [that he] stave off the more sexual consciousness which (particularly by 1916) had devel-

oped in [his] life and art" ("The Creative Uses of Homosexuality," 123). I suggest that although there is a relation between textual and biographical detail, the former is not an exclusive or obviously faithful expression of the latter.

40. Firbank, *Concerning The Eccentricities of Cardinal Pirelli* (1926), *The Complete Firbank,* 645–98. Subsequent references give pagination in main text.

41. See Jonathan Dollimore, "Homophobia and Sexual Difference," *Oxford Literary Review* 8.1–2, 1986, 5–12, and Eve Kosofsky Sedgwick, *Between Men: English Literature and Male Homosocial Desire,* New York: Columbia UP, 1985, 1, 20.

42. See Paul Davies, " 'The Power to Convey the Unuttered': Style and Sexuality in the Work of Ronald Firbank," *Lesbian and Gay Writing: An Anthology of Critical Essays,* ed. Mark Lily, London: Macmillan, 1990, 208. Mrs. Hurstpierpoint exclaims in *Valmouth:* "My tongue is over-prone perhaps to metaphor" (*The Complete Firbank,* 451).

43. Brooke, *Ronald Firbank,* 57. Consider also the following exchange between Madame Wetme and the Duchess of Varna in *The Flower Beneath the Foot:*

> "Indeed?"
> "My husband, you see . . ."
> ". . . . ."
> "Ah! well!"
> "Of course."
> "Have you made the request before?"
> "I have attempted."
> "Well?"
> "When the Lord Chamberlain refused me, I shed tears of blood,"
> Madame Wetme wanly retailed. (*The Complete Firbank,* 528–29)

8. In Defense of the Realm: Sassoon's Memoirs and "Other Opaque Arenas of War"

1. Siegfried Sassoon, *Memoirs of an Infantry Officer* (1930), London: Faber, 1991, 37. Subsequent references give pagination in main text.

2. Sassoon, *Memoirs of a Fox-Hunting Man* (1928), London: Faber, 1989, 266–67. Subsequent references give pagination in main text.

3. Sassoon, *Sherston's Progress,* London: Faber, 1936, 210.

4. T. S. Eliot, "East Coker" (1940), *Four Quartets, The Complete Poems and Plays of T. S. Eliot,* London: Faber, 1969, 182.

5. See Paul Fussell, *The Great War and Modern Memory,* Oxford: Oxford UP, 1975; Samuel Hynes, "The Irony and the Pity," *Times Literary Supplement,* December 18, 1981, 1469.

6. In this instance, I am using the word "real" to designate a specific historical event. My use of this term differs from all other uses of "real" in this chapter, which refer to Lacan's third topology—after the imaginary and symbolic orders—in which no symbol exists for the register of death, horror, and atrocity. Lacan argued that this register exists as a structural absence for the subject, that all symbolic identification negotiates this absence. The relevance of Lacan's "real" for Sassoon emerges in

his poem "Prelude: The Troops," in *Collected Poems 1908–1956,* London: Faber, 1947 (67):

> Yet these, who cling to life with stubborn hands,
> Can grin through storms of death and find a gap
> In the clawed, cruel tangles of his defence.

7. Fussell's *The Great War and Modern Memory* is an example of this historiography; his account comprises almost entirely literary references and autobiographical recollections.

8. Virginia Woolf, *To the Lighthouse* (1927), New York: Harcourt Brace Jovanovich, 1981, 134.

9. See Jeffrey C. Williams, "The Myth of the Lost Generation: The British War Poets and Their Modern Critics," *Clio* 12.1, 1982, 49; Fussell, "Arcadian Recourses," *The Great War and Modern Memory,* 231–69. Several critics have represented the war poets' "poetics of mourning" as the *cause* of Britain's post-War nostalgia, arguing that it created apathy among prominent writers and politicians of the time. See especially Correlli Barnett, *The Collapse of British Power,* New York: William Morrow, 1972, 62; Robert Wohl, *The Generation of 1914,* Cambridge, Mass.: Harvard UP, 1979; and Douglas Jarrold, *The Lie about the War: A Note on Some Contemporary War Books,* London: Faber, 1930.

10. Salman Rushdie, "Outside the Whale," *Granta* 11, 1984, 129. Examples include the Merchant-Ivory productions of Ruth Jhabvala's *Heat and Dust* (1983) and Forster's *A Room with a View* (1986), *Maurice* (1987), and *Howards End* (1992); David Lean's *A Passage to India* (1984); and the BBC Television adaptations of Evelyn Waugh's *Brideshead Revisited* (1981) and Paul Scott's *The Jewel in the Crown* (1984). Many other examples could be considered here; from Sassoon's poetry alone, consider "The Heritage," "October," and "Already Unheeding," *Collected Poems,* 52–55.

11. Examples of Sassoon's defiant poetry include "They," "The Hero," "Counter-Attack," "The Fathers," and "How to Die," *Collected Poems,* 23, 29, 68–74.

12. See John Middleton Murry, "Mr. Sassoon's War Verses," *The Evolution of an Intellectual,* London: Cape, 1927, 75–84; J. M. Gregson, "Siegfried Sassoon: Disillusion and Anger," *Poetry of the First World War,* London: Edward Arnold, 1976, 29–40; and Dominic Hibberd, "Some Notes on Sassoon's *Counter-Attack and Other Poems,*" *Notes and Queries* 29.227.4, 1982, 341–42.

13. On the sublime and its un/pleasures, see Frances Ferguson, "The Nuclear Sublime," *Diacritics* 14.2, 1984, 4–10.

14. See Eric Leed, *No Man's Land: Contact and Identity in World War I,* Cambridge: Cambridge UP, 1979, and John Onions, "Sassoon: The Hero Half-Redeemed," *English Fiction and Drama of the Great War, 1918–39,* London: Macmillan, 1990, 135–49.

15. Examples of this criticism include Paul Thompson, "War," *The Edwardians: The Remaking of British Society,* London: Weidenfeld and Nicolson, 1975, 276–88, and Philip Dodds, "Englishness and the National Culture," *Englishness: Politics and Culture, 1850–1920,* ed. Robert Colls and Philip Dodds, London: Croom Helm, 1984, 1–28.

16. See Julian Moynahan, "Pastoralism as Culture and Counter-Culture in English Fiction, 1800–1928," *Novel* 6.1, 1972, 20–35, and Northrop Frye, "Myth, Fiction, and Displacement," *Fables of Identity: Studies in Poetic Mythology,* New York: Harcourt, Brace and World, 1963, 21–38.

17. Onions, "Sassoon: The Hero Half-Redeemed," 136.

18. Sassoon, *The Old Century and Seven More Years* (1938), and *The Weald of Youth* (1942), London: Faber, 1986. Subsequent references to the latter give pagination in main text.

19. For an example of Thomas Hardy's nostalgia, see the last stanza to "In Time of 'The Breaking of Nations,' " *The Complete Poetical Works of Thomas Hardy,* vol. 2, ed. Samuel Hynes, Oxford: Clarendon, 1984, 296. For responses to the Second World War and British culture that differ from Sassoon's, see John Osborne, *Look Back in Anger,* London: Faber, 1957; Graham Greene, *The Quiet American,* London: Heinemann, 1955; C. P. Snow, *The New Men,* London: Macmillan, 1954; and Joe Orton, *Up Against It* (1967), London: Eyre Methuen, 1979. For a critical reading of this period, see Alan Sinfield, *Literature, Politics, and Culture in Postwar Britain,* Oxford: Blackwell, 1989.

20. Sassoon's phrase recalls Eliot's haunting question in *The Waste Land* (1922), 5, 359: "Who is the third who walks always beside you?" *The Complete Poems and Plays of T. S. Eliot,* 73.

21. See George L. Mosse, *Nationalism and Sexuality: Middle-Class Morality and Sexual Norms in Modern Europe,* Madison: U of Wisconsin P, 1985, and Paul Delaney, *The Neo-Pagans: Friendship and Love in the Rupert Brooke Circle,* London: Macmillan, 1987.

22. Sassoon, qtd. in Onions, "Sassoon: The Hero Half-Redeemed," 136. See also Bernard Knox, "Siegfried Sassoon," *Grand Street* 2.4, 1983, 144.

23. Onions, "Sassoon: The Hero Half-Redeemed," 135.

24. Knox, "Siegfried Sassoon," 147. His point refers to a memorial Sassoon gave for a friend's death: "So I wrote his name in chalk on the beech-tree stem, and left a rough garland of ivy there, and a yellow primrose for his yellow hair and kind grey eyes, my dear, my dear" (diary entry, qtd. in Knox, "Siegfried Sassoon," 148).

25. Sassoon, *Diaries 1920–1922,* ed. Rupert Hart-Davies, London: Faber, 1981. Subsequent references give pagination in main text.

26. For an account of this temporal arrangement, see Lacan, "Function and Field of Speech and Language," *Écrits: A Selection,* trans. Alan Sheridan, New York: Norton, 1977, 86.

27. As I argued in chapter 6, Forster's *Maurice* was written with these exact senti- ments in mind. The difference between the aim of Forster's novel and its resultant creative difficulties and suppression is analogous to my reading of Sassoon.

28. Forster, diary entry, April 8, 1922, unpublished manuscript held at King's Col- lege, Cambridge.

29. Roland Barthes represented the validation of the sign as a "warrior *topos,*" *The Pleasure of the Text,* trans. Richard Miller, New York: Hill and Wang, 1975, 28.

30. William Wordsworth, "The Happy Warrior" (1807), *Poetical Works,* ed. Thomas

Hutchinson, Oxford: Oxford UP, 1936, 386–87. Wordsworth's "Happy Warrior" stresses this character to suggest that

> . . . in himself [he must] possess his own desire . . .
> Tis finally, the Man, who, lifted high,
> Conspicuous object in a Nation's eye, . . .
> Finds comfort in himself and in his cause. (387)

31. Lacan, *The Four Fundamental Concepts of Psycho-Analysis,* ed. Jacques-Alain Miller, trans. Alan Sheridan, New York: Norton, 1978, 189; original emphasis.

32. Leed, *No Man's Land: Contact and Identity in World War I,* 104.

33. The 1914 Defence of the Realm Act was designed to restrict the movement of people and goods and the dissemination of information among foreign powers during wartime.

34. Francis Bacon, *De. Aug. Scient.,* 6, 3, qtd. in Jones, "War and Individual Psychology," *Essays in Applied Psycho-Analysis,* vol. 1, London: Hogarth, 1951, 68.

35. Dr. Chaim Shatan, qtd. in Leed, *No Man's Land,* 105.

36. Ernest Jünger, qtd. in Leed, *No Man's Land,* 114.

37. For an example of Sassoon's contempt for British colonial policy, see "Afterthoughts on the Opening of the British Empire Exhibition," *Collected Poems,* 127–29.

38. See Forster, "Notes on the English Character" (1920), *Abinger Harvest,* London: Edward Arnold, 1936: "The character of the English is . . . connected with the rise and organization of the British Empire. . . . Solidarity, caution, integrity, efficiency. Lack of imagination, hypocrisy" (13).

39. Rudyard Kipling, *Stalky & Co.* (1899), London: Macmillan, 1952, 187.

40. Thomas Hughes, *Tom Brown's Schooldays* (1857), London: Dent, 1899, 251–52.

41. See J. A. Mangan, *Athleticism in the Victorian and Edwardian Public School: The Emergence and Consolidation of an Educational Ideology,* Cambridge: Cambridge UP, 1981.

42. J. B. Priestley, qtd. in Fussell, *The Great War and Modern Memory,* 273–74.

43. See Sassoon, "To my Brother" and "Absolution" *Collected Poems 1908–1956:*

> The anguish of the earth absolves our eyes . . .
> And, fighting for our freedom, we are free. . . .
> Now, having claimed this heritage of heart,
> What need we more, my comrades and my brothers? ("Absolution," 11–12)

44. See Kristeva, *Powers of Horror: An Essay on Abjection,* 108–12, and Paul Schilder, *The Image and Appearance of the Human Body,* New York: International UP, 1978.

45. Sassoon's second-in-command made this remark, qtd. in Andrew Rutherford, "The Common Man as Hero," 85.

46. Rutherford, "The Common Man as Hero," 85.

47. Sassoon, *Sherston's Progress,* 242.

9. Saki/Munro: "Savage Propensities"; or, The "Jungle-boy in the Drawing-Room"

1. H. H. Munro (pseud. Saki) (1870–1916), "Gabriel-Ernest," *The Complete Saki,* Harmondsworth: Penguin, 1982, 67, and J. W. Lambert, introduction to *The Bodley Head Saki,* London: Bodley Head, 1980, 37. Subsequent references to *The Complete Saki* give pagination in main text.

2. Saki, *Commonplace Book,* qtd. in A. J. Langguth, *Saki: A Life of Hector Hugh Munro,* Oxford: Oxford UP, 1982, 69.

3. Henry James's *The Awkward Age* (1899), Harmondsworth: Penguin, 1966, is a novel concerning a young woman's "entry" into Edwardian society; it extends James's interest in dialogue to perhaps its furthest limit.

4. For elaboration on this argument, see Simon Stern, "Saki's Attitude," *GLQ: A Journal of Lesbian and Gay Studies* 1.3, 1994, 275–98, which is perhaps the only advanced and theoretical engagement with Saki to date, appearing just before this book was sent to press.

5. James, *The Tragic Muse* (1890), Harmondsworth: Penguin, 1978, 325, my emphasis.

6. Omar Khayyam, "The Rubaiyat," first translated by Edward FitzGerald in 1859, qtd. in Langguth, *Saki: A Life of Hector Hugh Munro,* 61–62.

7. Langguth, *Saki: A Life of Hector Hugh Munro,* 60–61. Writing to assume and diffuse the authority of one's literary forebears is a trope Harold Bloom famously interpreted in *The Anxiety of Influence: A Theory of Poetry,* Oxford: Oxford UP, 1973.

8. See Jacques Lacan, *The Four Fundamental Concepts of Psycho-Analysis,* ed. Jacques-Alain Miller, trans. Alan Sheridan, New York: Norton, 1978, 22, and Jean Laplanche, *Life and Death in Psychoanalysis,* trans. Jeffrey Mehlman, Baltimore: Johns Hopkins UP, 1976, 87–88.

9. Langguth, *Saki: A Life of Hector Hugh Munro,* 62.

10. In this sense, the name "Gabriel-Ernest" corresponds to Jacques Derrida's formulation of "dehiscence," in which the signifier is "grafted" onto already existing signifiers; each is metonymically associated, contingent on their relation to a principle Derrida deconstructs. See Derrida, "The Double Session," *Dissemination,* trans. Barbara Johnson, Chicago: U of Chicago P, 1981, especially 202 and 215 n. 27.

11. Oscar Wilde, *The Importance of Being Ernest* (1899), *Oscar Wilde: The Complete Plays,* London: Methuen, 1988, 213–99, and *The Picture of Dorian Gray* (1891), Harmondsworth: Penguin, 1982, especially 16–21.

12. Hélène Cixous, "Sorties," qtd. in Toril Moi, *Sexual/Textual Politics: Feminist Literary Theory,* New York and London: Methuen, 1985, 111. Betsy Wing's translation of this phrase, in *The Newly Born Woman,* (Minneapolis: U of Minnesota P, 1986, 80), gives "Empire of the Selfsame," a phrase I have generally repeated throughout this book; in this instance, however, I am adopting Moi's translation of *propre* as "proper," "appropriate," and "clean."

13. E. M. Forster, "Story of a Panic" (1904), *Collected Short Stories,* Harmondsworth: Penguin, 1954.

14. The tale gruesomely mimics Munro's own family history: in 1783 a tiger savagely mauled and killed Colonel Munro in India. See *The Gentleman's Magazine*'s report of 1793, qtd. in Lambert, introduction to *The Bodley Head Saki*, 8.

15. Saki, "Pau-Puk-Keewis," *Fortnightly Gazette,* May 10, 1915; my emphasis qtd. in Langguth, *Saki,* 261. Consider this commentary in *When William Came* (1913), especially *The Complete Saki,* 770.

16. Saki, qtd. in Langguth, *Saki: A Life of Hector Hugh Munro,* 251. Langguth comments: "it was a mistake but not an error. He was entering upon the last impersonation of his life" (251)—an observation with which I concur, though not with Langguth's conclusion that the "impersonation" always works.

17. For a detailed account of the fate of empire in this novel, see *The Complete Saki,* 714 and 732.

18. Munro/Saki advanced this critique in his political burlesque of Lewis Carroll's *Alice's Adventures in Wonderland,* titled *The Westminster Alice* (1902). Munro's contempt for the British Parliament's handling of the Boer War in 1899 is also notable in *The Westminster Alice* and his *Not-So Stories,* which deride Kiplingesque bravado.

19. For a contemporaneous example of anti-Semitism, see Olive Schreiner, *From Man to Man; or Perhaps Only . . .* (1926), London: Virago, 1982, especially chapter 11, and Arthur Schnitzler, *Dawn of Vienna* and *Professor Bernhardi* (1922), whose values Hitler cited in his diaries, and whose literature appeared to have influenced Munro because of the latter's ties with Vienna and Eastern Europe. Munro also wrote a short story—horrific in its pre-Holocaust fantasy and anti-Semitism—that imagined the violent death of a Jewish minority in an English village as a "practical joke." See "The Unrest Cure," *The Complete Saki,* 127–33.

20. See Ronald Hyam, *Empire and Sexuality: The British Experience,* Manchester: Manchester UP, 1990, 74.

21. See D. H. Lawrence, "The Prussian Officer" (1914), "The Fox" (1923), and *Aaron's Rod* (1922) for a resurgence of this masculine idealism. See also Klaus Theweleit, *Male Fantasies,* trans. Stephen Conway in collaboration with Erica Carter and Chris Turner, Minneapolis: U of Minnesota P, 1987, especially volume 1, "Women, Floods, Bodies, History," for an examination of the repudiation of femininity and the penalty that women suffer as a result of this ideal.

22. I have interpreted James's argument in " 'Thoughts for the Times on War and Death': Militarism and Its Discontents," *Literature and Psychology* 41.3, 1995, 1–12.

23. Munro, "An Old Love," *The Morning Post,* April 23, 1915. The name that accompanies this rhetoric is notable because it completes the shift from Saki to "Saki" to Munro.

24. For particular emphasis on the fascistic qualities of this phenomenon, see Theweleit, *Male Fantasies,* vol. 2, "Male Bodies: Psychoanalyzing the White Terror," 306–27.

25. For further discussion of *hommosexuelle* as a conceptual term, see Jacques Lacan, "Une lettre d'amour," *Le Séminaire, livre XX: Encore,* Paris: Seuil, 1975, 78; Luce Irigaray, "Commodities Among Themselves," *This Sex Which Is Not One,* trans.

Catherine Porter, Ithaca: Cornell UP, 1985, 192–97; and Craig Owens, "Outlaws: Gay Men in Feminism," *Men in Feminism,* ed. Alice Jardine and Paul Smith, New York: Methuen, 1987, 219–33.

26. The neologism is Lacan's. See "Seminar of 21 January 1975," *Feminine Sexuality: Jacques Lacan and the école freudienne,* ed. Juliet Mitchell and Jacqueline Rose, trans. Rose, New York: Norton, 1982, 167.

27. Comus's mother, Francesca Bassington, resembles many of the women Firbank represents in *Vainglory* and *Valmouth*—though Comus considers her responsible for his exodus to West Africa.

28. Wyndham Lewis, "The Family and Feminism" and "The 'Vicious' Circle," *The Art of Being Ruled,* London: Chatto and Windus, 1926.

29. The parallel with Milton's *Comus* (1637) seems deliberate, though as a mock-epic equivalent: Milton's Comus was sent to seduce a woman; Munro's is all but seduced by a man.

30. Consider Lacan's formulation of masculinity as a "parade" here in contradistinction with femininity's "masquerade." See Lacan, *The Seminar of Jacques Lacan,* book 2, ed. Jacques-Alain Miller, trans. Sylvena Tomaselli, Cambridge: Cambridge UP, 1988, 37 and 227.

31. Ronald Firbank, *The Complete Firbank,* London: Duckworth, 1961, 674.

32. For a significant account of mentorship's eroticism, see Henry James's short story "The Pupil" (1899) and its critical reading by Michael A. Cooper, "Discipl(in)ing the Master, Mastering the Discipl(in)e: Erotonomies in James' Tales of Literary Life," *Engendering Men: The Question of Male Feminist Criticism,* ed. Joseph A. Boone and Michael Cadden, New York: Routledge, 1990, 66–83.

33. See Julian Mitchell, *Another Country,* Ambergate, Derbyshire: Amber Lane, 1982, and James Baldwin, *Another Country* (1962), New York: Dell, 1963.

34. As Comus's overidentification with his mother appears to illustrate, the distress of his exclusion from his former life in Britain carries a psychoanalytic resonance because it brings any "Oedipal static" to an abrupt halt (the phrase occurs in Paul Monette, *Becoming a Man: Half a Life Story,* New York: HarperCollins, 1992, 7).

35. Anne McClintock, "Maidens, Maps and Mines: *King Solomon's Mines* and the Reinvention of Patriarchy in Colonial South Africa," *Women and Gender in Southern Africa to 1945,* ed. Cheryl Walker, Cape Town: David Philip, 1990, 106.

36. Langguth argues that much of this text established Munro's antagonistic relation to his past: "He had set out to bury his youth, and in *The Unbearable Bassington* he provided an elegant coffin for it" (*Saki: A Life of Hector Hugh Munro,* 208). Munro did acknowledge that the novel contained some references to his past.

Epilogue: Britain's Disavowal and the Mourning of Empire

1. Alan Hollinghurst, *The Swimming-Pool Library,* Harmondsworth: Penguin, 1988, 171. Subsequent references give pagination in main text.

2. Salman Rushdie, "Outside the Whale," *Granta* 11, 1984, 129.

3. Ibid. See also Renato Rosaldo, "Imperialist Nostalgia," *Representations* 26, 1989,

107–22, and Richard Ben Cramer, "Little England: The Further Decline and Total Collapse of the British Empire," *Esquire,* December 1993, 84–152.

4. For an interpretation of the inseparability of these fantasies and their prevalence in Hollinghurst's novel, see Richard Dellamora, "Tradition and Apocalypse in Alan Hollinghurst's *The Swimming-Pool Library,*" *Apocalyptic Overtures: Sexual Politics and the Sense of an Ending,* New Brunswick: Rutgers UP, 1994, 173–91.

5. David Leavitt, "Did I Plagiarize His Life?" *New York Times Magazine,* April 3, 1994, 37.

6. Ibid.

7. For a more detailed account of the "repressive hypothesis," see Jeffrey Weeks, *Sexuality and Its Discontents: Meanings, Myths and Modern Sexualities,* London and Boston: Routledge, 1985, 91–108, 248–51.

8. Jeffrey Meyers, *Homosexuality and Literature 1890–1930,* London: Athlone, 1977: "The fear of social condemnation and judicial punishment forced homosexuals to assume a protective posture in life and to devise a strategy of art that would allow them to express their private thoughts in a public genre" (10).

9. Freud, "Mourning and Melancholia," *Standard Edition,* vol. 14, 243–44.

10. Ibid., 244.

11. Rushdie, "Outside the Whale," 129. See also Edward W. Said, "Orientalism Reconsidered," *Literature, Politics and Theory: Papers from the Essex Conference 1976–84,* ed. Francis Barker et al., London: Methuen, 1986, 210–29.

12. Hanif Kureishi, *Sammy and Rosie Get Laid* (Frears, 1987). For an apposite reading of this film's racial and homo/sexual complexity, see Gayatri Chakravorty Spivak, *"Sammy and Rosie Get Laid,"* *Outside in the Teaching Machine,* New York: Routledge, 1993, 243–54.

Bibliography

Historiography, Psychoanalysis, and Sexuality

Ariès, Philippe. "Thoughts on the History of Homosexuality." *Western Sexuality: Practice and Precept in Past and Present Times.* Ed. P. Ariès and A. Béjin. Oxford: Blackwell, 1986. 62–76.

Bersani, Leo. *A Future for Astyanax: Character and Desire in Literature.* 1969. Boston: Little, Brown, 1976.

———. "Sexuality and Aesthetics." *October* 28 (1984): 27–42.

———. *The Freudian Body: Psychoanalysis and Art.* New York: Columbia UP, 1984.

———. *The Culture of Redemption.* Cambridge, Mass.: Harvard UP, 1990.

———. *Homos.* Cambridge, Mass.: Harvard UP, 1995.

Boothby, Richard. *Death and Desire: Psychoanalytic Theory in Lacan's Return to Freud.* New York: Routledge, 1991.

Brousse, Marie-Hélène. "L'homosexualité masculine dans les structures clinique." *Traits de perversion.* Ed. Fondation du champ freudien. Paris: Navarin, 1990. 162–71.

Butler, Judith. *Gender Trouble: Feminism and the Subversion of Identity.* New York: Routledge, 1990.

———. *Bodies That Matter: On the Discursive Limits of "Sex."* New York: Routledge, 1993.

Carpenter, Edward. *The Intermediate Sex: A Study of Some Transitional Types of Men and Women.* London: Allen and Unwin, 1908.

———. "Homogenic Love and Its Place in a Free Society." 1895. London: Redundancy, n. d.

Cohen, Ed. *Talk on the Wilde Side: Towards a Genealogy of a Discourse on Male Sexualities.* New York: Routledge, 1993.

Cooper, Emmanuel. *The Sexual Perspective: Homosexuality and Art in the Last 100 Years in the West.* New York: Routledge, 1986.

de Oliveria, Prado. "La libération des hommes ou la création de la pathogénèse." *Cahiers confrontation.* Paris: Aubier-Montagne 6 (1981): 187–95.

Dollimore, Jonathan. "Homophobia and Sexual Difference." *Oxford Literary Review* 8.1–2 (1986): 5–12.

———. "The Dominant and the Deviant: A Violent Dialectic." *Futures for English.* Ed. Colin MacCabe. Manchester: Manchester UP, 1988. 179–92.

———. "Different Desires: Subjectivity and Transgression in Wilde and Gide." *Textual Practice* 1.1 (1987): 48–67.

———. *Sexual Dissidence: Augustine to Wilde, Freud to Foucault.* Oxford: Clarendon, 1991.

Duberman, Martin B., Martha Vicinus, and George Chauncey Jr., eds. *Hidden from History: Reclaiming the Gay and Lesbian Past.* New York: North American Library, 1989.

Edelman, Lee. "Homographesis." *Yale Journal of Criticism* 3.1 (1989): 189–207.

———. *Homographesis: Essays in Gay Literary and Cultural Theory.* New York: Routledge, 1994.

Ferenczi, Sándor. *Sex in Psycho-analysis: Contributions to Psycho-analysis.* Boston: Gorham, 1916.

Fineman, Joel. "The Structure of Allegorical Desire." *October: The First Decade.* Ed. Annette Michelson, Rosalind Kraus, Douglas Crimp, and Joan Copjec. Cambridge, Mass.: MIT P, 1987. 373–92.

Flower MacConnell, Juliet. *The Regime of the Brother: After the Patriarchy.* New York: Routledge, 1991.

Fone, Byron R. S. *Hidden Heritage: History and the Gay Imagination.* New York: Irvington, 1981.

Foucault, Michel. *The History of Sexuality.* Vol. 1: *An Introduction.* 1976. Trans. Robert Hurley. Harmondsworth: Penguin, 1984.

Freud, Sigmund. *The Standard Edition of the Complete Psychological Works of Sigmund Freud.* Ed. and trans. James Strachey. 24 vols. London: Hogarth, 1957–74.

———. *The Interpretation of Dreams.* 1900. *Standard Edition.* Vol. 5. 339–627.

———. *The Psychopathology of Everyday Life.* 1901. *Standard Edition.* Vol. 6. 1–279.

———. *Three Essays on the Theory of Sexuality.* 1905. *Standard Edition.* Vol. 7. 135–72.

———. " 'Civilized' Sexual Morality and Modern Nervous Illness." 1908. *Standard Edition.* Vol. 9. 181–204.

———. "A Special Type of Choice of Object Made By Men (Contributions to the Psychology of Love I)." 1910. *Standard Edition.* Vol. 11. 163–75.

———. "Psychoanalytic Notes on an Autobiographical Account of a Case of Paranoia (Dementia Paranoides)." 1911. *Standard Edition.* Vol. 12. 1–82.

———. *Totem and Taboo.* 1913 (1912–13). *Standard Edition.* Vol. 13. 1–162.

———. "The Unconscious." 1915. *Standard Edition.* Vol. 14. 159–215.

———. "Remembering, Repeating and Working-Through (Further Recommendations on the Technique of Psycho-Analysis II)." 1914. *Standard Edition.* Vol. 12. 145–56.

———. "On Narcissism: An Introduction." 1914. *Standard Edition.* Vol. 14. 69–102.

———. "Repression." 1915. *Standard Edition.* Vol. 14. 146–58.

———. "Instincts and Their Vicissitudes." 1915. *Standard Edition.* Vol. 14. 117–40.

———. "Thoughts for the Times on War and Death." 1915. *Standard Edition.* Vol. 14. 273–302.

———. "Mourning and Melancholia." 1917. *Standard Edition.* Vol. 14. 237–58.

————. "From the History of an Infantile Neurosis." 1918 (1914). *Standard Edition.* Vol. 17. 1–123.

————. "The 'Uncanny.' " 1919. *Standard Edition.* Vol. 17. 217–56.

————. *Group Psychology and the Analysis of the Ego.* 1921. *Standard Edition.* Vol. 18. 67–143.

————. "Some Neurotic Mechanisms in Jealousy, Paranoia and Homosexuality." 1922 (1921). *Standard Edition.* Vol. 18. 221–32.

————. "A Seventeenth-Century Demonological Neurosis." 1923 (1922). *Standard Edition.* Vol. 19. 67–105.

————. *The Ego and the Id.* 1923. *Standard Edition.* Vol. 19. 1–66.

————. "A Note upon the 'Mystic Writing-Pad.' " 1924. *Standard Edition.* Vol. 19. 227–34.

————. *Inhibitions, Symptoms and Anxiety.* 1926 (1925). *Standard Edition.* Vol. 20. 77–175.

————. *Civilization and Its Discontents.* 1930 (1929). *Standard Edition.* Vol. 21. 57–145.

————. "The Dissection of the Psychical Personality." 1933. *Standard Edition.* Vol. 22. 57–80.

————. "Splitting of the Ego in the Process of Defence." 1940. *Standard Edition.* Vol. 23. 275–78.

Gallop, Jane. *The Daughter's Seduction: Feminism and Psychoanalysis.* Ithaca: Cornell UP, 1982.

————. *Reading Lacan.* Ithaca: Cornell UP, 1985.

Girard, René. *Deceit, Desire, and the Novel: Self and Other in Literary Structure.* Trans. Yvonne Freccero. Baltimore: Johns Hopkins UP, 1988.

Gonzalez-Crussi, F. *On the Nature of Things Erotic.* New York: Harcourt Brace Jovanovich, 1988.

Greenson, Ralph R. "Dis-Identifying from the Mother—Its Special Importance for the Boy." *International Journal of Psychoanalysis* 49 (1968): 370–74.

Greimas, Algirdas Julien, and Jacques Fontanille. *The Semiotics of Passions: From States of Affairs to States of Feeling.* Trans. Paul Perron and Frank Collins. Minneapolis: U of Minnesota P, 1993.

Hall, Lesley A. *Hidden Anxieties: Male Sexuality 1900–1950.* Cambridge: Polity, 1991.

Halperin, David M. *One Hundred Years of Homosexuality and Other Essays on Greek Love.* New York: Routledge, 1990.

Hammond, Dorothy, and Alta Jablow. "Gilgamesh and the Sundance Kid: The Myth of Male Friendship." *The Making of Masculinities: The New Men's Studies.* Ed. Harry Brod. Boston: Allen and Unwin, 1987. 241–58.

Hartmann, Heinz. "Notes on the Theory of Sublimation." *The Psychoanalytic Study of the Child* 10 (1955): 9–29.

Herzer, Manfred. "Kertbeny and the Nameless Love." *Journal of Homosexuality* 12.1 (1985): 1–23.

Hilliard, David. "UnEnglish and Unmanly: Anglo-Catholicism and Homosexuality." *Victorian Studies* 25.2 (1982): 181–210.

Hocquenghem, Guy. *Homosexual Desire.* 1972. Trans. Daniella Dangoor. Preface by Jeffrey Weeks. London: Allison and Busby, 1978.

Jones, Ernest. "War and Individual Psychology." 1915. *Essays in Applied Psycho-Analysis*. Vol. 1. London: Hogarth, 1951. 55–76.

———. "War and Sublimation." 1915. *Essays in Applied Psycho-Analysis*. Vol. 1. London: Hogarth, 1951. 77–87.

———. "War Shock and Freud's Theory of the Neuroses." 1918. *Papers on Psycho-Analysis*. 3d ed. New York: William Wood, 1923.

———. "La jalousie." *Revue française de psychanalyse* 3.2 (1929): 228–42.

Jung, Carl. "In Memory of Sigmund Freud." 1939. *The Collected Works of C. G. Jung*. Vol. 15. Ed. Sir Herbert Read, Michael Fordham, Gerhard Adler, and William McGuire, London: Routledge, 1979. 41–49.

Klein, Melanie. *Love, Guilt and Reparation, and Other Works, 1921–1945*. London: Virago, 1975.

Lacan, Jacques. "L'étourdit." *Scilicet* 4 (1973): 5–52.

——— . *Écrits: A Selection*. 1966. Trans. Alan Sheridan. New York: Norton, 1977.

———. *The Four Fundamental Concepts of Psycho-Analysis*. 1973. Ed. Jacques-Alain Miller. Trans. Alan Sheridan, New York: Norton, 1978.

———. *Feminine Sexuality: Jacques Lacan and the école freudienne*. Ed. Juliet Mitchell and Jacqueline Rose. Trans. Rose. New York: Norton, 1982.

———. *The Seminar of Jacques Lacan. 1954–1955: The Ego in Freud's Theory and in the Technique of Psychoanalysis*. Ed. Jacques-Alain Miller. Trans. Sylvana Tomaselli, with notes by John Forrester. Cambridge: Cambridge UP, 1988.

———. *The Seminar of Jacques Lacan, 1959–1960: The Ethics of Psychoanalysis*. Ed. Jacques-Alain Miller. Trans. Dennis Porter. New York: Norton, 1992.

Lagache, Daniel. "Contribution à l'étude des idées d'infidelité homosexuelle dans la jalousie." *Revue français de psychanalyse* 10 (1938): 709–19.

Lane, Christopher. "Describing the Boundaries of an Impossible Society." *Discourse* 16.3 (1994): 175–84.

———. " 'Thoughts for the Times on War and Death': Militarism and Its Discontents." *Literature and Psychology* 41.4 (1995).

———. "Is There a Homosexual in This Text?: Identity, Opacity, and the Elaboration of Desire." *GLQ: A Journal of Lesbian and Gay Studies* 2.4 (1995).

———. "Sublimation, Male Homosexuality, Esprit de Corps: Shattering the Dream of a Common Culture." *Homosexuality and Psychoanalysis*. Ed. Tim Dean. London: Macmillan, 1995.

Laplanche, Jean. *Life and Death in Psychoanalysis*. Trans. Jeffrey Mehlman. Baltimore: Johns Hopkins UP, 1976.

———, and J.-B. Pontalis. *The Language of Psychoanalysis*. London: Karnac, 1988.

Lewes, Kenneth. *The Psychoanalytic Theory of Male Homosexuality*. New York: Meridian, 1988.

Loewald, H. W. *Sublimation: Inquiries into Theoretical Psychoanalysis*. New Haven: Yale UP, 1990.

Mangan, J. A., and J. Walvin, eds. *Manliness and Morality: Middle-Class Masculinity in Britain and America, 1800–1940*. Manchester: Manchester UP, 1987.

McIntosh, Mary. "The Homosexual Role." *Social Problems* 16.2 (1968): 182–92.

Miller, Jacques-Alain. "Michel Foucault and Psychoanalysis." *Michel Foucault: Philosopher*. Trans. Timothy J. Armstrong. New York: Routledge, 1992. 58–64.

Mort, Frank. *Dangerous Sexualities: Medico-Moral Politics in England Since 1830.* New York: Routledge, 1987.

Nunberg, Herman, and Ernst Federn. *Minutes of the Vienna Psychoanalytic Society.* Vol. 1: *1906–1908.* Trans. M. Nunberg. New York: International UP, 1962.

Owens, Craig. "Outlaws: Gay Men in Feminism." *Men in Feminism.* Ed. Alice Jardine and Paul Smith. New York: Methuen, 1987. 219–33.

Phillips, Adam. *On Kissing, Tickling, and Being Bored: Psychoanalytic Essays on the Unexamined Life.* Cambridge, Mass.: Harvard UP, 1993.

Reynaud, Emmanuel. *Holy Virility: The Social Construction of Masculinity.* Trans. Ros Schwartz. London: Pluto, 1983.

Roper, Michael, and John Tosh, eds. *Manful Assertions: Masculinities in Britain since 1880.* New York: Routledge, 1991.

Rose, Jacqueline. *Sexuality in the Field of Vision.* London: Verso, 1986.

———. *Why War?: Psychoanalysis, Politics, and the Return to Melanie Klein.* Oxford: Blackwell, 1993.

Sedgwick, Eve Kosofsky. *Between Men: English Literature and Male Homosocial Desire.* New York: Columbia UP, 1985.

———. "A Poem Is Being Written." *Representations* 17 (1987): 110–43.

———. *Epistemology of the Closet.* Berkeley: U of California P, 1990.

———. *Tendencies.* Durham: Duke UP, 1993.

Silverman, Kaja. "Masochism and Male Subjectivity." *Camera Obscura* 17 (1988): 31–66.

———. "White Skin, Brown Masks: The Double Mimesis; or, With Lawrence in Arabia." *Differences* 1.3 (1989): 3–54.

———. "Historical Trauma and Male Subjectivity." *Cinema and Psychoanalysis.* Ed. E. Ann Kaplan. New York: Methuen, 1990. 110–27.

———. *Male Subjectivity at the Margins.* New York: Routledge, 1992.

Smith, F. B. "Labouchère's Amendment to the Criminal Law Amendment Bill." *Historical Studies* 17 (1976): 165–73.

Symonds, John Addington. *Sexual Inversion.* 1897. New York: Bell, 1984.

Theweleit, Klaus. *Male Fantasies.* Vol. 1. Trans. Stephen Conway in collaboration with Erica Carter and Chris Turner. Minneapolis: U of Minnesota P, 1987.

———. *Male Fantasies.* Vol. 2. Trans. Erica Carter and Chris Turner, in collaboration with Stephen Conway. Minneapolis: U of Minnesota P, 1989.

Walkowitz, Judith. *Prostitution and Victorian Society: Women, Class, and the State.* Cambridge: Cambridge UP, 1980.

Weeks, Jeffrey. " 'Sins and Diseases': Some Notes on Homosexuality in the Nineteenth Century." *History Workshop* 1 (1976): 211–19.

———. *Coming Out: Homosexual Politics in Britain, from the Nineteenth-Century to the Present.* New York: Quartet, 1977.

———. *Sexuality and Its Discontents: Meanings, Myths and Modern Sexualities.* London, Boston: Routledge and Kegan Paul, 1985.

Žižek, Slavoj. *The Sublime Object of Ideology.* New York: Verso, 1989.

———. "The Real and Its Vicissitudes." *Newsletter of the Freudian Field* 3.1–2 (1989): 80–101.

———. *Tarrying with the Negative: Kant, Hegel, and the Critique of Ideology.* Durham: Duke UP, 1993.

Critical Theories

Barthes, Roland. *Empire of Signs*. 1970. Trans. Richard Howard. New York: Hill and Wang, 1982.

———. *The Pleasure of the Text*. 1973. Trans. Richard Miller. New York: Hill and Wang, 1975.

———. *A Lover's Discourse: Fragments*. 1977. Trans. Richard Howard. New York: Hill and Wang, 1985.

———. *Incidents*. Paris: Seuil, 1987.

Cixous, Hélène, and Catherine Clément. *The Newly Born Woman*. Trans. Betsy Wing. Minneapolis: U of Minnesota P, 1986.

Davis, Richard Conn, ed. *The Fictional Father: Lacanian Readings of the Text*. Amherst: U of Massachusetts P, 1981.

de Man, Paul. "Autobiography as De-Facement." *MLN* 94 (1979): 919–30.

Derrida, Jacques. *Of Grammatology*. Trans. Gayatri Chakravorty Spivak. Baltimore: Johns Hopkins UP, 1974.

———. *Dissemination*. Trans. Barbara Johnson. Chicago: U of Chicago P, 1981.

———. *The Truth in Painting*. Trans. Geoff Bennington and Ian McLeod. Chicago: U of Chicago P, 1987.

———. "The Politics of Friendship." *The Journal of Philosophy* 85.11 (1988): 632–48.

Eisenstein, Hester, and Alice Jardine, eds. *The Future of Difference*. New Brunswick: Rutgers UP, 1987.

Fletcher, Angus. *Allegory: The Theory of a Symbolic Mode*. Ithaca: Cornell UP, 1964.

Fuss, Diana. *Essentially Speaking: Feminism, Nature, and Difference*. New York: Routledge, 1989.

———, ed. *Inside/Out: Lesbian Theories, Gay Theories*. New York: Routledge, 1991.

Greenblatt, Stephen J., ed. *Allegory and Representation*. Baltimore: Johns Hopkins UP, 1986.

Harpham, Geoffrey Galt. *The Ascetic Imperative in Culture and Criticism*. Chicago: U of Chicago P, 1987.

Heidegger, Martin. *What Is Called Thinking?* Trans. J. Glenn Gray. New York: Harper & Row, 1968.

Hoad, T. F., ed. *The Concise Oxford Dictionary of English Etymology*. Oxford: Clarendon, 1986.

Kristeva, Julia. *Powers of Horror: An Essay on Abjection*. Trans. Leon S. Roudiez. New York: Columbia UP, 1982.

Lukacher, Ned. *Primal Scenes: Literature, Philosophy, Psychoanalysis*. Ithaca: Cornell UP, 1986.

Macherey, Pierre. *A Theory of Literary Production*. Trans. Geoffrey Wall. London, Boston: Routledge and Kegan Paul, 1978, 189.

Miller, D. A. *The Novel and the Police*. Berkeley: U of California P, 1988.

Monnet, Georges. "Picasso and Cubism." Trans. Dominic Faccini. *October* 60 (1992): 51–52.

Nietzsche, Friedrich. *Beyond Good and Evil*. 1886. Trans. R. J. Hollingdale. Harmondsworth: Penguin, 1984.

Vance, Norman. *The Sinews of the Spirit: The Ideal of Christian Manliness in Victorian Literature and Religious Thought.* Cambridge: Cambridge UP, 1985.

Colonialism and Cultural Contexts

Abbeele, Georges van den. *Travel as Metaphor: From Montaigne to Rousseau.* Minneapolis: U of Minnesota P, 1991.

Abel, Elizabeth. "Race, Class, and Psychoanalysis? Opening Questions." *Conflicts in Feminism.* Ed. Marianne Hirsch and Evelyn Fox Keller. New York: Routledge, 1990. 184–204.

Anderson, Benedict R. *Imagined Communities: Reflections on the Origins and Spread of Nationalism.* London: Verso, 1983.

Angell, Norman. *The Defence of the Empire.* London: Hamish Hamilton, 1937.

Barnett, Correlli. *The Collapse of British Power.* New York: Eyre Methuen, 1972.

Behdad, Ali. *Belated Travelers: Orientalism in the Age of Colonial Dissolution.* Durham: Duke UP, 1994.

Bennett, George, ed. *The Concept of Empire.* London: Adams and Charles Black, 1962.

Berger, Mark T. "Imperialism and Sexual Exploitation: A Response to Ronald Hyam's 'Empire and Sexual Opportunity.' " *Journal of Imperial and Commonwealth History* 17.1 (1988): 83–98.

Bhabha, Homi. "Of Mimicry and Man: The Ambivalence of Colonial Discourse." *October* 28 (1984): 125–33.

———. "Representation and the Colonial Text: A Critical Exploration of Some Forms of Mimeticism." *The Theory of Reading.* Ed. Frank Gloversmith. Brighton: Harvester, 1984. 93–122.

———. "Signs Taken for Wonders: Questions of Ambivalence and Authority Under a Tree Outside Delhi, May 1817." *Critical Inquiry* 12.1 (1985): 144–65.

Boahen, A. Adu. *African Perspectives on Colonialism.* Baltimore: Johns Hopkins UP, 1987.

Bodelson, C. *Studies in Mid-Victorian Imperialism.* London: Heinemann, 1960.

Bongie, Chris. *Exotic Memories: Literature, Colonialism, and Fin de Siècle.* Stanford: Stanford UP, 1991.

Brantlinger, Patrick. *Rule of Darkness: British Literature and Imperialism, 1830–1914.* Ithaca: Cornell UP, 1988.

Bristow, E. Joseph. *Vice and Vigilance: Purity Movements in Britain Since 1700.* Dublin: Gill and Macmillan, 1977.

Bristow, Joseph. *Empire Boys: Adventures in a Man's World.* London: Harper-Collins, 1991.

Bruckner, Pascal. *The Tears of the White Man: Compassion as Contempt.* Trans. William R. Beer. New York: Free, 1986.

Busia, A. P. A. "Miscegenation as Metonymy: Sexuality and Power in the Colonial Novel." *Ethnic and Racial Studies* 9 (1986): 360–72.

Buzard, James. *The Beaten Track: European Tourism, Literature, and the Ways to "Culture," 1800–1918.* Oxford: Oxford UP, 1993.

Colls, Robert, and Philip Dodds, eds. *Englishness: Politics and Culture, 1850–1920.* London: Croom Helm, 1984.

Coward, Rosalind. *Patriarchal Precedents: Sexuality and Social Relations.* London, Boston: Routledge and Kegan Paul, 1983.

Cramer, Richard Ben. "Little England: The Further Decline and Total Collapse of the British Empire." *Esquire* (December 1993): 84–152.

Dunbar, Moodie T. "Migrancy and Male Sexuality on the South African Gold Mines." *Journal of Southern African Studies* 14 (1988): 228–56.

Dunton, Chris. "Wheyting Be Dat?: The Treatment of Homosexuality in African Literature." *Research in African Literatures* 20.3 (1989): 422–48.

Eagleton, Terry. *Exiles and Émigrés: Studies in Modern Literature.* New York: Schocken, 1970.

———, Fredric Jameson, and Edward W. Said. *Nationalism, Colonialism, and Literature.* Minneapolis: U of Minnesota P, 1990.

Etherinton, Norman. *Theories of Imperialism: War, Conquest and Capital.* Totowa, NJ: Barnes and Noble, 1984.

Fanon, Frantz. *Black Skin, White Masks.* Trans. Charles Lam Markmann. New York: Grove, 1967.

Fetter, Bruce, ed. *Colonial Rule in Africa: Readings from Primary Sources.* Madison: U of Wisconsin P, 1979.

Fussell, Paul. *The Great War and Modern Memory.* Oxford: Oxford UP, 1975.

———. *Abroad: British Literary Traveling Between the Wars.* Oxford: Oxford UP, 1980.

Gilman, Sander L. *Difference and Pathology: Stereotypes of Sexuality, Race, and Madness.* Ithaca: Cornell UP, 1985.

———, and J. Edward Chamberlain, eds. *Degeneration: The Dark Side of Progress.* New York: Columbia UP, 1985.

Goldberg, David Theo, ed. *Anatomy of Racism.* Minneapolis: U of Minnesota P, 1990.

Green, Martin. *Seven Types of Adventure Tale: An Etiology of a Major Genre.* University Park: Pennsylvania State UP, 1991.

———. *The Adventurous Male: Chapters in the History of the White Male Mind.* University Park: Pennsylvania State UP, 1993.

Howe, Susanne. *Novels of Empire.* New York: Columbia UP, 1949.

Huxley, Aldous. "Wordsworth in the Tropics." *Do What You Will.* London: Chatto and Windus, 1929. 113–29.

Hyam, Ronald. *Britain's Imperial Century 1815–1914: A Study of Empire and Expansion.* London: Batsford, 1976.

———. "Empire and Sexual Opportunity." *Journal of Imperial and Commonwealth History* 14.2 (1986): 34–89.

———. "Concubinage and the Colonial Service: The Crewe Connection (1909)." *Journal of Imperial and Commonwealth History* 14.3 (1986): 170–86.

———. " 'Imperialism and Sexual Exploitation': A Reply." *Journal of Imperial and Commonwealth History* 17.1 (1988): 90–98.

———. *Empire and Sexuality: The British Experience.* Manchester: Manchester UP, 1990.

JanMohamed, Abdul R. "The Economy of Manichean Allegory: The Function of Racial Difference in Colonialist Literature." *Critical Inquiry* 12 (1985): 59–87.

————. "Sexuality on/of the Racial Border: Foucault, Wright, and the Articulation of 'Racialized Sexuality.'" *Discourses of Sexuality: From Aristotle to AIDS.* Ed. Donma C. Stanton. Ann Arbor: U of Michigan P, 1992. 94–116.

Jarrold, Douglas. *The Lie about the War: A Note on Some Contemporary War Books.* London: Faber, 1930.

Kovel, Joel. *White Racism: A Psychohistory.* New York: Columbia UP, 1984.

Kristeva, Julia. *Strangers to Ourselves.* Trans. Leon S. Roudiez. New York: Columbia UP, 1991.

————. *Nations without Nationalism.* Trans. Leon S. Roudiez. New York: Columbia UP, 1993.

Lawrence, T. E. *Seven Pillars of Wisdom: A Triumph.* 1926. Harmondsworth: Penguin, 1962.

Mannoni, Octave. *Prospero and Caliban: The Psychology of Colonization.* Trans. Pamela Powesland. New York: Praeger, 1956.

Mosse, George L. *Nationalism and Sexuality: Middle-Class Morality and Sexual Norms in Modern Europe.* Madison: U of Wisconsin P, 1985.

Nandy, Ashis. *The Intimate Enemy: Loss and Recovery of Self Under Colonialism.* Oxford: Oxford UP, 1983.

Nordau, Max. *Degeneration.* 1894. New York: Fertig, 1968.

Parker, Andrew, Mary Russo, Doris Sommer, and Patricia Yaeger, eds. *Nationalisms and Sexualities.* New York: Routledge, 1992.

Pick, Daniel. *Faces of Degeneration: A European Disorder, c. 1848–1918.* Cambridge: Cambridge UP, 1989.

Porter, Bernard. *Critics of Empire: British Radical Attitudes to Colonialism in Africa 1895–1914.* London: Macmillan, 1968.

Porter, Dennis. *Haunted Journeys: Desire and Transgression in European Travel Writing.* Princeton: Princeton UP, 1991.

Pratt, Marie-Louise. *Imperial Eyes: Studies in Travel Writing and Transculturation.* New York: Routledge, 1992.

Richards, Thomas. *The Imperial Archive: Knowledge and the Fantasy of Empire.* New York: Verso, 1993.

Rosaldo, Renato. "Imperialist Nostalgia." *Representations* 26 (1989): 107–22.

Ross, R. "Oppression, Sexuality and Slavery at the Cape of Good Hope." *Historical Reflections* 6 (1979): 421–33.

————, ed. *Racism and Colonialism: Comparative Studies in Overseas History.* The Hague: Nijhoff, 1982.

Rowe, J. A. "The Purge of Christians at Mwanga's Court." *Journal of African History* 5 (1964): 55–71.

Rushdie, Salman. "Outside the Whale." *Granta* 11 (1984): 125–38.

Said, Edward W. *Beginnings.* New York: Basic, 1975.

————. *Orientalism.* 1978. Harmondsworth: Penguin, 1985.

————. "Notes on Exile." *Granta* 13 (1984): 157–72.

————. "Orientalism Reconsidered." *Literature, Politics and Theory: Papers from the Essex Conference 1976–84.* Ed. Francis Barker et al. London: Methuen, 1986: 210–29.

————. "Nationalism, Geography, and Interpretation." *New Left Review* 180 (1990): 81–97.

Sandison, Alan. *The Wheel of Empire: A Study of the Imperial Idea in Some Late Nineteenth and Early Twentieth-Century Fiction.* New York: St Martin's, 1967.

Spies, S. B. *Methods of Barbarism?: Roberts and Kitchener and Civilians in the Boer War Republics, January 1900–May 1992.* Cape Town: Human and Rousseau, 1977.

Spivak, Gayatri Chakravorty. "Imperialism and Sexual Difference." *Oxford Literary Review* 8.1–2 (1986): 225–40.

———. *In Other Worlds: Essays in Cultural Politics.* New York: Routledge, 1988.

———. "Can the Subaltern Speak?" *Marxism and the Interpretation of Culture.* Ed. Cary Nelson and Lawrence Grossberg. Urbana: U of Illinois P, 1988. 271–313.

Spurr, David. *The Rhetoric of Empire: Colonial Discourse in Journalism, Travel Writing, and Imperial Administration.* Durham: Duke UP, 1993.

Stokes, John. *In the Nineties.* New York: Harvester Wheatsheaf, 1989.

Stone, Lawrence. *The Family, Sex, and Marriage in England 1500–1800.* London: Weidenfeld and Nicolson, 1977.

Street, Brian V. *The Savage in Literature: Representations of "Primitive" Society in English Fiction 1858–1920.* London, Boston: Routledge and Kegan Paul, 1975.

Suleri, Sara. *The Rhetoric of English India.* Chicago: U of Chicago P, 1992.

Talbot, E. S. *Degeneracy: Its Causes, Signs and Results.* London: Walter Scott, 1898.

Thompson, Paul. *The Edwardians: The Remaking of British Society 1900–1914.* London: Weidenfeld, 1984.

Thoopen, J. P. *Black Martyrs.* London: Sheed and Ward, 1941.

Thornton, A. P. *The Imperial Idea and Its Enemies: A Study in British Power.* London: Macmillan, 1959.

Tidrick, Kathryn. *Empire and the English Character.* London: Tauris, 1992.

Vogt, Carl. *Lectures on Man: His Place in Creation, and in the History of the Earth.* Ed. James Hunt. London: Longman, Green, 1864.

Walter, Richard D. "What Became of the Degenerate?: A Brief History of the Concept." *Journal of the History of Medicine and the Allied Sciences* 11 (1956): 422–29.

Wohl, Robert. *The Generation of 1914.* Cambridge, Mass.: Harvard UP, 1979.

Wrigley, C. C. "Christian Revolution in Buganda." *Comparative Studies in Society and History* 2 (1959–60): 33–48.

Young, Robert. *White Mythologies: Writing History and the West.* New York: Routledge, 1990.

Young, Wayland. *Eros Denied.* 1964. London: Corgi, 1969.

Modernism and Homo/sexual Writing and Criticism

Ackerley, J. R. *Hindoo Holiday: An Indian Journal.* 1932. Harmondsworth: Penguin Travel, 1988.

Aldrich, Robert. *The Seduction of the Mediterranean: Writing, Art and Homosexual Fantasy.* New York: Routledge, 1993.

Annan, Noël. "The Cult of Homosexuality in England, 1850–1950." *Biography* 13.3 (1990): 189–202.

Bergonzi, Bernard. *The Myth of Modernism and Twentieth Century Literature.* Brighton: Harvester, 1986.

———. *Wartime and Aftermath: English Literature and Its Background 1939–1960.* Oxford: Oxford UP, 1993.

Boone, Joseph A. "Mappings of Male Desire in Durrell's *Alexandria Quartet.*" *Displacing Homophobia: Gay Male Perspectives in Literature and Culture.* Ed. Ronald R. Butters, John M. Clum, and Michael Moon. Durham: Duke UP, 1989. 73–106.

———. "Vacation Cruises; or, The Homoerotics of Orientalism." *PMLA* 110.1 (1995): 89–107.

Bradford, E. E. *The New Chivalry.* London: Routledge, 1918.

Brown, Dennis. *The Modernist Self in Twentieth-Century English Literature: A Study in Self-Fragmentation.* London: Macmillan, 1989.

Coote, Stephen, ed. *The Penguin Book of Homosexual Verse.* Harmondsworth: Penguin, 1983.

Craft, Christopher. *Another Kind of Love: Male Homosexual Desire in English Discourse, 1850–1920.* Berkeley: U of California P, 1994.

Dellamora, Richard. *Masculine Desire: The Sexual Politics of Victorian Aestheticism.* Chapel Hill: U of North Carolina P, 1990.

Eliot, T. S. *The Complete Poems and Plays of T. S. Eliot.* London: Faber, 1982.

Genet, Jean. *Prisoner of Love.* 1986. Trans. Barbara Bray. London: Picador, 1989.

Gide, André. *Travels in the Congo.* 1927–28. Trans. Dorothy Bussy. Harmondsworth: Penguin Travel, 1986.

Hollinghurst, Alan. *The Swimming-Pool Library.* Harmondsworth: Penguin, 1988.

Kenner, Hugh. *A Sinking Island: The Modern English Writers.* New York: Knopf, 1988.

Kopelson, Kevin. *Love's Litany: The Writing of Modern Homoerotics.* Stanford: Stanford UP, 1994.

Leavitt, David. "Did I Plagiarize His Life?" *New York Times Magazine* (April 3, 1994): 36–37.

Meinertzhagen, Richard. *Kenya Diary (1902–1906).* 1957. New York: Hippocrene, 1983.

Meyers, Jeffrey. *Homosexuality and Literature 1890–1930.* London: Athlone, 1977.

Reade, Brian, ed. *Sexual Heretics: Male Homosexuality in English Literature from 1850 to 1900.* London, Boston: Routledge and Kegan Paul, 1970.

Sarotte, Georges-Michel. *Like a Brother, Like a Lover: Male Homosexuality in the American Novel and Theater from Herman Melville to James Baldwin.* Trans. Richard Miller. New York: Doubleday-Anchor, 1978.

Showalter, Elaine. *Sexual Anarchy: Gender and Culture at the Fin de Siècle.* London: Virago, 1992.

Taylor, Brian. "Motives for Guilt-Free Pederasty: Some Literary Considerations." *Sociological Review* 24 (1976): 97–114.

Woolf, Virginia. *To the Lighthouse.* 1927. New York: Harcourt Brace Jovanovich, 1981.

Max Beerbohm

Beerbohm, Max. "The Pervasion of Rouge." 1894. *Works and More*. London: John Lane, 1930. 86–110.

———. *The Happy Hypocrite: A Fairy Tale for Tired Men*. 1896. London: John Lane, 1920.

———. "Pretending." 1898. *More*. London: John Lane, 1907. 55–61.

———. "A Pathetic Imposture." 1900. *Yet Again*. New York: Knopf, 1923. 77–81.

———. *A Peep into the Past, and Other Prose Pieces*. Ed. Rupert Hart-Davis. Battleboro, Vt.: Stephen Greene, 1972.

———. *Letters of Max Beerbohm 1892–1956*. Ed. Rupert Hart-Davis. London: John Murray, 1988.

Cecil, David. *Max*. Boston: Houghton Mifflin, 1965.

Danson, Lawrence. *Max Beerbohm and the Act of Writing*. Oxford: Oxford UP, 1989.

Kermode, Frank. "Whom the Gods Loathe." *Encounter* 24 (March 1965): 74–75.

Milton, John. *Paradise Lost*. 1667. *Milton: Poetical Works*. Ed. Douglas Bush. Oxford: Oxford UP, 1966.

Muggeridge, Malcolm. "A Survivor." *New York Review of Books* 5.8 (November 25, 1965): 31–33.

Scott, Robert, ed. *Greek-English Lexicon*. 9th ed. Oxford: Oxford UP, 1983.

Shelley, Percy Bysshe. "The Triumph of Life." 1822. *The Complete Poetical Works of Percy Bysshe Shelley*. Ed. Thomas Hutchinson. London: Oxford UP, 1929. 503–16.

Joseph Conrad

Baines, Jocelyn. *Joseph Conrad: A Critical Biography*. New York: McGraw-Hill, 1960.

Berman, Jeffrey. "The Ambiguities of *Victory*." *Joseph Conrad: Writing as Rescue*. New York: Astra, 1977. 163–79.

Bignami, Marialuisa. "Joseph Conrad, the Malay Archipelago, and the Decadent Hero." *The Review of English Studies* 38.150 (1987): 199–210.

Bonney, William W. " 'Eastern Logic under My Western Eyes': Conrad, Schopenhauer, and the Orient." *Thorns and Arabesques: Contexts for Conrad's Fiction*. Baltimore: Johns Hopkins UP, 1980. 3–30.

———. "Narrative Perspective in *Victory*: The Thematic Relevance." *Critical Essays on Joseph Conrad*. Ed. Ted Bill. Boston: G. K. Hall, 1987. 128–41.

Boyle, Ted E. *Symbol and Meaning in the Fiction of Joseph Conrad*. The Hague: Mouton, 1965. 218–38.

Bradbrook, Murial C. "The Hollow Men." *Joseph Conrad: Poland's English Genius*. Cambridge: Cambridge UP, 1941. 41–67.

Burg, B. R. "Buccaneer Sexuality." *Sodomy and the Pirate Tradition: English Sea Rovers in the Seventeenth-Century Caribbean*. New York: New York UP, 1984. 107–38.

Butler Haugaard, Janet. "Conrad's *Victory*: Another Look at Axel Heyst." *Literature and Psychology* 31.3 (1981): 33–46.

Chon, Soo Young. "Conrad's *Victory:* An Elusive Allegory." *English Language and Literature* 35.1 (1989): 83–101.

Collits, Terry. "Imperialism, Marxism, Conrad: A Political Reading of *Victory.*" *Textual Practice* 3.3 (1989): 303–22.

Conrad, Joseph. *Tales of Unrest*. 1898. Harmondsworth: Penguin, 1977.

———. *Lord Jim*. 1900. London: Dent, 1923.

———. *Typhoon and Other Stories*. New York: Doubleday, Doran and Co., 1902.

———. *Nostromo: A Tale of the Seaboard*. 1904. Harmondsworth: Penguin, 1990.

———. *Victory: An Island Tale*. 1915. Harmondsworth: Penguin, 1989.

———. "Geography and Some Explorers." 1924. *White Man in the Tropics: Two Moral Tales*. Ed. D. Daiches. London: Harcourt, 1962. 114–18.

———. *Joseph Conrad's Letters to R. B. Cunningham Graham*. Ed. C. T. Watts. Cambridge: Cambridge UP, 1969.

Cox, C. B. "Outcasts in *Chance* and *Victory.*" *Joseph Conrad: The Modern Imagination*. London: Dent, 1974. 118–36.

Curle, Richard. "*Victory*—1915." *Joseph Conrad and His Characters*. London: Heinemann, 1957. 219–54.

Daleski, H. M. "*Victory* and Patterns of Self-Division." *Conrad Revisited: Essays for the Eighties*. Ed. Ross C. Murfin. Tuscaloosa: U of Alabama P, 1985. 107–24.

Davidson, Arnold E. *Conrad's Endings: A Study of the Five Major Novels*. Ann Arbor: UMI Research, 1984. 87–101.

Deurbergue, Jean. "The Opening of *Victory.*" *Cahiers d'études et de recherches victoriennes et édouardiennes* 2 (1975): 239–70.

Dike, Donald A. "The Tempest of Axel Heyst." *Nineteenth-Century Fiction* 18 (1962): 101–20.

Dobrinsky, Joseph. "From Coal to Diamond: Axel Heyst's Progress in *Victory.*" *The Artist in Conrad's Fiction: A Psychocritical Study*. Ann Arbor: UMI Research, 1989. 101–11.

Gillon, Adam. "Betrayal and Redemption in Joseph Conrad." *Polish Review* 5 (1960): 18–35.

Gross, Seymour L. "The Devil in Samburan: Jones and Ricardo in *Victory.*" *Nineteenth-Century Fiction* 16.1 (1961): 81–85.

Guerard, Albert. *Conrad the Novelist*. Cambridge: Cambridge UP, 1958.

Guillaume, André. "The Psychological Approach in *Victory.*" *L'époque conradienne*. Limoges: Société conradienne française, 1981. 119–54.

Hawthorne, Jeremy. *Joseph Conrad: Narrative Technique and Ideological Commitment*. London: Edward Arnold, 1990.

Hay, Eloise K. *The Political Novels of Joseph Conrad: A Critical Study*. Chicago: U of Chicago P, 1963.

Hollingworth, Alan M. "Freud, Conrad, and the Future of an Illusion." *Literature and Psychology* 5.4 (1955): 78–83.

Hunter, Allen. *Joseph Conrad and the Ethics of Darwinism: The Challenges of Science*. London: Croom Helm, 1983.

Jean-Aubry, G. *Joseph Conrad: Life and Letters*. Vol. 1. Garden City: Doubleday, Page, 1927.

Kaehele, Sharon, and Howard German. "Conrad's *Victory:* A Reassessment." *Modern Fiction Studies* 10.1 (1964): 55–72.

Leavis, F. R. *The Great Tradition: George Eliot, Henry James, Joseph Conrad*. 1948. Harmondsworth: Peregrine, 1983.

Lee, R. F. *Conrad's Colonialism: Studies in English Literature*. The Hague: Mouton, 1969.

Lewis, John F. "Plain Mr. Jones and the Final Chapter of *Victory*." *Conradiana* 9.1 (1984): 4–14.

Lordi, R. J. "The Three Emissaries of Evil: Their Psychological Relationship in Conrad's *Victory*." *College English* 23 (1961): 136–40.

McCall, Dan. "The Meaning of Darkness: A Response to a Psychoanalytical Study of Conrad." *College English* 29 (1968): 620–27.

Meyer, Bernard C. *Joseph Conrad: A Psychoanalytic Biography*. Princeton: Princeton UP, 1967.

Meyers, Jeffrey. "Conrad and Roger Casement." *Conradiana* 5 (1973): 64–69.

Moser, Thomas. *Joseph Conrad: Achievement and Decline*. Cambridge, Mass.: Harvard UP, 1957.

Palmer, John A. "*Victory*—The Existential Affirmation." *Joseph Conrad's Fiction: A Study in Literary Growth*. Ithaca: Cornell UP, 1968. 166–97.

Parins, James W., Robert J. Dilligan, and Todd K. Bender. *A Concordance to Conrad's Victory*. New York: Garland, 1979.

Park, Douglas B. "Conrad's *Victory:* The Anatomy of a Pose." *Nineteenth-Century Studies* 31 (1976): 150–69.

Parry, Benita. *Conrad and Imperialism: Ideological Boundaries and Visionary Frontiers*. London: Macmillan, 1983.

Raval, Suresh. "Conrad's *Victory:* Skepticism and Experience." *Nineteenth-Century Fiction* 34.4 (1980): 414–33.

Sherry, Norman, ed. *Conrad: The Critical Heritage*. London, Boston: Routledge and Kegan Paul, 1973.

Tanner, Tony. " 'Gnawed Bones' and 'Artless Tales' —Eating and Narrative in Conrad." *Joseph Conrad: A Commemoration*. Ed. Norman Sherry. London: Macmillan, 1976. 17–36.

———. "Joseph Conrad and the Last Gentleman." *Critical Quarterly* 28.1–2 (1986): 109–42.

Watts, Cedric. *The Deceptive Text: An Introduction to Covert Plots*. Brighton: Harvester, 1984. 99–110.

Willy, T. G. "Measures of the Heart and of the Darkness: Conrad and the Suicides of New Imperialism." *Conradiana* 14.3 (1982): 189–98.

Ronald Firbank

Aercke, Kristiaan P. "Two Decadents' Fragrant Prayers." *Neohelicon: Acta Comparationis Litterarum Universarum* (Budapest) 15.1 (1988): 263–74.

Alford, Norman W. "Seven Notebooks of Ronald Firbank." *Library Chronicle of the University of Texas, Austin* 8.3 (1967): 33–39.

Barnhill, Sarah. "Method in Madness: Ronald Firbank's *The Flower Beneath the Foot*." *English Literature in Transition* 32.3 (1989): 291–300.

Benkovitz, Miriam J. *A Bibliography of Ronald Firbank*. London: Hart-Davis, 1963.

———. *Ronald Firbank: A Biography*. New York: Knopf, 1969.

Braybrooke, Neville. "Thorns and Vanities: Ronald Firbank Revisited." *Encounter* 31.3 (1968): 66–74.

Brooke, Jocelyn. *Ronald Firbank.* New York: Roy, 1951.

Brophy, Brigid. *Prancing Novelist: A Defence of Fiction in the Form of a Critical Biography in Praise of Ronald Firbank.* London: Macmillan, 1973.

Davies, Paul. " 'The Power to Convey the Unuttered': Style and Sexuality in the Work of Ronald Firbank." *Lesbian and Gay Writing: An Anthology of Critical Essays.* Ed. Mark Lily. London: Macmillan, 1990. 199–214.

Davis, Robert Murray. "Hyperaesthesia with Complications: The World of Ronald Firbank." *Rendezvous* 3.1 (1968): 5–15.

Firbank, Ronald. *The Complete Firbank.* London: Duckworth, 1961.

Fletcher, Ifan Kyrle. *Ronald Firbank: A Memoir.* London: Duckworth, 1930.

Forster, E. M. "Ronald Firbank." 1929. *Abinger Harvest.* Harmondsworth: Penguin, 1967. 129–35.

Hollinghurst, Alan. "The Creative Uses of Homosexuality in the Novels of E. M. Forster, Ronald Firbank, and L. P. Hartley." Unpublished M.Litt thesis. Oxford: Bodleian Library, 1980.

Horder, M., ed. *Ronald Firbank: Memoirs and Critiques.* London: Duckworth, 1977.

Irwin, W. R. *The Game of the Impossible: A Rhetoric of Fantasy.* Urbana: U of Illinois P, 1976.

Kiernan, Robert F. "Aestheticism Empurpled: Ronald Firbank." *Frivolity Unbound: Six Masters of the Camp Novel: Thomas Peacock, Max Beerbohm, Ronald Firbank, E. F. Benson, P. G. Wodehouse, Ivy Compton-Burnett.* New York: Continuum, 1990. 49–65.

Merritt, James Douglas. *Ronald Firbank.* New York: Twayne, 1969.

Potoker, Edward Martin. *Ronald Firbank.* New York: Columbia UP, 1969.

Ross, Andrew. "Uses of Camp." *No Respect: Intellectuals and Popular Culture.* New York: Routledge, 1989. 135–70.

Seidel, Michael. *Exile and the Narrative Imagination.* New Haven: Yale UP, 1986.

Sontag, Susan. "Notes on Camp." *Against Interpretation and Other Essays.* London: André Deutsch, 1964. 275–92.

Woodward, A. G. "Ronald Firbank." *English Studies in Africa* 11 (1968): 1–9.

E. M. Forster

Adams, Stephen. "Only Connect: E. M. Forster and J. R. Ackerley." *The Homosexual as Hero in Contemporary Fiction.* London: Vision, 1980. 106–30.

Annan, Noël. "Love Story." *New York Review of Books* 17.6 (October 21, 1971): 12–19.

Bharucha, Rustom. "Forster's Friends." *Raritan* 5.4 (1986): 105–22.

Doherty, Gerald. "White Circles/Black Holes: Worlds of Difference in *A Passage to India.*" *Orbis Litterarum* 46 (1991): 105–22.

Editorial. "A Canker in Imperial Administration." *The Spectator* (December 12, 1908): 980–81.

Finkelstein, Bonnie Blumenthal. *Forster's Women: Eternal Differences.* New York: Columbia UP, 1975.

Fletcher, John. "Forster's Self-erasure: *Maurice* and the Scene of Masculine Love."

Sexual Sameness: Textual Differences in Lesbian and Gay Writing. Ed. Joseph
Bristow. New York: Routledge, 1992. 64–90.

Forster, E. M. *The Longest Journey.* 1907. Harmondsworth: Penguin, 1988.

———. *Howards End.* 1910. Harmondsworth: Penguin, 1954.

———. *Maurice: A Romance.* 1913–14; 1971. Harmondsworth: Penguin, 1987.

———. "Kanaya." c. 1922. *Hill of Devi and Other Indian Writings.* Ed. E. Heine.
London: Arnold, 1983. 310–24.

———. "Reflections in India I: Too Late?" *Nation and Athenæum* 30.17 (January 21,
1922): 641b.

———. *A Passage to India.* 1924. Harmondsworth: Penguin, 1984.

———. "Fantasy." *Aspects of the Novel.* 1927. Harmondsworth: Penguin, 1990.
101–15.

———. "The New Censorship." *Nation and Athenæum* 43 (September 1, 1928): 696.

———. "The 'Censorship' of Books." *The Nineteenth Century and After* 105 (1929):
444–45.

———. *Abinger Harvest.* 1936. Harmondsworth: Penguin, 1967.

———. *Collected Short Stories.* 1947. Harmondsworth: Penguin, 1954.

———. *Two Cheers for Democracy.* London: Arnold, 1951.

———. *Albergo Empedocle and Other Writings.* Ed. George H. Thomson. New
York: Liveright, 1971.

———. *The Life to Come and Other Stories.* 1972. Harmondsworth: Penguin, 1989.

———. *Arctic Summer and Other Fiction.* London: Edward Arnold, 1980.

———. *Selected Letters of E. M. Forster: 1879–1920.* Vol 1. Ed. Mary Lago and P. N.
Furbank. London: Collins, 1983.

———. *Diary.* Unpublished manuscript. Cambridge: King's College Library.

Gardner, Philip, ed. *Forster: The Critical Heritage.* London, Boston: Routledge and
Kegan Paul, 1973.

Hampshire, Stuart. "*The Cave and the Mountain: A Study of E. M. Forster* by
W. Stone," *The New York Review of Books* VI.8 (May 12, 1966): 14–16.

Herz, Judith Scherer. "From Myth to Scripture: An Approach to Forster's Later
Short Fiction." *English Literature in Transition* 24.4 (1981): 206–12.

———. *The Short Narratives of E. M. Forster.* New York: St. Martin's, 1988.

———, and Robert K. Martin, ed. *E. M. Forster: Centenary Revaluations.* London:
Macmillan, 1982.

Hynes, Samuel. "A Chalice for Youth." *Times Literary Supplement* 3,632 (October 8,
1971): 1215–16.

Kipnis, Laura. "The Phantom Twitchings of an Amputated Limb: Sexual Spectacle
in the Post-Colonial Epic." *Wide Angle* 11.4 (1989): 42–51.

Lawrence, D. H. *Aaron's Rod.* 1922. Harmondsworth: Penguin, 1976.

———. *The Letters of D. H. Lawrence.* Vol. 2. Ed. George J. Zytaruk and James T.
Boulton. Cambridge: Cambridge UP, 1981.

Letters. *Times* (January 8, 1909): 15.

Martin, Robert K. "Edward Carpenter and the Double Structure of *Maurice.*" *Literary Visions of Homosexuality.* Ed. Stuart Kellog. New York: Haworth, 1983.
35–46.

"Minutes of Evidence." *Report of the Select Committee on Obscene Publications.*
London: HMSO, 1958. 15–18.

Page, Norman. *E. M. Forster's Posthumous Fiction.* Victoria, B.C.: U of Victoria P, 1977.

Perry Levine, June. "The Tame in Pursuit of the Savage: The Posthumous Fiction of E. M. Forster." *PMLA* 99.1 (1984): 72–88.

Rahman, Tariq. "E. M. Forster and the Break Away from the Ephebophilic Literary Tradition." *Études anglaises* 40.3 (1987): 267–78.

Salter, Donald. "That Is My Ticket: The Homosexual Writings of E. M. Forster." *London Magazine* 14.6 (1975): 5–53.

Sayre Martin, John. *E. M. Forster: The Endless Journey.* Cambridge: Cambridge UP, 1976.

Shusterman, David. *The Quest for Certitude in E. M. Forster's Fiction.* New York: Haskell House, 1973.

Steiner, George. "Under the Greenwood Tree." *The New Yorker* 47 (October 9, 1971): 158–69.

Stone, Wilfred. "Overleaping Class: Forster's Problem in Connection." *Modern Language Quarterly* 39 (1978): 386–404.

Toynbee, Philip. "Forster's Love Story." *Observer Review* (October 10, 1971): 32.

Welty, Eudora. "The Life to Come." *New York Times Review of Books* (May 13, 1973): 27–30.

Woolf, Virginia. *The Death of the Moth and Other Essays.* New York: Harcourt, Brace and World, 1938.

———. *Collected Essays.* Vol. 1 Ed. Leonard Woolf. London: Chatto and Windus, 1967.

H. Rider Haggard

Bartowski, Fran. "Travelers v. Ethnics: Discourses of Displacement." *Discourse* 15.3 (1993): 158–76.

Bass, Jeff D. "The Romance as Rhetorical Dissociation: The Purification of Imperialism in *King Solomon's Mines.*" *The Quarterly Journal of Speech* 67.3 (1981): 259–69.

———, and Richard Cherwitz. "Imperial Mission and Manifest Destiny: A Case Study of Political Myth in Rhetorical Discourse." *Southern Speech Communication Journal* 43 (1978): 213–32.

Baym, Nina. "Melodramas of Beset Manhood: How Theories of American Fiction Exclude Women Authors." *American Quarterly* 33.2 (1981): 123–39.

Bunn, David. "Embodying Africa: Woman and Romance in Colonial Fiction." *English in Africa* 15.1 (1966): 1–26.

Chrisman, Laura. "The Imperial Unconscious?: Representations of Imperial Discourse." *Critical Quarterly* 32.3 (1990): 38–58.

Crawford, Claudia. "She." *SubStance* 29 (1981): 83–96.

De Moor, Marysa. "Andrew Lang's Letters to H. Rider Haggard: The Record of a Harmonious Relationship." *Études anglaises* 40.3 (1987): 313–22.

Ellis, Peter Berresford. *H. Rider Haggard: A Voice from the Infinite.* London, Boston: Routledge and Kegan Paul, 1978.

Epstein, Sir Jacob. *Epstein: An Autobiography.* New York: Dutton, 1955.

Etherington, Norman. "South African Sources of Rider Haggard's Early Romances."
   Notes and Queries 24 (1977): 436–38.
———. "Rider Haggard, Imperialism, and the Layered Personality." *Victorian
   Studies* 22.1 (1978): 71–87.
———. *Rider Haggard.* Boston: Twayne, 1984.
Gilbert, Sandra M., and Susan Gubar. "Heart of Darkness: The Agon of the Femme
   Fatale." *No Man's Land: The Place of the Woman Writer in the Twentieth
   Century.* Vol. 2. *Sexchanges.* New Haven: Yale UP, 1989. 3–46.
Haggard, H. Rider. *King Solomon's Mines.* 1885. Oxford: Oxford UP, 1989.
———. *She: A History of Adventure.* 1887. Oxford: Oxford UP, 1991.
———. *Allan Quatermain.* London: Longman, Green, 1887.
———. "About Fiction." *The Contemporary Review* 2 (February 1887): 172–80.
———. *Eric Brighteyes.* London: Longman, Green, 1891.
———. *Nada the Lily.* London: Longman, Green, 1892.
———. Introduction to *Monomotapa (Rhodesia): Its Monuments, and Its History
   from the Most Ancient Times to the Present Century.* A. Wilmot. London:
   Fisher Unwin, 1896. xvii–xix.
Hartley, L. P. *The Go-Between.* London: Hamish Hamilton, 1953.
Hinz, Evelyn J. "Rider Haggard's *She:* An Archetypal 'History of Adventure.' "
   Studies in the Novel 4 (1972): 416–31.
Katz, Wendy R. *Rider Haggard and the Fiction of Empire: A Critical Study of British
   Imperial Fiction.* Cambridge: Cambridge UP, 1987.
le Carré, John. *Tinker, Tailor, Soldier, Spy.* New York: Knopf, 1974.
McClintock, Anne. "Maidens, Maps and Mines: *King Solomon's Mines* and the
   Reinvention of Patriarchy in Colonial South Africa." *Women and Gender in
   Southern Africa to 1945.* Ed. Cheryl Walker. Cape Town: David Philip, 1990.
   97–124.
Minter, William. *King Solomon's Mines Revisited.* New York: Basic, 1986.
Munich, Adrienne Auslander. "Queen Victoria, Empire, and Excess." *Tulsa Studies
   in Women's Literature* 6.2 (1987): 265–81.
Patteson, Richard F. "*King Solomon's Mines:* Imperialism and Narrative Structure."
   Journal of Narrative Technique 8 (1978): 112–23.
Pittock, Murray. "Rider Haggard and *Heart of Darkness.*" *Conradiana* 19.3 (1967):
   206–8.
Scheick, William J. "Adolescent Pornography and Imperialism in Haggard's *King
   Solomon's Mines.*" *English Literature in Transition* 34.1 (1991): 19–30.
Siegel, Carol. "Male Masochism and the Colonialist Impulse: Mary Webb's Return
   of the Native Tess." *Novel* 24.2 (1991): 131–46.
Stott, Rebecca. "The Dark Continent: Africa as Female Body in Haggard's
   Adventure Fiction." *Feminist Review* 32 (1989): 69–89.
Vasbinder, Samuel H. "Aspects of Fantasy in Literary Myths about Lost Civilisa-
   tions." *The Aesthetics of Fantasy Literature and Art.* Ed. Roger C. Schlobin.
   Brighton: Harvester, 1982. 192–210.

Henry James

Cameron, Sharon. *Thinking in Henry James.* Chicago: U of Chicago P, 1989.

Felman, Shoshana. "Turning the Screw of Interpretation." *Literature and Psychoanalysis: The Question of Reading — Otherwise.* Ed. Felman. Baltimore: Johns Hopkins UP, 1977. 94–208.

Funston, Judith E. "James's Portrait of the Artist as Liar." *Studies in Short Fiction* 26.4 (1989): 431–38.

Getz, Thomas H. "The Self-Portrait in the Portrait: John Ashbery's 'Self-Portrait in a Convex Mirror' and James's 'The Liar.' " *Studies in the Humanities* 13.1 (1986): 42–51.

James, Henry. "The Art of Fiction." 1884. *Henry James: Selected Literary Criticism.* Ed. Morris Shapira. New York: Horizon, 1981. 49–67.

———. "The Liar." 1888. *The Complete Tales of Henry James.* Vol. 6 (1884–1888). Ed. Leon Edel. London: Hart-Davis, 1963. 383–441.

———. *The Tragic Muse.* 1890. Harmondsworth: Penguin, 1978.

———. "The Pupil." 1891. *The Turn of the Screw and Other Stories.* Harmondsworth: Penguin, 1983. 123–70.

———. "The Beast in the Jungle." 1903. *The Jolly Corner and Other Stories.* Ed. Roger Gard. Harmondsworth: Penguin, 1990. 64–107.

———. "The Jolly Corner." 1908. *The Jolly Corner and Other Stories.* Ed. Roger Gard. Harmondsworth: Penguin, 1990. 161–93.

James, William. "The Hidden Self." *Scribner's Magazine* 7 (Jan.–June 1890): 361–73.

Ron, Moshe. "The Art of the Portrait According to James." *Yale French Studies* 69 (1985): 222–37.

Sedgwick, Eve Kosofsky. "The Beast in the Closet: James and the Writing of Homosexual Panic." *Epistemology of the Closet.* Berkeley: U of California P, 1990. 182–212.

Silverman, Kaja. "Too Early/Too Late: Subjectivity and the Primal Scene in Henry James." *Novel* 21.2–3 (1988): 147–73.

White, Allon. " 'The Deterrent Fact': Vulgarity and Obscurity in James." *The Uses of Obscurity: The Fiction of Early Modernism.* London, Boston: Routledge and Kegan Paul, 1981. 130–62.

Rudyard Kipling

Achar, Radha. "The Child in Kipling's Fiction: An Analysis." *The Literary Criterion* 22.4 (1987): 46–53.

Brock, Michael. "Outside His Art: Rudyard Kipling in Politics." *Essays by Divers Hands: Being the Transactions of the Royal Society of Literature.* Ed. Richard Faber. London: Boydell, 1988.

Buchanan, Robert. "The Voice of the Hooligan." *Contemporary Review* 76 (1899): 775–89.

Carrington, Charles E. *Rudyard Kipling: His Life and Work.* London: Macmillan, 1955.

Caserio, Robert L. "Kipling in the Light of Failure." *Grand Street* 5.4 (1986): 179–212.

Croft-Cooke, Rupert. *Kipling.* London: Home and Van Thal, 1948.

Crook, Nora. *Kipling's Myths of Love and Death.* London: Macmillan, 1989.

Cust, Robert Needham. *Pictures of Indian Life: Sketched with the Pen from 1852–1881.* London: Trubner, 1881.

Edwardes, Sir Herbert, and Herman Merivale. *Life of Sir Henry Lawrence.* Vol. 2. London: Smith, Elder, 1872.

Eliot, T. S. Introduction to *A Choice of Kipling's Verse.* London: Faber, 1941.

Holmes, T. Rice. *A History of the Indian Mutiny.* London: Macmillan, 1904.

Islam, Shamsul. *Kipling's "Law."* London: Macmillan, 1975.

Karim, M. "Rudyard Kipling and the Lodge Hope and Perseverance." *Kipling Journal* 189 (1974): 4–12.

Kipling, Rudyard. *Plain Tales from the Hills.* 1890. Harmondsworth: Penguin, 1987.

———. *Life's Handicap: Being Stories of Mine Own People.* 1891. Harmondsworth: Penguin, 1988.

———. *The Light That Failed.* 1891. Harmondsworth: Penguin, 1988.

———. *Wee Willie Winkie.* 1895. London: Macmillan, 1918.

———. *Stalky & Co.* 1899. London: Macmillan, 1952.

———. *Soldiers Three: The Story of the Gadsbys in Black and White.* London: Macmillan, 1899.

———. *Kim.* 1901. Harmondsworth: Penguin, 1989.

———. *Many Inventions.* London: Macmillan, 1909.

———. *A Song of the English.* London: Hodder and Stoughton, 1909.

———. *A Diversity of Creatures.* 1917. Harmondsworth: Penguin, 1987.

———. *A Book of Words: Selections from Speeches and Addresses Delivered Between 1906 and 1927.* London: Macmillan, 1928.

———. *Something of Myself, for My Friends Known and Unknown.* 1936. Harmondsworth: Penguin, 1988.

———. *Rudyard Kipling's Verse: Definitive Edition.* London: Hodder and Stoughton, 1943.

———. *Rudyard Kipling: Selected Verse.* Ed. James Cochrane. Harmondsworth: Penguin, 1977.

———. *Kipling: Interviews and Recollections.* Vol. 2. Ed. H. Orel. Totowa, NJ: Barnes and Noble, 1982.

———. *Early Verse by Rudyard Kipling, 1879–1889.* Ed. Andrew Rutherford. Oxford: Clarendon, 1986.

———. *A Choice of Kipling Prose.* Ed. Craig Raine. London: Faber, 1987.

Lawrence, Walter. *The India We Served.* Boston: Houghton, Mifflin, 1929.

Mallett, Phillip, ed. *Kipling Considered.* London: Macmillan, 1989.

McClure, John A. *Kipling and Conrad: The Colonial Fiction.* Cambridge, Mass.: Harvard UP, 1981.

———. "Problematic Presence: The Colonial Other in Kipling and Conrad." *The Black Presence in English Literature.* Ed. David Dabydeen. Manchester: Manchester UP, 1985. 154–67.

Mohanty, Satya P. "Drawing the Color Line: Kipling and the Culture of Colonial Rule." *The Bounds of Race: Perspectives on Hegemony and Resistance.* Ed. Dominick LaCapra. Ithaca: Cornell UP, 1991. 311–43.

Moore-Gilbert, B. J. "Rudyard Kipling: Writing and Control." *Literature and Imperialism*. Ed. B. J. Moore-Gilbert. Guilford: U of Surrey P, 1983. 93–117.

———. *Kipling and "Orientalism."* London: Croom Helm, 1986.

Moss, Robert F. *Rudyard Kipling and the Fiction of Adolescence*. London: Macmillan, 1982.

Paffard, Mark. *Kipling's Indian Fiction*. London: Macmillan, 1989.

Parry, Benita. "The Content and Discontent of Kipling's Imperialism." *New Formations* 6 (1988): 49–64.

Pinney, Thomas, ed. *Kipling's India: Uncollected Sketches 1884–88*. London: Macmillan, 1986.

Rai, A. "Colonial Fictions—Orwell's Burmese Days." *Economic and Political Weekly* 18.5 (1983): 47–52.

Ramachandran, C. N. "Kipling as the Chronicler of the Empire: Ambivalences and Archetypes." *The Literary Criterion* 22.4 (1987): 12–21.

Rao, K. Raghavendra. "Collective Identity in Kipling's *Kim:* Deconstructing Imperialism." *The Literary Criterion* 22.4 (1987): 22–30.

Ross, Angus, ed. *Kipling 86*. Conference Papers. Falmer, Sussex: U of Sussex Library, 1987.

Rutherford, Andrew, ed. *Kipling's Mind and Art*. London: Oliver and Boyd, 1964.

Said, Edward W. "*Kim:* The Pleasures of Imperialism." *Raritan* 7.2 (1987): 27–64.

Seed, David. "Disorientation and Commitment in the Fiction of Empire: Kipling and Orwell." *Dutch Quarterly Review of Anglo-American Letters* 14.4 (1984): 269–80.

Seymour-Smith, Martin. *Rudyard Kipling*. London: Queen Anne, 1989.

Smith, R. Bosworth. *Life of Lord Lawrence*. Vol. 2. New York: Scribner's, 1885.

Solomon, Eric. "Notes Toward a Definition of the Colonial Novel." *North Dakota Quarterly* 57.3 (1989): 16–23.

Stephen, James Fitzjames. *Liberty, Equality, Fraternity*. London: Smith, Elder, 1874.

Sullivan, Zohreh T. "Kipling the Nightwalker." *Modern Fiction Studies* 30.2 (1984): 217–35.

———. "Memory and the Colonial Self in Kipling's Autobiography." *Prose Studies* 12.1 (1989): 72–89.

Tompkins, Joyce M. S. *The Art of Rudyard Kipling*. Lincoln: U of Nebraska P, 1965.

Wilson, Angus. *The Strange Ride of Rudyard Kipling: His Life and Works*. London: Panther, 1979.

Woolf, Virginia. *A Room of One's Own*. 1929. London: Panther, 1984.

Wurgraft, Lewis D. *The Imperial Imagination: Magic and Myth in Kipling's India*. Middleton, Conn.: Wesleyan UP, 1983.

A. E. W. Mason

Green, Roger Lancelyn. *A. E. W. Mason*. London: Max Parrish, 1952.

Mason, A. E. W. *The Philanderers*. 1897. London: Hodder and Stoughton, 1926.

———. *The Four Feathers*. 1902. London: Smith, Elder, and Co., 1907.

———. *The Broken Road*. 1907. London: Hodder and Stoughton, 1924.

W. Somerset Maugham

Allen, Walter. "The Novel from 1881 to 1914." *The English Novel: A Short Critical History*. London: Phoenix House, 1954. 312–15.

Amis, Kingsley. "Mr. Maugham's Notions." *The Spectator* (July 7, 1961): 23–24.

Archer, Stanley. "Artists and Paintings in Maugham's *Of Human Bondage*." *English Literature in Transition* 14 (1971): 181–89.

Benson, A. C. *Memoirs of Arthur Hamilton BA of Trinity College, Cambridge, Extracted from His Letters and Diaries by His Friend Christopher Carr of the Same College*. London: Kegan Paul, Trench, 1886.

Braendlin, Bonnie Hoover. "The Prostitute as Scapegoat: Mildred Rogers in Somerset Maugham's *Of Human Bondage*." *The Image of the Prostitute in Modern Literature*. Ed. Pierre L. Horn and Mary Beth Pringle. New York: Frederick Ungar, 1984. 9–18.

Brion, Marcel. "Les 'carnets' de Somerset Maugham." *Revue des deux mondes* (août 15, 1950): 741–49.

Buckley, Jerome Hamilton. "Of Bondage and Freedom: Later Novels of Youth." *Season of Youth: The Bildungsroman from Dickens to Golding*. Cambridge, Mass.: Harvard UP, 1974. 248–55.

Burt, Forrest D. "William Somerset Maugham: An Adlerian Interpretation." *Journal of Individual Psychology* 26 (1970): 64–82.

Connolly, Cyril. *Enemies of Promise*. 1938. London: André Deutsch, 1973.

Curtis, Anthony, and John Whitehead, eds. *W. Somerset Maugham: The Critical Heritage*. London, Boston: Routledge and Kegan Paul, 1987.

Dobrinsky, Joseph. "The Dialectics of Art and Life in *Of Human Bondage*." *Cahiers victoriens et édouardiens* 22 (1985): 33–55.

———. "Les non-dits de la psychologie amoreuse dans *Of Human Bondage*." *Études anglaises* 41.1 (1988): 37–47.

Doren, Carl Van. "Tom Jones and Philip Carey: Heroes of Two Centuries." *The Century Magazine* 110 (1925): 115–20.

Dreiser, Theodore. "As a Realist Sees It." *New Republic* (December 25, 1915): 202.

French, Philip. "The Stammerer as Hero." *Encounter* 27 (1966): 67–75.

Frierson, William C. *The English Novel in Transition: 1885–1940*. New York: Cooper Square, 1965. 174–77.

Harris, Wendell V. "Molly's 'Yes': The Transvaluation of Sex in Modern Fiction." *Texas Studies in Literature and Language* 10 (1968–69): 107–18.

Howe, Susanne. "Meredith and the Moderns." *Wilhelm Meister and His English Kinsmen*. New York: Columbia UP, 1930. 287–90.

Lowes Dickinson, G. *The Autobiography of G. Lowes Dickinson and Other Unpublished Writings*. Ed. Dennis Proctor. London: Duckworth, 1973.

Mansfield, Katherine. "Inarticulations." *Nation and Athenæum* (May 9, 1919): 302.

Maugham, Robin. *Somerset and All the Maughams*. London: Longman, 1966.

Maugham, W. Somerset. *The Explorer: A Melodrama in Four Acts*. 1908. London: Heinemann, 1912.

———. *Of Human Bondage*. 1915. London: Mandarin, 1990.

———. *The Moon and Sixpence*. 1919. London: Mandarin, 1990.

————. *The Summing Up.* 1938. New York: New American Library, 1964.

————. *A Writer's Notebook.* 1949. London: Pan, 1978.

————. "Of Human Bondage with a Digression on the Art of Fiction: An Address by W. Somerset Maugham, April 20, 1946." *The Maugham Enigma.* Ed. Klaus W. Jonas. New York: Citadel, 1954. 121–28.

————. *A Traveller in Romance: Uncollected Writings 1901–1964.* Ed. John Whitehead. London: Anthony Blond, 1984.

Melville, Herman. *Billy Budd, Sailor.* 1891. *Billy Budd, Sailor and Other Stories.* Harmondsworth: Penguin, 1983. 317–409.

Nichols, Beverley. *A Case of Human Bondage.* London: Secker, 1966.

Pritchett, V. S. "Man of the World." *New Statesman* (December 24, 1965): 1008.

Routh, H. V. "Leading Interpreters of the InterWar Period: William Somerset Maugham." *English Literature and Ideas in the Twentieth Century.* London: Methuen, 1946. 146–153.

Schoenburg, Arnold. *Moses and Aron.* London: Friends of Covent Garden, 1965.

Sontag, Susan. *Illness as Metaphor.* Harmondsworth: Penguin, 1983.

Swinnerton, Frank. "William Somerset Maugham." *The Georgian Literary Scene: A Panorama.* London: Heinemann, 1935. 208–215.

Wittgenstein, Ludwig. *Tractatus Logico-Philosophicus.* London: Kegan Paul, Trench, Trubner, 1922.

H. H. Munro (pseud. Saki)

Hartwell, Ronald. "Fallen Timbers—A Death Trap: A Comparison of Bierce and Munro." *Research Studies* 49.1 (1981): 61–66.

Lambert, J. W. Introduction to *The Bodley Head Saki.* London: Bodley Head, 1980. 7–62.

Langguth, A. J. *Saki: A Life of Hector Hugh Munro.* Oxford: Oxford UP, 1982.

Larreya, Paul. "Pragmatique linguistique et analyse de discours: L'implicite dans Wratislav, de Saki." *Reserches anglaises et americaines* 17 (1984): 95–107.

Lewis, Wyndham. *The Art of Being Ruled.* London: Chatto and Windus, 1926.

Munro, H. H. (pseud. Saki.) *The Westminster Alice.* 1902. New York: Viking, 1929.

————. "The Political Jungle Book." *Westminster Gazette.* (Feb. 11, 1902): 1–2.

————. "Not So Stories." *Westminster Gazette* (Oct. 15, 1902): 1–2; (Nov. 5, 1902): 1–2.

————. *The Complete Saki.* Harmondsworth: Penguin, 1982.

Orel, Harold. "H. H. Munro and the Sense of a Failed Community." *Modern British Literature* 4.2 (1979): 87–96.

Porterfield, Alexander. "Saki." *London Mercury* XII.70 (Aug. 1925): 385–94.

Stern, Simon. "Saki's Attitude." *GLQ: A Journal of Lesbian and Gay Studies* 1.3 (1994): 275–98.

Cecil Rhodes

Flint, John. *Cecil Rhodes.* London: Hutchinson, 1976.

Fryde, Robin. "Cecil Rhodes and Paul Valéry." *Quarterly Bulletin of South African Liberation* 35 (1960): 68–69.

Marlowe, J. *Cecil Rhodes: The Anatomy of Empire*. London: Elek, 1972.

Millin, S. G. *Rhodes*. London: Chatto, 1933.

Rotberg, R. I., and M. F. Shore. *The Founder: Cecil Rhodes and the Pursuit of Power*. Oxford: Oxford UP, 1988.

Shepperton, G. "C. J. Rhodes: Some Biographical Problems." *South African Historical Journal* 15 (1983): 53–67.

Shore, Miles F. "Cecil Rhodes and the Ego Ideal." *Journal of Interdisciplinary History* 10.2 (1979): 249–65.

Siegfried Sassoon

Blunden, Edmund. *Undertones of War*. London: Cobden-Sanderson, 1928.

Burgess, Keith. "The Domestic Impact of Imperialism in Britain: 1880–1910." *Literature and Imperialism*. Ed. Bart Moore-Gilbert. Guilford: U of Surrey P, 1983. 48–68.

Craig, David, and Michael Egan. "Literature and Crisis." *Extreme Situations: Literature and Crisis from the Great War to the Atom Bomb*. London: Macmillan, 1979. 1–63.

Delaney, Paul. *The Neo-Pagans: Friendship and Love in the Rupert Brooke Circle*. London: Macmillan, 1987.

Douglas, Mary. *Purity and Danger: An Analysis of the Concept of Pollution and Taboo*. New York: Praeger, 1966.

Eliot, T. S. "Tradition and the Individual Talent." 1917. *Selected Essays*. London: Faber, 1932. 13–22.

———. *The Complete Poems and Plays of T. S. Eliot*. London: Faber, 1969.

Ferenczi, Sándor, ed. *Psychoanalysis and the War Neuroses*. London: International Psycho-Analytical, 1921.

Ferguson, Frances. "The Nuclear Sublime." *Diacritics* 14.2 (1984): 4–10.

Field, Frank. *British and French Writers of the First World War: Comparative Studies in Cultural History*. Cambridge: Cambridge UP, 1991.

Frye, Northrop. "Myth, Fiction, and Displacement." *Fables of Identity: Studies in Poetic Mythology*. New York: Harcourt, Brace and World, 1963. 21–38.

Gilbert, Sandra M., and Susan Gubar. "Soldier's Heart: Literary Men, Literary Women, and the Great War." *No Man's Land: The Place of the Woman Writer in the Twentieth Century*. Vol. 2: *Sexchanges*. New Haven: Yale UP, 1989. 258–323.

Gregson, J. M. "Siegfried Sassoon: Disillusion and Anger." *Poetry of the First World War*. London: Edward Arnold, 1976. 29–40.

Hibberd, Dominic. "Some Notes on Sassoon's *Counter-Attack and Other Poems*." *Notes and Queries* 29.227.4 (1982): 341–42.

Hughes, Thomas. *Tom Brown's Schooldays*. 1857. London: Dent, 1899.

Hynes, Samuel. "The Irony and the Pity." *Times Literary Supplement* (December 18, 1981): 1469.

James, William. "The Moral Equivalent of War." 1910. *Essays in Religion and Morality*. Cambridge, Mass.: Harvard UP, 1982. 162–73.

Jameson, Fredric. "From National Allegory to Libidinal Apparatus." *Fables of Aggression: Wyndham Lewis, The Modernist as Fascist*. Berkeley: U of California P, 1979. 87–104.

Jerrold, Douglas. *The Lie about the War: A Note on Some Contemporary War Books.* London: Faber, 1930.

Knox, Bernard. "Siegfried Sassoon." *Grand Street* 2.4 (1983): 140–51.

Lane, Arthur E. *An Adequate Response: The War Poetry of Wilfred Owen and Siegfried Sassoon.* Detroit: Wayne State UP, 1972.

Leed, Eric. *No Man's Land: Contact and Identity in World War I.* Cambridge: Cambridge UP, 1979.

Leffler, Konnie. "Sassoon's 'Repression of War Experience.' " *Explicator* 45.3 (1987): 45–47.

Mangan, J. A. *Athleticism in the Victorian and Edwardian Public School: The Emergence and Consolidation of an Educational Ideology.* Cambridge: Cambridge UP, 1981.

———. " 'The Grit of Our Forefathers': Invented Traditions, Propaganda and Imperialism." *Imperialism and Popular Culture.* Ed. John M. Mackenzie. Manchester: Manchester UP, 1986. 113–39.

Marcus, Jane. "Corpus/Corps/Corpse: Writing the Body in/at War." *Arms and the Woman: War, Gender, and Literary Representation.* Ed. Helen M. Cooper, Adrienne Auslander Munich, and Susan Merril Squier. Chapel Hill: U of North Carolina P, 1989. 124–67.

Marr, H. C. *Psychoses of the War.* London: Henry Froude, 1919.

Moynahan, Julian. "Pastoralism as Culture and Counter-Culture in English Fiction, 1800–1928." *Novel* 6.1 (1972): 20–35.

Murry, John Middleton. *The Evolution of an Intellectual.* London: Cape, 1927.

Onions, John. *English Fiction and Drama of the Great War, 1918–39.* London: Macmillan, 1990.

Richards, Frank. *Old Soldiers Never Die.* London: Faber, 1933.

Rivers, W. H. R. *Instinct and the Unconscious.* 2d ed. Cambridge: Cambridge UP, 1922.

Rutherford, Andrew. "The Common Man as Hero: Literature of the Western Front." *The Literature of War: Studies in Heroic Virtue.* 2d rev. ed. London: Macmillan, 1989. 64–112.

Sassoon, Siegfried. *Memoirs of a Fox-Hunting Man.* 1928. London: Faber, 1989.

———. *Memoirs of an Infantry Officer.* 1930. London: Faber, 1991.

———. *Sherston's Progress.* London: Faber, 1940.

———. *The Weald of Youth.* 1942. London: Faber, 1986.

———. *Siegfried's Journey 1916–1956.* London: Faber, 1945.

———. *Collected Poems 1908–1956.* 1947. London: Faber, 1987.

———. *Diaries 1920–1922.* Ed. Rupert Hart-Davies. London: Faber, 1981.

Scarry, Elaine. "Injury and the Structure of War." *Representations* 10 (1985): 1–51.

Shawen, Edgar. "Sassoon's 'Attack.' " *Explicator* 42.1 (1983): 34.

Showalter, Elaine. "Male Hysteria: W. H. R. Rivers and the Lessons of Shell Shock." *The Female Malady: Women, Madness and English Culture, 1830–1980.* London: Virago, 1987. 167–94.

Thorpe, Michael. *Siegfried Sassoon: A Critical Study.* Oxford: Oxford UP, 1966.

Williams, Jeffrey C. "The Myth of the Lost Generation: The British War Poets and Their Modern Critics." *Clio* 12.1 (1982): 45–56.

Wordsworth, William. *Poetical Works*. Ed. Thomas Hutchinson. Oxford: Oxford UP, 1936.

Paul Scott

Boyer, Allen. "Love, Sex, and History in *The Raj Quartet*." *Modern Language Quarterly* 46.1 (1985): 64–80.

Degi, Bruce J. "Paul Scott's Indian National Army: *The Mark of the Warrior* and *The Raj Quartet*." *Clio* 18.1 (1988): 41–54.

Hitchens, Christopher. "A Sense of Mission: *The Raj Quartet*." *Grand Street* 4.2 (1985): 180–99.

McBratney, John. "The Raj is All the Rage: Paul Scott's *The Raj Quartet* and Colonial Nostalgia." *North Dakota Quarterly* 55.2 (1987): 204–9.

Petersone, Karina. "The Concept of History in Paul Scott's Tetralogy *The Raj Quartet*." *Zeitschrift-für-Anglistik-und-Amerikanistik, Leipzig* 37.3 (1989): 228–33.

Rao, K. Bhaskara. *Paul Scott*. Boston: Twayne, 1980.

Scanlan, Margaret. "The Disappearance of History: Paul Scott's *Raj Quartet*." *Clio* 15.2 (1986): 153–69.

Scott, Paul. *The Jewel in the Crown*. 1966. New York: Avon, 1979.

Shahane, Vasant A. "Kipling, Forster and Paul Scott: A Study in Sociological Imagination." *The Twofold Voice: Essays in Honor of Ramesh Mohan*. Ed. S. N. A. Rizvi. Salzburg: Salzburg UP, 1982.

Singh, Satya Brat. "Rudy Wiebe, Paul Scott and Salman Rushdie: Historians Distanced from History." *The Commonwealth Review, New Delhi* 1.2 (1990): 146–56.

Weinbaum, Francine S. "Psychological Defenses and Thwarted Union in *The Raj Quartet*." *Literature and Psychology* 31.2 (1981): 75–87.

Oscar Wilde

Cohen, Ed. "Writing Gone Wilde: Homoerotic Desire in the Closet of Representation." *PMLA* 102.5 (1987): 801–13.

Cohen, William A. "Willie and Wilde: Reading *The Portrait of Mr. W. H.*" *Displacing Homophobia: Gay Male Perspectives in Literature and Culture*. Ed. Ronald R. Butters, John M. Clum, and Michael Moon. Durham: Duke UP, 1989. 207–33.

Wilde, Oscar. "The Happy Prince." 1888. *The Complete Works of Oscar Wilde*. London: Collins, 1966. 285–91.

———. *The Portrait of Mr. W. H.* 1889. *The Riddle of Shakespeare's Sonnets*. Ed. E. Hubler et al. New York: Basic, 1962. 163–255.

———. *The Picture of Dorian Gray*. 1891. Harmondsworth: Penguin, 1982.

———. "Pen, Pencil and Poison: A Study in Green." 1891. *The Complete Works of Oscar Wilde*. London: Collins, 1966. 993–1008.

———. "The Truth of Masks: A Note on Illusion." 1891. *The Complete Works of Oscar Wilde*. London: Collins, 1966. 1060–78.

———, and others. *Teleny; or, The Reverse of the Medal.* 1893. Ed. John McRae. London: Gay Men's, 1986.

———. *De Profundis.* 1987. De Profundis *and Other Writings.* Harmondsworth: Penguin, 1954.

Index

Esprit de corps, 22. *See also* Camaraderie; Fraternity
Etherington, Norman, 60, 64–65
Eton, 55
Eurocentrism, 227
Evangelism, 59, 161. *See also* Christianity; Missionaries
Event, the, 80, 102, 116, 194, 197
"Evil," 124, 158, 168
Exile, 12, 63, 66–67, 171, 177, 226, 277 n. 22. *See also* Émigrés; Expatriates
Expatriates, 108, 119, 127. *See also* Émigrés
Exploration, 71, 127, 140–43
Expropriation, 14, 56

Failure, 1, 9, 55, 92, 114, 146, 154, 160–62, 167; homosexuality as masculine, 190; marital, 225; masculine, 222; of symbolic reference, 97, 149, 207
Familiarity, 63, 65
Family, 130; and repetition, 189; "romance" (Freud), 140; "values," 65
Fanon, Frantz, 55, 220
Fantasy: colonial, 6, 12, 15, 36, 40, 78, 80, 124, 147, 169, 177; as genre, 152–56, 175–77; group, 15, 63; and masculinity, 11, 85, 104, 117, 127; of "otherness," 164–65; problem of managing, 169; racial, 146, 172–75; sexual, 2, 9, 79, 96–97, 113, 172, 207; of unavailable woman, 136. *See also* Fascism; Race; Stereotype
Fascism, 215, 223; and fantasy, 24, 29, 218, 222–23, 233; fascination of, 223
Fathers, 53–54, 65, 102; and homosexuality, 137; and Law, 107–8, 189; legacy of, 109; and patricide, 121, 249 n. 57; precepts of, 104, 107, 109; retribution of, 110, 210. *See also* Affiliation; Paternal metaphor
Fatigue, 101, 105, 119
Female body, 57, 248 n. 30. *See also* Femininity; Women
Femininity, 134, 222; ideal of, 134; "mystique" of, 137
Ferenczi, Sándor, 138
Firbank, Ronald, 12, 22, 56, 176–92, 213, 222, 224, 227; *The Flower Beneath the Foot,* 181–82, 186, 227; *The New Rythum* [*sic*], 179; *Prancing*

Nigger, 179, 182–84, 227, 276 n. 17; *Santal,* 186–90, 227; *Vainglory,* 213; *Valmouth,* 180, 185, 188, 191
First World War, 12–13, 43, 50, 152, 194–95, 199, 205–6
Fixation, 116, 133. *See also* Condensation; Obsession; Projection
Fliess, Wilhelm, 138–39
Forster, E. M., 7, 12, 56, 145–57, 161–77, 186, 190; *Abinger Harvest,* 176; *Arctic Summer,* 150; *Aspects of the Novel,* 155, 177; "The Celestial Omnibus," 156–57; *The Celestial Omnibus,* 153; "The 'Censorship' of Books," 150; "The Curate's Friend," 157; diary of, 149; *The Eternal Moment,* 153; and female characters, 148; *Hill of Devi and Other Indian Writings,* 173; *Howards End,* 146, 148; and ideal, 146; on imperialism, 165; on "indecency," 204; "Kanaya," 173–74; "The Life to Come," 146, 157, 161–71, 173, 183, 186; *The Life to Come and Other Stories,* 146, 153, 155, 175; on literary "greats," 177; *The Longest Journey,* 148, 154, 261 n. 8; *Maurice,* 46, 148, 150–52, 157, 163–66, 171; *Nottingham Lace,* 150; "The Other Boat," 24, 146, 163–65, 171–74, 183, 186; "The Other Kingdom," 157; "The Other Side of the Hedge," 156; "outing" of, 147; *A Passage to India,* 146, 148–50, 152–57, 163–65, 172, 175, 271 n. 53; and politics, 146; and Siegfried Sassoon, 170, 203; "Story of a Panic," 156–57, 163, 169, 171, 217; on the "tame" and "savage," 163–64; on tolerance, 166; "What I Believe," 165–66, 170; *Where Angels Fear to Tread,* 148; and working class fantasy, 163–64
Foucault, Michel, 6
Fraternity, 21, 35, 66, 69, 71, 209–10; Forster's idealism of, 170. *See also* Camaraderie; Esprit de corps
Frears, Stephen, 233
French empire, 28, 157, 186
Freud, Sigmund, 3, 10–11, 31–33, 53, 136–39; on bisexuality, 138; *Civilization and Its Discontents,* 110; "The Dissection of the Psychical Person-

ality," 30; "Dostoevsky and Parricide," 137–38; on his dreams, 59; on drives, 53, 60, 125; *Group Psychology and the Analysis of the Ego,* 218; on homoeroticism, 136; *Inhibitions, Symptoms and Anxiety,* 31; "Instincts and Their Vicissitudes," 10, 125; on jealousy, 136; letter to Fliess, 138–39; on male homosexuality, 137; "Mourning and Melancholia," 232–33; on the negative oedipal relation, 137; "A Note upon the 'Mystic Writing-Pad,'" 86; on paranoia, 77; on parapraxes, 128; on people of mixed race, 274 n. 94; "The 'Rat Man,'" 10; "Repression," 3; "A Seventeenth-Century Demonological Neurosis," 137; "Some Neurotic Mechanisms in Jealousy, Paranoia and Homosexuality," 137; "A Special Type of Choice of Object Made by Men," 136–38; on stammers, 128; *Three Essays on the Theory of Sexuality,* 137–39; *Totem and Taboo,* 66

Friendship, 21, 25, 42, 69–73, 103, 130, 133–35, 153, 165, 171, 203, 224. *See also* Camaraderie; Homophilia

Gallop, Jane, 140
Garnett, Edward, 153
Gay: desire, 230–32; identity, 5. *See also* Drives; Homosexuality; Lesbianism
Genet, Jean, 185
"Gentleman," 90, 120, 124. *See also* Buccaneers
German empire, 28; and Germans, 205, 209–11, 220
Girard, René, 127
God, 29, 39, 43, 57, 162. *See also* Catholicism; Christianity
Graves, Robert, 194–95
Green, Roger Lancelyn, 49, 51
Greene, Graham, 199
Grenfell, Julian, 211
Guilt, 86–91, 104, 109–12, 123–28, 161, 211; and the white man, 157, 163–64; and the black man, 157, 163–64

Haggard, H. Rider, 12, 56–67, 71, 92, 160, 185; *Eric Brighteyes,* 60, 64;

feminist critiques of, 64; *Heart of the World,* 59; *King Solomon's Mines,* 31, 57–65; *Nada the Lily,* 56, 59–70; on psychoanalysis, 60; *She,* 31, 57–62
Hall, Radclyffe, 150; *The Well of Loneliness* (trial of), 150
Hampshire, Stuart, 172
Hardy, Thomas, 199, 203
Harris, Frank, 93; *Oscar Wilde, His Life and Confessions,* 93
Hartley, L. P.: *The Go-Between,* 63
Heaven, 170. *See also* Arcadia; Eden
Hedonism, 87. *See also* Enjoyment; *Jouissance;* Masculinity and pleasure
Heidegger, Martin, 92
Heidelberg, 141
Herz, Judith Scherer, 169
Heterosexuality, 19, 131; and "complacency," 135, 224–25; Freud on, 139; as imperative, 92, 148; as interruption of homophilia, 21, 29–30, 66, 69–70, 135; and masculinity, 144; as masquerade, 148, 224–25; and narrative closure, 125, 148–50; and "Nature," 6; as "recovery" from homosexuality, 52–54, 70; semiotics of, 225
Hierarchy, 33, 62
Hinduism, 159
History, 232; and distortion, 79–80
Hollinghurst, Alan, 177–78, 184–90, 229–31; *The Swimming-Pool Library,* 229–32
Holocaust, 199
Homoeroticism, 80, 117, 134, 138, 221; structural, 208. *See also* Homophilia; Homosexuality; Fraternity; Friendship
Homophilia, 12, 21–23, 30, 42, 56, 69–70, 130, 135, 146; Forster on, 164–65; Greek, 164; Neo-Hellenist revival of, 195; relation to homosexuality, 165. *See also* Friendship
Homophobia, 8, 69–70, 146, 171, 227, 247 n. 23
Homosexuality: and aesthetics, 269 n. 37; African representations of, 161–62, 167, 271 n. 46; and allegory, 2; and the "anal zone" (Freud), 137; analogy with racial difference, 180–81; and betrayal, 4; and censor-

Homosexuality (*continued*)
ship, 151; and colonialism, xi, 1–2,
231; conservative lineage of, 4–5,
12; and constructivism, 6; and contagion, 151; and cowardice, 50; as
"deficient," 190; denaturing of, 122;
denial of, 114, 144; and hetero binary,
138; and *hommosexuelle* (Lacan),
222; and indeterminacy, 149; integration of, 4; as "inversion," 204;
and *jouissance,* 168; and masculinity,
2, 15, 20–25, 73, 126, 190, 213–14;
and maternal attachment, 137, 188–
90; and meaning, 6–8, 73, 91, 157,
203, 253 n. 35; and mobility, 4, 97;
and modernism, 7, 232, 286 n. 8; and
narcissism, 137; as narrative code,
155; and negative oedipal relation,
137; and obscurity, 5, 73; and panic,
127–32, 157, 167; and pornography,
148; and the "Primal Horde," 22;
radical lineage of, 4–5, 101, 125; and
redemption, 167; and scandal, 46–48,
51; and sibling rivalry, 137; truth of,
5, 73. *See also* Bisexuality; Drives;
Gay; Homophilia; Lesbianism;
Masculinity; Virility
Homosocial: criticism, 8–9, 12, 127,
130; exchange, 8, 67, 127, 138. *See
also* Triangular relationships
Hughes, Thomas: *Tom Brown's Schooldays,* 208
Huxley, Aldous, 179
Hyam, Ronald, 2
Hybridity, 40
Hynes, Samuel, 148, 177
Hypocrisy, 84, 91–97, 161; British, 231;
Christian, 162–63, 166–68

Ideal, 25, 46–47, 85, 198; companion,
200–1; and idealism, 42, 98, 164–
65, 170, 175; and idealization, 39, 49,
139, 164; masculine, 142, 147, 190;
religious, 167; spiritual, 182. *See also*
Resistance; Voluntarism
Identification: with the colonized, 2–4,
64, 147, 186; and envy, 131; group,
3, 63, 90, 120–24, 209–10; masculine, 12–13, 48–51, 56, 66, 86, 92,
99, 107–8, 113, 117, 126–27, 137–
38, 141–42, 188–90, 213, 219, 256
n. 23, 257 n. 24–26; military, 214;

national/political, 42, 100, 118–20,
124, 232; psychic structure of, 3–4,
9, 40, 88, 97, 101, 112, 117, 214, 227–
28, 232; racial, 3, 40–42, 63–64, 101,
120; sexual, 11
Imaginary, 64, 79–80, 200; and colo-
nialism, 184; and defense, 119, 210;
and imperialism, 228; and topog-
raphy, 33, 119–20, 207. *See also*
Imago
Imago, 68, 89, 142; Caribbean, 177; fra-
ternal, 137, masculine, 135; Oriental,
177; paternal, 137, 210; racial, 184
Immolation, 34, 108, 129, 209
Imperialism, 4, 228, 232. *See also*
British; Colonialism empire
Imposture, 96. *See also* Dissimulation
Impotence, 129
Incorporation, 90
Indeterminacy, 104, 164. *See also*
Undecidability
India, 26, 49, 55, 77, 79, 180; and
"Indo-English Marriages," 159; and
1857 "Mutiny," 158; and suffering,
174
Infantilism, 38
Insemination, 207
Interracial desire, 145–47, 152, 157–
75, 174–75, 230, 271 n. 53. *See also*
Miscegenation; Race
Irwin, W. R., 178
Islam, 159, 188–89

James, Henry, 12, 46, 73–84, 92, 97,
213; *The Ambassadors,* 74; "The Art
of Fiction," 74–75; *The Awkward
Age,* 213; "The Beast in the Jungle,"
77; "The Jolly Corner," 77, 82; "The
Liar," 46, 73–86, 97; problem of
desire in, 73, 97; *Roderick Hudson,*
74; *The Sacred Fount,* 82; secrecy in,
82, 96; *The Tragic Muse,* 214; truth
in, 73; *The Turn of the Screw,* 82; on
Wilde's trials, 93
James, William, 85, 220; and "The
Moral Equivalent of War," 220
Jealousy, 12, 66, 117, 127–32, 136–38.
See also Envy; Rivalry; Triangular
Relationships
Jews: British, 220. *See also* Anti-
Semitism
Johnson, Barbara, 57

Marquis of Queensbury, 88
Marriage, 70, 115, 130, 143–44, 189, 258 n. 45; and foreign travel, 143; Indo-English, 159; and the martial, 225; and novels, 148
Masculinity: and beauty, 85–86; and colonial rapacity, 190; and desire, 126; and failure, 222; and fascism, 222–23; and heterosexuality, 66, 115; and homosexuality, 2, 21, 115, 190, 214, 219–22; and ideal, 128, 190, 222–23; and identity, 3, 54, 140, 212; and insufficiency, 190; and pleasure, 86–90, 100, 122, 140, 161; semiotics of, 122, 225; and strength, 17, 223; uncertainty about, 85, 115, 121, 214–15, 227. *See also* Heterosexuality; Homosexuality; Identification
Masks, 91–92, 96–97. *See also* Dissimulation; Hypocrisy
Masochism, 131, 139, 174, 192
Mason, A. E. W., 45–56, 62, 66–67, 71, 92; *The Broken Road,* 55–56; *The Four Feathers,* 45–56, 65–66, 70, 88–90; *The Philanderers,* 55–56
Masons, 26–27, 43
Masquerade: and inauthenticity, 96–99; masculine, 52, 73, 135–38, 181; racial, 40; social, 101, 224
Mastery: economic, 147; of the indigenous, 100, 106, 142, 190, 227; linguistic, 215; self-, 218, 228; sexual, 159; of women, 128
Masturbation, 70, 156
Maugham, W. Somerset, 12, 126–44; on autobiography, 143–44; *The Explorer,* 142; on homosexuality, 144, 265 n. 50; *Of Human Bondage,* 12, 20, 52, 126–44; on marriage, 266 n. 64; *The Moon and Sixpence,* 142–43; *A Writer's Notebook,* 142
Mediterranean, 141, 171
Meinertzhagen, Richard, 159–61; *Kenya Diary,* 159–61; and "pig-sticking," 160; and voyeurism, 160
Melancholia, 90, 232–33. *See also* Mourning; Nostalgia
Melodrama, 47, 56, 63, 114, 132; "of beset manhood" (Baym), 68, 143
Melville, Herman: "Benito Cereno," 4; *Billy Budd, Sailor,* 128

Memory, 12. *See also* Amnesia
Mendacity, 74–78, 89, 121. *See also* Dissimulation
Mentorship, 42, 53, 224
Meredith, George, 120; *The Egoist,* 120
Messianism, 38
Metalepsis, 36, 191, 217
Metonymy, 77, 119, 134, 179–81, 191
Meyers, Jeffrey, 7, 232
Militarism, 215, 221; and homosexuality, 212, 222; as redemptive, 227; and regression, 206
Miller, Jacques-Alain, 6
Milton, John, 96, 250 n. 61, 254 n. 52
Miscegenation, 35, 65, 157–62, 192. *See also* Interracial desire; Race
Misogyny, 222, 266 n. 58; structural, 127, 143. *See also* Mothers; Women
Missionaries, 157, 161–62; and religious zeal, 166–67
Mitchell, Julian, 226
Modernism, 7, 147; and European modernity, 196; and the canon, 7, 147; and homosexuality, 232; and interrogative writing, 195; and war, 205, 211
Mothers, 137, 188–90; and maternal body, 64, 189; and mother-son attachment, 137, 188–90. *See also* Body; Misogyny; Women
Mourning, 13, 105, 177, 194, 229, 232–33. *See also* Melancholia
Multiculturalism, 230
Munro, H. H. *See* Saki
Mwanga, Court of (Buganda), 161–62

Nandy, Ashis, 147
Narcissism, 94–95, 106, 137, 251 n. 21; and homosexuality (Freud), 137; and Narcissus, 216
Nation, 5, 26, 61, 101, 118–20; and heroism, 140; and identity, 146; and the intranational, 13, 127; and nationality, 67; and postnationalism, 230
National Front (Britain), 229, 233
"Nature," 17, 57, 62, 145, 219, 223; Forster on, 163; law of, 55
Nietzsche, Friedrich, 97; *Beyond Good and Evil,* 97
Nomadism, 30, 106, 181, 189, 216
"No Man's Land": as trope, 205–6, 211

Nomenclature: of friendship, 103, 135; of imperialism, 39; of romance, 92; of sexuality, 9, 138–39, 191

Nordau, Max, 58

"Normalcy," 134, 139, 144, 178

Nostalgia, 38, 46, 140–41, 197, 199; and aestheticism, 181; and nationalism, 182, 194–97, 232–33

Obscenity, 150; 1958 Select Committee on, 151. *See also* Censorship

Obsession, 117. *See also* Fixation

Occident: and materialism, 183. *See also* Orient

O.E.D., 71

Oedipus: complex, 66–68, 100; and imagery, 68; myth of, 66; and taboo, 107. *See also* Drives; Freud; Lacan

Oikos, 67, 118; and colony, 186

Ontology: and consistency, 97, 118; and crisis, 90, 97, 106, 125, 143, 189, 197, 210, 213; and desire, 9, 73, 125, 189, 225; and lack, 140, 201; and meaning, 97; and pleasure, 142; and truth, 76, 83, 97; and unpleasure, 87

Opacity: and character, 75; and eroticism, 122; and homosexuality, 77, 80, 191; and narrative, 5, 75, 82–83, 101, 191

Opprobrium, 88, 90, 150

Orient, 79, 141, 181; and Near East, 186–89; and Orientalism, 141, 168, 181, 186–89. *See also* Occident; Subaltern

Orientation, 12, 67

Origin, 67, 132

Orton, Joe, 199

Osborne, John, 199

"Other-alien," 31, 64, 118–20, 165, 183; as "noble savage," 183; potency of, 166–68; as a white man, 226–27

Overidentification, 46, 200. *See also* Identification

Owen, Wilfred, 194–95

Page, Norman, 171

Painting, 75–77, 82–85, 251 n. 9

Palimpsest, 28, 172

Pan, 156, 216–17, 270 n. 44

Paradox, 4, 15–16, 35, 83, 97, 218, 222

Paranoia, 34

Parapraxis, 76, 128, 219

Parataxis, 18

Pariah, 45–46, 56

Paris, 93, 130, 141

Park, Douglas, 102

Parry, Benita, 18, 40–42

Passion, 1, 86–87, 99, 115–17, 132; "animal," 159, 168, 203; "ruling," 76, 178, 222; for sin, 87; for unpleasure, 87

Paternalism, 29

Paternal metaphor, 107. *See also* Fathers; Law

Pathology, 73, 86, 90, 97

Peace Society, 62–63

Pedophilia, 162, 192

Penetration, 64

Penis, 112

Performance, 88–90, 96–98, 213, 225–26

Peripeteia, 32, 154, 174

Periphrasis, 191

Perry Levine, June, 163, 169–71

Persona, 75, 96–97; and personality, 75, 81

"Perversion," 167–69, 178, 222

Phallus, 68; dispossession of, 110; and power, 25. *See also* Castration; Penis

Philia, 22. *See also* Homophilia

Phillips, Adam, 9–10

Physiognomy, 58

Pioneer, 56–57, 71

Polygyny, 162

Porter, Dennis, 63

Portuguese empire, 28, 103, 108, 113, 157

Postcolonial: culture, 157, 228, 230–33; theory of, 145

Poststructuralism, 202

Potoker, Edward Martin, 177

Pound, Ezra, 223

Preterition, 174

Priestley, J. B., 209

"Primal Horde" (Freud), 22, 66, 218

"Primal Scene" (Freud), 68, 111–12, 133–34, 206, 209

Primitivism, 184, 278 n. 29

Projection, 9, 15, 24, 59, 76, 79–80, 95–97, 102, 106, 116–17, 122, 144, 152, 165–67, 184, 187, 194, 209

Prosopopœia, 89–92

Prostitution, 158; introduction of flogging for homosexual, 158
Protestantism, 161. *See also* Catholicism; Christianity
Proximity, 36; between colonizer and colonized, 63, 118–20, 160–64, 185–86; between men, 115, 118, 120, 162–64; between objects, 114; between romance and deception, 89–90
Psychic time, 196
Psychoanalysis, 6, 9–11, 31, 58, 63–64, 69, 82, 106, 110, 145, 200–2, 215. *See also* Freud; Lacan
Psychobiography, 148, 188–90, 197, 204
Psychosis, 56, 61, 77; and Britain, 231
Punjab, 16, 28
Purity movement, 158–59, 208

Queer, 55, 80, 144
Quiller-Couch, Sir Arthur, 49

Race: and conservatism, 183; and difference, 40, 55, 166; as enticing trap, 169; and equivalence, 12, 58–60, 101, 120, 146; erasure of, 165; and history, 120; and indeterminacy, 173; and presumed superiority, 119–20, 227. *See also* Proximity; Racism; Similarity; Stereotype
Racism, 182–83, 229–30; scientific, 58; sexual, 171. *See also* Race
Real (Lacan), 32, 199, 209, 279 n. 6
Recidivism, 100. *See also* Criminality; Degeneration
Reciprocity, 23–25, 69, 95, 129, 139
Redemption, 60, 170, 189, 227; from effeminacy, 221; from Satan, 124; from "savagery," 100, 167
Reparation, 56, 110
Repetition, 12, 63, 84, 106
Repression, 2, 108; and "repressive hypothesis," 231–32
Resistance, 9, 48, 77, 96–97, 126–29, 143, 154, 196, 207
Rhodes, Cecil, 4, 26
Rhodesia (Zimbabwe): Northern, 158, 161; Southern, 158, 161. *See also* Zambia; Zimbabwe
Rivalry, 12, 118, 127, 131, 136–39, 224–25. *See also* Envy; Homoeroticism; Homosocial; Jealousy

Roles, 97–98, 223–24. *See also* Symbolization
Romanticism, 196–97
Routledge, Mr. and Mrs. W. S. (Kenya), 158, 161
Rushdie, Salman, 231–33
Ruskin, John, 26

Said, Edward, 40
St. Paul, 166
Saki (H. H. Munro), 9, 12, 56, 212–28; "Birds on the Western Front," 219; "The Brogue," 222; "Esmé," 218; "Gabriel-Ernest," 215–18, 222; "The Goblin and the Saint," 218, 222; "Herman the Irascible," 222; "Laura," 217; "The Lumber Room," 217; "Mrs. Packletide's Tiger," 218; "The Quest," 218; "The Square Egg," 219; "Sredni Vashtar," 217; *The Unbearable Bassington,* vii, 12, 217, 223–27; *When William Came,* 219–23; "The Wolves of Cernogratz," 217
Salter, Donald, 153
Sassoon, Siegfried, 9, 12, 170, 193–211; on British colonialism, 282 n. 37; *Counter-Attack,* 195–96; *Diaries,* 197, 201, 204–5; *Memoirs of a Fox-Hunting Man,* 196–201, 209; *Memoirs of an Infantry Officer,* 206–11; *The Weald of Youth,* 199–200, 204
Satan, 124, 169
"Savagery," 58–62, 69, 100, 119; Conrad on, 100, 119; Firbank on, 190; Forster on, 162–64; Haggard on, 69; "noble," 183; Saki on, 216–18; and the unconscious, 169; the "universality" of, 60
Sayre Martin, John, 148
Schopenhauer, Arthur, 107, 126
Scott, Paul, 171, 273 n. 76
Sculpture, 130–32
Second World War, 199, 206
Secrecy, 23, 82, 88–92, 96, 103, 138. *See also* Enigma; Opacity
Sedgwick, Eve Kosofsky, 8, 127, 130, 251 n. 11
Seduction, 76, 87, 95, 117, 161
Sexes: and difference, 148, 190, 223; and indeterminacy, 146; as races, 145–46; and transgression, 170

Sexology, 8
Seymour-Smith, Martin, 24
Shame, 46–47, 50, 53, 70, 91, 95–97, 109, 130, 135, 153, 157, 172–74
Shelley, Percy Bysshe, 91
Shusterman, David, 154
Silberrad, Henry, 158, 161–62; and Kenyan *lobola,* 158; and pedophilia, 162
Silverman, Kaja, 64; on the "double mimesis," 64
Similarity, 12, 58–63, 99–102, 118–20, 185. *See also* Proximity; Race
"Sin," 86, 161–62, 166; as allegory in Milton, 96
Social Contract: colonialism as, 27–29, 42, 100
Sodomy, 88, 274 n. 90; as "crime against nature," 161
Sontag, Susan, 177, 262 n. 19
South Africa. *See* Africa
Spain, 132, 141; empire of, 28
Spectator (London), 159
Spender, Stephen, 231; *World Within World,* 231
Sperm, 174
Spinsters, 129, 188
Stammer, 126–28, 133
Steiner, George, 152, 180
Stephen, James Fitzjames, 16
Stereotype: of dialect, 179; racial, 55–58, 162, 168, 177, 183–87, 230; sexual, 157
Stott, Rebecca, 64, 67
Strachey, Lytton, 164
Street, Brian, 57
Subaltern, 152. *See also* Orient
Subjectivity. *See* Drives; Ego; Identification; Ontology; Unconscious
Sublimation, 2, 5, 9, 21, 100, 162, 169, 203, 208, 218
Sublime, 174, 196; and military, 211–13
Substitution, 102. *See also* Displacement; Metalepsis; Metonymy; Synecdoche
Sudan, 23–24, 48–51
Suffering: of the colonized, 24, 56, 60, 174, 187; of the colonizer, 15, 32, 35, 42, 64, 160; female, 113; homophobic, 48, 91, 116, 163, 203, 229; military, 222; national, 194, 230; ontological, 1, 100, 109, 187, 203;

racial, 174, 229–30. *See also* Abjection; Guilt; Melancholia; Mourning; Shame
Suffragette movement, 43, 222. *See also* Women
Suicide, 42, 203
Superego, 52, 110
Symbolization, 64, 101, 105, 138, 188–92, 218
Symbols, 3, 90–91, 97, 152–54, 192; chaos of, 197; dearth of, 148
Symonds, John Addington, xi, 85; and *Sexual Inversion* 151
Symptom, 6, 12, 20, 33, 36, 75–77, 82–84, 95, 106, 114, 123, 128, 140, 173
Synecdoche, 26, 82, 130, 141, 158, 161, 200, 208, 228

Taboo, 51, 73, 110; and literature, 149–50
Tanner, Tony, 119–20
Thomas, Edward, 194
Times (London), 159
Timor, 103, 121
Transcendental signifier, 17
Transference: and acting, 89; Lacan on, 254 n. 50; and love, 90; and nationalism, 13; and objects, 97; and travel, 63; and worship, 135
Travel, 49, 56, 127, 142; as cause of sexual panic, 171; as expiation of sexual panic, 143, 156. *See also* Nomadism
Treachery, 1, 4. *See also* Betrayal
Triangular relationships, 12, 127, 135, 223–25. *See also* Homosocial exchange
Tribalism, 61, 65, 68
Trope, 12, 18, 22, 57, 73, 80–81, 103, 124, 127, 167
Turner, Reggie, 93
Tyranny, 65

Unconscious, 2–3, 10, 31–32, 40–42, 61–63, 71, 78, 80, 116, 131, 215; as a black man, 172; Lacan on, 273 n. 82; as "proletarian," 172; and racial eroticism, 147; "savagery" of, 169, 172; and sexual difference, 163. *See also* Drives; Ego; Superego
Undecidability, 5

Unheimlich (uncanny), 65, 142, 209, 216
Unmaking, 52, 85
Unmanning, 30. *See also* Castration
Usurpation: racial, 42, 66; sexual, 207

Vagrancy, 158
Veracity, 76–78
"Vice," 94, 167
Victory, 124
Virility, 46, 66, 114–15, 135; and colonialism, 215; hyper-, 114, 219, 222. *See also* Masculinity
Vogt, Carl, 58
Voluntarism, 98; psychic, 226
Vorticism, 196, 223

Warrender, Hugh, 49–50
Weeks, Jeffrey, 8
Wharton, Edith: *The House of Mirth,* 213
White, 119, 147, 160–61, 249 n. 47; and Caucasian men, 57; "intrusion," 161; "man's burden," 36, 39, 145
Wilde, Oscar, 12, 48–53, 62, 69, 83, 85–93, 97–98, 188, 213, 218; on consciousness, 86–88, 95–97; *De Profundis,* vii, 46; "The Happy Prince," 94; *The Importance of Being Earnest,* 216; on love, 90; on masks, 92; "Pen, Pencil and Poison," 87; *The Picture of Dorian Gray,* 48–53, 83, 85–91, 94–97; *The Portrait of Mr. W. H.,* 93–94; on secrecy, 96; on

surfaces, 178; *Teleny; or, The Reverse of the Medal,* 48; 1895 trials of, 48, 50, 88, (Beerbohm on, 93), (James on, 93), 94, 158, 188, 218
"Will," 98, 107, 126, 168; "to power," 232. *See also* Drives; Schopenhauer
Wittgenstein, Ludwig, 129
Women: and clitoridectomy in Kenya, 162; as complication (Priestley), 209; as danger (Haggard), 71; as distraction (Kipling), 42; and Eve, 124; excluded from empire, 70; and feminine ideal, 134, 143; and femininity, 134; as foils (Forster), 148; and marriage, 115; as "menace" (Kipling), 30; men's deception of, 224; in need of "rescue," 136–38; and nostalgia, 141; as a nuisance (Munro), 222; and spinsters, 129; and suffrage in India, 159; as "vanishing mediators," 15, 117, 143, 225; and wombs, 68. *See also* Fantasy; Female body; Femininity
Woolf, Virginia: on Forster, 154; on Kipling, 39; *To the Lighthouse,* 102, 194
Wordsworth, William: "The Happy Warrior," 205, 221

Yellow Book, 50, 93

Zambia, 158
Zimbabwe, 158
Zulus, 60–64, 67

Christopher Lane is Assistant Professor of English and Comparative Literature
at the University of Wisconsin-Milwaukee and the author of several articles on
psychoanalysis, sexuality, and literature.

Library of Congress Cataloging-in-Publication Data

Lane, Christopher
The ruling passion : British colonial allegory and the paradox of homosexual desire /
by Christopher Lane.
    p.   cm.
Includes bibliographical references and index.
ISBN 0-8223-1677-3.   ISBN 0-8223-1689-7 (pbk.)
1. English literature—19th century—History and criticism.   2. Homosexuality and
literature—Great Britain—Colonies—History.   3. English literature—20th
century—History and criticism.   4. English literature—Men authors—History and
criticism.   5. Masculinity (Psychology) in literature.   6. Imperialism in literature.
7. Colonies in literature.   8. Gay men in literature.   9. Desire in literature.
10. Allegory.   I. Title.
PR468.H65L36   1995
820.9'353–dc20   95-6484

The Ruling Passion